BRITISH POLITICS SINCE THE WAR

Also by Bill Coxall and Lynton Robins

CONTEMPORARY BRITISH POLITICS

British Politics since the War

Bill Coxall

and

Lynton Robins

First published in Great Britain 1998 by
MACMILLAN PRESS LTD
Houndmills, Basingstoke, Hampshire RG21 6XS and London
Companies and representatives throughout the world

A catalogue record for this book is available from the British Library.

ISBN 0–333–54531–1 hardcover
ISBN 0–333–54532–X paperback

First published in the United States of America 1998 by
ST. MARTIN'S PRESS, INC.,
Scholarly and Reference Division,
175 Fifth Avenue, New York, N.Y. 10010

ISBN 0–312–21108–2

Library of Congress Cataloging-in-Publication Data
Coxall, W. N.
British politics since the war / Bill Coxall & Lynton Robins.
p. cm.
Includes bibliographical references (p.   ) and index.
ISBN 0–312–21108–2
1. Great Britain—Politics and government—1945–   2. World War,
1939–1945—Influence.   I. Robins, L. J. (Lynton J.)   II. Title.
DA589.7.C69 1997
941.085—dc21   97–35661
                                                        CIP

This book is printed on paper suitable for recycling and made from fully managed and sustained forest sources.

10   9   8   7   6   5   4   3   2   1
07   06   05   04   03   02   01   00   99   98

Printed and bound in Great Britain by
Creative Print and Design (Wales)
Ebbw Vale

Contents

List of Figures

List of Tables

List of Exhibits

List of Photographs

Preface

Recent history – the period covering their own and their parents' lives – is often the period about which students know least, and the authors have long been aware that, despite the existence of some excellent works of contemporary history of a more advanced kind, no satisfactory introduction to the subject has been available. This book is an attempt to fill that gap.

After a scene-setting survey of prewar and wartime Britain, the book opens with a straightforward account of post-Second World War British governments from Attlee to Major, focusing on the main electoral and national developments and events. For the most part it then proceeds thematically, combining discussions of developments in political ideas, institutions and behaviour (Chapters 4–8) with the treatment of specific policy areas (Chapters 9–11). The remaining chapters offer broad overviews. Thus Chapter 2 examines postwar British politics from the perspective of consensus, its breakdown and possible reemergence, Chapter 3 considers some important political consequences of social change, and Chapter 12 looks at the history of Britain since 1945 from the viewpoint of the main political ideologies.

As with *Contemporary British Politics*, for which it provides, if we may use the term, a 'prequel', the authors hope that the book will prove useful not only to A level and first-year university students but also to everyone with an interest in recent British political history.

We take this opportunity to express our thanks to our publisher Steven Kennedy for his encouragement and advice and to Houri Alavi (also of Macmillan) for her editorial assistance.

BILL COXALL
LYNTON ROBINS

Acknowledgements

The authors and publishers wish to thank the following for permission to use copyright material:

Guardian News Service Ltd for **Table 9.3** from *The Guardian*, 26.4.89;

Oxford University Press for **Table 3.9** from M. Burch and M. Moran, 'The Changing British Political Elite, 1945–83: MPs and Cabinet Ministers', *Parliamentary Affairs*, 38 (1985);

Talking Politics, Journal of The Politics Association, for an extract from Ian Holliday, 'The Welfare State 1979–93: Safe in Conservative Hands?' *Talking Politics*, 6: 2 (1994) pp. 82–94;

Central Office of Information, London, for photographs on pages 24, 34, 38, 43 and 47.

Centre for the Study of Cartoons and Caricature, University of Kent, Canterbury, for cartoons on pages 55, 123, 168, 210, 244 and 268, all copyright John Appleton, Solo Syndication Limited, London.

Colin Jones, copyright The Observer for photograph on page 72.

Hulton Images for photograph on page 216.

National Museum of Labour History for photographs on pages 18, 28 and 242.

Oxford University Press for maps on pages 264–5 from *The Oxford History of Britain: The Modern Age*, 1992, ed. by H. C. G. Matthew and K. O. Morgan.

Every effort has been made to trace all the copyright holders, but if any have been inadvertently overlooked the publishers will be pleased to make the necessary arrangement at the first opportunity.

This book is dedicated to Stephen, Matthew, Edward, Jonathan, Anne and Stephen

Introduction: Britain in 1945

This is a book on British politics since the Second World War. But there are no clean breaks in history: political parties, the role of government, the class system, the economy and external relations in 1945 were all profoundly shaped by developments before that date. So too were the politicians who ruled postwar Britain until the 1970s: their formative experiences were of economic depression and appeasement of the European dictators; they grew up in an age of empire. Accordingly we begin with a retrospective glance at British politics, posing the question: 'What are the major landmarks in these areas on "the road to 1945"'?

The Party System

As the last year of the Second World War began, Britain was ruled by a coalition government under Winston Churchill that had been in power since 1940. The parliament, however, had been elected ten years previously at the 1935 general election, when the mainly Conservative national government (432 seats) had won an overwhelming victory over Labour (154 seats) and the Liberals (20 seats). Despite by-election defeats, Conservative ascendancy over the other parties was still well over 200 when the war ended. During the war itself an electoral truce had operated in by – elections in which the party holding a seat when it fell vacant had the right to put forward a candidate unopposed by the other two parties. However there was no broader political truce. Labour maintained its organisation in the country, and although its membership of the coalition inhibited full-blooded criticism it kept up a limited opposition in parliament during the war.

Interwar Politics

The Conservatives had, however, not only dominated British politics between 1935 and 1945 but for the whole period since the First World War. All told, between 1918 and 1945 they governed alone for six years and as the main partner in coalition governments for a further eighteen years (Table I.1).

TABLE I.1 *Governments between 1918 and 1945*

1918–1922	Conservative–Liberal coalition
1922–23	Conservative
1924	Labour
1924–29	Conservative
1929–31	Labour
1931–40	National government
1940–45	Wartime coalition

The main reasons for the Conservatives' success in the interwar years were good leadership and superior organisation, combined with a strong attraction as a national party with a reputation for governing competence. In Stanley Baldwin, their leader between 1923 and 1937, they possessed the shrewdest and most effective politician of the period. His personal qualities – he exuded calmness, trustworthiness and a sense of decency – together with the party's post-1924 anti-Socialist stance and support for the social order and social reform had considerable electoral appeal in the anxious years of economic depression and the rise of the fascist dictators in Europe.

That the opposition was divided between the Liberals and Labour also worked in the Conservatives' favour. Both anti-Conservative parties were further handicapped by splits. The Liberals split after 1916 when Lloyd-George, having ousted Asquith as wartime premier, decided to continue the wartime coalition into the postwar period, and a further threefold division between National Liberals supporting the national government, independent Liberals and a small group under Lloyd-George appeared in the 1931 general election. The 1935 general election ended a calamitous two decades for the party (Cook, 1993, pp. 112–22).

In contrast, despite a major setback in 1931 the Labour Party advanced steadily during the interwar years. By no means a national party before 1914 – the most seats it achieved was 42 in December 1910 – the party emerged from the war in a much stronger position, having gained from its patriotic role in the war effort (it held several ministerial posts in the Lloyd-George coalition), from the growing influence of the trade union movement (whose membership rose from just over 4.0 million to 6.5 million between 1914 and 1919) and from the introduction of a new Socialist constitution and party programme in 1918. Ditching its 1903 electoral pact with the Liberals, Labour benefited as an independent party with a collectivist ethos from the 1918 extension of the vote to almost the entire working class. Disadvantaged by the timing and circumstances of the 1918 'Khaki' election, the party registered a relatively small parliamentary advance in 1918 but displaced the Liberals as the main opposition party as early as 1922.

Labour formed minority governments in 1924 and again between 1929 and 1931, when its handling of the financial crisis resulted in a major setback from which the Conservatives benefited for the rest of the decade. The second Labour government faced an economic crisis (unemployment was over one million when it took office), which soon deteriorated further, largely as a result of the Great Depression in the United States (1929–33), and then gravitated into financial crisis as a result of a major collapse of Austrian and German banks. Britain had to face the crisis with an over-valued currency (which occurred when the country returned to the gold standard in 1925) and small gold reserves, which made it difficult to cover its budgetary deficit of £120 million. In order to balance the budget whilst maintaining the value of sterling at parity (staying on the gold standard), the government tried but failed to agree on sizeable public spending cuts, including a 10 per cent reduction in unemployment benefit. In fact, the cabinet divided 12–9 in favour of the cuts. Because the minority included leading Ministers and because the TUC also opposed the cuts, Labour had little alternative but to resign.

But to the surprise of most of the cabinet the Prime Minister, Ramsay MacDonald, agreed to continue as the head of a national government that included the Conservatives, the Liberals and three of the Labour ministers. MacDonald probably acted out of a sense of duty, but from that moment he became for a generation and more a traitor in the eyes of the Labour movement. National crisis was thus turned into Labour crisis and party split.

A quickly-held general election resulted in the return of a Conservative-dominated national government with a massive majority and a 'doctor's mandate' to take the necessary economic measures. The national government had 554 seats and 67 per cent of the vote; Labour was reduced to a very small contingent of 52 MPs. Even before the election the national government had been forced off the gold standard, thereby effecting a substantial devaluation of the currency, which, accompanied by low interest rates, led eventually to economic recovery.

Under George Lansbury (1932–5) and then Clement Attlee, Labour's fortunes slowly revived first at the local level (it gained control of London County Council in 1934) and then in parliament. In the 1935 general election it returned 154 MPs, although it still faced a national government (432 seats) with a massive majority. Under the influential guidance of the leading trade unionist Ernest Bevin, as well as Clement Attlee and Hugh Dalton, the party recovered its morale, committing itself in 1937 to a wide-ranging programme of nationalisation at home and resistance to the fascist dictators abroad. Electorally, however, despite some by-election victories Labour was in no position to offer a realistic challenge to the Conservatives at the outbreak of war, popular voting intentions (according to a Gallup poll in February 1939) being 54 per cent national government, 30 per cent Labour (cited in Fielding, Thompson and Tiratsoo, 1995, p. 14).

The Weakness of the Political Extremes

Unlike many systems of representative government between the First and Second World Wars, British parliamentary democracy proved sufficiently robust to survive economic depression without collapsing into communist or fascist dictatorship. An important reason for the lack of success of the Communist Party of Great Britain (CPGB) was the dominance in working-class politics of the gradualist Labour Party, which rejected the CPGB's attempts at affiliation in the early 1920s, excluded individual communists from the party in 1924 and, after 1927, proscribed communists from attending its conferences even as trade union delegates. That left trade unions as the main vehicle for possible communist influence, and ten communists (the 'Fraction of 10 ') attended the 1925 Trades Union Congress. However union militancy encountered firm resistance from the Conservative government, which prosecuted twelve leading communists for sedition. Communist Party headquarters was raided for evidence and the twelve were found guilty and imprisoned, their sentences ranging from six months to one year. The TUC itself took strong action in 1934, forbidding trades councils to accept communists as delegates and urging trade unions to exclude them from office. The party took its orders from Moscow, which required it to attack social democratic parties as 'social fascists' after 1927 and to support left unity in the mid 1930s. Its subordination to external control by the USSR made it unappealing to the working class even during the depression, and its membership rose only slowly, reaching 18 000 in 1939. Apart from trade union support in South Wales and to a lesser extent in London, it mainly attracted middle-class intellectuals. Suggested reasons for communism's appeal to intellectuals have included the need to make a clear anti-fascist commitment after the rise of Hitler had polarised political forces in a universal struggle; the social guilt felt by many at the apparent inability of the democratic parties to take decisive action against unemployment; and, in Orwell's view, the fact that communism offered something to believe in – a secular faith – in a world in which old values had collapsed.

British fascism between 1932 and 1935 posed more of a threat. Sir Oswald Mosley's British Union of Fascists (BUF) made a strong nationalist appeal, calling for economic protectionism and self – sufficiency and a vigorous scapegoating of the 'old gang' of politicians as dupes of a Jewish conspiracy. Mosley, who had previously been a Conservative and then a Labour MP, claimed to have found a 'third way' between socialism and capitalism. In fact his concept of a corporate state entailed an authoritarian capitalist economy in which the rights of both employers and workers would have been severely curtailed. The momentary attractiveness of the BUF stemmed from the disillusionment among Conservatives over Baldwin's India policy, which involved the extension of virtual self-government and voting rights to millions of Indians, and disappointment on the left with Labour's economic orthodoxy in office and its unwillingness after 1931 to become involved in extra-parliamentary action on behalf of the unemployed. Its threat to parliamentary politics was twofold. First, there was the possibility that Mosley's appeal to disenchanted working-class Conservatives, especially in London and the North would win him constitutional power which he would then use to overturn democracy. Second, there was the potential menace of street violence encouraged by BUF meetings, rallies and marches. However, economic recovery from 1934 held back the growth of British fascism and the 1935 general election – which Mosley, with the BUF in decline, decided not to contest – confirmed the authority of the national government. In 1936 the government introduced the Public Order Act, which prohibited political uniforms and empowered the police to ban political processions. This 'virtually killed' off the fascist movement (Taylor, 1965, p. 374). In fact it had never really flourished, achieving a membership of only 20 000 at its peak. The main reason for its failure must be sought in the relatively mild impact of the world depression on Britain. Unlike elsewhere, no massive and rapid inflation wiped out the savings of the middle class and, equally significant, falling food prices meant rising living standards for the majority of working-class people.

Politics in the Second World War

Wartime developments enhanced Labour's position in two main ways. First, the circumstances in which the national government under Neville Chamberlain fell and the wartime coalition under Churchill came into being was highly favourable to the party of the left. When on 8 May 1940 Labour divided the House of Commons at the end of a two-day debate on the collapse of the British military expedition to Norway, Chamberlain's majority fell to 81 as a result of Conservative defections and abstentions. The prime minister had suffered a major moral defeat and confidence in his government was fading, and when he sought to remain in power by broadening his administration, Labour's refusal to serve in it effectively forced his resignation. Churchill – the people's choice as premier but not favoured by the king, most leading politicians or the Conservative Party – emerged as leader after a tense meeting between him, Chamberlain, the Conservative chief whip and his main rival, Lord Halifax. The Labour and Liberal Parties, both of which had turned down invitations to serve in Chamberlain's government at the outset of the war, now joined Churchill's coalition in significant numbers. Labour's important role in the coalition, with two posts in the war cabinet as well as several key home front ministries, did much to reestablish its reputation for competence in government after the disaster of 1931 as well as closely associating it in the public mind with patriotism and postwar social reconstruction (Pugh, 1994, pp. 223–5).

Second, public opinion shifted to the left during the war, a trend that reflected popular determination that the wartime schemes for social reform would be carried out. Between 1943 and 1945, three by-election victories over the Conservatives by the left-of-centre Commonwealth Party, together with six general election forecasts by the British Institute of Public Opinion that gave Labour a lead of 12 per cent or more, clearly indicated the leftward movement of opinion (Addison, 1994).

The Expansion of Government

The social and economic responsibilities of government had expanded from the late nineteenth century but remained quite limited in 1940 (Exhibit I.1).

However a precedent for large-scale state intervention in social and economic life had been set during the First World War, just as the Liberal social reforms of 1906 to 1912 had contained the seeds, especially in the principle of social insurance, of the later welfare state. These reforms were extended during the interwar period, notably in the spheres of health and unemployment insurance and housing, but less progress was made in education. As a result of this modest extension of state intervention, total government expenditure as a proportion of gross national product (GNP) increased from 26.1 per cent in 1920 to 30.1 per cent in 1938, whilst spending on the social services rose from 4 per cent of GNP in 1913 to 12 per cent in 1935–6. The increase of total government spending on the social services was relatively small – from £490.7 million in 1919 to £596.3 million in 1939. Nonetheless it has been claimed that the British social services 'taken all in all, were the most admired in the world in 1939' (Addison, 1975, p. 33) and that Britain was 'half-way to a national health service by 1939' (Pugh, 1995, p. 196). One effect of the gradual increase in social service expenditure was to achieve a slight redistribution of wealth and income from rich to poor.

The effects of government social policy intermeshed with trends in the economy and society to produce a marked improvement in the health and living standards of the British people in the interwar period. Assisted by a decline in prices of about 25 per cent, real income per head was about one third higher in 1939 than in 1913. With working-class wages growing five times faster than middle-class salaries between 1911 and 1938 and with family size declining, working-class living standards may have risen by as much as 70 per cent between 1914 and 1937–8 (Cronin, 1984, p. 87), although it is likely that much of the improvement took place during the war and in the immediate postwar years. As the pre-1914 trends towards declining infant mortality continued and deaths from killer diseases such as tuberculosis waned, the average life expectancy increased from 55 in 1910 to 66 in 1938 for a woman and from 52 to 61 over the same period for a man.

Nevertheless government welfare provision had proceeded piecemeal and without reference to any guiding principle. Hence it lacked universality and contained many gaps, defects and anomalies at the beginning of the Second World War. Male workers were covered by health insurance, but not their wives and children, who were deemed the responsibility of the 'breadwinner'. This meant that about 15 million people, mainly women and children under five, were excluded from the health insurance scheme. Nor did health insurance extend to hospital care. The provision of hospitals itself lacked comprehensiveness, being in the hands of a variety of agencies, including local authorities, the old Poor Law infirmaries (despite the formal 'abolition' of the Poor Law in 1929) and voluntary institutions. In 1936 less than half of the county councils and county boroughs provided a general hospital service. In housing, despite the large interwar housebuilding record and a sizeable slum clearance programme in the 1930s, overcrowding remained a problem,

EXHIBIT 1.1   *The growth of state welfare, 1870–1940*

Pensions	National health insurance	National unemployment insurance	Education	Housing
1908: non-contributory pension of 5 shillings (25p) per week, payable to those with income of less than £21 a year (raised to 10 shillings per week in 1919). 1925: contributory pension scheme – contributions from employers and employees provided 65–70-year-old workers with pensions of 10 shillings per week (£1 for married couples). At 70 worker transferred to non-contributory scheme.	1911: national health insurance scheme for all wage earners based on weekly contributions by employer, employee and state. Insured received sick pay of 10 shillings (50p) per week and free medical treatment but no allowances for dependants and no hospital provision. Scheme included 20 million workers by 1938.	1911: compulsory scheme based on weekly contributions from employer, employee and state giving a benefit of 7 shillings (35p) per week up to a maximum of 15 weeks. Scheme limited to workers in certain industries, including building, mechanical engineering and ship building. 1920: Unemployment Insurance Act extended insurance scheme to all workers earning up to £250 per annum. However, between 1918 and 1939 the contributory scheme broke down in the face of mass unemployment and was largely replaced by non-contributory, subsistence-level, means-tested benefits.	1870: Board schools, financed by local rates and central government grants, provided non-denominational elementary education where the need existed – covered 54 per cent of elementary schoolchildren in 1900. 1880: education made compulsory for 5–10 year olds. 1893: elementary education became virtually free. 1902: local authorities given responsibility for administration of education. 1906: meals for needy schoolchildren. 1907: school medical inspection. 1918: school leaving age raised to 14. 1921: free milk to needy schoolchildren.	1919: local authorities made responsible for remedying housing deficiencies. Government subsidies for local authority house building began: 1.1 million local authority houses built by 1939 – 10 per cent of housing stock. Four million houses built from 1919–39. 1923: subsidies to private builders of working-class housing – 400 000 houses built with such subsidies by 1939. 1930: subsidies to local authorities for slum clearance.

the 4 per cent national figure concealing a much higher incidence in certain parts of the country, for example 20 per cent in Sunderland.

The gravest problem facing governments between the wars was unemployment. The weakness of international trade, together with increasing world competion in British staple industries such as textiles and ship building, led to severe unemployment, which remained above one million between 1920 and 1939. During particular periods and in certain regions, unemployment rose to much higher levels: in 1932, 2.8 million insured workers were unemployed (22.1 per cent), and regional unemployment in northern England, Scotland and Northern Ireland (over 27 per cent) and Wales (over 36 per cent) was even worse. In some towns in the north-east and Wales, about two thirds of the workforce were out of work, for example Jarrow 67.8 per cent and Merthyr Tydfil 61.9 per cent. In 1938 1.8 million insured workers were still unemployed – 12.9 per cent of the insured workforce. Faced with joblessness on this scale, the 1911 unemployment insurance scheme, which had been designed to cope with relatively modest levels of unemployment, broke down. As the scheme was having to be subsidised by the Exchequer the government sought to keep costs down, and about three million applicants were refused benefit between 1921 and 1930. From 1931 a stringent test of household means, together with lower national scales of payment, disallowed or reduced relief for half of all claimants, leading to enduring bitterness among the unemployed and a determination among their political representatives that such a situation should not recur (Pugh, 1995, pp. 202–3; Digby, 1989, pp. 51–2).

Although the ruling ethos was anti-collectivist, modest government intervention also took place in the economy and in the developing relationships between government and the representatives of employers and trade unions. In creating public institutions such as the Central Electricity Generating Board to organise the distribution of electricity and in intervening directly by price-fixing in industries such as coal, interwar governments were implicitly expressing their doubt about the efficacy in all circumstances of unfettered private enterprise and moving towards regulated capitalism. Secondly, the outline of a 'system' of relationships between government, employers and trade unions, which has been described as 'corporate bias', had become evident by 1940. This tendency for closer collaboration between the state and the 'peak' representative institutions of both sides of industry – the Federation of British Industry (FBI, 1916) and the Trades Union Congress (TUC, 1868) – had developed out of a crisis in the nineteenth-century liberal (that is, *laissez faire*) state under the pressure of intensified foreign trading competition, industrial conflict and war after 1880. It had been generated by the state's need to promote greater social consensus and political agreement in order to achieve a more efficient, modernised economy and national survival in wartime. After 1928, encouraged by the government, the two main employers' organisations and the TUC had established joint machinery to discuss industrial legislation, unemployment and national economic policy on a joint basis. Between 1931–2 and 1938 the political importance of the unions had increased with the need for their cooperation in rearmament activities, and the TUC was accepted as 'a legitimate and valued presence in Whitehall'. By 1940 the peak organisations of both employers and unions were poised to become 'governing institutions' (Middlemas, 1979, pp. 68–265; Middlemas, pp. 463–9 and Taylor, pp. 503–9 in Seldon and Ball, 1994).

The Impact of the Second World War on Government

A huge expansion of the role of government occurred during the war which, when combined with the new enthusiasm for social reform, served as a precedent and a blueprint for large-scale state action in peacetime. The government exercised sweeping power over the use of national resources, with dramatic effects. By 1943 the conscription of over five million men and women into the armed forces, together with the call-up of an additional 2.9 million workers, including large numbers of women, into domestic industry and services had virtually eliminated unemployment, the scourge of prewar Britain. To maintain civilian morale in the face of the anticipated bombing of the towns and cities, the government administered a large-scale evacuation scheme under which over 20 million evacuations had taken place by 1942, and to ensure equality of sacrifice and continuity of supply of essential items it introduced rationing of food and clothing. The cabinet also authorised large increases in spending on children's welfare, subsidising school meals and milk, vitamin-enriched products for infants and milk for nursing mothers. The machinery of the state expanded: new ministries sprang up and the number of full-time, non-industrial civil servants increased by 80 per cent to 704 000.

Secondly, blueprints for the major renovation of postwar society emerged, inspired by Liberal reformers such as the social scientist W. H. Beveridge and the economist J. M. Keynes, both of whom became temporary civil servants during the war. Appointed chairman in 1941 of the government's Committee on Social Insurance, Beveridge was aware that large-scale reconstruction of welfare provision had enjoyed wide support among educated 'middle opinion' from the 1930s; hence he greatly broadened his initially modest remit to coordinate existing social insurance schemes. His report on *Social Insurance and Allied Services* (1942) proposed a sweeping social insurance scheme covering all contingencies 'from the cradle to the grave', with universal, compulsory insurance contributions bringing entitlement to a national minimum income. The basing of Beveridge's plan on social insurance with flat-rate contributions and benefits was later seen as rather conservative, but he was undoubtedly radical in perceiving that his scheme would need to be accompanied by broader policy changes involving a national health service that would be free at the point of use together with family allowances and full employment. The report, which sold 630 000 copies, was received with great enthusiasm by the public and, despite Churchill's concern that it might generate excessive expectations, generally prompted a positive response from the government. Before the end of the war, white papers had appeared on social insurance (virtually accepting the whole of the Beveridge Report) and a national health service, and important social legislation had brought major educational reform (the 1944 Butler Act) and introduced family allowances of five shillings per week for second and subsequent children. The white paper on *Employment Policy* committed the government to 'the maintenance of a high and stable rate of employment after the war', a major change in policy priorities from the 1930s and one that reflected the pressure of wartime public fear of a postwar slump.

Social Class, Culture and Politics

The most important division in British society was social class, with occupation as its main determinant. In 1931 approximately three quarters of the population belonged to the manual working class, just under one quarter (23 per cent) were middle class whilst a tiny minority (2 per cent) were upper class. Each major class contained significant internal divisions. The working class was divided into skilled, semi-skilled and unskilled, the middle class into a variety of statuses ranging from top professionals, businessmen and managers through a middle stratum that included executive-grade civil servants to a lower middle class of bank clerks, state school-teachers and shopkeepers. Each class contained a wide range of income groups, and there was considerable overlap in financial terms between the lower middle class and the skilled working class, with, for instance, male certificated teachers and skilled engineering workers both earning about £6 per week in the late 1930s. This overlap also appeared in education, with about 10 per cent of the children of semi-skilled and unskilled workers attending grammar school in 1938, and in housing, where about 20 per cent of the working class were homeowners by 1939.

An overlap between classes was also apparent in culture and voting behaviour. Individualist attitudes towards work and the making of money and consumerist attitudes towards the enjoyment of material possessions were more prevalent than once thought among large sections of the working class. So too was patriotism, which was diffused among the working class by the continuous stream of nationalist and imperialist propaganda called forth by the First World War and conflicts in defence of the British Empire (Benson, 1989, pp. 141–73). Cultural values thus inhibited the growth of class consciousness among many workers that would have translated directly into support for the Labour Party whilst also providing significant linkages between the middle class and sections of the working class. These considerations help explain the strong electoral support for the Conservatives between the First and Second World Wars and the significant Liberal share of the vote in the 1920s. According to one calculation, just over half (55 per cent) of the working class voted Conservative in 1931 and exactly half did so in 1935. Sociological explanations for working-class conservatism include deference – the belief that the Conservative elites possessed greater governing competence than other elites – and self-ascribed middle-class status, whereby many working-class people considered themselves middle class probably because they judged class by income and consumption rather than by occupation or education (Benson, 1989, pp. 153–4).

Nonetheless, with class divisions more apparent at the time than class overlap, what most impressed observers of the interwar working class was its social separateness. Typically, between 1918 and 1939 middle-class children were educated privately or in fee-paying secondary schools and working-class children in all-age state elementary schools. About two thirds of middle-class families in 1939 were home owners whereas the working classes predominantly rented from private landlords or, a small minority, from municipal authorities. Finally, up to 10 per cent of working-class families still lived in poverty in the 1930s, and a much larger number in insecurity and fear of poverty. Their inadequate diet and poor standard of housing, clothing and health care contributed to the extensive class differences in infant mortality, health and life expectancy. In 1937 the death rate per 1000 was 73 in middle-class Harrow but 138 in working-class Wigan.

International role

Empire

In 1940 the British Empire was the largest formal empire the world had ever seen and was perceived by politicians and public as sustaining Britain's status as a world power. There was always a contradiction in the very idea of a liberal empire, that is, in the notion of a country practising freedom for its own citizens at home while subjugating millions of people overseas. The contradiction was in part resolved, first, by the gradual evolution of the old settler colonies towards self-government, with New Zealand, Australia, Canada and South Africa governing their internal and external affairs by 1939, and second by the promise, not invariably or completely carried out, to prepare the rest of the empire politically and economically for self-government. In addition there was a logistical contradiction in the disproportion between the sheer size of the empire in territory and population and the resources possessed by the ruling power. In the Far East in the 1920s, for example, 304 000 Britons ruled over 334 million Asiatics. At its height the empire rested on a mixture of illusion and reality, but increasingly between the wars the illusion was undermined and the actual power became overstretched and under strain.

However, partly because of the defeat of Germany and the collapse of Russia, its two main rivals, partly because of the isolationism of the United States and partly because of judicious concessions to nationalists, especially in the Middle East and India, Conservative governments were able to conduct a successful 'holding' operation on the empire between the wars. Anti-imperialist progressives made little impact. The focus of empire shifted to Africa, the colonies there being valuable to Britain for the large quantity of metals they supplied, and the Colonial Development Act (1929) aimed to build a transport infrastructure that would facilitate the exploitation of the continent's economic potential. Symbolic of the close relationship between the empire and Britain's conception of its world role was the Singapore naval base, built to harbour the entire British fleet in the event of war with Japan and completed in 1938 at the huge cost of £60 million.

Ever since its massive expansion in the late nineteenth century, a prominent function of the empire had been to cushion Britain's relative economic decline by providing 'soft' markets for industry and outlets for external investment. Against the background of an overall shrinkage of Britain's foreign trade in the interwar period, trade with the empire increased: between 1910–14 and 1935–9 imports from the empire rose from 25 per cent of total imports to 39.5 per cent and exports to the empire increased from 36 per cent to 49 per cent of all exports. Investment within the empire also increased: from 46 per cent of all overseas investment in 1911–13 to 59 per cent in 1927–9. Somewhat paradoxically, the economic cushion provided by the empire may have undermined the domestic economy in the longer term since imperial trade and investment occurred to some extent at the expense of making the home economy more efficient and competitive.

Foreign policy

The main aim of Britain's foreign policy in the interwar years was the prevention of European war by appeasement. Appeasement involved a series of concessions to the fascist dictators, notably when Mussolini attacked Abyssinia (1935) and when Hitler remilitarised the Rhineland (1936) and absorbed Austria (1938) and Czechoslovakia (1939). The policy ended in failure on 3 September 1939 with the declaration of war against Germany after it invaded Poland. Appeasement involved negotiating with the dictators over what were considered their legitimate demands. Its underlying assumption was that modern warfare was so terrible that only the protection of national interests justified risking it. A book entitled *Guilty Men* (1940), written under the pseudonym 'Cato' by Peter Howard, Michael Foot and Frank Owen, contained a judgement of appeasement that persisted well into the postwar period. It was a ferocious polemic against the political leaders (MacDonald, Baldwin, Neville Chamberlain and others) who presided over Britain's humiliating retreat before the dictators. In the 1950s, historical 'revisionism', which found some justification for appeasement, gained influential adherents but several decades later, encouraged to some extent by Thatcherism, harsher judgements on the appeasers appeared again. The historical controversy on the subject continues. But just as important were the practical lessons drawn from the episode by politicians and elite and public opinion. At all these levels, appeasement was thoroughly condemned. Negotiation backed by the strongest possible military weapons became the foreign policy stance of all postwar governments, no matter what their political complexion.

The case for appeasement at the time and later rested on public support for the policy together with the reasonableness of conciliation. Thus when Chamberlain returned from the Munich negotiations with Hitler over Czechoslovakia, only one cabinet minister resigned, only one newspaper condemned the settlement, and a mere 30 Conservatives abstained when Labour divided the House of Commons against the motion approving the Munich Agreement. Throughout the late 1930s Conservative opponents of appeasement numbered no more than forty, including Churchill. Politicians operated within the limits set by a public opinion that considered Germany had been treated unjustly in the Treaty of Versailles (1919), and hence believed in the reasonableness of making concessions until Germany's grievances were remedied. British public opinion was still scarred by the horror of the First World War, fearful of the consequences of aerial bombardment and imbued with a belief in a policy of collective security pursued through the League of Nations. In addition there was the fact that German aggression in 1938 took place in Central and Eastern Europe, a region that was not seen as involving any British national interests; in Chamberlain's words it was 'a quarrel in a far-away country of which we know nothing'. In any case Britain lacked the military means to support a European land war and, worse still, would have been defenceless against retaliatory air attacks. Finally, reliable allies did not exist. Although it possessed vast military superiority over Germany in 1938, France was considered to lack the will to fight, the United States was isolationist and the Soviet Union was adjudged unreliable and of doubtful military potential. In the circumstances, so the argument goes, appeasement was the only reasonable option available.

The case against the governments of the 1930s is first that they failed to rearm, thereby ensuring that the country was in a state of military unpreparedness when war broke out. Rearmament began too late (1934), proceeded too slowly and was based on the wrong priorities, leading to an imbalance between the armed services. In addition Britain lagged too far behind Germany in rearming, spending perhaps as little as one third as much between 1933 and 1938. Not until 1939 was there a rough parity between the two countries' military spending. In 1939 only the British navy was in a position of superiority over its German counterpart. Moreover the priority given to the navy and airforce in the late 1930s undermined the capacity of the army to fight a defensive war in support of Britain's allies in 1940. The Foreign Office knew about German rearmament in 1931, but serious British rearmament did not begin until 1936–7.

Second, appeasement was based on a misreading of public opinion by the politicians, who believed that the British people would be unwilling to sanction any use of force in support of foreign policy goals. For example the result of the 'Peace Ballot', organised by the League of Nations Union in October 1934, is often invoked as inhibiting the national government from rearmament and from a firm response to international aggression, whereas it in fact suggested that the public would have countenanced a League of Nations initiative, backed by military means if necessary, to check the fascist dictators (Pugh, 1995, pp. 209–10). The popularity of the League of Nations with the public could have been used as a non-controversial reason for rearmament but, somewhat paradoxically, practically no one advocated rearmament in order to support the League of Nations. In practice, rearmament and support for the League of Nations were seen as rival, and mutually incompatible, policies (Taylor, 1965, p. 368).

Finally, British governments failed to realise the cumulative effects of concessions both in feeding Hitler's ambitions and in undermining the morale of Britain's allies (Taylor, 1965, pp. 351–438; Reynolds, 1991, pp. 114–44; Pugh, 1995, pp. 205–20).

The Impact of the Second World War

The Economy

The Second World War inflicted heavy costs on the British economy. Just over one third of its shipping tonnage was sunk and nearly half a million houses were destroyed. More serious than the heavy material damage, however, were the trading and financial losses. By 1944 exports had fallen to a mere 34 per cent of the 1938 level. The negotiation in 1941 of a credit agreement with the United States (Lend-Lease) just as its own resources were nearing exhaustion enabled Britain to maintain its war effort without bothering about keeping up exports to sustain its balance of payments. Lend-Lease provided Britain with large quantities of munitions, ships and other essential supplies but at the price of a large $21 000 million debt to the United States at the end of the war. In addition, in order to finance the war effort Britain sold off more than one third of its overseas assets and one third of its gold reserves, and ran up war debts totalling £3.5 billion, the equivalent of 40 per cent of its GNP in 1945 (Alford, 1988, p. 22). However this gloomy picture of Britain's prospects was balanced by the fact that the economies of most of Western Europe and Japan had been devastated too. In addition the war had stimulated innovation in key industries such as chemicals, electronics and aircraft. Despite its wartime losses and pressing financial problems,

Britain was still one of the richest countries in the world in 1945, being exceeded on the continent only by Sweden and Switzerland (neutral during the war) and elsewhere only by the United States and Canada (Pollard, 1984, p. 2).

World Role

If in one sense the Second World war brought Britain's 'finest hour' when the country stood more or less alone against Nazi Germany in 1940, it also weakened its standing as a world power by further undermining the already shaky foundations of the empire and by ushering in the era of the super-powers: the United States and the USSR. In the Far East, the sinking of the British battleships *Repulse* and the *Prince of Wales* in 1942 by the Japanese not only brought to an end British pretensions to international naval mastery, but also finally undermined British prestige in Asia and Africa. Colonial hopes of independence were raised by the Atlantic Charter, agreed by Churchill and US President Roosevelt in 1941, which proclaimed 'the right of all peoples to choose the form of government under which they live'. Britain responded with arrests and repression to the call by the Indian Congress to 'quit India' immediately, but in the face of strikes, rioting and mutinies in the armed forces, it had effectively lost control of India by 1945.

Between 1940 and 1941 Britain faced the military strategists' nightmare of war in three theatres simultaneously – the North Atlantic, the Mediterranean and the Far East. Britain's decision to fight in 1940 was its greatest contribution to the defeat of Hitler, its salvation in the Battle of Britain being owed to a combination of air superiority through its fighter aircraft and radar and to Hitler's unwillingness and lack of capacity to launch a major attack. Thereafter its survival owed most to the strategic errors that led Hitler to invade the Soviet Union in June 1941 and the Japanese to launch an aerial assault on the US fleet at Pearl Harbour in December 1941, errors that culminated in the crushing of German power in Europe by the Soviet Union and the destruction of Japanese power in the Far East by the United States. However Britain's preoccupation with defeating the Axis forces in the Mediterranean and the United States' concentration on defeating the Japanese in the Pacific delayed the opening of a western front against Germany in support of the Soviets. The consequence was the Russian advance into Eastern Europe after their defeat of Germany, which British leaders perceived as posing a threat to postwar international stability well before the war ended. During the final conferences of the war (Yalta, February 1945, and Potsdam, July–August 1945), East–West divisions between the Allies were already appearing over the postwar settlement in Germany and Eastern Europe. Ultimately, only the close involvement of the United States would guarantee European security and global balance as the new age of the Cold War dawned.

The Ending of the Wartime Coalition

The war in Europe ended on 8 May 1945 (Victory in Europe, or VE Day) and almost immediately debate began within the wartime coalition government over its continued existence. Prime Minister Churchill wanted the Labour ministers to remain in the government until victory had been achieved over Japan. But the Labour Party was adamant that its leaders should withdraw from the coalition forthwith, and on 20 May Attlee and the other Labour ministers accordingly resigned. Churchill quickly formed a 'caretaker' Government, consisting entirely of Conservatives and National Liberals, and called a general election for 5 July. With parliament being dissolved on 15 June, party warfare could begin again with an election campaign.

Further reading

Addison, P., *The Road to 1945*, 2nd edn (London: Pimlico, 1994).

Benson, J., *The Working Class in Britain, 1850–1939* (London: Longman, 1989).

Brivati, B. and H. Jones (eds), *What Difference did the War Make?* (Leicester: Leicester University Press, 1993).

Brooke, S., *Labour's War: The Labour Party during the Second World War* (Oxford: Clarendon Press, 1992).

Cronin, J. E., *Labour and Society in Britain, 1918–1979* (London: Batsford, 1984).

Digby, A., *British Welfare Policy: Workhouse to Workfare* (London: Faber, 1989).

Johnson, P. (ed.) *Twentieth Century Britain* (London: Longman, 1994).

McKibbin, R., *The Ideologies of Class* (Oxford: Oxford University Press, 1991).

Middlemas, K., *Politics in Industrial Society* (London: André Deutsch, 1979).

Porter, B., *The Lion's Share: A Short History of British Imperialism 1850–1983*, 2nd edn (London: Longman, 1984).

Reynolds, D., *Britannia Overruled: British Policy and World Power in the Twentieth Century* (London: Longman, 1991).

1
The Governments of Postwar Britain

The Labour Governments, 1945–51

Labour's huge victory in the 1945 general election was based on the national desire for social change that was generated during the Second World War. Having gained a reputation for patriotism and governing competence since 1940, Labour was closely linked to the popular desire for government-sponsored social betterment, while the Conservatives were associated with the unemployment and appeasement of the 1930s. The polls pointed to a Labour victory, but were generally disbelieved as most commentators considered that Churchill's wartime reputation would be sufficient to ensure Conservative success. In the event Labour achieved a landslide victory, gaining over 200 seats from the Conservatives on a 12 per cent swing and increasing its vote by 3.75 million compared with 1935. It took office in late July with an experienced team. Unpretentious but shrewd and experienced, the Labour leader, Clement Attlee, proved one of Britain's most effective postwar prime ministers and he was well supported by the other members of Labour's 'Big Five'. The former TGWU leader, Ernest Bevin, was an inspired choice as foreign secretary; Herbert Morrison, leader of the House of Commons and lord president of the Council, ably supervised the government's legislative programme; whilst Hugh Dalton, who had presided over Labour's recovery of intellectual credibility in the 1930s, was chancellor of the exchequer until a political error over the budget forced him to give way to the austere Sir Stafford Cripps, who gained increasing influence over the inner sanctum of the government.

Labour presided over six years of considerable achievement, laying the foundations of Britain's social, economic and foreign policy for the next thirty years. Much of this programme, including the extension of public ownership to more than one fifth of the economy, the creation of the welfare state and the granting of independence to India and Pakistan, was carried out by 1948. The signing of a multinational treaty for the defence of Western Europe, the North Atlantic Treaty Organisation, followed in 1949. But this straightforward statement of achievements should not obscure the fact that this was an embattled government, facing huge responsibilities with considerably diminished resources. Its most acute political problems stemmed from the country's financial predicament, its defence requirements in the new

BOX 1.1   *The Labour governments, 1945–51*

Personalities

- Clement Attlee (Prime Minister)
- Hugh Dalton (Chancellor of the Exchequer, 1945–7)
- Sir Stafford Cripps (Chancellor of the Exchequer, 1947–50)
- Hugh Gaitskell (Chancellor of the Exchequer, 1950–1)

- Ernest Bevin (Foreign Secretary, 1945–51)
- Herbert Morrison (Lord President of the Council, 1945–51; Foreign Secretary, 1951)
- James Chuter Ede (Home Secretary)
- Aneuran Bevan (posts included Minister of Health, 1945–51)

Attlee Cabinet: (standing, left to right) Aneuran Bevan, George Isaacs, Lord Stansgate, George Hall, Lord Pethick-Lawrence, Jack Lawson, Joseph Westwood, Emmanuel Shinwell, Tom Williams; (seated, left to right) Viscount Addison, Lord Jowett, Sir Stafford Cripps, Arthur Greenwood, Ernest Bevin, Clement Attlee, Herbert Morrison, Hugh Dalton, A. V. Alexander, James Chuter Ede, Ellen Wilkinson.

Events

- VE (Victory in Europe) Day, 8 May 1945
- VJ (Victory over Japan) Day, 15 August 1945
- End of Lend-Lease and negotiation of US Loan ($3750 m.), 1945

- Devaluation of the pound from $4.03 to $2.80, 1948
- NATO Treaty signed, 1948
- Outbreak of Korean War, 1950
- Formation of European Coal and Steel Community (ECSC), 1951

Box 1.1 continued

Legislation/Policies

- National Health Service Act, 1946
- National Insurance Act, 1946
- Nationalisation of coal (1946), civil aviation (1946), gas (1948), electricity (1948), railways, canals and road transport (1948), iron and steel (1949)
- Repeal of 1927 Trade Disputes Act, 1946
- Decision to manufacture A-Bomb, 1946

- Independence for India, Pakistan (1947), Burma and Ceylon (1948)
- Policy of full employment
- Wage and dividends freeze, 1948
- Rationing and control of production in many spheres
- Parliament Act, 1948, reducing delaying power of House of Lords from two years to one year

Issues

- Handling of 1947 fuel crisis
- Continuation of rationing
- Nationalisation of iron and steel and possible further nationalisations

- Huge rise in defence expenditure after outbreak of Korean war and imposition of prescription charges

General Elections

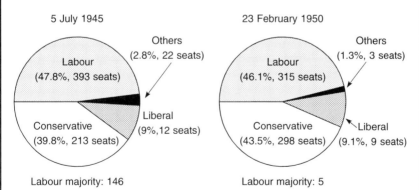

5 July 1945

Labour (47.8%, 393 seats)
Others (2.8%, 22 seats)
Liberal (9%, 12 seats)
Conservative (39.8%, 213 seats)

Labour majority: 146

23 February 1950

Labour (46.1%, 315 seats)
Others (1.3%, 3 seats)
Liberal (9.1%, 9 seats)
Conservative (43.5%, 298 seats)

Labour majority: 5

nuclear age, and its problematic relationship with its wartime allies, the United States and the Soviet Union.

Already facing large overseas debts and a massive loss of shipping, exports and overseas investment at the end of the war, Britain's economic difficulties worsened when the United States abruptly terminated Lend-Lease immediately after VJ Day in August 1945. Britain's 'financial Dunkirk' was countered by the immediate negotiation of a large American loan at 2 per cent interest, in return for which Britain was required to accept the Bretton Woods Agreement (1944) on the world monetary system, and to remove all restrictions on the exchange of sterling into dollars (convertibility) in early 1947. Britain was also under pressure from the United States to dismantle the empire, and it suffered further disappointment in 1946 when the McMahon Act effectively terminated atomic cooperation between the US and British governments (Britain had done important early work on the atomic bomb and in 1943–4 had reached an agreement with the United States on postwar cooperation on atomic matters and British approval of any deployment of the bomb). The Labour government responded with the secret decision to manufacture a British A-bomb. With Britain perceiving itself as under threat from the Soviets and uncertain of the United States' foreign policy intentions, this policy was reasonable at the time, despite the huge economic strain it imposed, as was the 1947 decision to continue conscription, an unprecedented move in peacetime. The Attlee government also allowed US bombers (which had atomic capability from 1949) to be stationed in Britain and participated in an airlift of supplies to Berlin when it was blockaded by the Soviets in 1948–9. However the weakness of the economy forced major retrenchments in Britain's world-wide commitments in 1947, with the government withdrawing from Greece and Turkey and referring the Palestine problem to the United Nations. By 1949 international stability, and with it Britain's position, had been improved by the revolution in US foreign policy, whereby the United States assumed responsibility for Western military security through the signing of the NATO and other treaties.

If a more secure world was the major aim of Labour's foreign policy, recovery was the principal goal of its economic policy. This involved achieving a smooth transition from a wartime to a peacetime economy and rebuilding the country's shrunken export markets. Much of this had been done by 1948, when demobilisation of the forces into civilian occupations was complete and a fourfold increase in exports, together with import restrictions and continued rationing, had brought the current account balance of payments back into balance. Beginning in late 1948 the government began to remove economic controls, and by 1951 it had abandoned clothing, petrol and sweet rationing and relaxed the rationing of food. Between 1948 and 1950 Britain's postwar recovery was boosted by $2.7 million of the $12 million provided by the United States under the Marshall Plan for European Recovery. However shortages of essential supplies such as coal, the needs for welfare and defence spending and the financial conditions imposed by international allies such as the United States brought severe periodic crises. In 1947 a coal shortage during severe winter weather led to a fuel crisis that resulted in a 20 per cent loss of exports, and this was followed by the convertibility crisis of 15 July 1947, which was only solved by suspending convertibility in August and making cuts in public spending. Considered a national humiliation at the time and badly-handled by the government, the devaluation of the pound sterling in 1949 from $4.03 to $2.80 later came to be seen primarily as a technical and necessary adjustment of the exchange rate. Finally, the government had to cope with rising prices: prices rose by 20 per cent between 1945 and 1949 as a result of postwar shortages, and by a further 20 per cent between 1949 and 1951 as a consequence of devaluation and the outbreak of the Korean War. The government responded to inflationary pressures by imposing a wage freeze in 1949 and invoking emergency powers to curb the ensuing trade union militancy, especially in the docks.

Labour fought the 1950 general election on its achievements: full employment, economic recovery, health, social security and education reforms. The main theme of the Conservative campaign was anti-socialism, socialism being equated with unnecessary controls, especially rationing, wasteful bureaucracy and nationalisation. Stressing 'consolidation' rather than advance, Labour promised a modest degree of additional nationalisation, including the nationalisation of cement and sugar; the Conservatives vowed to restore private ownership of iron, steel and road haulage and to introduce tax cuts whilst retaining full employment and preserving the welfare state. Labour suffered a 2.9 per cent adverse swing but still gained a narrow five-seat victory, although the result showed how much political ground the Conservatives had regained, especially in suburban and commuter areas.

Labour's 1950–1 administration was a troubled one, dominated by a furious internal row over the economic implications of military participation in the Korean War. Labour's decision to support the UN action by sending a contingent to help reverse the invasion of South by North Korea led to a huge rise in the defence budget and adversely effected exports and living standards. It also had serious political consequences: three ministers – Aneuran Bevan, John Freeman and Harold Wilson – resigned in April 1951 in protest against the scale of the rearmament programme and the introduction of prescription charges. The Labour government also prosecuted striking gas and dock workers, had to cope with an unexpected crisis in the Middle East when Persia nationalised the oil installations of the Anglo-Iranian Oil Company at Ibadan, faced fierce opposition harassment in Parliament in 1951 and was confronted by another balance of payments crisis in September 1951. By now it was a jaded administration, weakened by the ill-health of most of its leading figures and lacking in new ideas and legislative initiatives. The Conservatives held an eleven-point Gallup Poll lead in September 1951 when Attlee announced that a general election would be held in the following month.

The Conservative Governments, 1951–64

Labour cut the Conservative lead during the 1951 campaign and went on to poll its highest ever vote, a massive 14 million, thereby achieving a 'victory in votes'. However the Conservatives gained a small majority on a 0.9 per cent swing, and Winston Churchill thus resumed the premiership at the age of 77. His government included men who who would remain major figures in British politics for over a decade, all of them on the 'one nation' wing of Conservatism. His foreign secretary, and successor as prime minister in 1955, was Anthony Eden; R. A. Butler, who was later to become home secretary and then foreign secretary, was chancellor of the exchequer; Harold Macmillan, premier between 1957 and 1963, was in charge of housing; whilst another very influential figure, Iain Macleod, later minister of labour (1955–9) and colonial secretary (1959–61), became minister of health in 1952.

This was a moderate, cautious administration that was anxious to secure domestic peace. Hence it conciliated the trade unions, broadly maintained the level of social spending on health, education and pensions, kept its electoral promise to build more than 300 000 houses a year by 1953, and privatised modestly. It continued to scrap economic controls and finally ended food rationing in July 1954. Benefiting from the termination of the Korean War and the terms of trade moving back in Britain's favour, it introduced tax cuts in the 1955 budget. Labour's blend of strategic retreat combined with colonial economic development was also maintained, with decolonisation coming to a complete halt under Churchill. Much of the Administration's emphasis, as with successor Conservative governments in this phase, was on defence and foreign policy. Thus it presided over Britain's first A-bomb test, took the decision to develop the even more powerful H-bomb, devoted much diplomatic effort to securing German rearmament through the Atlantic Alliance rather than a European defence union and, after Stalin's death in 1953, initiated the attempt to broker détente between the superpowers through summit meetings.

Churchill, who had a serious stroke in June 1953, finally handed over to Eden in April 1955. The new prime minister held a general election within seven weeks of taking over. An electioneering budget, full employment, the final ending of wartime controls, Labour divisions, even the optimistic national mood occasioned by the coronation of Elizabeth II (1953), the conquest of Everest by a British-led team (1953) and the running by a Briton of the first four-minute mile (1954) probably contributed to the comfortable Conservative victory. But the party's delight was short-lived. By the end of the year a severe balance of payments crisis had brought the need for public expenditure cuts, and Butler had given way to Macmillan as chancellor.

Invited to the Messina talks on European integration in June 1955, Britain, which did not think the enterprise could succeed and in any case saw itself as superior to its European neighbours, unsuccessfully tried to undermine and obstruct the negotiations that later bore fruit in the creation of the European Economic Community with the signing of the Treaty of Rome (1957) (see Chapter 5). Finally, the Suez Crisis (1956), which involved a concerted but unsuccessful attack on Egypt by Britain, France and Israel after Egyptian President Nasser had nationalised the Suez Canal, destroyed Eden's political career and dealt a long-lasting blow to Britain's international prestige (see below, pp. 55-6, 261–3). On 9 January 1957 Eden resigned and was replaced by Macmillan.

Macmillan, who carefully cultivated an image of unflappability, set about restoring the government's reputation and with it party morale. Relations with the United States were repaired, although Britain had clearly become the dependent partner. As Britain's V-bomber force was obsolete and its medium-range missile, Blue Streak, would not be available until 1962–5, 60 US Thor missiles stationed in Britain would give it a nuclear capacity in the interim. Eisenhower also agreed to share US nuclear information with Britain. A start was made in 1957 in scaling down Britain's excessive spending on defence and overstretched overseas obligations. Decolonisation, having re-started under Eden with the granting of independence to the Sudan, moved slowly forward, with the Gold Coast (Ghana) and Malaya (Malaysia) becoming independent in 1957 and the military emergency in Cyprus gradually receding (after 1960 the retreat from empire went with a rush). However not all of the government's ventures succeeded so well. Worried about the likelihood of suffering discriminatory tariffs from the newly formed EEC, Macmillan sought to create a European free trade area in industrial goods comprising Britain, the six EEC partners and any other country wishing to join. But the effort broke down in November 1958 because of British unwillingness to accept a genuine customs union with Europe. The government moved on to negotiate an industrial free trade grouping with six other countries and the European Free Trade Area (EFTA) – the 'Outer Seven' – came into existence in July 1960. The government hoped thereby to 'build bridges' with the EEC six, but the possibility that its EFTA obligations might handicap a future attempt to join the Community appeared not to have occurred to it.

The Conservatives won their third victory in a row in the October 1959 general election with an increased majority. They benefited from the growing prosperity of the country and, in a close-fought campaign that Labour expected to win, from the Labour leader Gaitskell's error in maintaining that income tax would not be increased to pay for Labour's social programme. But the government was soon in difficulty. First, its nuclear weapons programme collapsed in early 1960 with the abandonment of Blue Streak on grounds of cost. Macmillan responded by negotiating the purchase of

BOX 1.2   *The Conservative governments, 1951–64*

Personalities

- Winston Churchill (Prime Minister, 1951–5)
- Sir Anthony Eden (Foreign Secretary, 1951–5; Prime Minister, 1955–7)
- Harold Macmillan (Foreign Secretary, 1955; Chancellor of the Exchequer, 1955–7; Prime Minister, 1957–63)
- Sir Alec Douglas-Home (Foreign Secretary, 1963–4; Prime Minister, 1963–4)
- R. A. Butler (Chancellor of the Exchequer, 1951–5; Home Secretary, 1957–62; Foreign Secretary, 1963–4)
- Peter Thorneycroft (Chancellor, 1957–8)
- Derek Heathcoat-Amory (Chancellor, 1958–60)

- Selwyn Lloyd (Foreign Secretary, 1955–60; Chancellor, 1960–2)
- Reginald Maudling (Chancellor, 1962–4)
- Sir David Maxwell-Fyfe (Home Secretary, 1951–4)
- Gwilym Lloyd-George (Home Secretary, 1954–7)
- Henry Brooke (Home Secretary, 1962–4)
- Lord Woolton (Lord President of the Council, 1951–2; Chancellor of the Duchy of Lancaster, 1952–5)
- Viscount Hailsham (renounced title to become Quintin Hogg in 1963) (posts included Lord President of the Council, 1957–9, 1960–4)
- Iain Macleod (posts included Colonial Secretary, 1959–61)

The Churchill Cabinet (1955): (standing, left to right) Osbert Peake, Peter Thorneycroft, Sir Walter Monckton, James Stuart, Gwilym Lloyd-George, Alan Lennox-Boyd, Derek Heathcoat-Amory, Sir David Eccles, Sir Norman Brook (cabinet secretary); (seated, left to right) Harold Macmillan, Lord Woolton, Lord Kilmuir, Anthony Eden, Winston Churchill, Lord Salisbury, R. A. Butler, Lord Swinton, Harry Crookshank.

Box 1.2 continued

The Macmillan Cabinet (1963): (Back row) Michael Noble, Julian Amery, Aubrey Jones, Jack Profumo, Tim Bligh, unidentified, Michael Fraser, Knox Cunningham, Freddy Erroll, Geoffrey Rippon, Keith Joseph, Richard Wood; (middle row) Peter Carrington, Christopher Soames, Edward Heath, Jack Maclay, Edward Boyle, Peter Thorneycroft, Hugh Fraser, unidentified, John Boyd-Carpenter, Bill Deedes; (front row) Enoch Powell, Ernest Marples, Iain Macleod, Henry Brooke, Rab, Harold Macmillan, Reggie Maudling, unidentified, Reggie Manningham-Buller, Quintin Hailsham.

Events

- Death of George VI and accession of Elizabeth II, 1952
- First US H-bomb, 1952
- British A-Bomb explosion, 1952
- First Soviet H-bomb, 1953
- Death of Stalin, 1953
- Suez expedition, 1956
- Soviet suppression of Hungarian rising, 1956
- Establishment of the EEC by Treaty of Rome, 1957

- Resignation of Chancellor of the Exchequer Thorneycroft over public expenditure policy, 1958
- Polaris agreement with US, 1962, after abandonment of British missile, Blue Streak
- Cuban missile crisis, 1962
- 'Night of the Long Knives': Macmillan's sacking of seven cabinet ministers, 1962

Legislation/Policies

- Scrapping of economic controls and ending of rationing
- Denationalisation of iron, steel and road haulage
- Rapid decolonisation, independence of most

former colonies by mid 1960s
- Life Peerage Act, 1958, allowing creation of non-hereditary peers and women to sit in House of Lords

Box 1.2 continued

- Formation of 'Outer Seven' trading bloc (EFTA), 1959
- National Economic Development Council, 1962
- Pay pause, 1961, followed by wage rise 'guiding light', 1962

- National Incomes Commission, 1962
- Unsuccessful application to join EEC, 1962

Issues

- Britain's role in the world, especially with regard to capacity for independent military action (the Suez venture) and possession of an 'independent' nuclear deterrent

- Democracy in the Conservative Party arising out of the 'emergence' of Sir Alec Douglas-Home as leader in 1963

General Elections

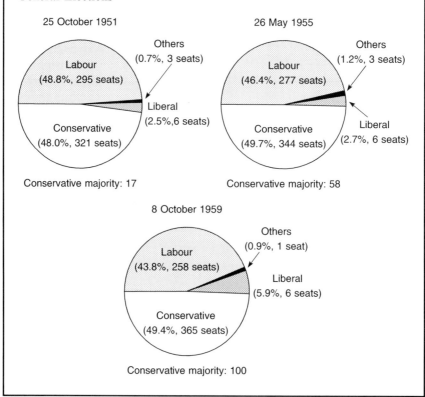

25 October 1951

Labour (48.8%, 295 seats)
Others (0.7%, 3 seats)
Liberal (2.5%, 6 seats)
Conservative (48.0%, 321 seats)

Conservative majority: 17

26 May 1955

Labour (46.4%, 277 seats)
Others (1.2%, 3 seats)
Liberal (2.7%, 6 seats)
Conservative (49.7%, 344 seats)

Conservative majority: 58

8 October 1959

Labour (43.8%, 258 seats)
Others (0.9%, 1 seat)
Liberal (5.9%, 6 seats)
Conservative (49.4%, 365 seats)

Conservative majority: 100

Skybolt, a US air-to-ground missile, and when this programme was cancelled in November 1962, leaving Britain without nuclear weapons, he persuaded President Kennedy to allow Britain to purchase Polaris submarine-launched missiles on favourable terms. Although Britain was permitted to use these weapons independently when 'supreme national interests' were at stake, its nuclear dependence on the United States was confirmed by this episode, leading critics to complain that Britain's deterrent was neither British nor independent nor a deterrent. Second, by early 1961 the government was in economic difficulties. To counter an adverse balance of payments, tax increases and public expenditure cuts were imposed together with a public sector 'pay pause' in July. New initiatives followed, including a swing towards greater economic interventionism through the formation of corporatist-style institutions such as the National Economic Development Council, and an application to join the EEC, which was vetoed by the French President de Gaulle in January 1963. Third, the government was further embarrassed by the Profumo affair: the secretary of state for war, Jack Profumo, was forced to resign in June 1963 after admitting he had lied to the Commons about his affair with a call-girl, who was also involved with the Soviet naval attache. Now the butt of the new TV satirists, the government was on the run. Labour's lead in the polls, which had been continuous since August 1961, was seemingly impervious to anything the prime minister tried to do to remedy the situation, including the drastic step of sacking one third of his cabinet in July 1962. When Macmillan was forced to step down through ill-health in October 1963, his successor Sir Alec Douglas-Home faced the virtually impossible task of restoring the government's fortunes in the twelve months before the next election.

The Labour Governments, 1964–70

Labour's lead over the Conservatives narrowed before the October 1964 general election. It finally took office with a very slender majority of four, in the knowledge that it would have to go to the electorate again within the next two years. Its election success rested on a combination of public disaffection with the Conservatives' record, dubbed 'thirteen wasted years' by Labour, and its leader Harold Wilson's widely believed claim to superior economic competence over his Conservative rival. Key personalities in the governments led by the politically adroit Wilson included the Labour deputy leader, the rumbustious George Brown – a volatile figure first at the newly created Department of Economic Affairs (DEA), then as foreign minister before his resignation in 1968 – and James Callaghan, who was chancellor of the exchequer until 1967, when he was reshuffled to the home secretaryship after the devaluation he had resisted had taken place. The influence of Roy Jenkins – a liberal and reforming home secretary before becoming a tough chancellor of the exchequer – increased steadily. Denis Healey proved both

BOX 1.3   *The Labour governments, 1964–70*

Personalities

- Harold Wilson (Prime Minister)
- James Callaghan (Chancellor of the Exchequer, 1964–7, Home Secretary, 1967–70)
- Roy Jenkins (Home Secretary, 1965–7, Chancellor of the Exchequer, 1967–70)
- Patrick Gordon-Walker (Foreign Secretary, 1964–5)
- Michael Stewart (Foreign Secretary, 1965–6, 1968–70, Minister of Economic Affairs, 1966–7)
- George Brown (Minister of Economic Affairs, 1964–6, 1966–8)
- Peter Shore (Minister of Economic Affairs, 1967–9)
- Sir Frank Soskice (Home Secretary, 1964–5)
- Richard Crossman (posts included Minister of Housing and Local Government, 1964–6, Minister of Health and Social Security, 1968–70)
- Anthony Crosland (posts included Minister of Education and Science, 1965–7)
- Barbara Castle (posts included Minister of Transport, 1965–8, Minister of Employment, 1968–70)

The Wilson Cabinet (July 1965): (standing, left to right) Fred Lee, Frank Cousins, Douglas Houghton, Anthony Crosland, Douglas Jay, Barbara Castle, Anthony Greenwood, Earl of Longford, Richard Crossman, Ray Gunter, Fred Peart, Tom Fraser, Sir Burke Trend (cabinet secretary), (seated, left to right) William Ross, Sir Frank Soskice, Michael Stewart, Lord Gardiner, George Brown, Harold Wilson, Herbert Bowden, James Callaghan, Denis Healey, Arthur Bottomley, James Griffiths.

Box 1.3 continued

Events

- Vietnam War, 1964–73
- Abolition of death penalty, 1965
- Liberalisation of the law on capital punishment (1965), homosexuality (1967), abortion (1967), divorce (1969) and censorship of the arts (1968)
- Wave of world-wide student protest, 1968
- Devaluation of the pound from $2.80 to $2.40, 1967
- Formation of National Front, 1967
- Enoch Powell delivers his 'rivers of blood' speech, 1968
- Royal Commission on Trade Unions and Employers Associations Report, 1968
- Civil rights marches in Northern Ireland, 1968
- British troops sent to restore order in Northern Ireland, 1969

Legislation/Policies

- National Economic Plan, 1964–7
- Prices and Incomes Board established, 1965
- Comprehensive education launched by Circular 12/65, 1965
- Prices and Incomes Act, 1966, following prices and incomes standstill
- Economic sanctions against Rhodesia after Rhodesia's unilateral declaration of independence, 1965
- Failure of application to join the EEC, 1967
- White paper &it,In Place of Strife&tf, proposed 28-day 'conciliation pause' and pre-strike ballots in industrial disputes, 1969

Issues

- Immigration and race relations
- Civil rights and public order in Northern Ireland
- Devaluation, 1967
- Rhodesian sanctions policy
- Trade union reform

Box 1.3 continued

General Elections

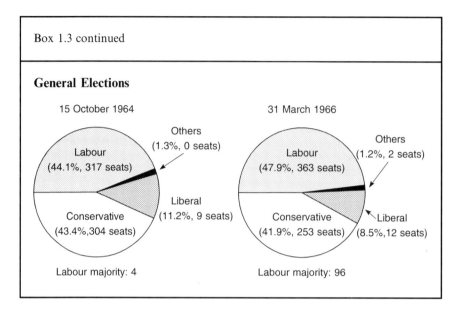

15 October 1964

Others
(1.3%, 0 seats)

Labour
(44.1%, 317 seats)

Liberal
(11.2%, 9 seats)

Conservative
(43.4%,304 seats)

Labour majority: 4

31 March 1966

Others
(1.2%, 2 seats)

Labour
(47.9%, 363 seats)

Conservative
(41.9%, 253 seats)

Liberal
(8.5%,12 seats)

Labour majority: 96

an able and a ruthless defence secretary. Anthony Crosland, a notable reformer at the Department for Education in the mid 1960s, Richard Crossman, as minister of housing and local government, then social services, and Barbara Castle, despite the failure of her trade union reforms, all made an impact.

Labour inherited a huge trade deficit from the Conservatives and decided immediately against devaluation. The decisive arguments against devaluation for Wilson and his closest colleagues were the possibility that it would trigger competitive devaluations by other countries, the certainty that it would annoy the United States, the notion of the sacredness of sterling as an international status symbol, and, against the background of the earlier devaluation of 1949, an acute sensitivity to Tory gibes that Labour was 'the party of devaluation'. Instead Labour sought to boost exports by a 15 per cent import surcharge on manufactures followed by an emergency budget that raised income tax, national insurance contributions and petrol duty to bolster sterling. These measures and a 2 per cent increase in the bank lending rate failed to stem speculation against the pound, which was brought to a temporary end only by the negotiation, with US help, of a massive loan of $3000 million in credits from the central banks of leading industrial countries. This gave Labour the breathing space to proceed with its national plan for the growth of production and exports. Under the aegis of George Brown at the Department of Economic Affairs, a target figure of 25 per cent was set for the growth of national output between 1964 and 1970. Key

institutions in its achievement were to be the National Economic Development Council, chaired by Brown, and a National Board for Prices and
Incomes, chaired by a former Conservative MP, Aubrey Jones, which would
preside over prices and incomes policy. The experiment came to nothing,
foundering by 1966 on the Treasury's suspicion of a rival economic department, inadequate preparation and the trade unions' preference for free
collective bargaining.

In September 1965, after further speculative pressure against the pound,
Wilson made a secret deal with the United States to avoid devaluation and
retain a British military presence east of Suez in return for massive US
support of sterling on the foreign exchanges. This agreement revealed
Wilson's deepest political beliefs: the Anglo-American alliance, the Commonwealth and the status of sterling as a world currency. By retaining its
nuclear weapons and with US help, Britain could preserve for a little longer
its precarious status as a world power. The strategic reason was the volatility
of the situation in the Far East in the mid 1960s: China had just tested its
atomic bomb and was about to be thrust into the cultural revolution, and
Britain was committed to defending its Commonwealth ally, the Malaysian
federation, against Indonesian military infiltration. The decision shaped the
fortunes of the Wilson administration, setting sharp limits to the defence cuts
achievable by Healey and requiring another huge deflationary package in
July 1966, when a further bout of heavy pressure on sterling was made worse
by the effects of a lengthy seamen's strike. After this crisis a certain
reappraisal took place within the government, which, bolstered by a substantial Commons majority achieved in the general election of March 1966,
decided to make a second application for membership of the Common
Market. However this initiative was foiled by another French veto in May
1967. Worse followed. After further blows to exports by adverse world
circumstances in summer 1967 and a dock strike followed by the worst-ever
monthly trade deficit in October, another heavy run on sterling made
devaluation impossible to avoid. A 14.3 per cent devaluation from $2.80
to $2.40 took place on 18 November, accompanied by $3000 million stand-
by credits, largely from the International Monetary Fund (IMF). Thereafter
the new chancellor of the exchequer, Roy Jenkins, through the continual
economic restraints of 'two years hard slog', gave priority to eliminating the
prolonged balance of payments deficit. With the added assistance of a
recovery of world trade in 1969, he had achieved a surplus on Britain's
external account by 1970. In January 1968 came retreat on the east of Suez
policy with Wilson's announcement that the British military presence in the
Far and Middle East was to be wound up by the early 1970s.

The Wilson government faced other intractable problems over Northern
Ireland, Rhodesia and industrial relations. In Northern Ireland, following
serious sectarian rioting in Londonderry/Derry and Belfast in summer 1969,
the government deployed troops to keep order in the province and they were

still there when it left office in 1970. A new phase of the Irish troubles had begun. Labour continued the rapid decolonisation pursued after 1960 by the Conservatives, but when the white minority in Southern Rhodesia made a unilateral declaration of independence in November 1965 in order to prevent black majority rule, it proved unable to put down the rebellion, despite a series of dramatic meetings between Wilson and the premier of the illegal regime, Ian Smith. Ruling out force at an early stage, the government relied on oil sanctions, which were easily evaded even by British oil companies. Labour failed still more spectacularly in its attempt to reform industrial relations, to which it turned in 1968 in order to combat low productivity and frequent strikes. Its proposals in the white paper 'In Place of Strife' (1969) to curb the unions' strike power broke down in the face of opposition from the trade unions, the parliamentary Labour Party and from within the cabinet, ending with a worthless 'solemn and binding undertaking' by the TUC to monitor strikes and disputes itself. Labour's main achievements were in social policy: it accelerated the demise of the eleven-plus exams, pioneered the Open University, introduced rent rebates, encouraged more poor people to apply for national assistance, increased pensions and family allowances, legislated to outlaw racial discrimination and provided parliamentary time for the liberal reforms by private members that subsequently did much to turn Britain into a more decent and humane society.

The Conservative Government, 1970–4

Mainly because of Labour's poll lead in the weeks before voting but also because Harold Wilson was a more popular figure than his Conservative counterpart, Edward Heath, the Conservative victory in the general election of 1970 was a surprise. What may have tipped the scales towards the Conservatives was the announcement of an increased trade deficit a few days before the election. In fact public opinion had swung away from Labour between April 1967 and April 1970, giving the Conservatives an unbroken and often large lead in the polls and resulting in a record fifteen by-election defeats for Labour. Labour voter apathy may also have played a part, with potential Labour voters deterred from voting by their disappointment with the government's record. The Conservatives had a modest parliamentary majority of 30 on a 4.8 per cent national swing. Heath could call on experienced figures such as Sir Alec Douglas-Home and Reginald Maudling, and newer men such as James Prior, William Whitelaw and Peter Walker enhanced their reputations. But overall his government suffered from a lack of commanding personalities, especially when the death of Iain Maclead deprived Heath of his chancellor of the exchequer a mere month after taking office.

The politics of European membership, industrial relations and pay policy dominated the Heath years. Britain's only explicitly pro-European postwar prime minister, Heath took advantage of the more favourable situation occasioned by de Gaulle's death in 1970 to lodge a successful application to join the European Economic Community. But, as Britain joined after the rules had been laid down, Heath's bargaining position was weak and the terms obtained were less favourable than if Britain had joined at the outset. Moreover Heath took into the Community a country that was profoundly uncertain about the merits of membership, and whose economy, with its weak industry but efficient agriculture, was rather ill-suited to the EEC pattern of price support and tariffs on imports. The timing of entry, at the moment when the long postwar European boom was coming to an end, was also unfortunate. Like his predecessors Heath believed that the collapse of Britain's imperial destiny and the weakness of the Commonwealth option made entry to Europe imperative, but to the general public his government stressed the economic benefits of membership in terms of improved living standards and played down its costs. By the end of the 1970s, after a five-year transition period Britain was providing 20 per cent of EEC income, which was reasonably fair in relation to the size of its economy, but it received less than 10 per cent of EEC spending (Reynolds, 1991, p. 245).

When Heath came to power he was committed to full employment and the welfare state, but pledged himself to a different, less interventionist tack to regenerate the economy. This involved lower taxes and public expenditure, a rejection of government assistance to ailing industries, legal regulation of industrial relations and a move away from prices and incomes policy. Accordingly the Conservative government began by introducing tax and public spending cuts, abolishing the Prices and Incomes Board and passing tough industrial relations legislation aimed at curbing unofficial strikes by compulsory pre-strike ballots and 'cooling-off' periods. However by mid-1971 a combination of rapidly rising inflation and unemployment and stagnating industrial production had forced the government into a policy 'U-turn'. 'Lame duck' companies such as Rolls-Royce and Upper Clyde Shipbuilders were given financial assistance by the government, a very interventionist Industry Act was introduced and incomes policy was revived, with a Pay Board and Prices Commission being established in 1973. Moreover the government's industrial relations legislation unleashed a wave of trade union protest, which by 1972 had rendered this too a dead letter. These were years of almost continual industrial disorder: 24 million working days were lost to strikes in 1972 and the National Union of Mineworkers imposed a heavy defeat on the government in February.

Beginning in late 1973 a series of blows combined to bring down the government. First, the Egypt–Israeli War was the prelude to a massive fourfold increase in oil prices. Retail prices, which were already under pressure from the government's expansionist economic policy (the 'Barber boom'), suddenly surged by 10 per cent. Second, at the same time the government became embroiled in another dispute with the miners, who had

BOX 1.4   *The Conservative government, 1970–4*

Personalities

- Edward Heath (Prime Minister)
- Anthony Barber (Chancellor of the Exchequer, 1970–4)
- Sir Alec Douglas-Home (Foreign Secretary, 1970–4)

- Reginald Maudling (Home Secretary, 1970–2)
- Robert Carr (Home Secretary, 1972–4)
- William Whitelaw (posts included Secretary of State for Employment, 1973–4)

The Heath Cabinet: (standing, left to right) Earl Jellicoe, John Goodber, Peter Thomas, Peter Walker, Gordon Campell, John Davies, Maurice Macmillan, Sir Geoffrey Howe, Burke Trend (cabinet secretary), (seated, left to right) Geoffrey Rippon, James Prior, Lord Carrington, Anthny Barber, Sir Alec Douglas-Home, Edward Heath, Quintin Hogg, William Whitelaw, Robert Carr, Sir Keith Joseph, Margaret Thatcher.

Events

- Ending of dollar–gold convertibility by United States and hence of Bretton Woods era
- 'Bloody Sunday', Derry, 30 January 1972: 13 demonstrators shot dead by British troops
- Six week miners' strike ended by 22 per cent pay increase after Wilberforce Court of Inquiry, 1972

- Quadrupling of world oil prices following Arab–Israeli War, October 1973
- Miners' overtime ban followed by complete stoppage, 1973–4
- Kilbrandon Report, 1973, with majority recommending elected assemblies for Scotland and Wales
- Three-day week for industry to conserve fuel stocks, December 1973
- 'Who governs Britain?' election, February 1974

Box 1.4 continued

Policies/Legislation

- Floating exchange rate for sterling after ending of gold–dollar convertibility, 1971
- Industrial Relations Act, 1971 (establishing Industrial Relations Court with power to order pre-strike ballots and 'cooling-off' periods)
- Financial rescue of ailing Rolls-Royce (nationalisation) and Upper Clyde Shipbuilders (large subsidy), 1971

- Interventionist Industry Act, 1972
- European Communities Act, 1972, followed by British entry into European Economic Community, 1 January 1973
- Suspension of Northern Ireland Parliament, direct rule from Westminster, 1972
- Prices and incomes legislation, involving three-stage policy, 1972–4

Issues

- Trade union reform which provoked militant trade union response and large-scale industrial conflict

- Government 'U-turns' on non-intervention in industry and pay policy
- Governmental authority: February 1974 election fought on 'Who governs Britain?'

General Election

18 June 1970

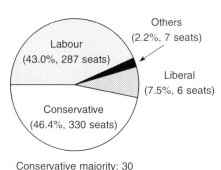

Others (2.2%, 7 seats)

Labour (43.0%, 287 seats)

Liberal (7.5%, 6 seats)

Conservative (46.4%, 330 seats)

Conservative majority: 30

called an overtime ban in November in support of a 40 per cent wage claim. Heath, who was also involved at that time with the demanding negotiations over Northern Ireland that led to the Sunningdale Agreement, declared a state of emergency to keep essential industries going, and a month later (13 December) announced that a three-day week would begin in January. By early February 1974 the country was in crisis: a record £1.5 billion balance of payments deficit for 1973 was announced and – with the government defending phase 3 of its prices and incomes policy and unable to find a compromise with the NUM – 81 per cent of miners voted for a national strike. Three days later (7 February) Heath called a general election for 28 February. In the circumstances the leading issue inevitably became 'Who governs Britain – the Government or the trade unions?' Apart from Europe, very little had gone right for the Heath government, neither in Rhodesia, where the illegal regime dragged on, nor in Northern Ireland, where there had been rising sectarian violence, the introduction of internment and the events of 'Bloody Sunday', nor, least of all, with industrial relations in Britain.

The Labour Governments, 1974–9

The main issues in the February 1974 general election were industrial relations and the economy, but unfortunately for the Conservatives the trade union issue was overtaken by the economy as the campaign proceeded, with the announcement of massive price rises and (three days before polling) a record trade deficit. With the public showing its loss of confidence in both major parties, the election produced a 'hung parliament'. Labour, as the largest party, held a four-seat lead over the Conservatives but lacked an overall majority, and the minor parties made considerable gains. Heath tried to remain in power by forging an agreement with the Liberals, but none was forthcoming and a minority Labour government took power. That another general election would take place in the near future was even more certain than it had been in 1964. By the October 1974 general election Labour had improved its position by settling the miners' strike, ending the three-day week, repealing the Industrial Relations Act and beginning to re-negotiate the terms of entry to the EEC, whilst support for the Conservatives had declined since February. The result was an overall majority of three for Labour on a small 2 per cent swing. Thus Harold Wilson, the supreme party manager, returned to power, with James Callaghan initially playing a pivotal supporting role as foreign secretary. Callaghan succeeded Wilson when the latter suddenly and surprisingly retired in 1976, probably because of ill-health. Denis Healey, the chancellor of the exchequer, was a leading figure under both prime ministers. Michael Foot (employment), Roy Jenkins (home secretary) and Barbara Castle (health and social security) until 1976, Anthony Crosland, foreign secretary until his death in 1977, and Shirley

Williams, as secretary of state for education and science from 1976, all played prominent roles in what were very experienced administrations.

The major challenges faced by Labour were once again the EEC, economic policy, especially the control of inflation, and relations with the trade unions. Northern Ireland, drifting into constitutional deadlock after the defeat of power sharing by the Ulster Workers Council strike and with the government adopting a tougher stance on security, remained a running sore whilst the possiblity of devolution in Scotland and Wales required considerable attention in the later stages, not least in order to ensure the government's own survival. On the EEC, serious divisions within the party had forced Wilson, before taking office, to promise to renegotiate the terms of entry and to hold a referendum on the renegotiated terms. After the renegotiations had led to concessions on Commonwealth products and on Britain's budgetary contributions, the government felt able to recommend that continued membership was in Britain's interest and on 5 June 1975 Britain voted in favour of remaining a member of the Community by a 2 to 1 majority: 67.2 per cent for and 32.8 per cent against, with a 64.5 per cent turnout. Believing that its enthusiasm for Europe had led the previous Conservative government to neglect Anglo–American relations, Labour set about strengthening Britain's links with the United States, the most obvious evidence of the renewal of the 'special relationship' being cooperation over nuclear weapons and especially Labour's decision to update Polaris in the Chevaline project.

Labour resumed office in the widespread belief that its social contract with the unions, in which the party promised to maintain living standards in return for union restraint on wage claims, gave it a stronger hand in the management of the economy than had been the case with the Conservatives. Healey's first budget included higher pensions, increased food subsidies and some redistribution of taxation; but, largely because of the inflationary effects of the oil crisis and EEC membership, union wage restraint was not initially forthcoming. Inflation rose by over 28 per cent and wage rates by 26.4 per cent in 1974. In 1976 confidence in sterling collapsed again, and when the pound sank to $1.70 the government was forced to seek a loan from the IMF. No fewer than twenty-six cabinet meetings were held to consider the IMF's terms. These proved to be harsh:in return for a $3 billion loan the government was forced to make massive public expenditure cuts of over £2.5 million in 1977–8 and 1978–9. However, assisted from mid 1975 by a TUC-backed policy of voluntary restraint for three years, Labour gradually achieved an improvement in the economy, reducing inflation to single figures (8.2 per cent) in 1978 and transforming a current account deficit on the balance of payments into a £1.2 billion surplus between 1974 and 1978. Unfortunately for the government, its proposed pay norm of 5 per cent for 1978–9 proved unacceptable to the unions and a wave of strikes followed. The disruption was particularly damaging in the public sector, and widespread publicity was given to uncollected rubbish and the unburied dead.

BOX 1.5   *The Labour governments, 1974–9*

Personalities

- Harold Wilson (Prime Minister, 1974–6)
- James Callaghan (Foreign Secretary, 1974–6; Prime Minister, 1976–9)
- Denis Healey (Chancellor of the Exchequer, 1974–9)
- Anthony Crosland (Foreign Secretary, 1976–7)
- David Owen (Foreign Secretary, 1977–9)

- Roy Jenkins (Home Secretary, 1974–6)
- Merlyn Rees (Home Secretary, 1976–9)
- Barbara Castle (Minister of Social Services, 1974–6)
- Michael Foot (posts included Secretary of State for Employment, 1974–6)

The Callaghan Cabinet: (standing, left to right) Sir John Hunt (cabinet secretary), John Smith, Bill Rodgers, Fred Mulley, John Silkin, Lord Peart, Albert Booth, John Morris, Bruce Millan, David Ennals, Joel Barnett, Roy Hattersley, Stan Orme, Harold Lever; (seated, left to right) Peter Shore, Tony Benn, David Owen, Denis Healey, Michael Foot, James Callaghan, Lord Elwyn Jones, Merlyn Rees, Shirley Williams, Eric Varley, Roy Mason.

Events

- Power-sharing executive in Northern Ireland broken by Ulster Workers' Council strike, 1974
- First landing of North Sea oil, 1975
- Referendum on continued membership of EEC, 1975: 2–1 vote for staying in

- Balance of payments crisis followed by large ($3 million) IMF loan in return for £2.5 billion public spending cuts, 1976
- Lib-Lab Pact, 1977–8
- Further OPEC (Organisation of Petroleum Exporting Countries) oil price rises, 1978–9

Box 1.5 continued

Events continued

- Serious public sector strikes: the 'Winter of Discontent', 1978–9

- Failure of devolution policy in Scottish and Welsh referendums, 1979

Policies/Legislation

- Social contract with the trade unions: voluntary wage restraint in return for congenial social and industrial policies, 1975–8

- Nationalisation of aircraft and shipbuilding industries, 1976.
- Scotland and Wales Acts, 1978

Issues

- 'Governability' of Britain in face of stagflation (combination of rising unemployment and rising inflation) and trade union militancy

- Scottish and Welsh nationalism
- Public order situation in Northern Ireland provoked by IRA and Protestant extremism

General Elections

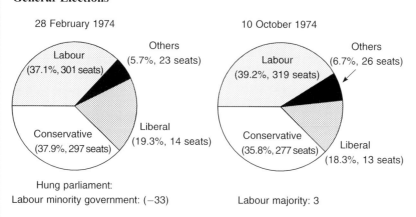

28 February 1974

Labour (37.1%, 301 seats)
Others (5.7%, 23 seats)
Conservative (37.9%, 297 seats)
Liberal (19.3%, 14 seats)

Hung parliament:
Labour minority government: (−33)

10 October 1974

Labour (39.2%, 319 seats)
Others (6.7%, 26 seats)
Conservative (35.8%, 277 seats)
Liberal (18.3%, 13 seats)

Labour majority: 3

At the end of this 'winter of discontent' in industrial relations, a parlia-mentary crisis caused by the failure of its devolution policy brought down the government. In 1976, when the latest in a series of by-election defeats had ended the government's majority, it had managed to continue in office by forming a pact with the Liberals. When this broke down in 1978, in order to survive Labour had sought the support of the Scottish and Welsh nationalist parties. However, with referenda in Scotland and Wales failing to produce the necessary support for its devolution policy, the government became vulnerable and on 28 March it was defeated on a vote of no confidence in its handling of the industrial crisis, with the Liberals, the Scottish Nationalists and most Ulster MPs voting against it. A general election followed on 3 May 1979.

The Conservative Governments, 1979–97

Had Labour called an election in October 1978 it might have won, but it had little chance of victory in May 1979 after the events of the winter had destroyed its claim to governing competence based on good relations with the unions. In a watershed election the Conservatives attacked Labour's economic record and promised a new direction in economic management with tax cuts, lower government spending, trade union reform and less government intervention in industry. Their poll lead declined during the campaign, but not sufficiently to deprive them of a 43-seat majority on a 5.1 per cent national swing. Labour's share of the poll at 36.9 per cent was its lowest since 1931, whilst the Conservative lead over Labour of two million votes was the biggest enjoyed by one major party over another since 1935. The victory began an 18-year period of Conservative dominance, with Labour suffering further defeats in 1983 and 1987 by Margaret Thatcher, and in 1992 by John Major. One contributory factor in 1983 may have been the surge in government popularity following the successful campaign to recover the Falklands in 1982 (see, however, Sanders, Ward and Marsh, 1987), but Labour extremism and divisions and the broader competition for votes between Labour and the SDP–Liberal Alliance certainly contributed to the result: a massive Conservative majority of 144 seats. A buoyant econo-my, which grew at the rate of 4.4 per cent in 1987, was the main reason for the Conservative victory in the next general election, although Labour's confusion on defence and the lack of unity in the Alliance leadership were other factors. In 1992, rather surprisingly, and with their majority reduced from 102 in 1987 to a mere 21, the Conservatives overcame the handicap of presiding over an economic recession to record their fourth consecutive electoral success. The party's new leader, John Major, enjoyed greater public support than his Labour rival, Neil Kinnock; the Conservatives' poll lead in economic competence more than offset Labour's advantage in health and education; and the tabloids' assault on Labour probably lost the party a small but significant number of votes.

Margaret Thatcher, Britain's most commanding postwar prime minister, dominated the 1980s, but Sir Geoffrey Howe (first as chancellor of the exchequer, then as foreign secretary), Nigel Lawson (as chancellor of the exchequer in the late 1980s), William Whitelaw (as a trusted close adviser) and Michael Heseltine (first by a dramatic resignation and then by challenging her for the leadership) all left their imprint on her premiership. The main ministerial influences in the Major administrations were Norman Lamont and Kenneth Clarke (his successive Chancellors of the Exchequer) and the other two leadership contenders in 1990, Douglas Hurd (as foreign secretary until 1995) and Michael Heseltine, who moved steadily through several posts to the deputy prime ministership in 1995. As Major's difficulties with his party over Europe intensified, the influence of right-wing, Euro-sceptic cabinet ministers Michael Portillo, Michael Howard and Peter Lilley increased.

Thatcher's foreign policy was characterised by blunt nationalism, especially in her relations with Britain's European partners. Her reputation as the 'iron lady' derived mainly from her resolute anti-Soviet stance in the Cold War of the late 1970s and early 1980s. This militant anti-communism chimed ideologically with the views of President Reagan and led to a renewal of the Anglo-American 'special relationship'. In 1980 Britain agreed to station American Cruise missiles on British soil and in return was offered the Trident missile system as a replacement for the obsolete Polaris. As well as enabling Britain to maintain its independent nuclear deterrent, US assistance was also crucial to the success of the naval task force despatched by Thatcher in 1981 to recover the Falkland Islands after their invasion by the Argentine General Galtieri (see pp. 270–2). The Falklands were regained at a cost of £1600 million, six ships sunk, 255 British dead and 777 wounded, and Thatcher used the victory to symbolise her courageous leadership in order to turn her flagging premiership around. Five years later she returned the American favour by allowing the United States to launch air strikes on Libya from British bases. In 1987 she moderated her former anti-Soviet stance to act as intermediary between Reagan and President Gorbachev in order to encourage détente, but was soon marginalised as the superpowers moved towards a bilateral reduction of nuclear weapons.

Unlike her stance on the Falklands, Thatcher's attitude towards decolonisation elsewhere was pragmatic. Her government finally achieved a settlement with Southern Rhodesia, which in 1980 became independent Zimbabwe, with black majority rule; and in 1984 an agreement was reached to return Hong Kong to Chinese jurisdiction in 1997. On Europe, the prime minister devoted her first five years to the forceful negotiation of a budget rebate for Britain, but from the mid 1980s she found it difficult to stem the accelerated progress towards European integration. She signed the Single

BOX 1.6   *The Conservative governments, 1979–97*

Personalities

- Margaret Thatcher (Prime Minister, 1979–90)
- John Major (Foreign Secretary, 1989; Chancellor of the Exchequer, 1989–90; Prime Minister, 1990–97)
- Sir Geoffrey Howe (Chancellor of the Exchequer, 1979–83; Foreign Secretary, 1983–9)
- Nigel Lawson (Chancellor of the Exchequer, 1983–89)
- Norman Lamont (Chancellor of the Exchequer, 1990–3)
- Kenneth Clarke (Home Secretary, 1992–3; Chancellor of the Exchequer, 1993–7)
- Lord Carrington (Foreign Secretary, 1979–82)
- Francis Pym (Foreign Secretary, 1982–3)
- Douglas Hurd (Home Secretary, 1985–9; Foreign Secretary, 1989–95)
- Malcolm Rifkind (Foreign Secretary, 1995–7)
- William Whitelaw (Home Secretary, 1979–83)
- Leon Brittan (Home Secretary, 1983–5)
- David Waddington (Home Secretary, 1989–90)
- Kenneth Baker (Home Secretary, 1990–2)
- Michael Howard (Home Secretary, 1993–7)
- Sir Keith Joseph (Minister of Industry, 1979–81; Minister of Education and Science, 1981–6)
- Cecil Parkinson (Paymaster General, 1981–2; Chancellor of the Duchy of Lancaster, 1982–3; Minister for Trade, 1983; Minister for Energy, 1987–9; Minister for Transport, 1989–90)
- Norman Tebbit (Minister for Employment, 1981–3; Minister for Trade, 1983–5, Chancellor of the Duchy of Lancaster, 1985–7)
- Michael Heseltine (Minister for Environment, 1979–83, 1990–2; Minister for Defence, 1983–6; President of the Board of Trade, 1992–7; Deputy Prime Minister, 1995–7)

Box 1.6 continued

The Thatcher Cabinet (1988): (standing, left to right) David Waddington, John Major, Lord Belstead, John Moore, Malcolm Rifkind, Kenneth Clarke, Kenneth Baker, John MacGregor, Paul Channon, John Wakeham, Cecil Parkinson, Tony Newton, Robin Butler (cabinet secretary); (seated, left to right) Nicholas Ridley, Norman Fowler, Peter Walker, Lord Mackay, Sir Geoffrey Howe, Margaret Thatcher, Nigel Lawson, Douglas Hurd, George Younger, Tom King, Lord Young.

The Major Cabinet (1992): (standing, left to right) Richard Ryder, Gillian Shephard, John Patten, David Mellor, William Waldegrave, David Hunt, Michael Howard, Peter Lilley, Ian Lang, Patrick Mayhew, Virginia Bottomley, Michael Portillo, Sir Robin Butler (cabinet secretary); (seated, left to right) Tony Newton, Malcolm Rifkind, Michael Heseltine, Norman Lamont, Lord Mackay, John Major, Douglas Hurd, Kenneth Clark, John MacGregor, John Wakeham, John Gummer.

Box 1.6 continued

Events

- Formation of Social Democratic Party (SDP), 1981
- Increasing tension between West and USSR; the new Cold War
- Falklands War, 1982
- IRA bomb explosion at Grand Hotel, Brighton, 12 November 1984. Five killed; narrow escape for Margaret Thatcher and other ministers
- East–West détente following accession of Gorbachev as Soviet leader, 1985, and policy of 'glasnost'
- Miners' strike, 1984–5: miners described as 'enemy within' by Margaret Thatcher in most serious industrial dispute since the war
- Westland affair, 1986: resignation of Michael Heseltine following government disagreement over future of Westland helicopter company
- US–Soviet arms reduction agreement, 1987
- Collapse of Soviet Empire in Eastern Europe followed break-up of USSR, 1989–90
- German reunification, 1990
- Fall of Margaret Thatcher and replacement by John Major, 1990
- Gulf War, 1991

Policies/Legislation

- Curbing trade union powers: Acts of 1980, 1982, 1984, 1988, 1990
- Privatisation of nationalised industries, including BT (1984), gas (1986), airways (1987), electricity (1990), water (1990) and railways (1996)
- Council tenants' 'right to buy' their homes: Housing Act, 1980
- Income tax cuts: 33% to 30% (1979), basic rate 25%, top rate 40% (1988)
- Monetarist economic policy, 1979–85, with priority given to curbing inflation rather than reducing unemployment
- Curbs on local government with abolition of GLC and six metropolitan authorities (1986), tougher control of council spending including rate capping, reform of local government finance (poll tax, 1990, council tax, 1993) and reduction of role in education and direct provision of services
- Reluctant, cautious, closer integration with European Community through Single European Act (1986) and Treaty of Maastricht (1992), with opt-outs on Social Chapter and monetary union; forced out of European

Box 1.6 continued

Policies/Legislation continued

Exchange Rate Mechanism (ERM), 16 September 1992 ('Black Wednesday'), with devaluation of pound from DM2.95 to DM2.65

- Anglo-Irish Agreement, 1985
- Downing Street Declaration, 1993
- IRA ceasefire, August 1994–February 1996

Issues

- Britain's membership of the European Community: retention versus pooling of sovereignty
- Social and urban unrest, as shown by riots in 1981, 1985 and 1991
- Poll tax, provoking campaign of non-payment and civil disturbances
- Market reforms of welfare state
- Large-scale unemployment, peaking at three million (1986)

General Elections

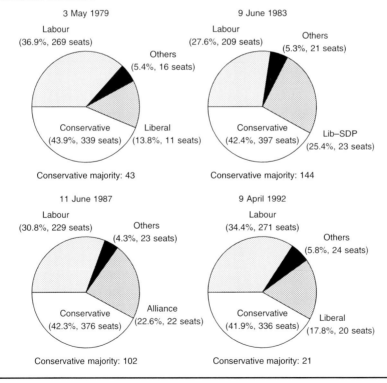

3 May 1979

Labour (36.9%, 269 seats)
Others (5.4%, 16 seats)
Conservative (43.9%, 339 seats)
Liberal (13.8%, 11 seats)

Conservative majority: 43

9 June 1983

Labour (27.6%, 209 seats)
Others (5.3%, 21 seats)
Conservative (42.4%, 397 seats)
Lib–SDP (25.4%, 23 seats)

Conservative majority: 144

11 June 1987

Labour (30.8%, 229 seats)
Others (4.3%, 23 seats)
Conservative (42.3%, 376 seats)
Alliance (22.6%, 22 seats)

Conservative majority: 102

9 April 1992

Labour (34.4%, 271 seats)
Others (5.8%, 24 seats)
Conservative (41.9%, 336 seats)
Liberal (17.8%, 20 seats)

Conservative majority: 21

European Act in 1986, which, in addition to providing for the launch of the single European market in 1992, increased the use of majority voting on the Council of Ministers and committed the Community to making 'concrete progress towards European unity'. But her Bruges speech in 1988, attacking the notion of 'a United States of Europe', made clear her implacable opposition to any form of federalism, and formed a rallying point for Conservative Euro-sceptics under her successor.

In economic policy, Thatcher introduced radical changes aimed at regenerating the ailing British economy. Rejecting the corporatist and Keynesian methods of the postwar era, she sought to 'roll back the frontiers of the state' and to create an entrepreneurial culture that would be more favourable to private enterprise. Controlling inflation rather than reducing unemployment became the primary policy objective and keeping strict control of the money supply (monetarism) the main policy weapon. Accordingly the Thatcher governments launched a large-scale attack on the public sector by means of a massive privatisation programme, which included the transfer of former public utilities such as British Telecom, gas, electricity and water into private ownership, the selling of council houses to their tenants on favourable terms and the 'contracting out' to private tender of a wide range of local government services. Direct taxation was sharply reduced, with top rates of income tax falling from 83 per cent to 40 per cent and basic rates from 33 per cent to 25 per cent by 1988. The power of the trade unions was curbed by a series of enactments that, among other things, abolished the closed shop, outlawed secondary picketing and made pre-strike ballots compulsory; and by government victories in pitched confrontations with the steel unions (1982) and especially the miners (1984–5). However the Conservative governments' overall record (1979–90) was a mixed one. Public expenditure proved difficult to control, largely because of surges in defence expenditure in the early 1980s and in social security payments as unemployment rose to three million (1986), whilst economic growth was relatively modest. Monetarism failed and was quietly dropped, but only after it had contributed to an unnecessarily severe recession in 1980–1 in which much manufacturing capacity was lost for good. When John Major took over as prime minister in 1990 the economy was in the first phase of another recession, to which the excessive expansion of the Lawson years had made a signal contribution.

John Major's main achievements as prime minister were replacing the poll tax, one of his predecessor's main policy mistakes, reducing inflation from about 10 per cent in late 1990 to 2.5 per cent in March 1994, negotiating important opt-outs from the Maastricht Treaty with regard to the single currency and the social chapter (1992) and introducing Citizens' Charters to improve standards in the public services. His government used high interest rates combined with British membership of the European Exchange Rate Mechanism to deflate the economy after the Lawson boom, but it suffered a

BOX 1.7   *The Labour government, 1997–*

Personalities

- Tony Blair (Prime Minister)
- Gordon Brown (Chancellor of the Exchequer)
- Robin Cook (Foreign Secretary)
- Jack Straw (Home Secretary)

- John Prescott (Deputy Prime Minister and Environment, Regions and Transport Secretary)
- Margaret Beckett (President of the Board of Trade)
- David Blunkett (Education and Employment Secretary)

The Blair Cabinet (1997): (standing, left to right) Nick Brown, Alistar Darling, David Clark, Clare Short, Mo Mowlam, Chris Smith, Frank Dobson, Ann Taylor, Harriet Harman, Ron Davies, Lord Richard, Gavin Strang, Sir Robin Butler (cabinet secretary); (seated, left to right) Donald Dewar, Margaret Beckett, Jack Straw, Robin Cook, John Prescott, Tony Blair, Gordon Brown, Lord Irvine, David Blunkett, Jack Cunningham, George Robertson.

General Election

1 May 1997

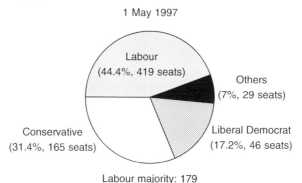

Labour (44.4%, 419 seats)

Others (7%, 29 seats)

Conservative (31.4%, 165 seats)

Liberal Democrat (17.2%, 46 seats)

Labour majority: 179

severe setback on 16 September 1992 – 'Black Wednesday' – when uncontainable speculation against sterling forced the pound out of the ERM and effectively devalued it. Major continued the 'Thatcher legacy' in key areas, including privatisation (coal and the railways), tax reform and reduction, market testing and contracting-out in the public sector, and 'market' reforms in health and education.

Further Reading

Childs, D., *Britain since 1939: Progress and Decline* (London: Macmillan, 1995).
Dorey, P., *British Politics since 1945* (Oxford: Blackwell, 1995).
Gourvish, T. and A. O'Day (eds), *Britain since 1945* (London: Macmillan, 1991).
Holland, R., *The Pursuit of Greatness Britain and the World Role, 1900–1970* (London: Fontana, 1991).
Morgan, K. *The People's Peace: British History 1945–1989* (Oxford: Oxford University Press, 1990).
Pugh, M., *State and Society: British Political and Social History 1870–1992* (London: Arnold, 1995).
Reynolds, D., *Britannia Overruled: British Policy and World Power in the Twentieth Century* (London: Longman, 1991).

2
The Rise and Fall of Consensus Politics

This chapter argues, first, that a broad consensus existed in British politics between the 1940s and the 1970s; second, that this consensus – especially with regard to the economy – was overturned by the Conservative governments after 1979; and third, that the emergence of a new right-of-centre political consensus in the making could be discerned in the 1990s.

The Postwar Consensus

The consensus was not simply a creation of the 1945–51 Labour governments but had deeper origins in the wartime coalition. The manifestos of the two main parties had much in common in 1945, a reflection of their recent cooperation in the coalition. Both committed themselves to full employment through government management of the economy, to a National Health Service and to a comprehensive system of social security based on national insurance; both stressed their determination to implement the 1944 Education Act and to tackle the housing crisis. On foreign policy, both parties supported the continuation of war-time cooperation with the United States and the USSR and were keen to play a full part in the creation of an international peacekeeping organisation. The only major difference was over industrial policy. Labour's nationalisation plans contrasted sharply with the Conservatives' obvious distaste for public ownership, which was variously referred to as the 'dead hand' and as bringing about undesirable state monopolies.

The broad agreement on the fundamentals of economic, social and foreign policies which constituted the postwar social democratic consensus emerged in the postwar decade. In that consensus the Labour governments of 1945–51, building upon the achievements of the wartime coalition, played the major shaping role whilst the Conservative government of 1951–5, by accepting the essentials of that settlement, ensured its continuance after 1951. Recent work that focuses on the 1940s and 1950s has drawn attention to the continuing ideological divergences between the major parties (Jefferys, 1987; Brooke, 1992; Jones and Kandiah, 1996); to the conflictual rather than consensual origins of the National Health Service (Webster, 1988, 1990); and to the differences between the economic management methods employed by the major parties in government (Rollings, 1994, 1996). The concept of consensus has been dismissed as 'a myth' (Pimlott, 1988). However these criticisms can be encompassed within a careful definition of the postwar consensus, which focuses not on the persisting differences of ideology and method between the parties, but on 'what governments actually do when they are in power' rather than what they say in opposition (Lowe, 1996, p.171). The 'agreement' underlying the consensus, therefore, should not be confused with total agreement between the major parties on all aspects of policy, or with ideological agreement, rhetorical agreement, agreement on detail, agreement between front benches or agreement between party activists (Seldon, 1994). In many respects the postwar consensus was more in the nature of a fragile compromise than a deep-rooted agreement.

Underlying strains and potential cracks in the consensus became increasingly evident as Britain moved into the 1970s. Nonetheless a consensus covering the whole spectrum of economic, social and foreign policy did exist between the elites of the two major parties in government, and it lasted for approximately two decades after 1955.

The Mixed Economy and Keynesian Economic Management

By 1949 Labour, by means of a series of nationalisation measures, had brought about a mixed economy. This was predominantly private sector but had a significant public sector, consisting mainly of the strategically important fuel, power and transport industries (Table 2.2). Much of this programme was put into effect without controversy, but not all. From 1947 onwards, the legislation on road haulage and then gas encountered stiff Conservative opposition in parliament, while the nationalisation of iron and steel, a late inclusion in the 1945 manifesto, provoked serious divisions within the Labour government itself. Rejected by the House of Lords in 1948, steel nationalisation did not become law until the end of 1949 after a deal had been made with opposition peers (Morgan, 1984, p.119). Nonetheless there were many reasons why the Conservatives accepted the bulk of the newly created public sector after 1951. Many of the industries concerned had had a long history of state involvement before nationalisation, including large-scale government intervention in wartime and wartime reports advocating greater state intervention in key industries such as coal, gas and electricity. Finally, the often generous compensation to owners, particularly in the coal industry, served to take the political heat out of the issue. Only relatively marginal changes in the sectoral balance of the mixed economy took place before the 1980s (Table 2.2).

A second theme of the postwar economic consensus was both major parties' acceptance of Keynesian demand management techniques to attain the goal of full employment. In 1951, 3 per cent unemployment was officially defined as full employment, and in practice the economy tended to be reflated when unemployment approached 2.5 per cent. Demand management became the main tool of government economic policy from 1947, when the budget was deliberately unbalanced as a counterinflationary measure, and this was supplemented by direct interventionism from the early 1960s. Full employment remained a priority of government policy until 1976, but debate continues on the extent to which government achievements in these years stemmed from Keynesian policies, or whether they were more the result of buoyant world trading conditions (cf. Lowe, 1996, pp.164–5, with Skidelsky, 1996, p. 51). Perhaps 'the ultimate attraction of Keynesianism . . . was essentially a negative and not a positive one' in that it allowed the basic ideological differences between (and within) the parties to remain unresolved (Lowe, 1993, p. 119)

A final part of the postwar economic consensus was cooperation with the trade unions. This proved particularly important in governments' attempts to minimise inflation in the quest to maintain full employment. Successful government collaboration with the unions began during the war with Bevin's enmeshing of the union leaders in 'key processes of the direction of production and control of the labour market' (Morgan, 1984, p. 28) and continued after it when the Labour government persuaded the trade unions temporarily to depart from their deep-rooted belief in free collective bargaining and agree to a three-year wage freeze (1948–50). After 1951 Churchill, who was keen to maintain good relations with the unions, appointed the conciliatory Walter Monkton as minister of labour with a brief to avoid industrial unrest. Nicknamed the 'oil-can' for the facility with which he calmed industrial trouble, Monkton dropped the plans to legislate on industrial relations, which might have annoyed the unions (Seldon, 1987, p. 80).

Spurred on by a concern to increase Britain's lagging economic growth, both Labour and Conservative governments intervened more actively in industry and the economy from the 1960s. Thus, in 1961 the Macmillan government brought government, management and unions together on the new National Economic Development Council (NEDC) in order to plan the development of British industry, whilst in 1964 the Wilson government expressed its belief in 'purposive physical intervention' by creating a new Department of Economic Affairs (DEA) to plan the long-term use of resources. A new Ministry of Technology was set up in 1964 to assist technology-based industries, and the Industrial Reorganisation Corporation (IRC) was established in 1966 to encourage industrial mergers with the aim of promoting greater international competitiveness in the key electronics and car industries. Although this interventionism was interrupted in 1970 with the abolition of the IRC, it was resumed in 1972 when the Industry Act gave the Department of Trade and Industry extensive powers of industrial intervention, and further extended by Labour's National Enterprise Board, which was given a sizeable budget to promote industrial modernisation.

Governments' concern to control inflation in order to promote faster growth while maintaining full employment also caused them to attempt to regulate prices and incomes through voluntary or statutory policies between 1961 and 1977 (Table 2.1). After 1977 union support for a wages agreement was no longer forthcoming and the Callaghan government unilaterally imposed upper limits on pay increases in 1977–8 and 1978–9, but this policy collapsed in the wave of strikes by public sector workers during the 'winter of discontent' (1978–9).

The period from the early 1960s to the late 1970s therefore saw increasingly interventionist governments involved in diverse ways of stimulating growth, promoting employment and reducing inflation, including indicative planning, nationalisation, industrial subsidies, the promotion of company mergers, regional policy and the regulation of prices, dividends and incomes. Heath's statement to the 1972 Conservative Party conference that 'the trade unions and employers [must] fully share with the government the benefits and obligations of running the economy' summed up the approach of both major parties in the 1960s and 1970s (cited in Kavanagh and Morris, 1994, p. 61; see further on interventionism, pp. 213–28).

As strikes, especially unofficial strikes, were increasingly seen as a drag on industrial competiteness, from the late 1960s both major parties also agreed on the need to curb the power of the trade unions. Cooling off periods in industrial disputes and ballots before strikes and in union elections were considered in Conservative circles in the mid 1950s, but were not acted upon for fear of antagonising the TUC (Barnes, 1987, p. 120). Although Labour's

TABLE 2.1 *Incomes policies, 1961–77*

	Government	*Voluntary/compulsory*
July 1961–March 1962	Conservative	Voluntary in private sector, imposed on public sector
April 1962–October 1964	Conservative	Voluntary 'pay norm'
December 1964–July 1966	Labour	Voluntary restraint (Statement of Intent)
July 1966–December 1966	Labour	Statutory (wage freeze)
January 1967–June 1967	Labour	Statutory (severe restraint)
April 1968–June 1970	Labour	Statutory (wage norm)
November 1972–February 1974	Conservative	Statutory (three-stages, starting with freeze)
March 1974–July 1974	Labour	Voluntary (social contract: wage restraint in return for social legislation desired by unions)
August 1975–July 1976	Labour	Compulsory (non-statutory)
August 1976–July 1977	Labour	Compulsory (non-statutory)

1969 proposals to introduce cooling off periods and pre-strike ballots were dropped, the fact that it was a Labour government that sought to introduce a legal framework for industrial relations has led to this episode being described as 'in many ways the high point of the postwar consensus' (Dutton, 1991, p. 59). The Heath government introduced far more stringent curbs on the unions in its Industrial Relations Act (1971), but the legislation soon foundered on union opposition (see p. 234).

The Welfare State

By 1955, with the election manifestos of both major parties committed to continuous improvement and expansion of its provisions, broad consensus also existed on the welfare state. Apart from the enactments on education (1944) and family allowances (1945), it was brought into being by the 1945–51 Labour governments, building on foundations laid during the war, especially by the Beveridge Report (1942). The welfare state had three main pillars: a universal system of social security dispensing 'cradle to grave benefits'; a comprehensive health service that was free to all at the point of receipt and financed mainly by taxation; and a large-scale housing programme devoted to alleviating long-term shortage, removing the slums and making up for wartime losses. In addition full employment, as well as being regarded as a primary economic goal, was seen by the parties as essential both to the relief of poverty and more broadly to the happiness and self-fulfilment of citizens.

Agreeing with Labour that the state should provide for a wide range of social needs, the Conservatives continued the welfare legacy after 1951. On the NHS, they dropped their plans for hospital charges, accepted the conclusion of the Guillebaud Committee (1956) that it was providing value for money and gradually increased spending on it. With regard to new housing, the Conservative average of just under 300 000 completions per annum compares favourably with the just over one million completions under Labour in six and a half years, although to the Labour total should be added the provision of over half a million temporary homes. In maintaining the welfare state with their redistributive tax and social policies, the Conservative governments ensured that the egalitarianism of the 1940s would continue. During the period 1945 to 1975 the real value of unemployment and supplementary benefits and retirement pensions approximately doubled, and the relative value of pensions and unemployment benefits remained relatively stable at 20 per cent of the average male manual earnings for a single person, 30 per cent for a couple and 40 per cent for a couple with two children (Lowe, 1993, pp. 151–3). The bipartisan consensus on the welfare state was also symbolised by a continual upward trend in welfare expenditure, which rose steadily between 1951 and 1976 both as a proportion of total public spending and of GDP (Figure 2.1).

FIGURE 2.1   *Welfare spending, 1951–88*

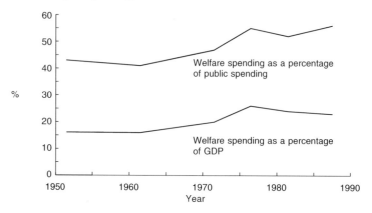

Foreign and Defence Policy

The foundations of postwar foreign and defence policy were laid by the Attlee governments and built upon with no significant changes by the Conservatives after 1951. Policy in these areas had three main features. First, the Attlee government worked closely with the United States on measures aimed at the global containment of Soviet communism, including the formation of NATO (1949) and strong diplomatic and military support for the United States during the Korean War (1950–3). Second, Labour began a gradual process of decolonisation that eventually transformed the British Empire into a multiracial Commonwealth, although, in keeping with its perception of Britain as a great power with important global interests to protect, Labour combined the retreat from empire with the maintenance of a series of global naval and military bases. Third, in order to sustain Britain's status as a leading power, Labour retained large conventional military forces and also developed a British atom bomb. This perception of Britain as a major power with a 'special relationship' with the United States and close trading and financial ties with a far-flung Commonwealth persuaded the Labour government to remain aloof from the movement towards European integration, which began with the Schuman Plan (1950) for a European Coal and Steel Community.

The Churchill government continued these policies after 1951. From early 1953 Churchill, who believed strongly in the 'special relationship', sought to use his influence with the United States to broker a summit peace conference with the USSR, but with little success. Notwithstanding Labour's 1951 manifesto warning that 'the Tory still thinks in terms of Victorian imperialism', the Conservatives continued Labour's policy of gradual retreat from empire by ending Britain's long-established military presence in Egypt. Moreover, like Labour the Conservatives held on to parts of the empire

SOLID ACHIEVEMENTS
OF MR. ATTLEE'S
LABOUR GOVERNMENT

GRANTING OF FREEDOM
TO INDIA, BURMA, etc...

FOUNDATION OF THE
WELFARE STATE
etc. etc...

Stepping down

Source: Vicky (Victor Weisz), *Daily Mirror*, 8 December 1955.

when this seemed justified for economic or strategic reasons, even by the use
of force (Reynolds, 1991, p. 221). Thus the Churchill government suppressed
a fierce rebellion in Kenya, which gave Britain a vital base at Mombasa
overlooking the Indian Ocean; fought a protracted military campaign to
maintain control of Cyprus, which was of increasing importance as a military
base after the withdrawal from the Suez Canal Zone in 1954; and continued
the struggle against communist terrorism in Malaya, whose rubber and tin
provided the sterling area with large dollar earnings.

There was also considerable continuity of policy on defence, with Churchill praising Labour for having taken 'several most important decisions about
our defence policy which . . . form the foundation on which we stand today'
(cited in Dutton, 1991, p. 47). His government placed increasing emphasis on
Britain's nuclear capability by developing the hydrogen bomb after 1954.
Finally, the Churchill government showed no more enthusiasm than Labour
for a European union, and was unwilling to participate either in the
proposed European Defence Community (1950–4) or in the negotiations
that led to the signing of the Treaty of Rome (1957).

Between the mid 1950s and the late 1970s Britain's world role collapsed,
the empire virtually disappeared, the significance of the Commonwealth
declined, the influence of Europe in Britain's affairs dramatically increased
and, especially in defence matters, Britain became increasingly dependent
upon the United States. The governing consensus between the two major
parties endured throughout these changes, although at times it came under

intense strain, for example over Suez (1956), when the Conservative government's resort to force provoked bitter condemnation by Labour. However, despite this massive setback the new prime minister, Macmillan, continued to pursue a world role for Britain by working to restore ties with the United States, by attempting to broker disarmament between the superpowers, by retaining military commitments 'East of Suez' in the Middle East and South-East Asia, and by keeping and upgrading an independent nuclear deterrent. After 1964 the incoming Labour government broadly maintained this international stance, and in November 1964 Prime Minister Harold Wilson declared 'We are a world power and a world influence or we are nothing'. By the late 1960s, however, the bid to preserve Britain as a front-rank power was at an end. Genuine nuclear independence ended in February 1960 with the cancellation of the surface-to-surface missile 'Blue Streak', whilst the failed Paris summit of May 1960 was 'the last time that a British Government appeared on the international stage as a great and independent power in the traditional sense of this description' (Holland, 1991, p. 285). Britain's commitment to keep a military presence east of Suez was terminated in 1967 with Labour's promise to withdraw British forces from Singapore and Malaysia in the mid 1970s. Meanwhile decolonisation accelerated under both parties in the 1960s. By 1979 it was nearly complete and the British Empire virtually extinct (see pp. 257–72). Except in Heath's premiership, the foreign policies of all governments were marked by a pro-American 'Atlanticism', with Britain totally dependent on the United States from 1962 for the supply of its nuclear weapons.

Finally, although opposed to the policy when in opposition, when in government Labour continued the Conservatives' attempt to enter the European Economic Community. In 1961 Macmillan had launched this major reorientation of Britain's external policy for a variety of reasons: British trade with the Commonwealth was declining while that with the EEC was increasing; the rate of economic growth in Britain was lagging far behind that achieved in the six EEC economies; the Commonwealth had failed to become the independent political force envisaged immediately after the Second World War; and above all, perhaps, the United States wanted Britain inside the Community to act as a counterpoise to France and West Germany. But Britain's applications to join the EEC in 1962 (Conservative) and 1967 (Labour) were rejected by General de Gaulle, largely on the ground that Britain's pro-American sympathies made it insufficiently European. Not until 1973 did Britain secure entry to the EEC (under the Conservative government of Edward Heath), and then on rather disadvantageous terms. Labour sought – and received – confirmation of British membership on newly negotiated terms in a referendum in 1975. As Kavanagh and Morris point out: 'There could hardly be a clearer example both of consensus and the elite nature of consensus politics' (Kavanagh and Morris, 1989, p. 107; see further pp. 116–30).

The Postwar Consensus in Historical Perspective

The main characteristics of the social democratic consensus that had emerged by the mid 1950s were egalitarianism, collectivism and statism. Terms frequently used to describe the consensus are 'welfare capitalism', the 'managed economy' and the 'Keynesian' or 'Beveridgean' settlement. It has also been well summed up as 'a middle way, neither free market capitalist (as in the United States) nor state socialist (as was to emerge in Eastern Europe)' (Kavanagh and Morris, 1989, p. 6). It arose in the particular form it did and endured for over three decades for several reasons. First, the form it took – centralised delivery of health and social services, which was at variance with the tradition of decentralised, local provision – was the product of popular and elite confidence in state planning arising from the efficiency with which the coalition government had allocated resources for military and civilian use in wartime. Second, its main components – full employment, the welfare state and strong defence – were extremely popular with the electorate. In 1952 Churchill said that nine-tenths of the people agreed with what had been done with social services, foreign affairs and defence (Seldon, 1981, cited in ibid., 1989, p. 98). Third, the social democratic consensus was a product of political and ideological forces that conspired to present in a favourable light its blend of social and economic interventionism at home and anti-communism abroad. Both major parties accepted that the postwar settlement (reformed capitalism) was a necessary compromise that was in keeping with their ideology. Thus for Labour, state intervention by modifying market forces would eventually produce both a more efficient and a more equal society, whilst the Conservatives accepted the need for greater market regulation to counter poverty and unemployment, although not to produce greater equality. Against the background of the Cold War, the strongest affordable defence based on nuclear weapons and membership of collective security pacts were ideological and political imperatives for both major parties. For two decades after the early 1950s, both parties held to the political centre, the apparent success of the postwar settlement helping Labour to resist left-wing calls for further nationalisation and unilateral nuclear disarmament and the Conservatives to deflect the free market ideas of economic liberals and the continuing thoughts of empire on the far right. The leading ideas underlying the consensus fitted in not only with the ethical socialism of the Labour Party and the paternalist 'one nation' strand of Conservatism, but also with interventionist social Liberalism.

However, the existence of consensus in the postwar period by no means implies the absence of differences between the main parties. Sometimes these were merely a matter of emphasis, but on occasion they were more significant. Conservative social and economic policies, within the overarching consensus, favoured the private sector and private enterprise, and Conservatives often spoke of the 'opportunity' state rather than the welfare state.

Labour's bias was towards the public sector and state provision. On public ownership and welfare policy, each party interpreted the consensus according to its own ideological bias. Thus on nationalisation Labour favoured modest extensions, while the Conservatives supported limited denationalisation, although they failed to achieve it between 1970 and 1974.

On welfare there were different emphases in education, housing, pensions and taxation. On education the Conservatives emphasised private schooling and the grammar school/secondary modern division in the state sector, whereas Labour would have liked to integrate the public schools into the state sector in the mid 1960s, although it failed to do so. However Labour did launch comprehensive schools in 1965, and although these were continued by the Conservatives after 1970 they would certainly never have initiated this policy. On housing the Conservatives remained more sympathetic to private landlordism (although they failed to prevent the steady decline of the private rented sector) and private house building for owner occupation: their political rhetoric emphasised the need to create a 'property-owning democracy'. In contrast Labour stressed 'fair rents' and security of tenure in the privately rented sector (the Conservatives had removed rent controls), and encouraged the building of local authority houses to a greater extent than the Conservatives. However, despite these contrasting ideological sympathies, when in government each party accepted that the sector it favoured least had an important role to play in housing, with the result that between 1945 and 1979 the public rented and the owner-occupied sectors both increased whilst the private rented sector declined (Figure 2.2). By the late 1960s and 1970s there was increasing bipartisan endorsement of owner occupation, with total mortgage relief rising by 146 per cent in real terms between 1967–8 and 1976–7 (Malpass and Murie, 1990, pp. 62–86; Digby, 1989, pp. 79–82).

FIGURE 2.2   *Housing tenure, 1945–89 (per cent)*

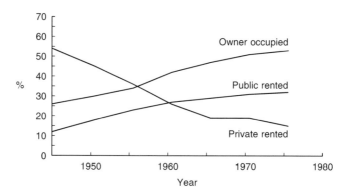

Source: Lowe, 1993, p. 251; Ball, Gray and McDowell, 1989, p. 220; Malpass and Murie, 1990, p. 14.

In pensions policy the Conservatives, as 'reluctant collectivists', wanted to minimise the role of the state and encourage contracting out and occupational pensions, whereas Labour had redistributionist aims and in particular wanted to provide inflation-proof state pensions worth at least 50 per cent of the average wage. The Conservative National Insurance Act (1959) was the only measure not to be overturned by electoral defeat in this period. The Act increased funding for national pensions by permitting additional income-related contributions that would earn contributors a small extra pension, but it also allowed for contracting out into occupational pensions (Lowe, 1993, pp. 158–9). On taxation, whilst the tax burden for low- and middle-income groups increased under both parties in this period, taxation of the better-off (those with twice the average earnings or more) fell under the 1951–64 and 1970–4 Conservative governments and increased under the 1964–70 and 1974 Labour administrations (Field, Pond and Meacher, 1977, p. 23).

Finally, the progressive social legislation of the 1960s – on capital punishment, abortion, divorce and homosexuality – was the consequence of private members' initiatives, but it was a Labour government that made time for it and it might not have reached the statute book under a Conservative administration (Dutton, 1991, p. 62)

The Consensus Under Strain

The social democratic consensus persisted for over thirty years despite these differences but came under increasing strain in the 1970s and finally broke down in 1979 when the Thatcher government made a sharp change of direction. Broadly, what caused the breakdown of consensus was a loss of confidence in its leading ideas – especially in Keynesianism – because of the steady deterioration of Britain's economic circumstances. Thus unemployment, which had averaged an annual one third of a million in the 1950s and under half a million in the 1960s, increased dramatically in the 1970s, reaching three quarters of a million between 1970 and 1974 and one and a quarter million between 1974 and 1979. Inflation, which had been running at approximately 3 per cent per annum in the 1950s and 4–5 per cent in the 1960s, rose to 9 per cent between 1970 and 1974 and 15 per cent between 1974 and 1979. Economic growth, which averaged 2.8 per cent per annum between 1949 and 1973, declined to a mere 1.4 per cent per annum between 1973 and 1979. In the face of 'stagflation' (a combination of rising unemployment, accelerating inflation and declining growth) Keynesian economic policy lost credit. As an economic theory Keynesianism had 'failed to renew itself intellectually'; in particular 'it could offer no theoretical explanation of the acceleration of inflation between 1968–1973' (Skidelsky, 1996, pp. 61, 63).

At the same time governments lost political authority because they seemed incapable of imposing their will on powerful interest groups, especially the trade unions. Thus Wilson's attempt at trade union reform was destroyed by his own (union-based) party whilst Heath's industrial relations legislation foundered on the opposition of militant trade unionism. When Ford workers and lorry drivers and then the public sector unions broke through the Callaghan government's pay norm, corporatist government too was perceived by the public to have failed.

Finally, slow growth accompanied by a steady increase in public spending brought apparent problems in financing the welfare state. With slowing growth, the rising revenue necessary to pay for the welfare state was no longer forthcoming. Meanwhile public expenditure was rising, partly for demographic reasons (the product of an ageing population), partly because of higher unemployment, partly as a consequence of rising expectations and a demand for higher standards born of greater affluence, and partly as a result of a comparative increase in public sector employment. The burden of taxation increased with the rise in public spending. By the mid 1970s the average wage earner with two children paid a quarter of his or her income in direct taxes compared with a mere 3.3 per cent in 1955. In the mid 1970s average real take-home pay after tax fell for the first time since 1945; real consumer expenditure also declined in 1974, 1975 and 1977 (Glennerster, 1995, pp. 171–2). Despite the large-scale increase in taxation, the gap between public expenditure and revenue (the public sector borrowing requirement) also rose dramatically. Against this troubled social and economic background, anti-consensual ideas both on the left and the right became increasingly prominent, with the socialist left advocating further nationalisation and state control of industry together with import and exchange controls and the new right proposing monetarist economics, tax cuts, a reduced role for the state and selective concentration on the neediest rather than universality in welfare.

The Breakdown of the Consensus, 1979 to the 1990s

The Labour government began to depart from the economic consensus in the late 1970s. The Heath government's earlier attempt to break with parts of the consensus by abandoning state intervention in industry and incomes policies had collapsed in a spectacular 'U-turn' in 1971–2. But Labour departed from the consensus in three main ways. First, Denis Healey's 1975 Budget effectively abandoned the postwar commitment to full employment by reducing the government's deficit rather than increasing demand in the face of rising unemployment. Instead the emphasis of government policy shifted to the control of inflation. Second, during the sterling crisis of 1976 chancellor Healey set formal limits for the growth of the money supply in order to reduce inflation, thereby indicating a shift to monetarist economics. Third, Labour moved away from the Public Expenditure Survey Committee system (PESC) of controlling public expenditure, whereby public spending plans were not adjusted when growth proved to be lower and inflation higher than predicted, and turned instead to cash limits. Under cash limits, introduced by the Treasury in July 1976, each spending programme received a cash limit for the year and was required to keep within its budget. However it was the Conservative government of Margaret Thatcher that made the definitive break with the Keynesian consensus by extending these new directions and formalising them into a philosophy of government.

The Economy: Privatisation, Monetarism and the end of Corporatism

The Thatcher governments broke the consensus on the economy in four main ways: (1) by seeking a significant reducation in public expenditure as a proportion of GDP; (2) by shifting the balance of the mixed economy away from the public sector by large-scale privatisations; (3) by abandoning Keynesian demand management in favour of the monetarist economics of Milton Friedman and the 'Chicago School'; and (4) by replacing the corporatist tripartite approach to industrial relations with arm's length dealings with employers and unions and curbs on union power.

The Conservative government believed that high public spending was at the heart of Britain's economic difficulties, first because excessive absorption of resources by the state prevented their more efficient and productive use by the private sector, and second because it rested upon a regime of heavy taxation, which undermined individual initiative. One of the government's primary aims, therefore, was to reduce public spending as a proportion of GDP and to cut the standard and higher rates of income tax. However, largely because of the growth of the social security budget as a result of rapidly rising unemployment, public spending rose as a proportion of GDP in the early 1980s and did not decline until the later years of the decade (Figure 2.3). It then rose again to 45 per cent of GDP in 1993–4. The top and standard rates of income tax both fell, but with National Insurance contributions and VAT both increasing the overall burden of taxation rose from 34 per cent of GDP in 1978–9 to 38 per cent in 1989–90 (Riddell, 1991, p. 32).

FIGURE 2.3   *Public spending as a proportion of GDP, 1970–90*

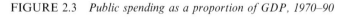

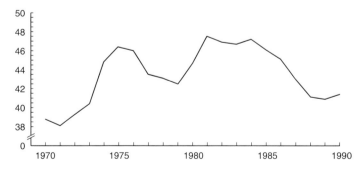

Source: Budge and MacKay, 1993, p. 20.

Privatisation did not figure much in the 1979 manifesto, emerging only gradually as a major plank in the Conservative programme. By 1991 two thirds of state-owned industries had been transferred to the private sector. These sell-offs increased the number of individual share owners from three million in 1979 to 11 million in 1990. At the same time Conservative governments sold council houses to sitting tenants on advantageous terms, with the consequence that by 1988–9 more than 1.2 million tenants had bought their own homes and council house sales accounted for 43 per cent of privatisation proceeds (Kavanagh and Morris, 1994, p. 33). Privatisation was the most dramatic break with the postwar consensus and became the Thatcherite flagship, widely admired and copied round the world (Table 2.2).

The government formally abandoned full employment as the main goal of economic policy, giving priority instead to the control of inflation. To this end it rejected Keynesian demand management as a mechanism of economic policy in favour of monetarism (the setting of 'publicly-stated targets for the growth of money supply') together with a gradual reduction in the public sector borrowing requirement. However, by the mid 1980s, because of the difficulty of finding a reliable measure of the money supply, strict monetarism had been abandoned and a stable exchange rate had been adopted as the most effective disciplinary measure, first by linking sterling to the German mark and then by entry to the European Exchange Rate Mechanism (ERM) in 1990. Despite the controversial nature of monetarism, there is little doubt that 1979 was a genuine watershed in economic policy, marking the transition from Labour's 'reluctant' or 'unbelieving' monetarism to Mrs

TABLE 2.2 *From the mixed to the privatised economy, 1945–97*

Nationalised industries, 1945–79	Privatisation, 1979–97	
The Bank of England (1946)	British Petroleum	British Airways (1987)
Civil aviation (1946)	(1979–87)	Royal Ordnance (1987)
Cable and wireless (1946)	British Aerospace (1981,	Rolls-Royce (1987)
Coal (1946)	1985)	British Airports Authority
Road and rail transport (1946), road	British Sugar Corporation	(1987)
haulage denationalised 1953	(1981)	Rover Group (1988)
Land development rights (1947)	Cable and Wireless (1981,	British Steel (1988)
Electricity (1947)	1983, 1985)	Water Companies (10)
Gas (1948)	Amersham International	(1989)
Iron and steel (1949; denationalised	(1982)	Electricity Companies (12)
1953; renationalised 1967)	National Freight	(1990)
Rolls-Royce (1971; shares vested in	Consortium (1982)	National Power/Powergen
National Enterprise Board, 1975)	Britoil (1982, 1985)	(1991)
British Leyland (1975; shares vested	Associated British Ports	Scottish Electricity
in NEB, 1975)	(1985)	Companies (1991)
British National Oil Corporation	Enterprise Oil (1984)	British Coal (1994)
(1976)	Sealink (1984)	Railtrack (1995)
British Aerospace (1977)	Jaguar (1984)	British Energy (1996)
British Shipbuilders (1977)	British Telecom (1984–94)	Rail passenger franchises
	British Gas (1986)	(1996–7)

Thatcher's 'believing' monetarism. Labour's adoption of monetarist positions after 1975 was always qualified, there being an element of temporary suspension rather than final rejection of the full employment alternative as well as the use of other counterinflationary weapons (for example incomes policy) in addition to monetary targets (Thain, 1992, pp. 228–30). For the Conservatives, however, monetarism provided a way of controlling inflation on 'automatic pilot', without the need for government to compromise its authority by close involvement with big producer groups (Kavanagh, 1990, p. 283).

The rejection of corporatist-style collaboration with employers and unions in running the economy was the fourth way in which 1979 marked a departure from consensual government. The Thatcher government regarded 'cosy deals' between government, business and the unions as having undermined the role of the market in economic decision making, ratcheting up inflation and holding down productivity. In particular it saw the excessive bargaining power and legal privileges of trade unions as having played a significant role in Britain's economic decline. Accordingly the Conservatives moved to a more distant relationship with employers and unions, downgraded and then abolished consensual institutions such as the National Economic Development Council, launched a sustained legislative drive to curb the power of the unions and singlemindedly set out to win industrial confrontations, for example the miners' strike in 1984–5.

The Welfare State

The main motivating ideas of the Conservatives were that the universal welfare state was too costly and that excessive dependence upon the state undermined the self-reliance of individuals and families and weakened voluntary effort and private charity. Accordingly Conservative governments in the 1980s would have liked to cut back severely on publicly provided welfare, but the strong public support for the NHS, the social security system and free state education forced them to temper this ambition. Rather than root-and-branch reform, the first two Thatcher administrations sought to contain rising costs by looking for greater efficiency and value for money in welfare provision, by targeting benefits on the most needy and by encouraging an enhanced role for the private sector in housing, healthcare, pensions and education. The effect was to 'nibble away' at the margins of welfare. For example pension increases were reduced by linking them to inflation price rises not to whichever rose the most, prices or incomes; child benefit was not uprated annually after 1987 and declined in real terms; from the 1990–1 academic year onwards students were no longer eligible for housing benefit, supplementary benefit and income support; and stiffer criteria were imposed on those claiming unemployment benefit. However, despite the government's frequently expressed wish to end the 'dependency culture', spending on social security increased by almost two fifths in real terms during the 1980s. The main reasons for this were the greater demand for pensions owing to the steady rise in the number of older people, the huge increase in unemployment (which rose by more than two million between May 1979 and July 1986) and the inability of labour-intensive social services to match the productivity gains in other sectors (Lowe, 1994, p. 361).

Fundamental changes in health and education finally came in the late 1980s, with reforms designed to create 'internal markets' in both services. In both cases the services remained taxpayer-financed and free at the point of use. A key aim of the reforms was to break the grip of the existing authorities (local government and local health authorities), professionals (doctors and teachers) and public sector unions by increasing choice and competition among the providers of these services to the benefit of their 'consumers' – patients, parents and pupils. In addition private medical insurance and private education were encouraged and hospital pay beds restored, dental charges were increased, free eye tests were abandoned and charges for prescriptions rose tenfold between 1979 and 1989. Of the major welfare items, spending on health rose as a proportion of GDP in the 1980s, spending on education held steady and although spending on housing (as conventionally defined) fell very sharply as a proportion of GDP from 2.7 per cent to 0.9 per cent, this fall was more apparent than real because of the switch from funding through subsidies towards a mixture of public and private funding.

The total impact of Conservative taxation and welfare policies reversed the consensus philosophy of redistributing resources from the better-off to the poor. Thus, after housing costs are taken into account, the poorest 10 per cent of families in 1990 were 14 per cent worse off in 1990 than in 1979. With Conservative tax policy (a shift from direct to indirect taxation, a large reduction in top income tax rates, the introduction of flat-rate regressive taxes such as the poll tax) predominantly benefiting the better-off, inequality increased in the 1980s for the first time since the war. The gulf between the prosperous south-east and the rest of the country also widened during the 1980s.

Foreign and Defence Policy

The Thatcher governments continued the main elements of the postwar consensus but combined them with a a more strident patriotism and a more aggressive assertion of British interests. The new Cold War provided Margaret Thatcher with the opportunity first to renew the 'special relationship' with the United States by voicing an outspoken anti-communism, and second, from 1984, by cultivating relations with the Soviet Union, to resume the role of mediator between the superpowers that had been pursued byearlier prime ministers (Buller, in Ludlam and Smith, 1996, p. 231).

However, after the bilateral US–Soviet arms reductions (1987), the replacement of Reagan by Bush as US president and the emergence of a new US–German alliance it became apparent that the 'special relationship' had always meant more in London than in Washington, where Britain was certainly seen as a reliable ally, but also as just one amongst several medium-ranking European powers.

On Europe, Thatcher devoted the early 1980s to a campaign to gain greater equity in British contributions to the Community budget before moving to negotiation and acceptance of the Single European Act (1986), which gave increased momentum to the achievement of a single market for goods and services within the Community by 1992. Thereafter she fiercely resisted 'Euro-federalism' and delayed British entry into the European Exchange Rate Mechanism (ERM) until October 1990. Elsewhere, decolonisation continued (see pp. 266–8, 270–2), with the Thatcher government dealing pragmatically with 'imperial hangovers' such as Rhodesia, Hong Kong and, first negligently but then decisively, with the Falklands. Finally, the Conservative governments made an increased commitment to defence. A new, more powerful generation of nuclear weapons (Trident) was commissioned and defence spending was increased by one fifth between 1979 and 1989, this form of public spending being deemed an unequivocal good. The defence budget was actually 28 per cent higher in 1985–6 than in 1978–9, but declined to about 20 per cent higher in real terms by the late 1980s (Riddell, 1991, p. 200).

The 1990s: Towards a New Consensus?

By the time of the 1997 general election there were clear signs that Labour had accepted much of Thatcherism and that a new, right-of-centre, post-Thatcherite consensus had emerged, in sharp contrast to the social democratic consensus of the postwar era. The Labour policy shift to the right began under Neil Kinnock: unilateral nuclear disarmament, support for large-scale nationalisation, hostility to market forces and opposition to the European Community were all abandoned under his leadership. Even when John Major succeeded Margaret Thatcher in 1990, surveys showed that the public could see few significant differences between the two, now moderate, parties (Kavanagh and Seldon, 1994, p. 149). By the 1992 general election, with both major parties agreeing on membership of the ERM as the main counterinflationary weapon and Labour having accepted the majority of Conservative privatisations and trade union reforms, one political scientist suggested that 'arguably there were fewer policy differences between the Conservative and Labour parties than at any time this century'. The 'new consensus' was described as 'a post-Thatcher settlement of the "social market" within the European Community, in which the state's role is limited to the supply side of the economy and selective, targeted welfare' (Crewe,

1993, pp. 110–11). Assuming the validity of this general observation, what is the new consensus likely to involve in detail?

Answering this question requires a brief review of trends in both major parties in the early 1990s. Broadly, the Conservative governments under John Major continued Thatcherite policies on the economy, that is, supply side economics with priority being given to the fight against inflation; the welfare state, with reforms introducing 'quasi-markets' in health, education and community care, and giving council tenants the right to choose their landlords; privatisation, with the government privatising coal, nuclear power and the railways but being prevented by its backbenchers from selling off the Post Office; and further anti-trade-union legislation and other measures designed to promote labour market flexibility. Although Major steered the government's diplomatic approach away from hostility towards Europe, his actual policy followed the anti-federalist principles laid down by Thatcher (George and Sowemimo, in Ludlam and Smith, 1996, p. 261). The main departures from Thatcherism were the swift replacement of the poll tax with the new council tax, and the Citizens' Charter – Major's initiative aimed at improving standards in the public services. Meanwhile, modernisation of the policies and structure of the Labour Party continued under John Smith, who set up the Borrie Commission on Social Justice on reform of the welfare state, and Tony Blair, who presided over the dropping of Clause 4, the public ownership commitment, from the party constitution.

In short the mid-1990s trends in both parties suggested convergence in key areas (Exhibit 2.1). On the economy, both parties gave priority to a low income tax regime with tight control over public spending, especially over public borrowing (PSBR), and to supply-side economics, with a greater focus than in the 1980s on bringing about improvements in education and training. Both parties emphasised the strengthening of manufacturing, Labour with tax reforms to encourage long-term industrial investment by financial institutions, the Conservatives by focusing on a 'new partnership' involving initiatives aimed at stimulating industry's ability to generate wealth (Kavanagh and Seldon, 1994, pp. 199–200, 214, 220). The existing public sector/ private sector balance seemed likely to remain, with the emphasis on improving the system of regulation of privatised utilities. Labour supported a tougher regulatory regime than did the Conservatives and also was likely to seek ways of providing more commercial freedom for the Post Office. Both parties' macroeconomic policy prioritised the control of inflation. However there were differences over the minimum wage, which was promised by Labour but opposed by the Conservatives. On welfare policy, the Thatcherite reforms of health, education and housing seemed likely to continue, although Labour favoured a large expansion of nursery education, greater equity in funding between schools and using the income generated by council house sales to build new council houses. The search continued for greater efficiency in the delivery of welfare services, as did the political debate on paying for

EXHIBIT 2.1   *Consensus and new consensus*

Subject area	Old consensus (1940s–1970s)	New consensus (1990s)
Nature of consensus	Social democratic	Neoliberal
Role of state	Provider	Enabler and regulator
Economy	Mixed	Free market
Macroeconomic policy	Main emphasis on preserving full employment	Main emphasis on curbing inflation
Public expenditure and taxation	Steady increase as percentage of GDP. Rising taxation	Tight control. Low tax regime
Industry	Interventionist in order to regulate working of market (pay policies, industrial reorganisation regional policy)	Non-interventionist. Sovereign markets. 'Global economy'
Business and trade unions	Corporatist: business and unions seen as parteners of government. Trade unions have legal privileges and powerful position.	Anti-corporatist, arm's length attitude to business and privileges and unions. Reduction of union power and privileges.
Welfare state	State-provided 'cradle to grave' welfare, guaranteeing all citizens minimum income, social security and access to optimum range of services in health care and education	Reform of welfare state: 'quasi-markets' introduced in health, education and housing. Search for greater efficiency in service delivery and greater public accountability. Rethinking of service delivery by state (more selectivity and opting out) and search for new ways of financing services (higher charges and private provision)
Foreign and defence policy	World power with key role in resistance to Soviet Communism based on 'special relationship' with US, Commonwealth leadership and possession of nuclear weapons. Decolonisation. Resistance (before 1960s) to joining European Community. High (but declining) expenditure on defence as percentage of GDP and of government spending.	Middle ranking, post-imperial European state but with resources to play significant role in regional conflicts, for example Gulf War, Bosnia. Retention of nuclear weapons. Entry to European currency if in national interest and after referendum. Post-Cold-War search for big cuts in defence as part of peace dividend.

welfare, with the precise balance between general taxation, insurance-related benefits, hypothecated taxes, increased charges and loans a matter for vigorous controversy.

In broad terms, both major parties accepted the growing role of the state as enabler, that is, as contractor, regulator and empowerer rather than direct provider. But in the future there will probably be greater emphasis on matters that were largely neglected in the 1980s, such as redefining and encouraging a public service ethos; devising and enforcing criteria of performance quality across the private and the public sector (where a start was made with the Citizens' Charters); developing ways of ensuring greater accountability of quasi-governmental organisations; and enforcing greater control of administrative costs, especially in the NHS and local government. Both parties (although with significant and, in the case of the Conservatives, strident minorities disagreeing) saw Britain's future as firmly inside the European Union. But both recognised that the public would have to be persuaded about the next step – monetary union – and that there would probably have to be a referendum. The principal difference between the main parties was over constitutional reform, with Labour committed to devolution, freedom of information and reform of the House of Lords, and the Conservatives opposed to these and other constitutional reforms.

Further Reading

Cairncross, A. K., *The British Economy since 1945* (Oxford: Blackwell, 1992).

Dutton, D., *British Politics since 1945: The Rise and Fall of Consensus* (Oxford: Blackwell, 1991).

Glennerster, H., *British Social Policy since 1945* (Oxford: Blackwell, 1995).

Hennessy, P. and A. Seldon (eds), *Ruling Performance: British Governments from Attlee to Thatcher* (Oxford: Blackwell, 1987).

Jones, H. and M. Kandiah (eds), *The Myth of Consensus: New Views on British History 1945–1964* (London: Macmillan, 1996).

Kavanagh, D. and P. Morris, *Consensus Politics from Attlee to Thatcher*, 2nd edn (Oxford: Blackwell, 1994).

Kavanagh, D., *Thatcherism and British Politics: The End of Consensus?* (Oxford: Oxford University Press, 1990).

Marquand D. and A. Seldon (eds), *The Ideas that shaped Post-War Britain* (London: Fontana, 1996).

Pimlott, B., 'The myth of consensus' (1988), reprinted in *Frustrate their Knavish Tricks* (London: HarperCollins, 1995).

Riddell, P., *The Thatcher Era and its Legacy*, 2nd edn (Oxford: Blackwell, 1991).

3
Society, Economics and Politics

The half century after 1945 brought a transformation in British society. The white-collar and professional middle class expanded; the manual working class continued its century-long decline. Women's participation in the workforce increased whilst men's fell. With the expansion of the ethnic minority population, Britain became a multiracial, multicultural society. As prosperity and educational opportunities increased patterns of participation changed. The influence of the media rose steadily. This chapter examines the significance of these changes for British politics. After outlining the main changes in postwar society, it focuses on three themes: changes in the social composition of political elites; trends in political participation; and the political impact of the mass media.

Social and Economic Change, 1945–95

Britain after the Second World War

Britain was an acutely class-divided, class-conscious society in 1945 and a large social gulf divided the middle class from the working class majority. By the 1990s class differences had been moderated and softened but not extinguished, and society contained a much larger middle class and a much reduced working class. During the 1980s non-manual groups became the majority of the working population for the first time.

The pronounced social division between the upper/middle classes and the working class in 1945 was expressed in type of work, pay differentials, job security, status at work, trade union membership, housing, health, accent, dress and material possessions. Middle-class jobs were normally in the white-collar professions, business, administration and clerical work. Working-class jobs were mainly blue-collar manual occupations in manufacturing, construction, transport and agriculture (men), and textiles, clothing, catering, cleaning and shop work (women). Middle-class occupations were more secure than working-class occupations, which typically were vulnerable to economic fluctuations. Higher professionals received 191 per cent of average male earnings in 1955–6, whereas semi-skilled manual workers received 58 per cent and unskilled manual workers 54 per cent. The superior status of the middle classes at work was reflected in dining arrangements (staff dining rooms for management, works canteens at best, 'snap' tins on the factory floor at worst, for the working class), methods of payment (monthly salaries for professional employees, weekly wages for manual workers) and occupational pensions (generally lacking in manual jobs).

Owner occupation was still a predominantly middle-class phenomenon in 1951. Working-class people normally rented their properties, mostly from private landlords but also from local councils. Whereas the middle classes were mainly educated in grammar or public schools (untouched by the Butler Act and taking in about 5 per cent of the school population), working-class children predominated in the markedly less well-funded secondary modern schools. With university education in the 1950s limited to about 4 per cent of the relevant age-group, a mere 25 per cent of undergraduates had fathers in manual occupations and less than 25 per cent of all full-time higher education students were women. Significant class and gender inequalities occurred in health too, with both sexes in the unskilled manual worker category experiencing the highest mortality rates (Malpass and Murie, 1990, p. 14; Halsey, 1988, pp. 419–20). Finally, class inequalities in wealth, income and job status were reflected in inequalities in holidays and material possessions, with middle-class people in 1948 enjoying longer holidays than working-class people and monopolising the ownership of cars and televisions (Halsey, 1972, pp. 549, 551).

A Changing Society, 1951 to the 1990s

Rapid economic change transformed British society in the postwar period (Figure 3.1). The first major source of this change was deindustrialisation, which began in the 1970s. Manufacturing industry employed 36 per cent of the workforce and generated 36 per cent of GDP in 1951. Manufacturing employment peaked in 1966 with 8.5 million workers but then went into a decline that accelerated in the 1980s. In 1992, the manufacturing sector employed a mere 4.59 million workers, just over one-fifth of the total workforce, and produced less than a quarter of GDP. Meanwhile the service sector rose in importance: in 1992 it accounted for nearly three quarters of total employment and over two thirds of GDP, compared with about half in 1950 (*Social Trends*, 1993, pp. 56–7; *Britain 1993: An Official Handbook*, p. 214). A large expansion of middle-class occupations and a significant contraction in working-class occupations accompanied the shift from industry to services. Between 1951 and 1981 the non-manual workforce increased from 36 per cent to 52 per cent whilst the manual workforce declined from 64 per cent to 48 per cent (Halsey, 1988, pp. 162–3).

The second major transforming influence on postwar Britain was economic growth, with real GDP per head rising by a factor of 2.4 between 1948 and 1992 (Figure 3.2) (Butler and Butler, 1994, p. 384). Spurred on by the welfare state, three decades of full employment, the rapid development of technology and the large increase in the number of women in paid employment, growing affluence changed all sections of society, albeit unequally. Its most

FIGURE 3.1   *Changes in the workforce, 1951–81*

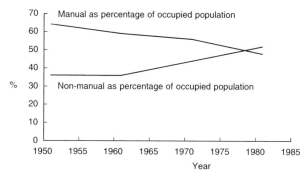

Source: Halsey, 1988, p. 164

FIGURE 3.2   *The growth of the British economy, 1951–92*

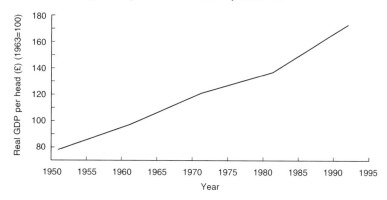

Source: Butler and Butler, 1994, p. 384

observable effect was the acquisition by most groups of material possessions on a hitherto unparallelled scale. This spread of consumer goods did much to transform working-class homes into households that differed little from their middle-class counterparts (Rubinstein, 1986, p. 84). In 1990, with the general expansion of home ownership, three fifths of skilled workers, two fifths of semiskilled and a quarter of unskilled workers were buying their houses on a mortgage. By 1990, as a result of privatisation, 21 per cent of the population were shareholders compared with 7 per cent in 1979. In 1987 almost two fifths (37 per cent) of manual workers held shares. The number of individuals covered by private health insurance increased from 2.4 million in (1978) to 5.2 million in (1989). The rapid postwar rise in living standards had ushered in a prosperous consumer society.

As well as a much wealthier society, Britain became a better educated society. The age threshold of compulsory schooling rose to 16 in 1973, and

Liverpool dockers, November 1962

the number of those choosing to stay on after 16 also increased, slowly at first, and then rapidly in the 1980s and 1990s (Table 3.1). However, although by 1991 86 per cent of secondary pupils attended comprehensive schools and less than 4 per cent went to grammar schools, class divisions remained, with 8 per cent of 11–15 year olds and 20 per cent of students aged 16 and over being educated in the private sector. Moreover a lower proportion of over-16 year olds continued in full-time education than in other advanced countries. In addition, by the 1990s there was mounting concern about the standards of achievement in British schools.

Girls took greater advantage than boys of the very rapid expansion of further education in the 1980s, accounting for 86 per cent of the increase; by 1990–1, there were more female than male students in further education. In higher education, whereas in 1961 5.5 per cent of men but only 2.8 per cent of women attended university, thirty years later female students made up almost half of all students on full-time degree courses.

The postwar era has also been notable for women's increasing participation in the workforce. Women still constituted less than one third of the

TABLE 3.1 *Percentage of age group in full-time education, 1938–90*

	1938	1962	1980	1990
16 year olds	4	15	27	43
19 year olds	2	7	12	18

Source: Butler and Butler, 1994, p. 343.

labour force in 1951 but by 1991 made up over two fifths of employed workers. The main change occurred in the proportion of married women in paid work: in 1951 just over one quarter of married women were in paid employment (itself a large increase on the roughly one tenth of married women who worked before the war), but this proportion rose steadily to reach seven tenths in 1991 (Table 3.2). Economic factors underlying this process included the postwar expansion of certain types of industrial employment, such as the light engineering and electrical goods industries, and of clerical, administrative and lower professional jobs in the service and public sectors. Social factors included women's desire to improve the living standards of their families, the greater willingness of managements to employ women, downward trends in the birth rate and improvements in women's health and educational qualifications. The very considerable increase in part-time work in the 1980s was also a factor: by 1992 one quarter of employees worked part time, and four fifths of part-time workers were women. Between 1971 and 1992 the number of women in paid employment rose by more than two million whilst the number of men in work declined by about 2.5 million.

Another significant change in British society after 1945 was the shift in ethnic composition, primarily as a consequence of immigration from the West Indies and the Indian subcontinent. Postwar governments encouraged this immigration in order to counteract the shortage of domestic labour, although by the 1960s the unskilled labour shortage had virtually disappeared. In the meantime a number of extremist organisations had emerged to exploit anti-immigrant feeling and violent clashes had occurred between members of the black and white communities in Notting Hill, London, and Nottingham in 1958. From 1962 this unrest led to restrictions on Commonwealth immigration, which eventually reduced the volume of black immigration, although at the cost of separating many families. Black people were given a legal means of seeking redress against the widely prevalent discrimination in housing and employment by the passing of the Race Relations Act (1965), which also established the Race Relations Board, subsequently the Community Relations Commission. However political exploitation of racial prejudice by groups and parties on the extreme right continued, as did racial incidents on the streets. By the 1970s and 1980s a new generation of black

TABLE 3.2 *Women in the labour force, 1951–91*

	1951	1961	1971	1981	1991
Women as percentage of labour force	31	33	37	40	44
Women aged 20–64 in labour force (%)*	36	42	52	61	71
Married women aged 15–59 in labour force (%)*	26	35	49	62	70

*16–59 in 1991.

Britons had emerged who were generally much better integrated in British society. Black sportsmen and women were achieving widespread recognition and black politicians were being elected to local government and parliament. In 1990 the black population numbered 2.62 million, 4.8 per cent of the total population. The highest proportion of ethnic minority people lived in the south-east (mainly Greater London), with significant numbers in the Midlands, Yorkshire and the north-west.

The social distance between the prosperous and relatively affluent majority and the rest of society increased in the 1980s. The main underlying reasons for this trend were increasing income differentials, the regressive effects of the shift from direct to indirect taxation, a steep increase in lone parent families (nearly one fifth of all families in 1993) and a rapid rise in unemployment (Table 3.3). Furthermore, high unemployment combined with Conservative legislation aimed at curbing the unions' power and privileges undermined trade union membership, which, having risen steadily to a postwar peak in 1979, fell by over four million to approximately nine million in 1993, a mere 31 per cent of the employed workforce (Figure 3.3). To some social observers a large new 'underclass' had come into existence by the 1990s. It consisted of the long-term unemployed, the homeless, the

TABLE 3.3 *Unemployment, 1965–92*

	Number	*Percentage*
1965	338 200	1.4
1975	929 000	3.6
1980	1 667 600	6.3
1986	3 027 900	13.1
1990	1 661 700	5.8
1992	2 970 000	10.5

FIGURE 3.3   *Trade Union Membership, 1945–97 (millions)*

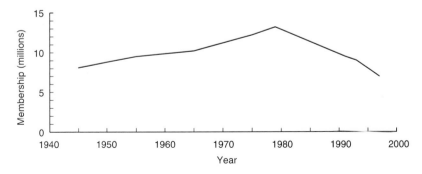

educationally unqualified and a large group consisting of one-parent families, pensioners and ethnic minorities. Despite official attempts to deny the connection, rising crime in the 1980s and periodic riots in towns and inner-city areas such as Brixton and Toxteth (1981), Handsworth (1985) and Tyneside and other places in 1991 and 1992 were obviously linked to increasing unemployment and relative deprivation. In addition, with the fall in full-time tenured jobs from 55.5 per cent to 35.9 per cent of the working population between 1975 and 1993, and with the increase in full-time untenured, part time and self-employed work, a second large category – the newly insecure – had emerged by the mid-1990s. By that time, according to one critic, Britain had become a '40/30/30' society, consisting of the top 40 per cent, most of whom were in full-time tenured employment, the newly insecure, who had enjoyed some material gains in the 1980s but whose position in the job market had become more precarious, and the bottom, absolutely disadvantaged group of unemployed and economically inactive (Hutton, 1995, pp. 105–10).

Hence postwar egalitarian trends suffered a setback in the 1980s, but nonetheless Britain in the 1990s was a very different society from Britain in 1945. There existed by the 1990s a property-owning majority whose aspirations for themselves and their children had been transformed by the steady growth of material prosperity, improved access to education and the long-term trend towards 'psychological equality' (Rubinstein, 1986, p. 126). The large increase of married women in jobs, leading to a high proportion (60 per cent in 1995) of two-income households, helped maintain and equalise consumption standards, as did the strongly unionised, fully employed workforce in the 1970s and the major extension of credit facilities in the 1980s which resulted in over three quarters of adults possessing credit or debit cards by 1995. Direct taxation was extended in the postwar period to cover virtually the whole of society: before 1939 a relatively small proportion of the community, largely the better-off, paid income tax (3.7 million), but by the mid 1970s 85 per cent of the working population (20.7 million) were tax payers, including all manual and clerical workers (Field *et al.*, 1977, p. 46). Trends towards uniformity in education and exposure to the mass media, with weekly viewing hours in winter averaging 20 in the 1970s and rising even higher in the 1980s, led to a greater similarity of cultural experiences and a certain flattening of class differences.

Finally, the shape of the class system changed as a consequence of the expansion of better-paid white-collar and professional occupations and a contraction of the worst-remunerated manual jobs. Occupational change was the main cause of the increase in absolute rates of social mobility. A 1983 study showed that almost one quarter (23.6 per cent) of men of working-class origin had moved into the middle class compared with 16 per cent in 1972 (Goldthorpe and Payne, 1986, cited in Halsey, *Social Trends*, 1987, p. 18).

Political Elites

The Major Parties

The overwhelming majority of Conservative MPs in the postwar period came from socially privileged backgrounds (Figure 3.4). From the mid 1970s, however, the party began to move away from its patrician, upper-middle-class foundation towards a more meritocratic one. Both the public school and the Oxbridge elements declined, the proportion educated at top public schools falling particularly sharply from nearly one quarter in October 1974 to about one seventh in 1992. Conservative MPs over the whole postwar period have been drawn predominantly from business and the professions, and company directors, company executives and barristers have been especially prominent. A negligible proportion have had working-class origins (Figure 3.5). Although their numbers increased after 1979, there were still only 20 Conservative women MPs in 1992 (Table 3.4). The party gained a single ethnic minority MP in 1992 (Table 3.5). Based, in Ingle's phrase, on 'an unusually narrow channel of recruitment', the Conservative Party in the House of Commons has been socially homogeneous, almost wholly male and middle class, and extremely resistant to social change (Ingle, 1989, pp. 76–97).

FIGURE 3.4   *The educational background of MPs in the two main parties, 1951–92*

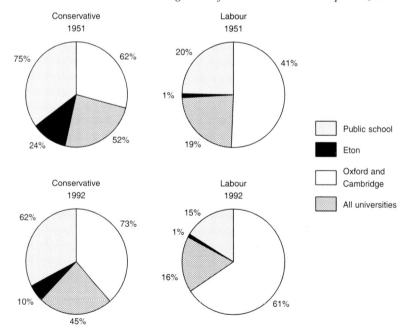

Source: data from Butler and Pinto-Duschinsky, 1970, p. 303 and Butler and Kavanagh, 1992, p. 224.

FIGURE 3.5   *The social background of MPs in the two main parties, 1918–92*

(a) 1918–35 (Average)

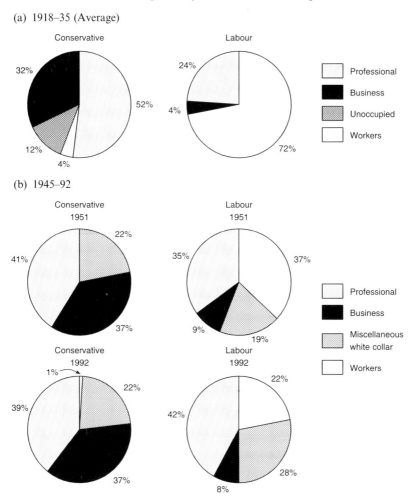

(b) 1945–92

Source: data extracted from Butler and Butler, 1986, p. 178 and Butler and Kavanagh, 1992, p. 226.

The social composition of the Conservative Party since the war has been unrepresentative both of society at large and of its voters. A 99 per cent non-manual parliamentary party drawing most of its MPs from the moneyed business and professional middle class, the party has been regularly supported at elections by about one third of the manual working class, which, despite its shrinkage since 1945 still constitutes about half the population. A second major difference between party and public is in education: 62 per cent of the parliamentary party in 1992 had attended public school compared with a mere 5 per cent of the population and less than 8 per cent of its voters.

TABLE 3.4 *Women MPs, 1945–97*

	Conservative	Labour	Women as % of total
1945	1	21	3.8
1950	6	14	3.4
1951	6	11	2.7
1955	10	14	3.8
1959	12	13	4.0
1964	11	18	4.6
1966	7	19	4.1
1970	15	10	4.1
1974 (Feb.)	9	13	3.6
1974 (Oct.)	7	18	4.3
1979	8	11	3.0
1983	13	10	3.5
1987	17	21	6.3
1992	20	37	9.2
1997	13	101	18.2

Although differences between the main parties decreased after 1945, the educational and social backgrounds of Labour MPs contrast sharply with those of the Conservatives (Figures 3.4 and 3.5). In contrast with the predominantly public-school-educated Conservatives, the greater proportion of Labour MPs have been educated at state schools, with neither public school nor Oxbridge elements forming more than a small minority of the party, and both declining further in the 1980s and 1990s. MPs with only elementary education made up over half the party in 1945 but then fell rapidly to 21 per cent in 1970 and under 1 per cent in 1992. Furthermore the traditionally predominant manual worker element declined sharply as Labour MPs came to be drawn increasingly from the white-collar, professional middle classes working mainly in the public sector. Trade-union-sponsored MPs formed a consistently high proportion of the parliamentary party (PLP), constituting just over one third in the 1950s and 1960s and rising to about half of a much-reduced PLP after 1979. But an increasing percentage of these union-sponsored MPs came from white-collar unions and decreasing numbers from traditional industrial unions. Generally, women and the ethnic minorities have been better represented in the Labour Party than in the Conservative Party (Tables 3.4 and 3.5).

As an increasingly middle-class party with two thirds of its MPs drawn from the salariat in 1987, Labour moved progressively further away from the working class, which provided 63 per cent of its vote in the 1987 general election. However it continued to possess a much larger working-class base than the Conservatives. Also, the mainly state-educated Labour Party was considerably more representative of the population than its main rival.

TABLE 3.5 *Ethnic minority MPs, 1970–97*

	Conservative	Labour	Total
1970	0	0	0
1974 (Feb.)	0	0	0
1974 (Oct.)	0	0	0
1979	0	0	0
1983	0	0	0
1987	0	4	4
1992	1	5	6
1997	0	9	9

Trends in the social composition of the main parties reflected changes in postwar society. First, the increasing proportion of graduates in both parties together with the dramatic decline in the percentage of MPs with minimal education in the Labour Party arose out of the long-term move towards a better-educated society. The expansion of educational opportunities after the war, with grammar schools providing a ladder to higher education for ambitious working-class children, was reflected in the growing proportion of meritocrats in the Labour Party. Thus whereas the typical Labour MP in the prewar era moved out of the working class by entering parliament, the typical Labour MP of the postwar period moved into the middle class by acquiring a university education, and then capped the process by election to the House of Commons (Moran, 1989, p. 158). Second, the expansion of the professional middle class was echoed in both parties. The declining number of Conservative MPs educated at public schools, especially the most socially prestigious ones such as Eton, indicated both the drift of the party away from the upper middle class and the movement of the upper middle class away from a political career, which was increasingly seen as less rewarding both in pay and status (Criddle, in Butler and Kavanagh, 1988, p. 201). Both major parties became more solidly middle class, with people from the 'talking professions' gaining at the expense of manual workers in the Labour Party, and professionals such as teachers and journalists gaining at the expense of military men and landed squires in the Conservative Party. The 'career politician' made significant advances, with both parties recruiting an increasing number of political organisers and researchers and people with experience in local government. But, despite some convergence in their social composition, each party represented different sections of the middle class, the Conservatives being orientated towards top business and the higher private sector professions, Labour towards public sector, white-collar and professional occupations.

The two main parties achieved only modest success in their efforts to become more representative with regard to class, gender and race. Conservative efforts to recruit more working-class candidates foundered on the prejudice against individuals from such backgrounds in the autonomous constituency associations (Greenwood, 1988, pp. 461–8). Despite anxiety in some quarters that the party was moving away from its working-class roots, Labour 'selectorates' continued to prefer middle-class to working-class candidates, who as a proportion of all candidates fell to less than 14 per cent in 1992 (Bochel and Denver, 1983, pp. 56–8).

The two parties adopted contrasting approaches to the problem of increasing the number of women candidates. Labour adopted positive discrimination in 1988, requiring the compulsory registration of women on shortlists, and went further in 1993 with a policy of women-only shortlists for half its winnable seats, although it subsequently dropped this policy. Believing in individual achievement and promotion on merit, the Conservatives rejected affirmative action. They tried officially to select more women candidates from 1947, but although financial barriers to women candidates were removed, social and cultural obstacles remained and the selection process remained biased against women (Lovenduski *et al.*, 1994, pp. 628–30).

Parliament

Predominantly middle class, male and white, parliament was far from a social microcosm in the postwar period, a characteristic it shared with most Western legislatures. Working-class underrepresentation was a persistent feature of postwar parliaments, with the working class forming over two thirds of the population but only 22 per cent of the House of Commons in 1945, and just under one half (48 per cent) of the population but a mere 10 per cent of MPs in 1992. If the working class had been represented in parliament in proportion to its size in the population, in 1992 there would have been 312 working-class MPs, not 63. Working-class underrepresentation was offset to some extent, especially between 1970 and 1995, by the very significant number of Labour MPs who had moved out of the working class by virtue of their education. In gender terms, the lack of representativeness in postwar parliaments has been even more striking. Women constitute slightly over half the population (52–3 per cent of voters) but between 1945 and 1992 the number of women MPs increased only modestly from 3.8 per cent to 9.2 per cent, an increase that did not begin until 1987. Had women been represented in the House of Commons in proportion to their numbers in the electorate, there would have been 339 women MPs in 1992, not 60. However, significant progress was made in 1997, when 119 women were elected, representing 18.2 per cent of the House of Commons. Finally, in 1992 ethnic minorities constituted approximately 5 per cent of the total population but ethnic minority MPs made up a mere 0.9 per cent of the House of Commons. If representation in the Commons had been strictly proportional, there would have been 30 or more black and Asian MPs (Norris and Lovenduski, 1995, pp. 99, 102, 106). The main constraints on increased representation of the working class, women and the ethnic minorities were the number of seats becoming vacant at each general election (about 60), the prejudices of selection committees and financial, occupational and psychological factors on the part of candidates.

Many would approve of the increasing trend towards the recruitment of MPs from the most highly educated stratum of the population: university graduates, who formed 3 per cent of the population in 1945 and 7 per cent in 1992, increased from under one half of the House of Commons to about two thirds between those years. But other aspects of the social unrepresentativeness of the House of Commons are generally seen as less desirable. Approximately 40 per cent of MPs in 1992 had been educated at public school, compared with 54 per cent in 1945, but in the population as a whole a mere 5 per cent had attended public school in the postwar era. If the composition of the House of Commons had been closer to a social microcosm there would have been about 33 MPs with public school backgrounds in 1992, not 258.

The Cabinet

With the number of aristocrats and those educated at top public schools falling steadily, Conservative cabinets became more solidly middle class between 1945 and 1984 (Table 3.6). However state-educated meritocrats made little headway before the 1980s and, even after a small increase in the proportion of state-educated members after 1983, ministers with socially exclusive public school backgrounds still predominated in the 1990s (Baker *et al.*, 1992, p. 661). Thus, after 1965, Conservative leaders with relatively modest social origins such as Edward Heath (a carpenter's son), Margaret Thatcher (a grocer's daughter), and John Major (a circus entertainer's son), were completely untypical of their party. The university-educated component of Conservative cabinets rose from 69 per cent in 1951 to nearly 82 per cent between 1955 and 1984, and to 90 per cent in Major's 1992 cabinet. The

TABLE 3.6 *The social and educational background of cabinet ministers, 1916–84 (%)*

| | 1916–55 | | 1955–84 | |
	Conservative	Labour	Conservative	Labour
All public schools	76.5	26.1	87.1	32.1
Eton/Harrow	45.9	7.6	36.3	3.5
Oxbridge	63.2	27.6	72.8	42.8
All universities	71.4	44.6	81.6	62.5
Elementary/Secondary	4.0	50.7	2.5	37.5
Aristocrat	31.6	6.1	18.1	1.8
Middle class	65.3	38.4	74.0	44.6
Working class	3.0	55.3	2.6	41.0

Source: extracted from Burch and Moran, 1985.

Oxbridge-educated contingent, which averaged just over 63 per cent of Conservative cabinets between 1916 and 1955, increased significantly in the four decades after 1955. Decreasingly aristocratic and patrician, more uniformly middle class but only slightly more meritocratic, increasingly university-educated but with Oxbridge predominance persisting, Conservative cabinets changed their social composition only very gradually and remained socially exclusive groupings throughout the 1945–95 era.

Postwar Labour cabinets contrasted very sharply with Conservative cabinets in social and educational background. Three fifths of the Labour cabinet of 1945 were of working-class origin, three quarters were state-educated and only half were university graduates. However in the 1960s and 1970s the manual worker element declined and Labour cabinets became much more middle class. The Labour cabinets of 1964, March 1974 and 1976 were on average nearly two thirds (64 per cent) middle class and under one third (28 per cent) working class. Both the university-educated element, which averaged 67 per cent for these three cabinets, and the Oxbridge component, which rose from 25 per cent in 1945 to an average of 48.5 per cent between 1964 and 1976, increased significantly. The small upper-class element in Labour cabinets immediately after the war had disappeared almost completely by the 1970s. The postwar trend towards the predominance of university-educated, middle-class meritocrats in Labour's elite continued in Labour shadow cabinets in the 1990s. Thus all 21 members of Tony Blair's 1995 shadow cabinet were university-educated but only four had attended Oxbridge, a much smaller proportion than in Labour cabinets of the 1960s and 1970s. Approximately three quarters were state-school products, most of these having attended grammar schools. Labour's 1995 front-bench team reflected both postwar social embourgeoisement and the consequences of the 1944 Education Act as a generator of upward social mobility. Whereas contemporary Conservative cabinets were predominantly public school and Oxbridge-educated and mainly derived from the worlds of law, commerce and finance, Blair's shadow cabinet was largely drawn from the 'communicating professions' university teaching, political research and journalism. It also contained more women: five compared with two in the 1992 Major cabinet.

Trends at cabinet level therefore mirrored developments in the respective parliamentary parties. Conservative cabinets shed their most socially patrician element after the war but 'the flattening of social profile' was 'painfully slow', even under John Major (Baker *et al.*, 1992, p. 661). Meanwhile Labour cabinets became more meritocratic and less working class. Neither the Conservative nor the Labour cabinets contained many women. Altogether in the 1945 to 1995 period there were nine women cabinet ministers, 22 women ministers and one woman prime minister: 32 in all, equally divided between the parties.

Elites in Postwar Britain

On the face of it, British society became less elitist in the half century after 1945 in four main ways. First, social and political deference (willing submission to the elite) declined after the 1960s when traditional authorities came under attack and more individualistic, egalitarian and 'permissive' social and political attitudes gained ground, preparing the way for demands for a more open and participatory democracy. Second, in the 1980s the liberal establishment of 'the great and the good', who had staffed the main cultural and political institutions of the state since 1945, came under fire from Thatcherite Conservatism. The Thatcherite new right championed an anti-establishment of entrepreneurs and right-wing newspapermen against such cultural bastions as the BBC and the universities, which were portrayed as complacent and out of touch with the 'real world'. Third, in the late 1980s and 1990s, hitherto widely respected institutions such as the monarchy lost support, in part as a consequence of the publicity surrounding the marital problems of the queen's children. Fourth, as well as enduring internal divisions over the ordination of women, the Church of England was increasingly seen as one religious minority among many and suffered calls for its disestablishment.

Society certainly became more egalitarian and less deferential, but to what extent did the radical, populist and feminist movements of the late 1960s and 1970s open the way to the top for the less privileged classes and groups and erode the social homogeneity of elites? One small-scale survey of top individuals suggested that since the war less change had occurred at the highest levels of British society than was claimed by the argument for a growing meritocracy. *The Economist* compared the social background of 100 top people from politics, business, finance, academia, the learned professions and the arts in 1992 to that of their counterparts in 1972. It found, first, that 'the public schools had retained their control of the commanding heights of Britain's social system'. Of the top group in 1992, 66 per cent had been educated at public schools and 54 per cent at Oxbridge, little different from the 1972 proportions of 67 per cent and 52 per cent respectively. However it had become more difficult to succeed without higher education: approximately one quarter did so in 1972 but a mere 11 per cent reached the top without it in 1992. The second major finding was that 'a quarter of a century after the modern feminist movement reached Britain' the national elite contained only 4 per cent of women, a tiny increase of 2 per cent since 1972 (*The Economist*, 19 December 1992). The clear conclusion from both this survey and our earlier review of political and social elites is that change at the highest level of British society was extremely slow in the postwar period. The main change was that it became more difficult to attain the highest social positions without a university education. But the leading political, social and cultural institutions remained socially unrepresentative and relatively unresponsive to social trends.

Political participation

The Political Parties

By far the most significant change in political participation was a massive fall in the membership of both major parties. Having peaked at 2.8 million in 1953, Conservative membership fell to about 1.5 million in 1975 and 1.2 million in 1984, but then more sharply to perhaps as little as 500 000 in 1993. Membership of the Young Conservatives, which in the late 1940s was a formidable agency for recruiting the middle class, declined just as drastically from a high point of over 160 000 in 1949 to 50 000 in 1968 and a mere 6000–9000 in 1993 (Seldon and Ball, 1994, p. 275). Individual membership of the Labour Party also fell rapidly from a peak of just over one million in 1952 to just over 300 000 in 1990.

There are three types of explanation – political, social and cultural – for the drop in party membership. Political explanations include, first, the rapid growth of alternative vehicles of political participation such as social movements and 'cause' pressure groups (see below, pp. 85–7). Second, the loss of powers and shrinkage of responsibilities of local government in the 1980s reduced the chances of a local political career. Third, partisan dealignment – the long-term decline in party identification by voters – led to a smaller pool of possible recruits for both parties. Electors identifying with the Conservatives fell only slightly from 39 per cent to 37 per cent between 1964 and 1987, but the proportion identifying with Labour fell much more heavily from 42 per cent to 30 per cent (Heath *et al.*, 1991, pp. 12–13). Fourth, disappointment on the left at the perceived failings of the Wilson and Callaghan governments in the 1960s and 1970s sapped the will to join or remain a member of the Labour Party, whilst the one-nation Conservatives' disillusionment with Thatcherism may have led to an exodus from the Conservative Party in the 1980s and 1990s.

Social factors also contributed to the process of grass-roots decay. The huge growth in women's participation in the workforce, especially the increase in married women workers, limited the time and energy available for the kind of heavy political commitment by women that in the past had done much to sustain Conservative constituency associations. The erosion of working-class communities by the virtual disappearance of heavy industry and the decay of the inner cities undermined the traditional sources of Labour strength. Second, the increasing trend towards television electioneering may well have reduced the sense of purpose of local party activists in both parties, even if it did not undermine the rationale of local party campaigning (Seyd and Whiteley, 1992, pp. 174–200). Third, the growing range of recreational and leisure activities undoubtedly diverted potential recruits away from voluntary political activity. Finally, cultural factors such as the decline in public respect for politicians probably played a part in discouraging people from joining the political parties.

Granted party members were a diminishing band, who were they? Evidence for both parties was sparse before the 1990s. A local study of Newcastle-under-Lyme in the 1960s portrayed the typical Conservative member as in a high occupational status group, Anglican, educated beyond 15, late middle-aged (50–59), and more likely to be female, but it was impossible to say how representative of the whole party this picture was (Bealey *et al.*, 1965). A study of Conservative constituency chairmen in 1969 suggested that they were mainly male (94 per cent), largely upper-middle-class, from business (66 per cent) rather than professional backgrounds, and generally educated at public or grammar school; only a tiny minority (1 per cent) were drawn from the manual working class (Butler and Pinto-Duschinsky, 1980). Labour's local leadership at that time was predominantly white collar (17 per cent), business (12 per cent) and professional (20 per cent), but also contained a significant proportion of manual workers (26 per cent) (Janosik, 1968). However national random sample surveys conducted in late 1989/early 1990 and 1992 provided comprehensive portraits of both memberships that revealed interesting similarities as well as differences. Whilst both parties were predominantly composed of middle-class owner occupiers, the Conservatives were shown to be an ageing party, with an average age of 62 compared with 48 for Labour. Although the Conservatives had a higher proportion of privately educated members than Labour, the majority of Conservatives, like Labour, had been educated at state schools. Over one quarter of Labour members but under one tenth of Conservatives were working class, nearly two thirds of Labour members were trade unionists, and a significant minority of Labour members but only a minute proportion of Conservatives rented their houses from a local authority. Whereas over three quarters of Conservatives belonged to a Protestant church, only 36 per cent of Labour members did so. Whereas Labour changed considerably after the war, its heavily working-class, minimally educated membership being displaced by a mainly middle-class, better-educated, public-sector-orientated, more affluent one, the Conservative Party appears to have changed much less since it has traditionally been seen as a middle-class organisation forming 'the political wing of Anglicanism' (Seyd and Whiteley, 1992, pp. 27–40; Whiteley *et al.*, 1994, pp. 42–52).

Pressure Groups and Social Movements

A considerable surge in political participation began in the late 1950s, bringing a significant increase in diversity and pluralism. New social movements were launched and older ones virtually reinvented; a large number of cause groups were founded; and minor parties experienced a generally steady but occasionally dramatic increase in membership and electoral support (see

Chapter 7). These trends in political participation reflected the social change towards a more affluent and better-educated society, in which white-collar and professional groups predominated and leisure time and opportunities expanded. A study by the American political scientist Ronald Inglehart in 1977 argued that, as its basic needs were met, postwar society moved from a materialist politics aimed at satisfying material needs to a post-materialist politics in which a better quality of life and improved social relationships displaced the traditional emphasis on raising living standards. The new life-style politics was not only a generational matter influencing the new postwar generation rather than the prewar one, but also a matter of social class, affecting the affluent and educated middle class more than the working class. Both the younger generation and the middle class, it was contended, became increasingly influenced by new life-style values (Inglehart, 1977). This theory helps to explain much if not everything about the reaction against class-based politics, the falling electoral support and membership of the two main parties, the explosion of cause and protest groups and social movements, and the trend towards greater pluralism of political affiliation, as shown in the rise of new political parties such as the Greens and the nationalist revival. In particular the peace, civil rights, animal rights and environmental movements with their associated protest and pressure groups, both local and national, are usefully seen in the context of post-materialist culture, as is the demand of 'second wave' feminism for a radical change in women's role in society. The welfare lobby, which emerged in the 1960s, however, is better viewed as part of the long movement on behalf of the poor and materially disadvantaged (Exhibit 3.1) (see Byrne, 1994; Garner, 1996; Young, 1993; Lovenduski and Randall, 1993).

Finally, the findings of the British Political Participation Study, conducted in 1984–5, confirmed the explanation of the upsurge in political participation in terms of the emergence of a wealthier, better-educated society with an expanded middle class. It found that graduates were among the top 12 per cent in the overall participation scale; that those who participate beyond voting come disproportionately from the professional and managerial salaried groups; and that gender bias among the politically active had largely disappeared, women being as well represented as men among the more active 25 per cent of citizens. Lastly, it showed that those concerned with the new values of environmentalism, peace, feminism and general 'quality of life' issues were more participatory than average and that such attitudes were distributed across a broader section of the population than hitherto (Parry and Moyser, 1990, pp. 155, 162, 168; Parry and Moyser, 1993, p. 21).

The Mass Media

The main trends in the postwar press were increasing concentration of ownership, a serious fall in the quality of tabloid newspapers and an

EXHIBIT 3.1 *Pressure groups and social movements*

Movement/area of concern	Group	Aims	Achievements
Feminism			
Liberal	Fawcett Society Six Point Group	Equal opportunities Equal pay	Equal pay in civil service (1954) and teaching (1955)
Radical	Women's liberation movement (1970)	Politicisation of sexuality and gender relations. Complete sexual equality in all spheres of life More women MPs	Defence of abortion reform (1967), equal pay; sex discrimination, maternity leave and domestic violence legislation (1970–7) Influence on Labour Party, especially
Social and moral reform	Groups advocating reform of law on abortion, divorce and homosexuality; abolition of capital punishment. Pro-life groups	Liberalisation of law on abortion, divorce, homosexuality; abolition of capital punishment Reversal of 1967 abortion legislation	Extension of right to abortion; introduction of 'no fault' divorce; decriminalisation of homosexuality between consenting adults aged 21 (reduced to 18, 1994); abolition of capital punishment
Welfare Reform (poverty lobby)	Child Poverty Action Group Shelter, Diasblement Income Group Low Pay Unit Age Concern National Council for One-Parent Families	Improved welfare for pensioners, one parent families, the mentally and physically disabled, the homeless and the poor	Small increase in family allowances (1967); additional allowances for lone parents (1975) improvements in circumstances of disabled and then carers. Sharp decline in receptivity of government in 1980s
Environmentalism			
Old established groups	National Trust Council for Protection of Rural England Royal Society for Nature Conservation	Preserving countryside as an amenity Nature conservation	Limited progress, mainly Wildlife and Countryside Act (1981), protecting endangered species of birds and mammals
New Groups	Friends of the Earth Greenpeace	Environmental protection; anti-pollution and resource-depletion	Limited progress in control of air and water pollution; creation of H M Inspectorate Pollution (1987), National Rivers Authority (1989). Some influence of green issues on political parties.
Animal lobby	RSPCA Anti-vivisection and anti-blood sports groups	Higher moral status for animals, stiffer control or banning of scientific experiments on animals; ban on blood sports	Stronger regulation of animal experiments (1986). Improved protection of wild mammals (1996) and of farm animals in transit (1995).
Nuclear disarmament	CND (1958)	Unilateral nuclear disarmament by British government	Adoption of unilateralism by Labour Party (1960–1, 1981–9)
Civil liberties	National Council for Civil Liberties; Liberty 1988 Campaign for Freedom of Information Charter 88	Human rights Open government Written constitution for UK	Moved these issues on to the political agenda: both Labour and the Liberal Democrats promised to introduce a Freedom of Information Act and to incorporate the European Convention on Human Rights into the UK law in their 1997 manifesto, and the Liberal Democrats also promised a Bill of Rights.

increasing Conservative bias in the press as a whole. The other major postwar development was the rapidly growing importance of television in political affairs.

The century-long trend towards concentration in press ownership continued after 1945, and by the early 1990s three quarters of national dailies and over four fifths of Sunday newspapers were owned by three syndicates. News International (Rupert Murdoch), which published *The Sun*, *The Times*, *Today*, the *News of the World* and *The Sunday Times*, had a total circulation of over 10 million, including a third of daily tabloid circulation and 45 per cent of the Sunday 'quality' market. In 1991 (the year of Maxwell's death), the Maxwell Foundation, whose publications included the *Daily Mirror*, the *Sunday People* and the *Sunday Mirror*, had sales of nearly 12 million, including a quarter of daily tabloid circulation. United Newspapers, which published the *Daily Express*, the *Daily Star* and the *Sunday Express*, had over one quarter of daily tabloid circulation. Associated Newspapers (Lord Rothermere) published newspapers with a combined circulation of over five million, including the *Daily Mail* and the *Mail on Sunday*. From the perspective of political pluralism, this concentration of the press in fewer hands was a disturbing trend, especially when combined with the steady fall in the number of newspaper titles.

Increasingly, moreover, newspapers were owned by giant corporations with substantial interests in other media, notably television, as well as non-media businesses. In 1995, for example, the media tycoon Rupert Murdoch headed a massive world-wide business that included satellite, cable and terrestrial television, films (twentieth Century Fox and Metromedia), book, magazine and journal publishing (for example Harper Collins), Reuters News Agency, and companies involved in property, transport, gas and oil. Concern about multimedia ownership in Britain surfaced in 1991 when Murdoch's Sky cable company merged with its main competitor, British Satellite Broadcasting, to create BSkyB. Although inconsistent with the cross-media ownership clauses of the 1990 Broadcasting Act and at variance with practice in Australia and the United States, where laws on cross-media ownership are more stringent, the merger was approved by the Independent Broadcasting Authority (Newton, 1995, pp. 159–62).

A second development in the decades after 1970 was the steady deterioration in the quality of the tabloid press. The tabloids increasingly regaled their readers with a diet of scandal, sensationalism, triviality and oversimplification and focused unrelentingly on so-called personalities from the worlds of film, television, pop music and the royal family. The tiny and diminishing pieces of genuine political information carried by some tabloids hardly entitled them to be called 'newspapers' at all. The intrusiveness of their reporting into the lives of the Royals and ordinary people led to widespread public concern in the 1980s and a demand by some critics for a privacy law. The rapid downmarket descent of the tabloids appeared the more serious in view of their taking an increasing proportion of readers. Whereas 50 per cent of voters read a tabloid in 1970, 80 per cent did so in 1995.

A third trend was increasing Conservative bias in the press. At the time of the 1945 general election a reasonable balance existed, with the Conservatives supported by newspapers with 52 per cent of circulation, Labour backed by newspapers with 35 per cent of circulation, and the Liberals by newspapers with 13 per cent of circulation. This rough equality between Conservative and anti-Conservative forces in the press lasted until 1970, but declined thereafter. In 1979 newspapers accounting for 71 per cent of circulation backed the Conservatives, with Labour receiving the support of the remainder. Conservative domination intensified in the 1980s: from 1983, seven dailies were pro-Conservative, one pro-Labour, none pro-Alliance. Not only did the balance of press allegiance change, the tone and intensity of partisanship moved from the relatively muted advocacy of the consensual 1960s and 1970s to the strident, often vicious, invective of the 1980s and 1990s.

Evidence of direct press influence on voting behaviour, previously unproven, increased in the 1980s. A study of the 1983 and 1987 general elections concluded that newspaper influence had had a substantial effect on the outcomes, and the closer the party battle, the bigger the newspaper effect (Newton, 1992). Another political scientist estimated that press bias was worth about 1 per cent to the Conservatives in 1983 and 1987. He also thought that newspaper bias appeared to have contributed both to the longer-term pro-Conservative swing between the second half of 1991 and the general election on 9 April 1992 and to the last-minute pro-Conservative swing in that election (Crewe, 1993, pp. 96–7). An authoritative 1991 study of the media and voters concluded that 'the press, but not television, had a significant influence on voter preferences' (Miller, 1991, p. 198).

Unlike the press, which is left to free-market principles, there is state regulation of broadcasting, whose political coverage is required to maintain balance, accuracy and impartiality. Nonetheless the postwar period saw a complete transformation in the manner in which the broadcasting authorities, especially television, covered elections. Deference towards politicians and rigorous self-restraint aimed at precluding any possibility of influencing the election results were the keynotes in the 1950s. The BBC's fourteen day rule excluded all reference to any matter likely to be discussed in both houses of parliament for the coming fortnight. The first party political broadcast appeared on television in 1951, and as news bulletins avoided all reference to the campaigns, party political broadcasts were the main campaign events on television for most of the 1950s. In 1959, however, late-night news bulletins began to report election events and politicians went in front of the cameras to be interviewed. Elections as media events had begun, and in 1964 viewers' questions were put to party leaders in 'Election Forum'. After that the parties increasingly conducted their campaigns on television. Constituency campaigning waned and was replaced by national media campaigns in which party news conferences were timed to fit in with news bulletins and old-style mass meetings gave way to all-ticket rallies in which entrance could be strictly controlled by the organisers.

Top politicians had to learn to use television to maximum effect. Good televisual performers such as Harold Wilson, the first national leader to make skilful use of the medium, were considerable assets to their parties whilst poor performers such as Home in 1964 and Foot in 1983 were political liabilities. Accomplished performances on television probably assisted the Liberal recovery under Jeremy Thorpe and David Steel in the 1970s and heavy exposure on television may have contributed even more to the mushroom growth of the Liberal–SDP Alliance in the 1980s. Election campaigns after 1979 were increasingly guided by advertising and marketing 'experts'. Special advisers were employed to guide Margaret Thatcher on voice production and personal appearance for television purposes. With party campaigns more and more designed for TV, producers were criticised by neutrals for being too compliant in reporting stage-managed party 'events' and contrived photo opportunities, and by the parties for pursuing 'their own agenda'. The TV campaigns became dominated by discussions of opinion polls, which were little used in 1945 but by the 1990s were seen as driving out more substantial issues. While the politicians moved into the television studios, the broadcasters moved into the political arena. Direct radio broadcasting from the House of Commons began in 1975; TV cameras moved into the House of Lords in 1985 and eventually into the House of Commons, at first on an experimental basis in1989 and then permanently in 1990. Colin Seymour-Ure described well the postwar shift from 'broadcasters being, first, observers of politics, to being, next, discreet participants, and finally to becoming . . . so essential as to be part of the structure' (Seymour-Ure, 1995, p. 36).

The public perceives the actual coverage of politics by TV news and current affairs programmes as generally accurate and impartial. Hence the concern about political bias that has emerged in relation to the press has not applied to the same extent to political coverage by the broadcasting authorities. However the continuing tension between radio and television broadcasters and the politicians does raise issues central to a democracy. During the 1980s, controversy arose over BBC television coverage of the Falklands War and the US bombing of Libya, and between the independent Television authorities and the government over coverage of the IRA and the security services. The first worry arising out of these episodes was that the government would engage in direct bans on specific areas of broadcasting, thereby eroding freedom of speech, a situation brought nearer when the broadcasting of the voices of Sinn Fein speakers was banned in 1989. The second was that, perhaps in anticipation of government bans or severe pressure, broadcasters would engage in self-censorship, as seemed to have happened when the BBC programme on Britain's proposed spy satellite, Zircon, was withdrawn in 1987. The BBC, which was dependent on the government for the renewal of its annual licence fee and also for a new charter in 1997, seemed especially vulnerable to such pressures.

Further Reading

Baker, D., A. Gamble and S. Ludlam, 'More Classless and Less Thatcherite? Conservative Ministers and New Conservative MPs after the 1992 Election', *Parliamentary Affairs*, vol. 45, no. 4 (1992).

Burch, M. and M. Moran, 'The Changing British Political Elite, 1945–1983: MPs and Cabinet Ministers', *Parliamentary Affairs*, vol. 38 (Winter 1985).

Byrne, P., 'Pressure Groups and Popular Campaigns', in P. Johnson (ed.) *Twentieth Century Britain* (London: Longman, 1994).

Crewe, I., 'Parties and Electors', in I. Budge and D. McKay (eds), *The Developing British Political System: the 1990s* (London: Longman, 1993).

Halsey, A. H., *Trends in British Society since 1900* (London: Macmillan, 1988).

Lovenduski, J., P. Norris and C. Burgess, 'The Party and Women', in A. Seldon and S. Ball (eds), *The Conservative Party since 1900* (Oxford: Oxford University Press, 1994).

Moran, M., *Politics and Society in Britain*, 2nd edn (London: Macmillan, 1989).

Newton, K., 'The Mass Media: Fourth Estate or Fifth Column?' in R. Pyper and L. Robins (eds) *Governing the UK in the 1990s* (London: Macmillan, 1995).

Norris, P. and J. Lovenduski, *Political Recruitment: Gender, Race and Class in the British Parliament* (Cambridge: Cambridge University Press, 1995).

Seyd, P. and P. Whiteley, *Labour's Grass Roots: The Politics of Party Membership* (Oxford: Clarendon Press, 1992).

Seymour-Ure, C., 'The Media in Postwar British Politics', in F. F. Ridley and M. Rush (eds) *British Government and Politics since 1945: Changes in Perspective* (Oxford: Oxford University Press, 1995).

Solomos, J., *Race and Racism in Contemporary Britain* (London: Macmillan, 1989).

Thane, P., 'Women since 1945', in P. Johnson (ed.), *Twentieth Century Britain* (London: Longman, 1994).

Whiteley, P., P. Seyd and J. Richardson, *True Blues The Politics of Conservative Party Membership* (Oxford: Clarendon Press, 1994).

4
The Territorial Dimension

Before the 1960s a chapter on 'territorial politics' probably would not have appeared in a book of this kind. For not only was the United Kingdom a unitary state, as it still is, it was also a homogenous state. The 'homogeneity thesis', which was widely held by British political scientists, argued that Britain's unitary constitution was underpinned by an increasingly uniform political culture in which religious, linguistic and national differences were overridden by differences based on social class. Hence separate discussion of the various national components of the UK was not required since these countries were becoming progressively more alike. But in the late 1960s and 1970s the emergence of nationalist movements in Scotland and Wales and of 'the troubles' in Northern Ireland provided a reminder of the complex, multinational nature of the UK. Its taken-for-granted unity disappeared as problems with the territorial management of Scotland, Wales and Northern Ireland by Westminster politicians pressed to the fore.

This chapter first examines the nature of Britain as a multinational state and describes the main cultural, social and economic features of its component nations. It then focuses on three themes: party politics in the peripheral countries since 1945; the system of territorial sub-government in the UK; and the constitutional challenge posed by the resurfacing of peripheral nationalisms together with the political responses made by British governments.

Britain as a Multinational State

The United Kingdom evolved slowly by means of the gradual extension of the political authority of England over the countries of the outer periphery of the British Isles. The absorption of Wales, Scotland and Ireland by Acts of Union in 1536, 1707 and 1801 respectively occurred in different ways, the particular circumstances of the Acts of Union influencing the later history of these countries' relationship with the Westminster parliament. The union was always a very unequal one, the populations of the individual countries in 1951 being England 43.7 million, Scotland 5.1 million, Wales 2.6 million and Northern Ireland 1.4 million. But each country retained a strong sense of national identity which was reinforced by geographical separateness and expressed through a particular culture and pattern of social institutions. A key aspect of the integration of the peripheral countries within the union was the constitutional doctrine of parliamentary sovereignty, which proved sufficiently flexible to permit decentralised political and administrative arrangements for their government whilst enshrining the idea of firm rule from the centre when necessary.

The union could have developed in several ways after 1880, including (at least) four different forms of unitary state, a federal state and the break-up of the union by the secession of one or more of the peripheral nations. The unitary alternatives were (1) a powerful central authority with a widely spread, deeply embedded unionist culture and a comprehensive constitution; (2) a system of 'internal colonialism' in which England exploited the weaker countries; (3) a decentralised state, with power devolved to the regional assemblies; and (4) a weak centre, dominated by the peripheral nations and regions. Broadly, the strength of cultural nationalism in Wales, Scotland and Northern Ireland in the two generations before 1940 prevented either of the first two alternatives becoming a reality whilst the integrating effects of late-nineteenth-century imperialism and of the First World War precluded the third and fourth alternatives and also served to dampen the appeal of federalism and to rule out substantial break-up (Bulpitt, 1983).

From the 1870s, nationalist movements pressed for home rule in all three countries, but the outbreak of war in 1914 led to suspension of the bill that would have given Ireland its own parliament. After the war a partial fragmentation of the UK occurred, with 26 of Ireland's 32 counties separating to achieve dominion status as the Irish Free State (Republic of Ireland 1949). The six counties of the north became a new province, which owed allegiance to the British crown, had its own parliament at Stormont from 1921 to 1972 and sent 12 representatives to Westminster (17 from 1983). In 1940 Scotland had 71 MPs and Wales 35. Although nationalist parties were formed in Wales in 1925 and Scotland in 1934, they made little headway in a situation in which, with the devolutionist Liberals a declining force, pro-union parties (the Conservatives and Labour) dominated the Westminster parliament. The rise of national socialism (Nazism) in Europe and the policies pursued by the the Irish Free State, which included 'gaelicisation', a 'special position' for the Roman Catholic Church, trade wars with Britain in the 1930s and neutrality in the Second World War, further undermined the appeal of nationalism in Wales and Scotland.

The Nations of Multinational Britain

Scotland, Wales and Northern Ireland all differ from England and from each other. The peripheral nations have in common their political domination by England and their constitutional subordination to the Westminster parliament by means of the doctrine of parliamentary sovereignty. But in terms of society, economy, culture, institutions and political behaviour they are all different. An important difference between Scotland and the other peripheral countries of the union is that Scotland was a state before its incorporation into the union in 1707, whereas Wales and Ireland were not. After union,

Scotland retained separate legal, religious and educational systems. Of all the peripheral nations, Wales became the most integrated into the UK and Northern Ireland remained the least integrated.

Differing patterns of religious observance lie behind national identity in the peripheral countries. Of the three, only Scotland has an established Church. In Wales, after a successful campaign by religious nonconformists the Church of England was disestablished in 1920. In England and Scotland the majority identify with the established Church – the Church of England (Anglican) and the Church of Scotland (Presbyterian) respectively – but Wales is more evenly divided between Anglicanism and nonconformity. However, although religion continued to shape cultural differences between the mainland countries, all three became more secular in the postwar period, in contrast to Northern Ireland, where religious divisions remained intense and politically significant. There Roman Catholics, who were a minority but are increasing relative to Protestants, account for about 40 per cent of the population and face a Protestant majority divided between Presbyterians, Church of Ireland adherents and members of Protestant sects, the largest of which is Methodism. In Northern Ireland religion broadly determines political and national loyalties, with Catholics tending to favour the nationalist cause and Protestants loyal to the Union.

Language differences remain significant only in Wales, where about one fifth of the population spoke both Welsh and English in 1971. Only a tiny proportion (roughly 1 per cent) spoke only Welsh, but as a consequence of the nationalist campaign for the wider recognition of the Welsh language, by the mid 1980s Wales had become 'officially, visibly and audibly a bilingual country' (Williams, 1985, p. 293). In contrast British policy successfully discouraged the variants of Gaelic spoken by about half the Irish and nearly one quarter of Scots in the early nineteenth century, and in the UK today less than 2 per cent of Scots speak Gaelic.

Although it would be too much to speak of a 'Scottish economy' or a 'Welsh economy', the economic experiences of the peripheral countries since 1945 were extreme manifestations of UK-wide economic developments. All were characterised by heavy structural unemployment as old staple industries declined: unemployment rates in the peripheral countries were persistently higher than in most English regions and also higher than the average unemployment figures for England and the UK as a whole. In 1969, for example, average unemployment was 2.5 per cent in the UK but 3.7 per cent in Scotland, 4 per cent in Wales and 7.1 per cent in Northern Ireland. By 1989 it had risen to 5.9 per cent in the UK but 7 per cent in Wales, 8.9 per cent in Scotland and 14.5 per cent in Northern Ireland. Accelerating deindustrialisation after 1960 created severe problems for the west of Scotland, south Wales and the Belfast region. Postwar per capita incomes in Wales, Scotland and Northern Ireland also lagged behind England, with per capita GDP in England standing at 102.3 per cent of the UK figure in 1988 compared with 93.9 per cent in Scotland, 84 per cent in Wales and 78 per cent in Northern Ireland.

Party Politics on the UK Periphery

Political behaviour in the UK has strong regional differences as well as important similarities. Scotland and Wales are broadly similar to England in that both the main UK parties, together with the Liberal Democrats, compete for votes, but different in that, from the 1960s, they possessed nationalist parties capable of winning seats at Westminster, thereby introducing four-party competition into these regions. In contrast the main UK parties did not contest elections in Northern Ireland until 1992, the province having continued to operate its own distinct party system throughout the postwar period. Necessarily in Northern Ireland, because of the different party system, but also in Scotland and Wales, because of the additional parties and their distinctive political cultures, voting behaviour differs from that in England. The main contrast is that whereas the Conservatives were dominant in England in the postwar period, failing to gain an electoral majority there only in 1945, 1964, October 1974 and 1997, they were quite unable to establish electoral ascendancy in Scotland and Wales.

During the postwar decade in Scotland the two main parties were in a roughly equal position with regard to seats (Table 4.1). But from 1959 the Conservative position deteriorated, steadily at first and then dramatically in the 1980s, when Labour gained the kind of ascendancy enjoyed by the Liberals before 1914. Overall, between 1955 and 1992 the Conservatives lost 25 seats and 15.8 per cent of the vote in Scotland. Scottish voting behaviour therefore showed an increasing divergence from English voting behaviour in this period. Nonetheless, drawing upon their strength in England, the Conservatives won six of the ten UK general elections held between 1955 and 1992.

Recent explanations of the differences in voting behaviour between the two countries stress cultural, political and economic factors. Theories that conservatism has declined since the late 1950s because Scotland is more working class than the rest of the UK or because of the fading influence of Protestantism, which formerly sustained its vote, have been questioned. Political scientists now seek to account for trends since 1959 in terms of such factors as the decline in 'the symbolic power of unionism' in Scottish political culture; the increasing perception of the Conservatives as the 'English' party in a society in which nationalism and devolution have become increasingly salient; the retention by Scotland of a relatively high commitment to the welfare consensus allied to the probability that it is more collectivist in outlook than southern England; and finally, the short-term economic record of the Conservatives, which 'at election times has been more

TABLE 4.1 *The leading mainland parties and Scottish National Party in general elections in Scotland, 1945–97*

	Conservative		Labour		Liberal		Scottish National Party	
	Seats	% of Scottish vote	Seats	% of Scottish vote	Seats	% of Scottish vote	Seats	% of Scottish vote
1945	27	41.1	37	47.6	–	5.0	–	–
1950	31	44.8	37	46.2	2	6.6	–	–
1951	35	48.6	35	47.9	1	2.7	–	–
1955	36	50.1	34	46.7	1	1.9	–	0.5
1959	31	47.2	38	46.7	1	4.1	–	0.8
1964	24	40.6	43	48.7	4	7.6	–	2.4
1966	20	37.7	46	49.9	5	6.8	–	5.0
1970	23	38.0	44	44.5	3	5.5	1	11.4
1974 (Feb.)	21	32.9	40	36.6	3	8.0	7	21.9
1974 (Oct.)	16	24.7	41	36.3	3	8.3	11	30.4
1979	22	31.4	44	41.6	3	9.0	2	17.3
1983	21	28.4	41	35.1	8	24.5	2	11.8
1987	10	24.0	50	42.4	9	19.3	3	14.0
1992	11	25.7	49	39.0	9	13.1	3	21.5
1997	0	18.0	56	46.0	10	13.0	6	22.0

Notes: The Conservative results from 1945–64 include National Liberal and Conservative. Under Liberal are Liberal–SDP Alliance, 1983–7, and Liberal Democrat, from 1992.
Source: data extracted from Craig, 1989, pp. 34–9; Butler and Kavanagh, 1992, p. 286; *The Times*, 3 May 1997.

unfavourable (to Scotland) than Labour's' (Seawright and Curtice, 1995, pp. 330–5, 339; Brown *et al.*, 1996, p. 149, 157; Midwinter *et al.*, 1991, pp. 18–20).

Labour dominance and Conservative weakness also characterised postwar politics in Wales (Table 4.2). Indeed Labour's strength in Wales was more pronounced than in Scotland: between 1945 and 1970 it always won over 70 per cent of the seats, peaking in 1966 with 86 per cent. The Conservative position in Wales improved briefly in 1979 and 1983, but fell back again in 1987 and even further in 1992. Both Liberals and nationalists had less success in Wales than in Scotland. Nonetheless from February 1974 a four-party system operated in Wales. Conservative improvement in the 1970s and 1980s, together with stronger competition from Plaid Cymru, the Liberals and the Liberal–SDP Alliance, reduced the Labour advantage over the Conservatives from an average of 22 seats between 1945 and 1970 to 13 between February 1974 and 1987, although it rose again to 21 in 1992.

Historical and social factors explain the Labour ascendancy in Wales. From the late nineteenth century Wales became even more anti-Conservative than Scotland, to the benefit first of the Liberals between 1874 and 1922, then of Labour between 1922 and the present. In its Liberal phase, Welsh anti-Conservatism was a compound of anti-landlordism, Welsh nonconformity and nationalist sentiment: its opponent was a Conservative Party

TABLE 4.2 *The leading mainland parties and Plaid Cymru in general elections in Wales, 1945–97*

	Conservative		Labour		Liberal		Plaid Cymru	
	Seats	*% of Welsh vote*	*Seats*	*% of Welsh vote*	*Seats*	*% of Welsh vote*	*Seats*	*% of Welsh vote*
1945	4	23.8	25	58.5	6	14.9	–	–
1950	4	27.4	27	58.1	5	12.6	–	–
1951	6	30.8	27	60.5	3	7.7	–	–
1955	6	29.9	27	57.6	3	7.3	–	3.1
1959	7	32.6	27	56.4	2	5.3	–	5.2
1964	6	29.4	28	57.8	2	7.3	–	4.8
1966	3	27.9	32	60.7	1	6.2	–	4.3
1970	7	27.7	27	51.6	1	6.8	–	11.5
1974 (Feb.)	8	25.9	24	46.8	2	16.0	2	10.7
1974 (Oct.)	8	23.9	23	49.5	2	15.5	3	10.8
1979	11	32.2	22	48.6	1	10.6	2	8.1
1983	14	31.1	20	37.5	2	23.2	2	7.8
1987	8	29.5	24	45.1	3	17.9	3	7.3
1992	6	28.6	27	49.5	1	12.4	4	8.8
1997	0	20.0	34	55.0	2	12.0	4	10.0

Notes: Conservative results 1945–64 include National Liberal and Conservative. Under Liberal are Liberal–SDP Alliance, 1983–7, and Liberal Democrat from 1992.
Source: Craig, 1989, pp. 34–49; Butler and Kavanagh, 1992, p. 286; *The Times*, 3 May 1997.

identified with Englishness and 'the unholy trinity of bishop, brewer and squire' (Morgan, 1981). Labour's dominance from 1922 rested on the intense class consciousness of the South Wales coalfields.

Elsewhere in Wales, Labour's embodiment of Welsh sentiment enabled it to win constituencies it could not have won in England (Dunbabin, 1980, p. 249). Unlike in Scotland, where the Conservatives gained a majority in 1931, 1935 and 1955, Labour's ascendancy in Wales remained unaffected by falls in Labour support elsewhere in mainland Britain.

In Northern Ireland, until 1972, the main party, the Ulster Unionists, had close links with the Conservatives, whose mass party organisation was named the National Union of Conservative and Unionist Associations. Before February 1974 Ulster Unionist votes were simply reckoned with the Conservatives in the House of Commons. But from the early 1970s Ulster Unionism drifted away from the Conservatives, the last formal links between the two parties being cut in 1990 (Seldon and Ball, 1994, p. 303). Effectively, however, the links were severed immediately after the inconclusive general election of February 1974, when the Unionists, alienated by the ending of the parliament in Stormont (1972) and the experiment of power sharing with Catholics, refused to back the Conservative prime minister, Edward Heath, thereby destroying his attempt to hold on to power.

Northern Ireland politics, like much else in the province, is organised around the Protestant–Catholic sectarian divide, and it entered its formative phase in the late 1960s and 1970s. Not only did the Ulster Unionists strike out on their own, the Catholics, through the formation of the Social Democratic and Labour Party (SDLP) in 1970, achieved their most effective representation since 1920. Formed in 1905 to defend the constitutional link with Britain, the Unionists won the majority of Northern Ireland seats in general elections. From the late 1960s, however, the Unionists began to divide, a split that was formalised in the late 1970s into two major groupings: the Official Unionists, led between 1979 and 1995 by James Molyneaux, and the Democratic Unionists, led by the Reverend Ian Paisley. Opposed to Protestant unionism are the two anti-Partition parties representing the Catholic community: the Social Democratic and Labour Party (SDLP), led initially by the moderate republican socialist Gerry Fitt (1970–9) and then by John Hume, and Provisional Sinn Fein, led by Gerry Adams. The main aim of the SDLP is the reunification of Ireland with the consent of the majority in the north. After 1982 the SDLP faced an electoral challenge from Sinn Fein, which has direct links with the IRA. The other significant development in the early 1970s was the formation of the moderate Alliance Party in 1970, a centrist group committed to uniting Catholics and Protestants behind a reform programme within a continuing link with Britain (Table 4.3).

In conclusion, in the postwar period politics on the periphery in some ways became more different from politics in England. First, after 1970 'geographical milieu . . . exerted an increasingly independent influence on the vote' in the UK: the movement away from the Conservatives between 1979 and 1992 in Scotland, Wales and the north combined with the movement towards conservatism in the Midlands and the south suggests that 'a more enduring geographical polarisation' occurred that had 'an independent behavioural impact on the vote' (Crewe, 1993, p. 103). Second, Conservative hegemony at the UK level between 1979 and 1997 meant that for almost two decades neither Scotland nor Wales voted for the governing party. This represented a real departure, since between 1945 and 1979 no nation was 'consistently excluded from a share in the Westminster government' (Rose, 1982, p. 81).

TABLE 4.3 *General elections in Northern Ireland, 1974–97 (number of seats)*

	Official Ulster Unionists (UUP)	Democratic Unionists (DUP)	Other Unionists	SDLP	Sinn Fein	Alliance	Other
1974 (Feb.)	7	1	3	1		–	–
1974 (Oct.)	6	1	3	1		–	1
1979	5	3	2	1		–	1
1983	11	3	1	1	1	–	–
1987	9	3	1	3	1	–	–
1992	9	3	1	4	–	–	–
1997	10	2	1	3	2	–	–

Source: Craig, 1989, pp. 43–49; Butler and Kavanagh, 1992, p. 313; *The Times*, 3 May 1997.

Not only was the main Northern Ireland political party closely linked to the Conservatives, but also three of the four UK nations usually voted for the governing party most if not all the time, with England backing the winning party for 78 per cent, Scotland for 74 per cent and Wales for 51 per cent of this period. Third, the rise of nationalist parties in Scotland and Wales meant that, from the 1970s, politics in those countries was based on a four-party rather than a three-party system, as in England.

However the party system has integrated the United Kingdom as well as dividing it. First, postwar Scottish and Welsh electorates have regularly voted predominantly for the main Westminster parties, even after the rise of the nationalists. Second, there has been a consistent overrepresentation of Scotland and Wales in the Westminster parliament: in 1992, if seats had been allocated strictly according to population, Scotland would have been entitled to 59 seats in the House of Commons rather than the 72 it actually had, and Wales would have had 32 rather than 38.

Governing the United Kingdom

The United Kingdom is a unitary state in which the Westminster government legislates and makes decisions for all parts of the kingdom. The major territorial elements (Scotland, Wales amd Northern Ireland) were incorporated into the British state at various times over the last five centuries and therefore do not possess their own systems of government. However the constitutional doctrine of parliamentary sovereignty coexists and is consistent with different systems of subordinate government in each of these countries.

Simultaneously 'in the centre and for a periphery' (Rhodes, 1988, p. 144) the Scottish, Welsh and Northern Ireland Offices operate within a dual political environment: Scottish, Welsh or Northern Irish *and* British. The functional responsibilities of these sub-governments are to oversee the implementation of centrally determined policy in their regions. None has any role in foreign and defence policy, which remain squarely the responsibility of the Westminster government; but in 1988 all had responsibilities in education and science, the environment, health, industry and heritage. Each office is headed by a secretary of state, assisted by a team of ministers. The offices came into existence in response to the changing circumstances of territorial politics. The main factors involved in the establishment of the Scottish Office (1885) and the Welsh Office (1964) were special territorial needs, nationalist dissatisfaction with distant Westminster government and the desire for greater political accountability. The Northern Ireland Office (1972) was formed when the Stormont government was abolished. The territorial sub-governments in Edinburgh, Cardiff and Belfast also mediate between the interests of their territories and the demands of the centre, and lobby Westminster or Whitehall on behalf of their regions.

Although departments of state, the various offices differ in several ways from the other departments headed by cabinet ministers. Responsible for a wide range of the functions of modern government, they are multifunctional rather than monofunctional; they have a key role in territorial management by the centre; and they are located in the peripheral countries and seek to advance their interests.

In addition to these arrangements for administrative devolution, special parliamentary procedures and institutions have evolved for dealing with territorial legislation. These include the Scottish Grand Committee (1894) and the Scottish Standing Committee (1957) to consider the committee stage of Scottish legislation, and the Select Committees on Scottish Affairs (1968), Welsh Affairs (1979) and Northern Ireland (1994) to improve the accountability of their respective offices. But the timing of their formation – with the Welsh committee, for example, being created in the wake of the devolution referendum (see p. 106) and the Northern Ireland committee after the Downing Street Declaration (see p. 113) – suggests that the development of political institutions to deal with the affairs of the peripheral countries was piecemeal and opportunistic. Such moves reflected the constantly shifting balance in their relations with the centre.

Territorial management by the centre became more difficult in the 1960s. During the preceding half century, contact between centre and periphery was mainly bureaucratic and depoliticised (Bulpitt, 1983). Nationalist sentiment certainly existed, as indicated, for example, by the Scottish Covenant, which between 1949 and 1951 attained over two million signatures in favour of a Scottish Parliament. However peripheral nationalisms were constrained by three major forces: a cultural framework that emphasised loyalty to the monarch and the British Empire; an ideological mind-set focusing on the attainment of collectivist ends such as welfare and redistributive taxation within a UK context; and a political context in which the Westminster government was preoccupied with maintaining the integrity of the UK against external threat. The successful pursuit by governments of the twin objectives of domestic welfare and external security brought clear benefits to Scotland, Wales and Northern Ireland from membership of the union and also a certain prestige. The threat from Germany and Japan until 1945 and from the USSR after the war boosted British nationalism whilst making any quest for home rule on the part of the peripheral nations seem both irrelevant and dangerous.

Other structural and political factors contributed to the persistence of what Bulpitt (1983) has termed the 'dual polity' phase of centre–periphery relations until the 1960s. This phrase denotes the coexistence of Westminster and local/regional politics in separate spheres. The relevant structural factor concerns the place of Northern Ireland, which, as a consequence of the Government of Ireland Act (1920), enjoyed devolved government by its own parliament at Stormont until 1972. In 1920, when southern Ireland chose dominion status and eventual independence, the north rejected both joining the south and reintegration with the rest of the United Kingdom in favour of home rule (Bogdanor, 1979, p. 46). For Northern Ireland, the possession of its own parliament was the surest safeguard against its greatest fear: being coerced into joining the south in a united Ireland.

The 1920 Act gave Stormont the power to make laws for its internal affairs; the Westminster parliament, as well as retaining supreme constitutional authority over Northern Ireland, reserved to itself specific powers over defence, foreign policy and external trade. In practice, although legally subordinate to Westminster, Stormont enjoyed quasi-federal status for over 45 years after 1920, and exercised a degree of autonomy that was 'more appropriate to that of a provincial unit in a federal system' (ibid., 1979, p. 50). This suited both the Unionists in Stormont, who wanted to rule undisturbed, and the Westminster governments, which were more concerned with global than with domestic affairs. Indifference in Westminster – for example no attempt was made to deal with allegations of religious discrimination against Roman Catholics – led to the development of 'a one-party (i.e. Unionist) statelet with powers of control and coercion unknown in the British periphery' (Bulpitt, 1983, chapter 5).

The political factors underlying the 'dual polity' phase were, first, the displacement of the pro-home-rule Liberal Party in Scotland and Wales by a Labour Party favouring a welfare-Keynesian centralist strategy, and second, the political weakness of the nationalist parties, which meant that the periphery lacked political leverage in Westminster. The situation prevailing between the 1920s and the 1960s contrasted with the pre-1914 position when both Ireland, with its more than 80-strong nationalist party, and Scotland and Wales, with the dominant Liberals expressing nationalist aims and aspirations, were able to exercise real pressure in Westminster. Post-1945, with the political focus of the centre squarely on international alliance building and the implementation of the welfare-Keynesian consensus, the union resumed its taken-for-granted status in a British polity that was dominated by an English majority scarcely aware of the existence of the other nations except in ethnic jokes of the 'An Englishmen, an Irishman, a Scotsman and a Welshman . . . ' variety. But during the 1960s the nationalist upsurge in Scotland and Wales and the outbreak of sectarian strife in Northern Ireland pushed territorial management to the forefront of British politics, reminded the UK of the distinct national identities comprising it and made apparent the provisional nature of a state that had already suffered one major secession in the twentieth century.

Nationalism and Devolution in Scotland and Wales

Nationalist parties in Scotland and Wales began to achieve electoral success in the mid-1960s by winning by-elections. After polling well at Glasgow

Pollak earlier in the year, the Scottish National Party (SNP) went on to win the Labour stronghold of Hamilton in November 1967, gaining 46 per cent of the vote. The seat was lost in 1970, but the party won the Western Isles, its first general election victory. The Nationalists, who had progressed steadily but slowly from the 1950s, suddenly made a rapid advance in 1970, with even greater success following in 1974 (Table 4.1). Membership of the party rose from 2000 in 1962 to a peak of 120 000 in 1968, and still stood at 85 000 in 1974. The foundations of the 1970s successes were laid by earlier developments that included the ending of multiparty membership in 1946, after which SNP membership could no longer be combined with membership of another party; the elimination of left–right divisions and the uniting of the party behind the goal of an independent Scotland by the late 1950s; and, after the high polls achieved at the Bridgeton (1961) and West Lothian (1962) by-elections, the recruitment of Ian Macdonald as a full-time organiser to build up the party at the grass roots.

Postwar changes in both British and Scottish politics and society help explain the nationalist upsurge. First, by the 1960s centralised government by Labour and the Conservatives no longer seemed to be working to Scotland's economic benefit. Second, the discovery of North Sea oil heightened the already existing Scottish debate about the value of membership of the union. An independent Scotland could use the oil revenues to boost employment and incomes in Scotland, whereas the Westminster government would use the additional income to improve the British balance of payments. Third, UK entry into the EEC (later the European Union) in 1973 suggested that Scotland would become more peripheral by remaining within the UK than by gaining independence and negotiating entry to the EEC directly. As a member of the EEC, an independent Scotland would retain the advantages of union, such as access to the British market, without the disadvantage of political domination by England. Disenchantment with the economic policy failures of the major British parties combined with the prospect of a wealthy independent Scotland made national consciousness, which had been undergoing a revival since 1945, politically salient. The organisational transformation of the SNP in the early 1960s 'from a party of activists into a modern mass party' (Webb, 1978, p. 133) ensured that it was the SNP that benefited from this electoral opportunity rather than the Liberals. The idea that the growth of support for the SNP was merely a 'protest' vote is belied by the fact that most SNP voters supported either devolution or independence. However the Nationalists did on occasion gain from tactical voting (Kellas, 1989, p. 139).

As with the SNP, by-election success at Carmarthen in July 1966 triggered a sudden improvement in the fortunes of the Welsh nationalist party, Plaid Cymru, albeit on a lower scale (Table 4.2). Although expanding its operations to industrial south-east Wales in the 1970s, it continued to derive the bulk of its support from Welsh-speaking rural constituencies in North and

West Wales. Also, whereas in Scotland the SNP far surpassed the Liberals, in Wales the Liberals remained a potent force, increasing their share of the vote from 6.8 per cent to 15.5 per cent between 1970 and October 1974. Plaid Cymru membership grew from just under 3500 in 1965 to 27 000 in 1967 and a probable figure of over 30 000 in 1976 (Birch, 1979, pp. 128–9).

Like the SNP, Plaid Cymru called for a national parliament, but made the Welsh language its central issue: the main goal from 1969 being the achievement of bilingualism throughout Wales by the year 2000. As well as providing the party with a practical target, the Welsh language demand was a means of expressing anti-materialist values and of linking contemporary life with traditional Welsh culture. As in Scotland, the rising support for the nationalist party in the 1960s owed much to broader British factors such as political disillusionment with the economic management of the major parties and a growing feeling of powerlessness in the face of remote bureaucratic government. However Welsh nationalism lacked the triggering effect provided for its Scottish counterpart by the discovery of oil. Nonetheless the two nationalist parties combined received nearly half a million votes in 1970 and over one million votes in October 1974. The emergence of peripheral mainland nationalisms on such a scale presented a considerable territorial-management challenge to the Westminster Government.

The Labour government responded to nationalist by-election successes by appointing a Royal Commission (1969–73) to consider whether constitutional change was necessary in the relations between the central legislature and the various nations and regions of the UK. No doubt it hoped that this would defuse the situation. However the proposals of the Kilbrandon Commission constituted a weak compromise which satisfied neither the nationalists nor the mainstream Westminster parties but which the political circumstances of the time dictated should be carried forward into legislation. The Kilbrandon Commission was unanimous only in rejecting federalism and in recommending a Scottish assembly elected by proportional representation (the single transferable vote). It rejected a federal solution to the relationship between the four major territorial units of the UK because it considered that federalism:

- was an inconvenient system of government that worked well in the United States, Switzerland and West Germany *despite* its inherent disadvantages;
- would be unpopular with the English, who wanted neither a separate legislature nor regional legislative assemblies, federal or otherwise;
- would be unworkable in the UK because it would be dominated by the largest country, England; even if England were to be divided into provinces the system would still be unbalanced because it would be hard to prevent south-east England, which contained 31 per cent of the UK population, from dominating the federation (Birch, 1979, pp. 156–7).

Kilbrandon's recommendations, with a narrow majority of the thirteen members supporting legislative devolution for Scotland and Wales but not for England, certainly shaped the ensuing constitutional debate. But Kilbrandon's divisions, which revealed the complexity of the devolution issue, were also reflected in it. A Memorandum of Dissent signed by two members of the Commission argued that devolution should be based on the principle of equality of rights for all citizens of the UK, and accordingly should be extended to the English regions. The dissentient minority recommended executive, but not legislative, devolution to seven elected assemblies in Scotland, Wales and five English regions.

The report was debated only briefly in the House of Commons and neither major party promised devolution in its February 1974 manifesto. However the gains made by the nationalist parties in the February 1974 general election and the emergence of a minority Labour government dependent on the support of the Liberals and nationalists forced Labour into concessions. These concessions were reluctant mainly because of the party's ideological dislike of nationalism and firmly-held belief that economic prosperity and social justice would be catered for most effectively by a centrally administered economy and welfare system. Two white papers in 1974 prepared the way for the Scotland and Wales Bill (1976), whose main proposals were:

- An elected legislative assembly for Scotland and an elected executive assembly for Wales.
- The powers devolved to the Scottish assembly to be those pertaining to existing Scottish legislation and Scottish Office functions, but not to include powers over industry, the economy, agriculture or energy policy (oil).
- The secretary of state for Scotland to possess a power of veto over the Scottish Assembly, subject to parliamentary approval.
- Neither assembly to possess independent revenue-raising powers but to be financed mainly through a block grant allocated by parliament.
- Scotland and Wales to retain their existing number of seats in the Westminster parliament.
- The secretaries of state for Scotland and Wales to retain their places in the Cabinet.

The weak form of devolution suggested in this legislation contained many anomalies and raised as many problems as it solved. First, the very limited nature of the devolved powers were a grave disappointment to nationalists. The SNP resented the lack of revenue-raising power and the ruling out of control over the economy, and also disliked the allocation of a veto to the Scottish secretary. For Plaid Cymru the Welsh Assembly was even more of a political sop, a feeble institution that would effectively be no more than a large county council with powers to allocate a government block grant to the social services. Second, for many critics the legislation involved unfairness to England, raising the question that, if devolution was appropriate for Scotland and Wales, why was it not suitable for England also? Under the proposed scheme Yorkshire, with a population of over four million, would lack the regional powers of Wales, with a population of around 2.75 million. Third, the proposal that Scotland and Wales, although gaining elective assemblies, should retain their current representation in the Westminster parliament smacked of 'a crude gerrymander' by a Labour government anxious to appease nationalist opinion without undermining its electoral predominance in either country (Birch, 1979, p. 163). When the Northern Ireland Parliament was established in 1921, the Westminster representation of Northern Ireland was cut to two thirds of the seats to which its population size entitled it without devolution. Had a similar principle been applied in 1976, Scotland would have received 38 seats and Wales 21: that is, two thirds of the seats the countries would merit on population grounds, not two thirds of the seats they actually possessed in 1976.

The devolution bill gained the assent of the House of Commons with difficulty and only after significant concessions by the government. Much of the problem stemmed from the government's slender majority, which disappeared completely in November 1976 after by-election defeats. But it was also the consequence of diehard opposition to the bill within its own party. When the bill passed its second reading by 292 votes to 247, more Labour MPs voted against (10) and abstained (30) than Conservative MPs voted for (5) or abstained (28). Moreover, with the dissentient Conservative pro-devolutionists largely returning to the fold in voting at the committee stage, the government was forced into conceding referendums in Scotland and Wales after the bill became an Act in order to win back its own dissidents. The ploy failed, and with 22 Labour MPs voting against and 23 abstaining, a guillotine motion was defeated by 312 votes to 283 in February 1977, thereby in effect killing the Scotland and Wales Bill.

When the government revived the legislation as two separate bills for Scotland and Wales, further concessions were necessary in order to get them through the House of Commons, which on a free vote would have overturned them. The first concession was acceptance of a proposal from a Labour backbencher, George Cunningham, to the effect that, if devolution received the support of less than 40 per cent of the Scottish electorate in a referendum, the Scotland Act would be repealed. The second was made in response to the so-called 'West Lothian question' named after the MP for West Lothian, the Labour MP Tam Dalyell. The question was whether it was fair for Scottish MPs to be able to vote in the House of Commons on matters such as health, education and housing affecting the rest of the UK, when as devolved issues these could not be voted on by non-Scottish MPs when under consideration in Scotland. An amendment proposed by a Conservative front-bencher, Lord Ferrers, sought to deal with this question by stipulating that, if any Commons vote on a matter devolved to Scotland were passed by the votes of Scottish MPs, a second vote could be taken two weeks after the first, at which point, it could be presumed, pressure would be exerted on the Scottish MPs not to vote.

Both countries rejected devolution in the referendums held on 1 March 1979, Scotland by a narrow margin (Table 4.4). The rejection ratio was nearly 4:1 in Wales. In Scotland, the majority of voters supported devolution, but as only 62.9 per cent of the electorate registered a vote, the required endorsement by 40 per cent of the electorate was not attained. Nationalists argued that because there was a majority for a Scottish Assembly the government should press ahead with devolution for Scotland. However the argument was not persuasive, especially when it was borne in mind that the 37.1 per cent of abstentions were in effect 'no' votes, so all the government would offer was 'all-party' talks. As the Lib–Lab Pact, which had sustained it in office between 1977 and 1978, had ended the Labour government entered a vulnerable phase. It was brought down on 28 March 1979 when, responding to a Conservative 'no confidence' motion, the SNP threw its weight against the government. The voting was ayes, 311 – 279 Conservative, 13 Liberal, 11 SNP, 8 Ulster Unionist; 'noes', 310 – 303 Labour, 2 Scottish Labour, 3 Plaid Cymru, 2 Ulster Unionist. The devolution issue had been the main factor in unseating a British Government.

TABLE 4.4 *The Devolution Referendums, 1979*

		Vote	*% of vote*	*% of electorate**
Scotland	Yes	1 230 937	51.6	32.5
	No	1 153 502	48.4	30.4
Wales	Yes	243 048	20.2	11.8
	No	956 330	79.8	46.5

*Percentage who did not vote: Scotland, 37.1%; Wales, 41.7%.

Northern Ireland, 1945–72

As they considered that the 'Irish question' had been settled by the constitutional changes of 1921, British governments pursued a 'hands off' policy towards Northern Ireland between the 1920s and the 1960s. A convention adopted in 1923, that matters within the responsibility of Stormont should not be raised in the House of Commons, was strictly adhered to for forty years. But the 1921 partition arrangements were never accepted by Irish nationalists. The claim of Article 2 of the 1937 Irish Constitution that 'the national territory consists of the whole island of Ireland, its lands and its territorial seas' received considerable support among the Catholics of Northern Ireland. Northern Ireland nationalists in fact refused to take the title of loyal opposition before 1965 as a way of showing their allegiance to the idea of a united Ireland. When the Irish Free State left the Commonwealth upon becoming a republic in 1949, the Attlee government guaranteed the constitutional status of Northern Ireland by declaring that no change in its constitutional position would occur without the consent of the Stormont parliament, and the Stormont government showed itself able to maintain order when the IRA resumed its attacks between 1954 and 1962.

However events in Northern Ireland began to impinge on British public opinion in late 1968 as a result of violent clashes with police and loyalists by civil rights activists in Londonderry/Derry. Behind the worsening relations between the Catholic and Protestant communities were, first, increasing Catholic anger over their treatment by the Protestant majority. Roman Catholics suffered from the denial of political and civil rights by the Protestant majority, most notably the lack of democracy in local government, gerrymandering of local government boundaries, and discrimination in employment and municipal housing. By the mid 1960s middle-class Catholics were no longer prepared to tolerate this discrimination, and hence formed the Campaign for Social Justice (1964), the Northern Ireland Civil Rights Association (NICRA, 1967) and the student-led 'People's Democracy'. NICRA's demands included one man, one vote in local elections; no gerrymandering of constituency boundaries; fair distribution of council housing; and the disbanding of the 'B' Specials, a part-time, exclusively Protestant auxiliary force.

In addition to the radicalisation of Catholic opinion, a second reason for the renewal of the Irish troubles was the backlash provoked amongst Protestants by the reforming policies of the Stormont prime minister, Terence O'Neill, after 1965. O'Neill sought to build bridges both with the Irish Prime Minister and with the Catholic community in the north. At his invitation, the Irish prime minister made a first-ever visit to Stormont in 1965. Then, under pressure from the civil rights movement and the British government, O'Neill announced a package of reforms in late 1968. However his reforms lost him more support among Protestants than they gained among Catholics and further violence followed early in 1969, when a People's Democracy march from Belfast to Derry was attacked by Protestant extremists at Burntollet Bridge. The emergence of irreconcileable working-class Protestantism under the leadership of the Reverend Ian Paisley, with its stance of fundamental opposition to all change and no concessions to Catholics, created a severe strain in Ulster Protestantism. An election called by O'Neill in February 1969 not only exposed increased divisions within the Unionist Party but also led to considerable change in other areas of Northern Ireland politics.

O'Neill won the election but was severely damaged by the election of 11 anti-O'Neill Unionists. Gains were also made by civil rights activists, three of whom, including John Hume, were elected, thereby successfully challenging the major opposition Nationalist Party. Moreover, within a few months Paisley won O'Neill's seat, the latter having resigned as prime minister in April 1969 after further splits in his party and cabinet. O'Neill's moderate reforms had provoked a crisis in unionism, which now divided three ways: constitutional supporters of reform, constitutional opponents of reform, and diehard fundamentalist opponents of it in the shape of Paisley's followers, whose membership overlapped with Protestant paramilitaries such as the Ulster Volunteer Force, which had been refounded in 1966 (Foster, 1989, pp. 586–7).

To some historians O'Neill's departure marked a turning point in the postwar history of Northern Ireland, his essential reforms having failed because by then they were insufficient to satisfy Catholic demands whilst going too far for the Unionists (Gourvish and O'Day, 1991, p. 293). On the other hand O'Neill has been seen both as 'an unconvincing Liberal', more interested in economic reforms to consolidate Protestant unionism by undermining the Northern Ireland Labour Party than in civil rights reform to assist Catholics, and as 'an inept tactician' whose incompetently administered reforms inadvertently triggered chronic political destabilisation (Foster, 1989, p. 585).

Although mainly political in origin, the renewed trouble in Northern Ireland also had deep-rooted economic causes. Paradoxically the disturbances of the late 1960s reflected the benefits enjoyed by Northern Ireland under the British welfare state as well as the long-term structural unemployment that the province had experienced since the 1920s. In order to ensure that public spending on education, health, pensions and social services in Northern Ireland was on a par with that in the rest of the UK, a Treasury subsidy of £45 million a year was required by the early 1960s, which gave the region a far higher standard of social welfare than prevailed in the Republic. In particular, Catholic access to higher education improved considerably after 1946, and this creation of a better-educated Catholic middle class lay behind the upsurge of protest against discrimination in the 1960s. Finally, with its traditional textile, engineering and ship-building industries in decline, Northern Ireland also suffered from high unemployment, which helped fuel the disturbances.

The security situation in Northern Ireland deteriorated rapidly from the late 1960s, culminating in the ending of devolved Stormont government in 1972. First, sectarian riots in Derry and Belfast in August 1969 led the British government to send in troops, initially on a temporary basis, to help an exhausted RUC restore order. The 'B Specials', who had been prominent in the violence in Belfast, were disbanded and replaced by the Ulster Defence Regiment, a locally raised force controlled from London; the RUC were disarmed. Initially the troops were welcomed by the Catholic community, but this was to change. The British government, which had responded only reluctantly to the Northern Ireland prime minister's request for the British

Army to be deployed there, was now fully involved in the affairs of the province. In the words of James Callaghan, Labour home secretary in 1969, it had been 'sucked into the Irish bog' (quoted in Madgwick and Rose, 1982, p. 112).

Second, the Irish Republican Army (IRA) gradually emerged after 1968 as defender of the Catholic community loyalist attacks and from repression by the security forces. Humiliated by its inability to defend the Catholic areas of Belfast against loyalist mobs in August 1969, in 1970 the IRA split into the hard-line Provisional and the Official wings, with the former dedicated to a violent guerilla campaign and the latter largely concerned with mainstream politics. The immediate objective of the Provisionals was to secure the withdrawal of British troops, who were perceived as a 'foreign' army on Irish soil, but their long-term goal was a united, thirty-two county, republican Ireland. They were soon receiving arms and money from the United States and elsewhere. During the early 1970s recruitment to the Provisionals was helped considerably by some inept military activities by the British Army, including insensitive house searches and even the shooting of unarmed Catholics during security operations. From its point of view the British Army had reasons for extreme nervousness when approaching Catholic areas: not only did terrorists receive shelter there, but also house searches in Catholic areas had uncovered large stores of firearms, ammunition and explosives (Madgwick and Rose, 1982, pp. 113–14). The formation in 1970 of the SDLP provided a focus for constitutional Catholic opposition to Unionism, but it was the extremist politics of the paramilitary groups on both sides that continued to make the headlines.

Third, in response to increasing disorder on the streets, a mounting number of police, army and civilian deaths and the launching in February 1971 of a guerrilla campaign by the Provisional IRA, the British government introduced internment in August 1971. Large numbers of republican suspects were rounded up by the British Army for interrogation. However, largely because the arrests were made on the basis of out-of-date files that failed to distinguish properly between political and terrorist activity, internment turned into a political disaster. The main result of imprisonment without trial was 'to unite the whole Catholic community in opposition to the Stormont regime and to increase both the flow of recruits to the IRA and the level of terrorist activity' (Boyle and Hadden, 1985, p. 65). Deaths caused by the violent conflict in the province rose from 174 in 1971 to 467 in 1972.

Fourth, the spiral of violence accelerated on 30 January 1972 when 13 civilians were killed by the British soldiers at a demonstration in Derry. Faced with an international outcry and the burning of the British embassy in Dublin, the British government responded to the events of 'Bloody Sunday' by assuming direct responsibility for security and the administration of justice. When the Unionist government resigned, British Prime Minister Edward Heath imposed direct rule on the province. Originally intended to be temporary, the suspension of Stormont turned out to be permanent, thereby ending over fifty years of devolved government. William Whitelaw became the first secretary of state for Northern Ireland.

Northern Ireland, 1972 to the 1990s

Two themes predominated in Northern Ireland affairs under direct rule from Westminster after 1972. These were (1) British political initiatives aimed at creating a framework under which a viable settlement of the future of the province could emerge, and (2) the development of a security policy capable of containing the violence while political initiatives proceeded. Of the many political initiatives between 1972 and 1990, two were particularly important: the 1974 attempt to devolve authority to a power-sharing executive; and the 1985 Anglo-Irish Agreement.

The Northern Ireland Constitution Act (1973) provided first for an assembly elected by proportional representation and a power-sharing executive; and second for a Council of Ireland with vague functions but including representatives from the Republic as well as from Northern Ireland. However, many Unionists were bitterly opposed both to the idea of sharing power with Catholics and nationalists and to any involvement of the Republic in Northern Ireland affairs. Although the elections to the new assembly in June 1973 produced a power-sharing majority (50 out of 78), 28 of the 50 Unionists were against sharing power with those whom they perceived as a disloyal minority. Faced with such opposition the power-sharing executive, composed of moderate Unionists, the SDLP and the Alliance, lasted a mere five months from its inception on 1 January 1974. It was seriously undermined almost immediately by events at the February 1974 general election, when anti-power-sharing Unionists grouped together as the United Ulster Unionist Council (UUUC) and won eleven of the twelve Northern Ireland seats in Westminster. Brian Faulkner, the premier of the executive, responded by seeking to backtrack on his commitment to the Council of Ireland, which had been agreed between the British and Irish governments and representatives from Northern Ireland in December 1973 at Sunningdale. But he failed to save the executive, which was finally destroyed by the Ulster Workers' Council strike of 15–29 May 1974. Industrial action, backed by intimidation from the Protestant paramilitary organisations (especially the Ulster Defence Association (UDA), brought the province to a standstill. With the British government unwilling to deploy troops to safeguard essential power supplies, the extra-parliamentary action succeeded in bringing down the power-sharing executive. Although attempts by Westminster governments to get Northern Ireland politicians to agree on some form of devolved power-sharing administration continued, most notably in 1975, 1979 and 1981, none succeeded. However increasing concern about the problem of security, together with a growing recognition by the British government of the need to involve the Irish Republic in a Northern Ireland settlement, led to the next major initiative in 1985.

From the early 1970s the British government faced the most ruthless, persistent and sophisticated terrorist movement in Europe, whose campaign did much to undermine the quality of British life and British democracy. Quality of life suffered because of continuing outrages that on average caused the death of more than 200 people a year during the 1970s and 75 a year between 1980 and 1986. Altogether, deaths from sectarian violence in Northern Ireland numbered 3169 between the beginning of the troubles in 1969 and the IRA ceasefire of 31 August 1994. In addition there were 119 deaths in Great Britain, 100 in the Irish Republic and 18 in Europe. About two thirds of the dead were civilians. As many as 38 680 people were injured in Northern Ireland and there were over 10 000 bombings. Over the whole period Republican groups, which included the Irish National Liberation Army (INLA) as well as the IRA, killed more people than died at the hands of loyalist groups, although in the two years preceding the ceasefire this situation was reversed.

The IRA revealed a capacity to hit a wide range of military, civilian and economic targets. Its aims were fourfold: (1) to create maximum chaos and instability, from which it hoped to seize a political advantage; (2) to achieve spectacular symbolic successes in mainland Britain in order to persuade British public opinion of the need to withdraw troops from Northern Ireland; (3) to provoke the British government into overreaction, thereby gaining an international propaganda victory; and (4) to make the cost to the British state of retaining Northern Ireland too great to bear (Gearty, 1991, pp. 120–3). Prominent people killed by the terrorists included the British ambassadors to Dublin and The Hague; Airey Neave, the Conservative spokesman on Northern Ireland; Ian Gow MP, a close associate of Margaret Thatcher; and Lord Mountbatten, who was blown up in his boat off the coast of Ireland in 1979. One of the IRA's most sensational attacks was the bombing of the Grand Hotel in Brighton during the Conservative Party conference, when five people died and Prime Minister Thatcher had a narrow escape. The cost of Britain's commitment to Northern Ireland escalated: its expenditure in the province amounted to £52 million more than it raised there in taxation in 1966–7, £1 billion more in the late 1970s and a massive £1.7 billion more in the early 1990s. From its peak at 30 000 troops in 1972, the size of the British Army presence in Northern Ireland was scaled down to about half that number in the mid 1980s. The number stood at 17 600 in 1994, when the cost of military support to the Royal Ulster Constabulary was put at £477 million.

The struggle against terrorism damaged British democracy in many ways. First, internment without trial, which was reintroduced in 1971 under the 1922 Special Powers Act and subsequently admitted to be a mistake by a former secretary of state for Northern Ireland, led to British humiliation when the European Court of Human Rights judged in 1978 that the post-internment interrogation techniques used by the British Army constituted 'inhuman and degrading treatment'. Second, from 1972 trial by jury for those accused of terrorist offences was abandoned in favour of non-jury or 'Diplock' courts, named after the British judge (Lord Diplock) who had recommended them. Diplock was concerned about the intimidation of jurors and witnesses in jury trials. Third, a spectacular atrocity on the British mainland – the Birmingham pub bombings (1974), which killed 21 people – led to the introduction of the Prevention of Terrorism Act (1976), which abrogated certain civil rights of suspected terrorists. Fourth, IRA trials in Britain resulted in some major miscarriages of justice, for example the convictions of the Guildford Four, the Birmingham Six and the Maguire Seven were all quashed between 1989 and 1991. Pressure on the police from an outraged public opinion had played a part in these faulty verdicts. Fifth, Britain's alleged 'shoot to kill' policy in Northern Ireland led to continuing controversy throughout the 1980s, particularly with regard to two incidents: the killing of six people – five known IRA or INLA members but also one innocent 17 year-old – by the security forces in November to December, 1982; and the shooting dead by the security forces of three IRA members in Gibraltar in March 1988. Finally, the steady withdrawal of the 'special status' of IRA prisoners after 1976 led to a series of protests by them, including a refusal to wear prison clothing ('going on the blanket') and a refusal to use toilet facilities (the 'dirty protest'), and culminating in the death by hunger fast of Bobby Sands and nine other IRA prisoners in the Maze prison in 1982. During this episode, Sands fought and won the Fermanagh/South Tyrone by-election from his deathbed. The hunger strikes resurrected the Republican cause and constituted a considerable propaganda success in Ireland and the United States.

The growth of support for Sinn Fein in the early 1980s accelerated the new rapprochement between the British and Irish governments. For the British government, greater cooperation with Ireland would assist the security situation as well as blunting American criticism of Britain's handling of Northern Ireland; for the Irish government, it might play a role in reducing the violence that often spread south of the border. Improved relations between Britain and the Republic from 1980 came to fruition in the Anglo-Irish Agreement (1985), by which both governments guaranteed that any change in the constitutional status of Northern Ireland would only come about with the consent of the people of Northern Ireland. It also provided for an intergovernmental conference to meet regularly to discuss political, legal and security matters, and the promotion of cross-border cooperation; and for the development of a devolved power-sharing form of government for the province. However the agreement encountered immediate and bitter opposition from the Unionists who, against the background of a higher Catholic than Protestant birthrate, feared the consequences of making the constitutional status of Northern Ireland dependent upon majority wishes, and also disliked the role accorded to the Dublin government in Northern Ireland affairs. The agreement was also opposed by Sinn Fein on the ground that it merely reaffirmed the territorial status quo in Northern Ireland. Terrorist and sectarian outrages continued.

The next important initiative occurred in December 1993, when talks between the heads of the British and Irish governments (John Major and Albert Reynolds) led to the 'Downing Street Declaration'. The British prime minister, on behalf of the government, reaffirmed support for the wishes of the majority in Northern Ireland on the question of whether they preferred to support the Union or a sovereign united Ireland. This was the furthest any British government had ever gone towards recognising Irish unity as a legitimate aspiration. Major also reiterated that the British government had 'no selfish strategic or economic interest in Northern Ireland'. On behalf of the Irish government, Reynolds declared that it would be wrong 'to impose a united Ireland, in the absence of the freely given consent of the majority of the people of Northern Ireland'. A new and controversial element in the declaration was the offer to Sinn Fein and the IRA that, provided they abandoned terrorism and violence, they would be permitted to join in the future dialogue between the two governments and the Northern Ireland parties. This put pressure on the IRA to seek influence through constitutional means and to renounce the Armalite in favour of the ballot box, and thus it paved the way for the announcement of an IRA ceasefire as of midnight on 30 August 1994.

In February 1995 a Joint Framework Document on the future of Northern Ireland was issued by the British and Irish governments. It envisaged a 90–strong regional assembly elected by proportional representation, together with a series of cross-border forms of cooperation. In the new Northern Ireland assembly, a complex system of checks and balances would be established to prevent the nationalist minority being continually outvoted. The magnitude of the political task ahead was demonstrated by a poll taken immediately after publication of the document: 92 per cent of the Protestants questioned said they wanted Northern Ireland to stay in the United Kingdom whereas 56 per cent of the Catholics wanted it to become part of an all-Ireland republic (cited in the *Guardian*, 25 February 1995). An IRA bomb explosion in the Docklands area of London on 9 February 1996, which killed two people and ended the 17-month IRA ceasefire, further underlined the problem of achieving a permanent settlement in Northern Ireland.

Scottish and Welsh Nationalism in the 1980s and 1990s.

The electoral fortunes of the Scottish and Welsh nationalists declined after the failure of the devolution legislation in 1979. Both parties recovered in the late 1980s and 1990s, but without regaining the heights of popularity enjoyed in the 1970s (Tables 4.1 and 4.2). It was only small consolation that Plaid Cymru gained more MPs than ever in 1992, whilst the SNP came second to Labour and gained more seats (36) than the Conservatives (25). In fact neither had made an electoral breakthrough, as Labour remained by far the strongest party in their regions, and each had found it particularly hard to make progress in the more industrialised urban areas of their countries: Plaid Cymru in south-east Wales and the SNP in the west of Scotland. As national pressure groups, however, they had made devolution a leading political issue and a realistic future possibility. Whilst the stronger Scottish nationalists had achieved more on the constitutional issue, the Welsh nationalists had made many cultural advances, including the Welsh Language Act (1967), which gave the Welsh language equal status with English for official, governmental and legal purposes; an increase in the number of schools teaching primarily in Welsh; and a fourth TV channel broadcast in Welsh (1981).

From the United Kingdom perspective, the nationalist campaigns partially arrested and in Scotland potentially reversed several centuries of political integration produced by mass education, a cheap newspaper press, a modern communications system and UK-wide political parties. The rise of the nationalists also forced new divisions in the politics of both the centre and the periphery. In Westminster after 1975, a strongly anti-devolutionist pro-status quo Conservative Party confronted a (largely) devolutionist Labour Party and devolutionist Liberals/SDP/Liberal Democrats. In Scotland and Wales public opinion was divided between three options: a degree of greater self-government within the UK, independence, or retaining the constitutional status quo. Whilst the constitutional debate was more intense in Scotland, Wales became riven by the language issue, which divided the English-speaking from the Welsh-speaking Welsh, thereby creating 'a new shadow-line' across the country (Williams, 1985, p. 293). A language that had seemed to be in inexorable decline was reinvigorated and the English language, which paradoxically established itself even more firmly in this period as the premier world language, was put on the defensive. The capacity of West-minster politicians to hold together a divided kingdom had become more problematic than seemed possible in the immediate postwar decades.

Conservative anti-devolutionism seemed to intensify as its electoral position weakened on the periphery. In 1992, of the 110 Scottish and Welsh seats the Conservatives won a mere 17 and Labour 76, respectively 15 per cent and 69 per cent of the total. In 1997, with both Labour and the Liberal Democrats advocating a Scottish assembly with tax-raising powers, the Conservatives played on the threat to the union posed by their opponents' devolution plans, arguing that a Scottish assembly constituted the first step on a slippery slope to an independent Scotland.

Meanwhile both Plaid Cymru and the SNP stressed the benefits of independence: governments that would be entirely dedicated to the improvement of their respective economies, as in Ireland; larger EU subsidies, especially in the case of Wales; and, for Scotland, 90 per cent of Britain's oil revenues. Both disputed Treasury figures showing that the Scots enjoyed 25 per cent and the Welsh 20 per cent more public expenditure than the English, although academic studies suggest that public expenditure had indeed been consistently higher in Scotland and Wales than in England since 1945 (Rose, 1982, p. 135; Midwinter *et al.*, 1991, p. 99; Brown *et al.*, 1996, p. 92). Per capita public expenditure in all three peripheral territories was higher than in England, which in 1989–90 received £693.7 per head, compared with £743.6 in Scotland, £745.9 in Wales and £801.3 in Northern Ireland, which largely reflected their higher levels of unemployment, social deprivation and need compared with England.

Further Reading

Arthur, P. and K. Jeffery, *Northern Ireland since 1988* (Oxford: Blackwell, 1988).

Birch, A. H., *Political Integration and Disintegration in the British Isles* (London: George Allen and Unwin, 1979).

Bogdanor, V., *Devolution* (Oxford, Oxford University Press, 1979).

Brown, A., D. McCrone and L. Paterson, *Politics and Society in Scotland* (London: Macmillan, 1996).

Bulpitt, J., *Territory and Power in the United Kingdom* (Manchester: Manchester University Press, 1983).

Catterall, P. and S. McDougall (eds), *The Northern Ireland Question in British Politics* (London: Macmillan, 1996).

Crick, B. (ed.), *National Identities* (Oxford: Blackwell, 1991).

Foster, R., *Modern Ireland 1600–1972* (London: Penguin, 1989).

Gamble, A., 'Territorial Politics', in P. Dunleavy, A. Gamble, I. Holliday and G. Peele (eds), *Developments in British Politics 4* (London: Macmillan, 1993).

Hadfield, B. (ed.) *Northern Ireland: Politics and the Constitution* (Buckingham: Open University Press, 1992).

Kellas, J. G., *The Scottish Political System*, 4th edn (Cambridge: Cambridge University Press, 1989).

Levy, R., 'Governing Scotland, Wales and Northern Ireland', in R. Pyper and L. Robins (eds) *Governing the UK in the 1990s* (London: Macmillan, 1995).

Madgwick, P. and R. Rose (eds) *The Territorial Dimension in United Kingdom Politics* (London: Macmillan, 1982).

Midwinter, A., M. Keating and J. Mitchell, *Politics and Public Policy in Scotland* (London: Macmillan, 1991).

O'Day, A., 'Britain and the Two Irelands', in T. Gourvish and A. O'Day (eds), *Britain since 1945* (London: Macmillan, 1991).

Rose, R., *Understanding the UK* (London: Longman, 1982).

5
Britain and Europe

The idea of a more closely integrated Europe was not conceived in the twentieth century, but reaches back at least to the Holy Roman Empire. Even in the twentieth century, proposals for a Pan-European union and a common market were first made in 1923, predating the eventual establishment of the EEC by well over thirty years. The origins of what became the European Union drew from this tradition of thought, gathering salience in the minds of key politicians and administrators as a solution to the old as well as the new problems their continent faced.

In Italy, France and, crucially, Britain, there appeared to be support for the development of Europe as a more integrated entity. A variety of groups from different parts of the political spectrum advocated closer forms of European unity, generally for different reasons, and frequently for motives closely tied to their respective domestic politics. Britain's wartime leader, Churchill, was president of the authoritative European Movement, a campaigning body launched by the Congress of Europe. This seemed fitting, since in the dark days of the war he offered the beleaguered French joint citizenship with Britain in a Franco-British union, and again in 1946 he called for a creation of a United States of Europe. From the outset, however, Churchill's enthusiasm was for greater European integration in principle and not for Britain's participation in practice. Churchill harboured personal doubts about the possibility of Britain resuming its world role after the Second World War, but he did not see Britain's reduced circumstances necessarily meaning that Britain's new role would have to be a regional one. In any case there was a distinction, which became clearer as time passed, between the Anglo-Saxon version of Europeanism, which was compatible with Atlanticist and world ties, and continental Europeanism, which was integrationist and confined to the nations of Western Europe. At the time Churchill's Europeanism was restricted to urging other countries to integrate for their own good; some might describe his behaviour as 'gesture politics'. But with the exception of Edward Heath, a committed pro-European prime minister, Churchill was the first in a long line of British leaders willing to play politics with the European issue.

Other European leaders assumed that Britain, having played an heroic role in the Second World War, would continue to play a leading peacetime role in constructing the European project. For them, a new-style integrated Europe promised to solve the basic enmities that had resulted in two world wars as well as provide future defence in in the event of a third. They looked back on a war-torn Europe where the costly struggle against fascist forces had left them with crippled economies. They looked forward and saw an increasingly dangerous Soviet Union, seemingly bent on an ideological struggle with the West. They believed that an economically strong, integrated Europe that included Germany and thereby reduced the risk both of a return of German militarism and revived German territorial ambitions to the East, and where national armies might be replaced by a European army, would provide stability and defence in the Cold War struggle. Politicians from many countries were anxious to solve the 'German problem', which they viewed in the context of an historical thread linking Prussian militarism, World War One, the rise of fascism and World War Two. In the years following the end of the war with Hitler, German militarism was the key problem that linked the conflict they had recently ended with the one they were about to begin. For not only were the French fearful of a revived (and rearmed) Germany but given their terrible losses at German hands, so too were the people of the Soviet Union.

The Schuman Plan

There were a number of early initiatives involving European political, economic and military organisation, many of which were based on wartime patterns of cooperation. The Hague conference in 1948 launched the Council for Europe. Economic cooperation was stimulated by US Marshall Aid. The United States abruptly ended the wartime 'lend-lease' loans but then grew concerned that the weakness of many European economies could result in political unrest and increased communist influence. General Marshall argued that it made good sense for the United States to resume economic assistance since without sound economies there could be no political stability and no assured peace. Consequently Marshall Aid was offered to all countries, including the Soviet Union. The Soviets declined, as many anticipated they would, and Marshall Aid, in the formal structure of the European Recovery Programme (ERP), was channelled into European economies. The organisation set up to manage this programme developed into the Organisation for European Economic Co-operation (which was transformed into the Organisation for Economic Co-operation and Development in 1960). Military cooperation came principally in the form of the North Atlantic Treaty Organisation (NATO).

A number of politicians from different countries had very different views on the ways – politically, economically and militarily – in which Western Europe should develop. In many respects they shared a mindset that approached the problems of European countries in ways very different from those of the Americans and the British (Exhibit 5.1). Firstly, they rejected existing initiatives since they all involved intergovernmental cooperation. These left nation-states, which were seen as the source of conflict, as the

EXHIBIT 5.1   *Continental and British mindsets*

> 'The difference is temperamental and intellectual. It is based on a long divergence of two states of mind and methods of argumentation. The continental tradition likes to reason *a priori* from the top downwards, from the general principles to the practical application . . . The Anglo Saxon likes to argue *a posteriori* from the bottom upwards, from practical experience.'
>
> (Harold Macmillan discussing British and Continental attitudes to the Schuman Plan, quoted in A. Sampson, *Macmillan: A Study in Ambiguity*, Harmondsworth, Penguin, 1967, p. 89.)

principal units. The alternative vision saw a pattern of cooperation based on supranationalism, which in the late 1940s was seen as involving a transfer of sovereign powers from national governments to a higher federal authority. Secondly, and despite the United States' decisive contribution to the Allied victory, there was considerable antagonism towards that country and its renewed dominance of European affairs. For many in the Labour Party, for example, the United States was 'an irresponsible, prodigiously powerful economic giant, controlled by a capitalist-dominated, reactionary Congress much influenced by military leaders' (Meehan, 1960, p. 70). Many Europeans shared similar anti-American sentiments, feeling that ERP and NATO were more about safeguarding markets for US exports than about benefits intrinsic to Europe. They wanted the major initiatives for economic recovery to be European in origin rather than American. Finally, Europeans did not share the US and British view of continental Europe as a potential battleground between the Soviets and the West. Rather their vision was of Europe developing into an independent 'third force' that could mediate between the Soviets and the West.

In this political climate, Robert Schuman, the French foreign minister, developed a plan for the alternative vision of European cooperation. Together with Jean Monnet, France's general commissioner for the modernisation plan, Schuman devised a plan to pool France and Germany's coal and steel industries under the control of a supranational authority. This idea had been mooted by the Free French during the war, had already been the subject of a parallel experiment by the Benelux countries, and was perceived at the time as a model for more extensive European integration. But coal and steel were seen as the most appropriate starting point; in the 1940s coal and steel were crucial war-fighting industries and pooling them symbolised reconciliation between traditional enemies, France and Germany. Interested parties met at an intergovernmental conference and agreed to establish the European Coal and Steel Community (ECSC). The Treaty of Paris, signed by France, Germany, Italy and the Benelux countries in 1951, formally established the ECSC.

Like other countries, Britain was invited to participate in the Schuman Plan; however it was made clear that acceptance of a supranational high authority was a precondition of acceptance. Attlee's Labour government was unable to accept the invitation to participate and maintained only tenuous, associational links with Schuman's experiment. Labour of course had its own plans: the nationalisation of Britain's coal and steel industries. Pooling these industries under the control of what Attlee described as an 'utterly undemocratic' high authority would have been unacceptable to the trade unions and effectively undermined Labour's version of socialism.

The return of a Conservative government to office in 1951 was not marked by a change in policy direction towards the ECSC. Churchill maintained a similar aloofness towards integration as had Attlee before him. Conservative prejudices, also present on Labour backbenches, supported official policy. During the 1940s and 1950s there was much suspicion of political Catholicism in continental Europe and the major players in the Schuman Plan were known to be devout Catholics. In this sense it was easy to see the ECSC as some sort of Catholic plot. In addition a British arrogance existed that saw the participants in the Schuman Plan as countries that in one way or another had been defeated in the Second World War. It was easy for them to perceive the ECSC as 'a losers' club' in which victorious Britain had no business.

The Pleven Plan

An increase in Cold War tensions in Europe, together with a hot war between communist North Korea and capitalist South Korea, emphasised the need for stronger military defence of the West. The United States was particularly anxious to strengthen Western defences by rearming West Germany. The flaw in this solution remained, however, that of opposition from those who had already suffered from Nazi aggression and who continued to fear that a rearmed West Germany would resume its old expansionist policies. The new mood of integrationism, which had produced the Schuman Plan, seemed to promise a compromise solution for rearming Germany that would reassure neighbouring countries. Before the ECSC Treaty had been signed, the French premier Rene Pleven proposed that German re-armament could take place through military integration within what was called the European Defence Community (EDC). The Pleven Plan involved pooling forces from national armies with all of West Germany's forces into a common European army. This solution would therefore get Germany rearmed without setting up a separate German army; the '"caterpillar of German rearmament" could be transformed "into the butterfly of supranational integration"' (quoted in DePorte, 1979, p. 159).

The Americans anticipated that Germany would be rearmed within the NATO structure, but after consideration they supported the Pleven Plan for setting up an EDC. Britain gave grudging support for the EDC but, as with the ECSC, did not intend that Britain would participate.

Establishing an EDC would have represented a giant step on the road to European integration. It was to be accompanied by a parallel proposal to create a European Political Community, which would have federated the ECSC and the EDC. Despite having initiated the idea, the French dithered with policy on the EDC for a variety of domestic political reasons. With the death of Stalin and the ending of the Korean War, events took the urgency out of the Pleven Plan and the proposal for an EDC finally collapsed when it was rejected by a substantial majority in the French assembly.

With the EDC idea dead, the British government fell back on the NATO framework as the means of rearming Germany. The Brussels Treaty was expanded to form a Western European Union (WEU), a diplomatic arm to NATO that 'provided a fig leaf of continued control of German rearmament' (DePorte, 1979, p. 162), in order to reduce anxieties about the German problem. In the event, the failure of the EDC brought the worst of all worlds to Europe's integrationists whilst satisfying the British. On the one hand, the second and third experiments in integration had failed and West Germany was to have its own national army. On the other hand, to British satisfaction the failure of the integrationist EDC contrasted with the success of the intergovernmental WEU. The British way of doing things, through national governments cooperating, appeared to point the way for future European development. The Atlanticist, NATO-based version of Europeanism had seemingly triumphed over the continental EDC-based version.

The Treaty of Rome

The failure of the Pleven Plan sent a misleading message to the British government, which assumed that the movement towards an integrated Europe had come to a halt. Whilst the EDC had collapsed, the ECSC overcame many practical difficulties and could be judged as successful overall. European disappointment with what came to be seen as an over-ambitious EDC did not mean an end of integrationism. In 1955 the six foreign ministers of the ECSC countries met at Messina in Italy to consider a proposal from the Benelux countries to develop a common market as the next step in developing a united Europe. A committee was established under Paul-Henri Spaak, the Belgian foreign minister, to explore such a possibility. Britain participated in the proceedings of the Spaak Committee until its proposals for a free trade area were rejected. The Spaak Report was accepted by the foreign ministers and subsequent negotiations resulted in two treaties being signed in Rome that established the European Economic Community (EEC) and the European Atomic Energy Community (Euratom).

The Treaty of Rome, establishing the EEC, set out to produce 'an ever closer union among the peoples of Europe'. In the foreseeable future this was to be achieved by the creation of a common market based on the free movement of labour and capital and the development of common policies for key areas such as agriculture, investment, commerce and social welfare. Whilst there would eventually be free trade within the common market, a common external tariff would protect the common market from external competition. Initially the ECSC, the EEC and Euratom had parallel institutional frameworks but these would later be brought together to comprise the European Community. The cooperation amongst the six member states produced a body that was unlike any other. The supranational element that administered the Treaty of Rome rested in the Commission; the intergovernmental element that dealt with the real politics of policy making was located in the Council of Ministers; a Court of Justice interpreted the Treaty in operation, and a parliamentary Assembly, albeit with limited legislative powers, represented the democratic element.

The British Position

Britain's initial response to the proposal for a European common market survived in spirit from 1955 to influence successive policy makers throughout the remainder of the century. The single-mindedness of Europeans in pursuing their integrationist goals confirmed in many minds the doctrinaire nature of continental politics, in sharp contrast to British pragmatism. The common external tariff was interpreted by many Britons as Europe turning its back on the rest of the world, whilst Britain faced in the opposite direction of the open seas. Finally, whilst Europeans strove for federal, legalistic and supranational solutions to their problems, what suited Britain was loose, functional and intergovernmental cooperation. Labour Chancellor Sir Stafford Cripps effectively spoke for both parties in the 1950s when he declared 'participation in a political federation, limited to Western Europe, is not compatible either with our Commonwealth ties, our obligations as a member of the wider Atlantic community, or as a world power' (quoted in Robins, 1979, p. 21).

In 1955 the British foreign secretary, Selwyn Lloyd, outlined his version of what was termed 'the grand design'; a means of simplifying the organisation of Western Europe. The latter component of the grand design was to form the basis of negotiations as Britain came to terms with the reality of 'the six'. At the end of 1956 an OEEC working party concluded that a free trade area scheme was feasible but that work on it should be delayed until the signing of the Rome treaties. Discussions on the free trade area were chaired by the paymaster-general, Reginald Maudling, and were to last for over a year. However opposition to the scheme grew as the six member countries suspected that it was a ploy to block their own progress whilst providing Britain with the benefits of access to their market without sacrificing preferential Commonwealth trading arrangements. In 1958 the French president, Charles de Gaulle, took action that resulted in the negotiations coming to a halt.

With the collapse of the Maudling negotiations, the British government explored the possibilities of establishing a much narrower free trade area. Britain approached countries outside the EEC and rapidly proceeded for those not in the 'inner six' to form the 'outer seven'. In November 1959 a convention was signed in Stockholm by which the European Free Trade Association (EFTA) was established. Along with Britain, EFTA would include Austria, Denmark, Norway, Portugal, Sweden and Switzerland. In contrast with the EEC, EFTA was a loosely knit, diverse organisation without distinctive political goals. Nevertheless the six suspected British motives in setting up EFTA and as a consequence diplomatic relations deteriorated between the EEC members and Britain.

Britain's Changing Policy

The British government became increasingly concerned that a politically integrated EEC would result in deep splits in Western Europe, which would then be at 'sixes and sevens'. A great concern of the government was that Britain would be leading the weaker seven. At the same time the EEC was proving to be an economic success, which contrasted with Britain's lacklustre performance, and there were growing fears of Britain's prospects outside a trading bloc with an ever rising external tariff. Also there was diplomatic pressure from the United States, which urged Britain to reconsider its attitude towards EEC membership.

In 1960 an interdepartmental committee chaired by Sir Frank Lee, who personally supported Britain's membership of the EEC, examined the options opened to the government. The committee reported that Britain's future lay within Europe, and that maximum advantage would come from full membership of the EEC rather than from looser associational links. A decision was announced on 2 August 1961 that the government intended to apply to join the EEC.

Conservative Prime Minister Harold Macmillan skilfully accomplished a significant change of direction in Britain's traditional foreign policy without provoking a rebellion on his party's backbenches. This was possible because the reappraisal of foreign policy was handled by Macmillan in a very low-key manner. He presented the EEC both to parliament and to the party as a trading arrangement and ignored the political implications of the Treaty of Rome. There was no attempt to convert his followers to the European ideal; to the contrary, Macmillan still talked of the importance of Britain's world role and special relationship with the United States. Indeed, even those who were enthusiastic about the EEC argued that Britain's membership would be the saviour, not the replacement, of Britain's importance to the Commonwealth and the United States.

"I FORBID THE BANNS!"

Source: David Low, *Evening Standard*, 24 March 1948

The Labour Party was slow to reach a decision on British membership. Most of the party's left-wing opposed membership on the grounds that the EEC was a capitalist club, an economic reflection of NATO that threatened socialist Eastern Europe, and which exploited a divided trade union movement. In contrast, leading Labour right-wingers campaigned in favour of EEC membership, arguing that it would bring Britain the benefits of higher economic growth and improved welfare services.

Most Labour MPs were concerned about the role of Germany in the EEC and the impact that British membership would have on the future of the Commonwealth. They looked to their party leader, Hugh Gaitskell, for reassurance but he tended to vacillate on the wisdom of British entry. Finally, he set out five essential conditions that must be met if Labour was to support the government's application. Contemporary commentators believed that the five conditions were so demanding that they were tantamount to rejecting Macmillan's EEC bid. This impression was almost confirmed by an emotional speech he made at the Labour conference in which he talked of Britain in Europe as ending a thousand years of history. He then cast his attention on Britain's prospective partners:

> Europe has had a great and glorious civilisation. Although Europe can claim Goethe and Leonardo, Voltaire and Picasso, there have been evil features in European history too – Hitler and Mussolini. . . .You cannot say what this Europe will be; it has two faces and we do not know as yet which is the one which will dominate.

Lengthy negotiations between Britain and the six focused on Commonwealth safeguards as well as protecting the interests of Britain's farmers and EFTA partners. Rather than commence with a decision in principle to join the EEC followed by detailed negotiations, Macmillan's application began with negotiations that frequently became bogged down in detail. As the negotiations entered what might have been their final phase in 1963, the French president casually announced that he did not think that Britain was yet ready to join the EEC. This amounted to a veto from de Gaulle on British entry, bringing the negotiations to an abrupt ending.

Britain's Second EEC Application

Labour presented itself to the electorate as 'the Commonwealth party': its 1964 manifesto contained a commitment to revive the Commonwealth and, in contrast to the Conservatives, 'though we shall seek to achieve closer links with our European neighbours, the Labour Party is convinced that the first responsibility of a British Government is still to the Commonwealth'. The manifesto was broadly in line with party attitudes expressed at the time of Macmillan's EEC application, when most Labour members were 'anti-EEC' because they were 'pro-Commonwealth'. Party attitudes developed in opposition, however, are not necessarily a useful guide to policy when in government. For Labour's experience in office was that the Commonwealth was not a realistic framework for Britain's foreign trade or world role. In fact the Commonwealth was becoming a problem for Britain, with conflict between member states, the collapse of parliamentary democracies into corrupt dictatorships, the South African issue and the Rhodesian rebellion. Whilst the EEC appeared able to resolve its diplomatic difficulties, in contrast the Commonwealth's problems seemed insurmountable.

In 1965 the Labour prime minister attempted to close the gap between the members of EFTA and the EEC. A 'bridge building' conference in Vienna brought all parties together, but it became clear that the six were not interested in closer links between the two organisations. After Labour was returned to office in the 1966 general election George Brown, a strong advocate of British membership of the EEC, was made foreign secretary. In November Prime Minister Harold Wilson announced that the government was about to start high-level investigations to discover if it would be possible to open negotiations for EEC membership. Wilson and Brown were anxious to avoid the humiliation of the veto that was visited on Macmillan, and they toured the EEC capitals in order to probe the likely response to a second British application. They were encouraged by what they heard, and in May the prime minister informed the House of Commons that Britain would be making a second application to join.

In his memoirs Harold Wilson recounted that his speech 'was taken as a strong lead in favour of an application, with no commitment about entry until the terms which emerged from the negotiations became known' (Wilson, 1971, p. 388). With characteristic 'Wilsonian' skill, the prime minister produced a major policy initiative at a time when his government was coming under increasing domestic pressure, but did so in way that kept his increasingly fractious party united. Firstly, by focusing on the terms of entry, both the left and the right of the party supported the application. The left's grudging support was based on the assumption that the terms would prove to be unacceptably high, and settle the question once and for all that Britain's role was outside the EEC. Labour's right saw the terms as a relatively minor issue to be sorted out through negotiations, and the principle of Britain in Europe was given enthusiastic support.

Secondly, as with the Macmillan bid for entry, the political implications of EEC membership were played down. Harold Wilson time and time again referred to the large-market framework that the EEC could provide for European technological development. George Brown argued that Britain's changing patterns of trade pointed to a new reality: 'Since 1958 . . . exports to the Community countries have doubled . . . similarly, our exports to EFTA have doubled. In contrast our exports to the Commonwealth countries remain almost static' (Figure 5.1).

The Labour Government's application was not successful in the short term: in 1967 de Gaulle again vetoed Britain's membership of the EEC. The Government's response, however, was not to withdraw its application but to leave it 'on the table' until such time as it might be reactivated. The major obstacle to Britain's entry was removed in 1969 when de Gaulle retired from public office. But it was to be the responsibility of the incoming Conservative administration, led by Edward Heath, a strong supporter of Europeanism, to resume negotiations on the terms of entry.

FIGURE 5.1   *The changing pattern of Britain's foreign trade*

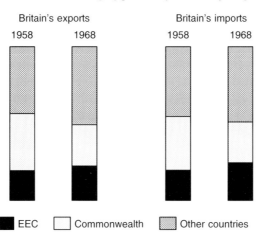

Britain's Entry to the EEC and Labour's Response

Edward Heath, the Conservative prime minister, was a committed European who had been in charge of negotiations during Macmillan's unsuccessful bid for membership of the Common Market. On this occasion, however, the negotiations were intended to be comparatively straightforward, and those issues that could not be settled before Britain's entry would be settled afterwards. Despite Heath's determination the negotiations on the terms of Britain's entry went through a very difficult period, but they were eventually concluded and the prime minister signed the Treaty of Accession on 22 January 1972, along with Ireland, Denmark and Norway. A referendum in Norway rejected membership, and so on 1 January 1973 the EEC was enlarged to a membership of nine.

It was inevitable that Harold Wilson's skilful strategy for uniting Labour on his government's EEC policy would change once Labour was in opposition, once the negotiations were the responsibility of a Conservative government truly detested by Labour's rank-and-file, and once the terms of entry emerged. In the last days of his government, Wilson prepared the ground for a change in EEC policy should the Conservatives win the approaching general election. In the House of Commons he maintained his bipartisan approach, stating that the Labour government was 'ready immediately to start negotiations. . . .We shall enter them in full determination to achieve success for we believe it to be in the interests not only of Britain but of Europe and of Europe's place in world affairs'. But when speaking to grassroot members he stressed the differences between himself and the Conservatives; 'the most fantastic aspect of their policies on Europe' was that 'they would be committed to paying a heavy price before negotiations, or even if there were no negotiations at all'. Once Labour was in opposition, Wilson ditched the bipartisan strand of policy in favour of a more distinctive Labour strand.

This change in the direction of Labour's EEC policy resulted in large part from the issue becoming entangled with domestic politics. When Harold Macmillan applied for Common Market membership in 1961 it was perceived basically as a foreign policy issue concerned with overseas trading arrangements. With Edward Heath's Conservative government negotiating EEC entry, however, it became understood as a domestic policy issue and a 'hot' one at that. Many Labour supporters came to see Conservative policies on trade union controls, higher council rents and welfare cuts as a means of preparing Britain for EEC membership, for they viewed the six existing members of the EEC in terms of their divided and weak trade union movements, their small welfare states and their restricted health services. These and other fears were expressed at a special Labour Party conference in 1971, where almost every adverse aspect of British life was linked to impending EEC membership. One delegate, for example, argued that 'housewives are worried too. . . . They are not just worried about prices – they do not want a reduced standard of living in Europe. They do not want to substitute margarine for butter or a pound of sausages instead of the weekend joint – and why should they?'

Labour's EEC policy became one of 'no entry on Tory terms': Harold Wilson told his party that he could not have recommended the terms negotiated by the Conservatives to a Labour cabinet. He argued that a future Labour government would recognise the treaty signed by Edward Heath but would renegotiate the terms of entry. Reluctantly he also accepted Tony Benn's proposal for a referendum on continued membership. Although holding a referendum was not normal British constitutional practice, Benn's proposal was acceptable since not only were other applicant countries holding them but France too was holding a referendum on whether Britain and the other applicants should be allowed to join the EEC.

Both the main parties contained EEC rebels. A substantial number of Conservatives opposed Britain's entry, whilst inside Labour a substantial minority supported the move and opposed their own party's drift towards opposing membership. The Conservative anti-EEC rebels were in a difficult political position because it was their leader who had decided in principle that Britain should enter the EEC. Labour pro-EEC rebels were in an exposed position because their leader had avoided such a strong commitment. The 'Wilsonian' style of party management was to avoid such a needless commitment, with Labour's stance on the EEC being one of 'no decision' in principle until such time as the final terms were known. Now, with the Conservatives in office, as far as Wilson was concerned the final terms would be those renegotiated by a future Labour government.

Labour's pro-EEC members, mostly on the right wing of the party and led by Roy Jenkins, became a beleaguered 'party within a party'. They were seen as traitors by their opponents, and the internal party conflict and accompanying emotions were such that a 'code of good order and discipline' was devised to limit the intensity of internal feuding. However this code of behaviour was largely ignored, and as a consequence Labour suffered a political crisis. For in the crucial Commons vote, Edward Heath's government received a majority of 112 votes, with 69 Labour MPs supporting him and a further 20 abstaining. In other words, if every Labour MP had voted in the same lobby the government would have been defeated and there might well have been a general election, and this could have resulted in the return of a Labour government. Labour's pro-EEC rebels had saved Edward Heath from the actions of his Conservative rebels. Labour's left wing was furious about the 'hand maidens of Tory survival' and their anti-EEC leader, Tony Benn, warned Labour rebels that 'no personal pledges about unity, no violent anti-Tory speeches' from them could solve the problems Labour now faced. In opposing the consequential legislation on Britain's EEC membership, the position of many Labour MPs moved increasingly towards outright opposition to membership. It became clear to political commentators at the time that should Labour form a future government, Harold Wilson's genius for holding the party together on potentially divisive issues would be tested as never before.

In the event Labour was returned to office in 1974 with a temporary truce between its opposed EEC factions. Harold Wilson had avoided any policy staightjacket on continued EEC membership, which allowed him to paper over the cracks in his party. However with the prospect of renegotiated terms of entry, Labour was approaching a final decision on Britain in Europe. Some political commentators wondered whether Labour, already internally damaged by the European issue, could survive yet another political storm on the way to reaching a final decision. What they had not taken account of was the party being saved from sinking by a 'little rubber life raft' (see below).

Labour duly renegotiated the terms of EEC entry (some critics claimed that the so-called renegotiations were simply the routine day-to-day conduct of EEC affairs, not the root-and-branch changes claimed by the prime minister) and these were completed on 18 March 1975. Prime Minister Harold Wilson announced that the renegotiated terms were in line with the safeguards in the party manifesto, and that he recommended their acceptance.

The extent of the crisis within Labour over Britain's membership of the EEC is indicated by the splits and alliances provoked by the issue. The ballot held during Labour's second special conference on the EEC resulted in 3 724 000 votes against and 1 986 000 for continued membership on the new terms. Within the trade union movement the two large general unions took opposing positions, with the General and Municipal Workers' Union in favour of the renegotiated terms and the Transport and General Workers' Union against. The PLP divided by 145 votes to 137 against continued membership, with 33 abstentions. The Labour cabinet was narrowly in favour of the renegotiated terms, and the party's NEC was against. Any thought that Labour could be held together under these circumstances flew in the face of the evidence, and the very deep divisions of opinion ran from the top to the bottom of the party. Collective responsibility on Europe for cabinet ministers was abandoned during the referendum campaign. The referendum – the 'little rubber life raft' referred to earlier – acted like a political safety valve for Labour for it helped to 'externalise' what might otherwise have been even more damaging internal conflict. In the referendum Labour's left wing found common cause with the Conservative right, most of whom opposed EEC membership. However this time cross-party cooperation did not result in accusations of betrayal or collaboration, as it had when Labour rebels supported Heath's EEC motion.

An ominous development for future governments in their handling of EEC issues was a clearer articulation of the political case against Britain's membership. Some on Labour's broad left continued to see the EEC as a capitalist organisation that would prevent Labour from pursuing socialist policies. Others shared the more specific concern of right-wing Conservative MPs such as Enoch Powell that the EEC was a threat to the sovereignty of parliament. Tony Benn developed the sovereignty theme in an open letter to his constituents, in which he outlined five basic democratic rights that had changed as a consequence of entry (Exhibit 5.2). In retrospect this cross-party interest in the constitutional implications of membership could be seen as a warning of political trouble ahead for any British government that (1) came into conflict with its EEC partners, (2) was seen as making significant concessions on any policy overseen by the EEC or (3) supported any measure that promoted further federalism within Europe.

Harold Wilson received a great deal of hostile criticism for his handling of the EEC issue, as he seemed to have put party considerations above the national interest. But such criticism overlooked the very great difficulties faced by Wilson in comparison with Conservative leaders in their dealings with Europe. Harold Macmillan was able to present the Common Market to his party as a rather low-key issue, an option not available to Wilson as Edward Heath's intervening administration sabotaged bipartisanship by incorporating EC membership into the 'Selsdon' manifesto and consequently raised the political profile of the issue. In addition the Conservatives put a much greater value on loyalty and were more willing to support policies

EXHIBIT 5.2   *Socialist fears about loss of British sovereignty*

The basis of Tony Benn's open letter to his constituents, 'What the Market Really Means', was published in the TGWU publication *Record* in February 1975:

'First, it [membership] subjects us to laws and taxes which your Members of Parliament do not enact, such laws and taxes being enacted by authorities you do not directly elect and cannot dismiss through the ballot box. Secondly, British membership means that Community laws and taxes cannot be changed or repealed by the British Parliament, but only by Community authorities not directly elected by the British people. Thirdly, the EEC requires the British courts to uphold and enforce Community laws that have not been passed by Parliament, and that Parliament cannot change or amend even when such laws conflict with laws passed by Parliament, since Community law overrides British law. Fourthly, British membership imposes duties and constraints upon British governments not deriving from the British Parliament; and thus, in discharging those duties ministers are not accountable to Parliament or to the British people who elect them. Fifthly, British membership, by permanently transferring sovereign legislative and financial powers to the Community authorities, who are not directly elected by the British people, also permanently insulates those authorities from direct control by the British electors, who cannot dismiss them and whose views, therefore, need carry no weight with them and whose grievances they cannot be compelled to remedy.'

associated with electorally successful leaders. The Conservative Party was also easier to manage insofar as it was generally less ideologically sensitive than Labour, less likely to perceive links between the EEC and revered party symbols, and in any case the EEC then appeared for the greater part the creature of conservative-minded European politicians, who might be expected to form a natural alliance with Conservatives in Britain. Finally, while Macmillan and Heath were able to conduct European policy unimpeded by challenges to their leadership, Wilson had to be mindful of the actions of his rivals. It may be the case that Wilson saw plots to remove him where none existed, but rivals did use the EEC issue to place themselves in positions that threatened him. In one famous incident James Callaghan, billed to make a speech on Labour and Europe, told a reporter to be there 'if you want to hear the next leader of the Labour Party' (Kitzinger, 1973, p. 300).

After a three-day debate on the renegotiated terms, the Commons voted to endorse continued EEC membership by 396 votes to 170. A majority of Labour MPs voted against the government, with the most recently elected members more anti-EEC than their colleagues of longer standing. Public opinions polls showed acceptance of the renegotiated terms by a two to one majority. These proportions were reflected in the result of the referendum held on 5 June: in a turnout of 63.2 per cent, 17 378 581 voted for continued membership and 8 470 073 voted for British withdrawal.

Thatcherism, Conservatism and Europeanism

After its defeat in the 1979 general election, Labour responded to the emergence of Thatcherism by moving leftwards in terms of party policies and constitutional changes, which increased grassroot influence within the party. Policy on Europe hardened to the point where Labour demanded Britain's withdrawal from the European Community. A small number of Labour MPs were not able to tolerate the leftward drift and defected to form the Social Democratic Party. In the eyes of Labour diehards, the SDP comprised elitist-minded members who were piqued at their own loss of influence and valued their European ideals over and above their Labour ideals. This perception was confirmed by the fact that the SDP leader was Roy Jenkins, once Labour's deputy leader and later president of the European Commission, and by the SDP's alliance with the fervently pro-EC Liberal Party.

Labour anticipated that, like Edward Heath who preceded her, Margaret Thatcher would be strongly committed to Britain's role in Europe. Her commitment was, however, to reduced public spending both in the form of Britain's contribution to the EC budget and in the EC budget as a whole. Consistent with her tough reputation in domestic politics, her image in Europe was one of 'handbagging' other national leaders in order to 'get Britain's own money back' from their profligate hands. At the time many problems arose over the financing of the Common Agricultural Policy, which involved subsidising the small family farms that are common in France and Germany.

For a variety of reasons, amongst them the impact of Thatcher's combative style of doing business, the European Community appeared to enter a period of decline. A number of European politicians recognised the danger of so-called 'Eurosclerosis' and the need to relaunch the European ideal. They saw the need to assess progress to date, to identify which policies needed to be reviewed, and to draw up plans for future developments. France and Germany proposed that the original Treaty of Rome should be updated whilst Jacques Delors, the federalist-minded president of the European Commission, proposed accelerating the transition of the EC from a customs union to a single market.

The twelve member states signed the Single European Act in 1986. In retrospect Margaret Thatcher might feel that she was misinformed about the purpose of this legislation, but at the time she raised no substantial objections. Indeed the idea of liberalising trade through the creation of a large free market fitted in well with Thatcherite economic principles. Others, however, saw a single European market as requiring a single European currency in order for it to work effectively. The vision of one currency for all EC members had no place in the Thatcherite philosophy.

As plans to rejuvenate the EC were discussed, so Thatcher's perception of the Community appeared to clarify and her attitudes towards it harden. In particular she was dismayed by Delors' widely reported view that within a decade 80 per cent of the economic and social legislation of all member states would be directed by the EC. She attacked these federal ambitions in an equally widely reported speech in Bruges in which she criticised many aspects of the way in which the Community conducted its business. At the Conservative Party conference she identified the social dimension of European renewal as the very enemy she was dedicated to slaying, telling delegates 'we haven't worked all these years to free Britain from the paralysis of socialism only to see it creep through the back doors of central control and bureaucracy in Brussels'.

Against her judgement, Thatcher was persuaded by her chancellor and foreign secretary that sterling should enter the Exchange Rate Mechanism of the European Monetary System. For some time sterling had been shadowing the German mark on the foreign exchanges, and it now appeared timely for it to enter the formal means of currency stabilisation as a step towards all EC currencies locking together, which in turn was a prelude to the creation of a single European currency. Thatcher's instinct, justified by subsequent events, was that such plans would ultimately end in failure since 'you can't buck the market'.

Thatcher's relations with Europe, sometimes vividly expressed in her own style of rhetoric, marked a continuity in British outlook rather than significant change. In the first place she reacted to EC affairs in a pragmatic manner rather than making prior commitments in principle. In much the same way as Attlee could not accept supranationalism as a precondition for participating in the ECSC, so Thatcher could not accept the necessity of a single currency as a means of developing the EU. The British compromise of a *common* European currency existing alongside the national currencies rather than a *single* currency replacing all national currencies was unacceptable to the other partners. Britain's proposal for a so-called 'hard Ecu' – which arguably was more feasible than a single currency since it was less ambitious – represented a pragmatic approach that was not rooted deeply in the European federal tradition. Debate over movement to a single currency appeared to reflect the contrasting mindsets described by Harold Macmillan (see Exhibit 5.1). Whilst European idealists insisted that the 1999 deadline would be met, British advocates such as Chancellor Kenneth Clarke argued that practical difficulties in meeting the convergence criteria would inevitably result in slippage.

In the second place, Margaret Thatcher's European ideals reflected the vision of Europe that was present in the unsuccessful Maudling negotiations for a Free Trade Area, in the successful creation of EFTA, and in Wilson's unsuccessful bridge building between the EEC and EFTA. Whilst Thatcher was far from *communautaire*, neither was she a Little Englander in her attitudes towards Europe. Speaking to the Czechoslovak parliament she said, 'We must create the sort of Community which you and others in Eastern and Western Europe truly want to join – a European Community which is fair, which is open, which preserves the diversity and nationhood of each of its members'. Later she added, 'I am a Europe idealist and I want a Europe, the larger Europe. Europe is older than the European Community. I want the larger wider Europe in which Moscow is also a European Power' (Jones and Robins, 1992, p. 253). What Thatcher was seeking, like three of her four predecessors, was a looser, outward-looking partnership of European nations that was not opposed to Atlanticist ties and was intergovernmental in character rather than based on the proto-federalist institutions of the Community.

In political terms the issue of Britain's relations with the Community cost Thatcher dear. In one way or another Europe was central to the Westland affair, which resulted in Michael Heseltine and Leon Brittan leaving her cabinet; the resignation of her chancellor, Nigel Lawson, resulted from a row concerning the EMS; the departure of Nicholas Ridley from the cabinet was provoked by an interview in which he expressed hostile views towards Europe, and the resignation of the deputy prime minister, Sir Geoffrey Howe, resulted from Thatcher's approach to the Community. This list of political casualties ended, of course, with her dramatic removal from the leadership of the Conservative Party and her departure from 10 Downing Street.

The Impact of Britain's Membership of the EEC

The impact of membership of the European Community on Britain's constitution was profound, moving many powers away from British institutions to institutions of the Community. Aspects of national life became subject to Community-wide policies, of which those concerned with agriculture and the environment received considerable media coverage. At the same time, it is true to say that many people in Britain were never fully aware of the extent to which these changes were affecting their lives. The *Factortame* case revealed that many in the political and administrative elite also failed to appreciate fully the developing consequences of Community membership. The potential impact of Community membership on Britain and other member countries is set out in the various treaties and acts that have directed the development of the European project. Yet the surprise, even shock, experienced by some politicians, lawyers as well as journalists at the *Factortame* judgement illustrated the limited understanding of the meaning of Europeanism in practice.

Basically, under the Common Fisheries Policy introduced in 1983, member countries' trawler fleets had limited access to each other's coastal waters. But Spanish fleet owners increased their access by registering their vessels in Britain, which enabled them to 'quota hop' into British waters. Under pressure from British fishermen, a Merchant Shipping Act was passed in 1988 designed to prevent Spanish registration. In 1991 a Spanish company, Factortame, challenged the Act and applied to the Queen's Bench Divisional Court for a ruling that the Act was incompatible with Community law, that the Single European Act of 1986, designed to create a single market, opened the way for all businesses to trade anywhere in the Community, and this included the fishing industry. As a result of the complex legal process that followed, including action by the Commission against the British government, the offending aspects of the Merchant Shipping Act were removed.

In what amounted to a milestone in British constitutional history, the supremacy of Community law over national law was established. In addition, it was established that British courts now had the power under Community law to grant injunctions against ministers of the crown. Parliamentary sovereignty, already threatened by developments such as majority voting in the Council of Ministers, was now clearly limited by European law. A number of parliamentarians and media opinion makers were prepared to reappraise the wisdom of continued membership. It was argued that the sovereignty of parliament could be reestablished only by repealing the 1972 European Communities Act. The number prepared to question continued British membership increased after the Maastricht Treaty (see below). The government responded with a damage limitation strategy, which involved Britain opting out of the most integrationist schemes. Should other member states proceed with European integration, and should such measures be generally successful, the political risks of British isolation within the EU would become all too apparent. Sooner or later other members would question whether Britain's multiple opt-outs constituted failing membership and begin their own appraisal of Britain's position in the EU.

Maastricht and Beyond

The Conservatives went through a rapid learning process on the nature of the emerging 'new' Europe, and as a result of this experience a Eurosceptic tide swept through the party. Conservative infighting on Europe, reinforced by other party divisions, plunged the party into a prolonged crisis that some commentators likened to those in 1846 concerning the repeal of the corn laws and 1903 over tariff reform. Where Harold Wilson's leadership tactics – avoiding making unnecessary decisions prior to membership, and renegotiation and a referendum after membership – had ensured both his own survival and that of European policy in a divided but predominantly Eurosceptic Labour Party, John Major found little success. For example his Thatcher-like gestures of 'getting tough' with Europe frequently failed and resulted in further humiliation, whilst promises to hold a referendum provoked conflict rather than resolving it. At the same time new fringe parties that were hostile to Europe, not normally seen as a threat, now looked as if they might steal a small percentage of traditional Conservative support in many crucial marginal seats. Panic, political gambles and desperate measures became the hallmark of Conservative leadership whenever Britain's relations with Europe were the focus of its policy making. John Major began his premiership with a declaration that he wanted Britain to be 'at the very heart of Europe', but within a few years a significant number in his party were contemplating the possibility of Britain's withdrawal from the EU.

The principal stimulus to rethinking Europe was the Maastricht Treaty (1993), which drew together a number of existing developments and new developments into what amounted to a new version of the Treaty of Rome. In order to smooth the passage of the treaty through parliament, the British delegation ensured that nowhere did the politically explosive word 'federal' appear in the final Treaty on European Union. From the early days of the Common Market debate to the emergence of the European Union, playing down the political impact of federalism had become a British political tradition. Successive prime ministers have either denied the possibility of federal developments or argued that they would not become a reality for many generations. However, because of the realities of the European debate it was easier for politicians to play down or ignore the federal issue before Maastricht than after. The relatively few voices to sound the implications of federalism, including those of Tony Benn and Enoch Powell, became a chorus of opposition in the days after Maastricht.

Essentially the Maastricht Treaty extended the competence of the EU to include education, health and the environment as well as providing for greater cooperation in defence and foreign policies, and justice and immigration. There was an emphasis on citizenship rights and a new Social Chapter, based on the old Social Charter, laid down a range of employment conditions. Finally, a timetable was established for economic and monetary union; new powers were given the European Parliament in an attempt to address the 'democratic deficit' and strengthen what until then had basically been a consultative assembly; a Committee of the Regions was set up; and the principle of subsidiarity was enshrined in the treaty where appropriate.

The Maastricht Treaty was not in tune with the Conservative mood, and mainstream thinking in the party swung against going along with Britain's European partners. Extreme Eurosceptics argued that the treaty provided reasons why Britain should withdraw from the EU and maintain trading links only. Mainstream Conservative Eurosceptics believed that Britain should remain inside the EU but 'stop the rot from Brussels' by blocking federal measures. Euroenthusiasts became increasingly beleaguered inside the Conservative ranks, and arguments that British negotiators had influenced the Maastricht package fell on deaf ears. Why did this issue divide Conservatives in such a bitter manner?

There remains a strong nationalistic element within conservatism. Indeed there is a tradition that equates 'being Conservative' with 'being British' or, more accurately, 'being English'. As a result many Conservatives are disturbed by arguments that the nation state is in decline, that powers will be lost upwards to a federal European Union and downwards as more power is given to regional government. In this context the European Union has become the enemy of conservatism.

Conservatives had not been reassured by the concept of subsidiarity, which seems akin to 'devolution' in British translation but closer to meaning 'federalism' in the thinking of continental partners. Many Conservatives were shocked by the *Factortame* affair and its consequences for the sovereignty of parliament, and were dismayed to discover the reality outlined by Tony Benn a decade earlier (Exhibit 5.2), namely the supremacy of Community law over national law.

Some commentators have argued that there are complex links between the Conservative crisis over the EU and what has happened to the structure of the economy. Basically, it has been argued that in the past capitalism developed within countries, so that in the case of Britain, being a capitalist, being a nationalist and being a Conservative fitted together. However the globalisation of economies no longer allows that neat fit. Whilst the small businessman in the Conservative grass roots sees the EU in terms of rules, regulations and bureaucratic red tape, international companies see the EU more in terms of the opportunities provided by the single market and the single currency.

Both Conservative and Labour have found it difficult to reconcile party ideology with Europeanism. MEPs in both parties still tend to be held at arm's length from the central organisational structures, and the behaviour of the electorate appears to reinforce their isolation from mainstream politics: a turnout of only 36.5 per cent in the fourth direct elections to the European Parliament in 1994 reflected widespread lack of interest. A rather different response, however, is found within commerce and industry, certain pressure groups and many trade unions, where the new European reality is accepted, often enthusiastically. Patterns of power have changed, and for such concerns Brussels has become an increasingly important focus for lobbying.

Tony Blairs' labour government is more receptive to many aspects of EU social policy than was its Conservative predecessor, but there remains considerable caution with respect to other aspects of federal development. In rebuilding the Conservative party after its electoral defeat in 1997, William Hague has made Euroscepticism the keystone of party policy towards EU developments.

Britain and Europe

Britain is not a fully participating member of the EU as it has either been non-committal about or has opted out from a number of integrationist developments such as the Social Chapter, the single currency and the Schengen Accord on the removal of internal borders. The expansion of the EU is likely to make the opting in/opting out pattern more commonplace than now as new members will tend to promote their various national interests. The creation of a free-trade European Economic Area made up of EFTA and EU members presents the possibility of even more fluid arrangements in the future. In a variable-geometry, two-speed Europe it seems inevitable that Britain will position itself off-centre and generally in a slower lane. If the events of the last fifty years have any logic, it is likely that, from the possibilities available, Britain will attempt to construct a set of arrangements with Europe that are intergovernmental rather than supranational in nature.

Further Reading

Camps, M., *European Unification in the Sixties* (London: Oxford University Press, 1967).

Carr, F. and S. Cope, 'Implementing Maastricht: the limits of European Union', *Talking Politics*, vol. 6, no. 3 (1994), pp. 166–70.

Cooper, M-. P., 'Understanding subsidiarity as a political issue in the European Community', *Talking Politics*, vol. 7, no. 3 (1995), pp. 178–83.

De Porte, A. W., *Europe Between the Superpowers* (New Haven, CT: Yale University Press, 1979).

George, S., *An Awkward Partner: Britain and the European Community* (Oxford: Oxford University Press, 1990).

Jones, B. and L. Robins (eds), *Two Decades in British Politics* (Manchester: Manchester University Press, 1992).

Kitzinger, U., *Diplomacy and Persuasion: how Britain joined the Common Market* (London: Thames and Hudson, 1973).

Meehan, E. J., *The British Left Wing and Foreign Policy* (New Brunswick: Rutgers University Press, 1960).

Norton, P., 'The impact of Europe on the British Constitution Pre-Maastricht', *Talking Politics*, vol. 6, no. 3 (1994), pp. 161–5.

Robins, L., *The Reluctant Party: Labour and the EEC 1961–75* (Ormskirk: Hesketh, 1979).

Urwin, D. W., *The Community of Europe* (London: Longman, 1995).

Wilson, H., *The Labour Government 1964–70* (London: Weidenfeld & Nicolson/ Michael Joseph, 1971).

6
The Constitution

This chapter focuses on the prevailing broad perceptions of the nature of the constitution; political debate, not just *party* political debate, about the constitution, in particular whether and how far reform was thought to be needed and how this might be accomplished; and the constitutional changes that actually occurred either through legislation or through informal processes. There were three main phases in the debate about and changes to the British constitution in the postwar era:

- 1945 to the early 1960s: relative contentment, limited debate and modest change.
- Early 1960s to 1975: growing doubts and the drive to modernise British institutions.
- 1975 to the present: radical discontent and the written constitution debate.

This chapter reviews each of these phases in turn.

1945 to the early 1960s: Relative Contentment, Limited Debate and Modest Change

Viewed from the 1990s, the period immediately after the Second World War appears as a time when there was general satisfaction with the workings of the British constitution among the major parties and political commentators alike (for the main characteristics of the British constitution, see de Smith and Brazier, 1991, pp. 15–22). The British constitution was widely perceived as 'a glorious example, to be envied by less fortunate nations, of a flexible and adaptable method of governing a modern democracy with the consent of the governed' (Lester in Jowell and Oliver, 1989, p. 345).

At its pinnacle, the monarchy remained a respected institution. Having survived the abdication crisis (1936), it quickly regained public affection, much assisted by the decision of King George VI and Queen Elizabeth to share the risk of German bombs with everyone else by remaining in London during the war, and by the popularity of royal events such as the marriage of Princess Elizabeth to Prince Philip Mountbatten in 1947 and the Coronation of Elizabeth II in 1953, accompanied as this was by much rhetoric about a rebirth of national greatness in the 'new Elizabethan Age' (Morgan, 1990, pp. 108, 126). The principal role of the monarch had already become almost entirely a ceremonial and symbolic one as head of state: the king or queen reigned but did not rule. The post-Victorian monarchy was required to act on the advice of the prime minister and maintain a politically neutral stance in public. Beyond this, its residual prerogative powers might permit the monarchy a constitutional role in times of national political crisis. For example after the war the monarch became involved when a prime minister failed to emerge from the normal party and electoral processes, with Queen Elizabeth playing a part in the consultations that led to the appointment of Macmillan in 1957 and Sir Alec Douglas-Home in 1963 following the resignation of their predecessors on grounds of ill-health. But the point about the monarchy's role as guardian of the constitution is precisely the unforeseeable nature of the situations in which it might be forced to act. Immediately after the war L. S. Amery cited Sir David Keir's comment that

'The King's prerogative, however circumscribed by conventions, must always retain its historic character as a residue of discretionary authority to be employed for the public good. *It is the last resource provided by the Constitution to guarantee its own working*' (cited by Amery, in Campion, 1952, p. 59, emphasis added; see also ibid., pp. 58–62; Morrison,1964, pp. 90–4).

For two decades or more after 1945 it was generally believed that the flexible, unwritten British constitution was infinitely superior to the rigid written constitutions of the United States and Western Europe. The unitary, centralised British system of parliamentary democracy with strong cabinets well served by a permanent independent civil service recruited on merit and directly accountable to a sovereign parliament appeared far preferable to systems with strict separation of powers or federal divisions of power. For most Britons, the effectiveness of their constitutional arrangements had been underlined during the Second World War, when a formidable concentration of executive power was achieved without dispensing with parliament, and after the war, when power was removed peacefully from the country's greatest wartime leader.

First, the British political system provided for *representative government* through the operation of the single member, simple majority electoral method, which helped to limit popular choice to two major parties and normally provided one of them with a clear-cut majority, thereby according it a mandate to implement its programme and security from defeat in parliament. In contrast the proportional representation systems of other European democracies such as France and Italy tended to produce weak, unstable and frequently short-lived coalitions.

Second, the British constitution provided for *responsible government* through the convention of ministerial responsibility, whereby ministers were held to be accountable to the House of Commons for decisions taken in their departments. In the Crichel Down affair (1954) the Minister of Agriculture, Sir Thomas Dugdale, resigned when it came to light that officials in his department had been guilty of unfair treatment of a Dorset landowner. This case was widely assumed at the time to have affirmed the importance of the doctrine that ministers should resign when administrative mismanagement by their officials is revealed, although it was later shown that the resignation followed strong pressure from Conservative backbenchers and that Dugdale had been personally involved in the maladministration for which he resigned. The courts also accepted the total validity of ministerial responsibility as a constitutional principle, thereby assuming they should not intervene in cases of alleged mismanagement by ministers and civil servants (Oliver, 1994, p. 631). This judicial deference to the governments of this period was well illustrated in the famous wartime case of Liversidge versus Anderson (1942), in which a detainee under the Defence (General) Regulations 1939 questioned in the courts whether the minister had the right to issue a detention order in the absense of objectively reasonable grounds for his belief that the detainee had hostile associations. The majority found in favour of the minister, supporting its refusal to review the grounds of his decision with the argument that the minister was responsible to parliament for the exercise of his power. A dissentient judge, who found for the detainee, remarked that the rest of the court was 'more executive-minded than the executive'.

Finally, contemporary political commentators were supremely confident that the unwritten British constitution afforded better protection for individual liberties than written declarations of rights in other systems of government. The lengthy statements of rights often found in foreign constitutions were suspect for two reasons. First, they were seen as hard to define and virtually impossible to agree upon, and second, they were seen as worthless unless backed, as they rarely were, by legal guarantees. Even rights that received effective constitutional support were criticised as undemocratic since they might obstruct the will of elected governments or provoke a habit of litigation. Written declarations of rights did not fit in with British traditions, and in any case were unnecessary since human rights were already adequately protected by other means. The civil liberties of Britons, it was believed, could be entrusted with complete safety to the vigilance of MPs; the integrity of an incorrupt civil service; a free press; and an independent judiciary, zealous in its application of legal remedies for wrongful encroachments on individual freedoms (Jowell and Oliver, 1989, pp. 92, 347).

The general satisfaction with the British constitution in the postwar period could not have been predicted before the war or even in 1945. After 1931, some leading socialist intellectuals had argued that a future Labour government would have to take new constitutional powers in order to overcome unconstitutional opposition from conservative institutions to its programme of radical social change. In the event the Labour governments of 1945–51 did not encounter significant opposition from the expected quarters, neither from the monarchy, even though, in Gaitskell's phrase, George VI was 'a fairly reactionary person', nor from the House of Lords, which Labour saw as an anachronism, nor the Civil Service, which was seen as a potentially hostile public-school-educated elite, nor the City, which occupied 'an even more sinister role in Labour demonology'. In return for a high level of cooperation with its reforms, the Labour Government 'displayed much institutional caution. It showed a conservative attitude towards the civil service, and almost a reverence for the consitution, from the monarchy and the House of Lords to the fabric of local government' (Morgan, 1984, pp. 81–93; 493–4).

The two major works on the British constitution in this era reflected the left–right constitutional consensus. These were *Thoughts on the Constitution* (1947) by the Conservative, L. S. Amery, and *Reflections on the Constitution* (1951) by the socialist H. Laski. Amery gave a top-down view of the constitution, in which the 'active and originating element' in the constitution was never the voter but always the government, with parliament occupying merely a supportive role. The British political system was 'one of democracy, but of democracy by consent and not by delegation, of government of the people, for the people, with, but not by, the people' (Amery, 1947, pp. 10, 15, 20–1). Rather surprisingly, Laski also subscribed to this government-centred, Tory view of the constitution. He considered that the first and most vital function of the electorate was to choose a stable executive with sufficient authority to drive an important and substantial programme through the House of Commons. Fearful in the 1930s that the British constitution would be unable to accommodate 'the fundamental challenge of Socialism', Laski had been convinced by the experience of Labour government between 1945 and 1951 that it was sufficiently flexible and adaptable to do so. For the Conservative Amery, the British tradition of a strong executive enshrined the need for governments to govern and be able to resist pressures from without; to the socialist Laski, it enabled a class party to enact its programme without hindrance (Laski, 1951, pp. 58, 55–6). Right and left agreed that a strong executive was the 'efficient secret' of the British constitution and that its natural expression was the two-party system (Wright, 1989, pp. 185–8).

The only persistently dissenting voices to the postwar Conservative–Labour constitutional consensus were Liberal ones focusing on the twentieth-century growth of an overmighty and inadequately checked executive, excessive centralisation of power in Westminster and the unfairness of the electoral system. The three main constitutional remedies proposed by Liberals in the 1950s were devolution of power from Westminster, the revitalisation of local government, and electoral reform based on the introduction of a system of proportional representation (Elliott Dodds, cited in Eccleshall, 1986, pp. 52, 240). Proportional representation was advocated both on grounds of fairness and also as a means of breaking the stranglehold that the 'party machines' had on the House of Commons (Fulford, 1959, pp. 10–38).

Unsurprisingly, given the high degree of satisfaction with the constitution expressed by the major political parties, the first two postwar decades saw relatively little constitutional legislation. The reforming statutes had three main targets: the system of justice; electoral machinery and the franchise; and the powers and composition of the House of Lords (Exhibit 6.1). The bulk of reforming attention in this period centred on the House of Lords. After 1945 the House of Lords, or rather the Conservative majority in it, adopted the self-limiting 'Salisbury doctrine' whereby its members accepted that it would be wrong for them to defeat at second reading any bill based on a government's electoral programme. Nonetheless the Attlee government legislated to reduce the upper house's delaying power, fearing its hostile use. Previously, all-party talks on reform of the House of Lords had broken down over a minor interparty difference over its delaying power, having reached agreement on the admission of women peers, peers' entitlement to stand for and vote in elections to the House of Commons and removal of the right to participate in the Lords solely because of inheritance.

As an institution, the House of Lords appeared to be dying on its feet in the 1950s. It was characterised by sparse attendance punctuated by the occasional heavy turn-out to vote down progressive reforms, as in 1956 when a private member's bill to abolish the death penalty was defeated by 238 votes to 95. Hence some reform was necessary to preserve the House. Accordingly, having provided for the creation of life peers and for women to enter the House for the first time, the Macmillan government later removed the anomaly whereby peers were unable to disclaim their peerages in order to stand for or remain in the House of Commons. This issue first arose in 1950 when Quintin Hogg was forced to move from the Commons to the Lords upon inheritance of his peerage, but cropped up in more urgent form in 1960 when, on becoming Lord Stansgate, Tony Benn refused to accept his translation to the Lords. Benn fought and won a by-election that had been called to elect his replacement in the Commons, a strategy that led to an act that enabled peers to renounce their peerages. Under this legislation not only did Benn renounce his peerage, but so too did Lord Hailsham (Quintin Hogg) and Lord Home (Sir Alec Douglas-Home) in order to take part in the Conservative leadership contest of 1963 (Shell, 1994).

A significant change in constitutional practice in the 1940s and 1950s was the greater and more systematic use of cabinet committees. Set up according to the 'Questions of Procedure for Ministers' 'to relieve the pressure on the cabinet itself by settling as much business as possible at a lower level', they have remained an indispensable feature of the British core executive ever since (James, 1994, p. 613–15). Other innovations included the establishment of a Select Committee on Statutory Instruments in 1946 in response to a concern about delegated legislation, and of the Select Committee on Nationalised Industries in 1956. The Procedure Committee rejected a proposed Select Committee on Colonial Affairs in 1959 on the ground that it would be

EXHIBIT 6.1 *The constitution and political institutions: main changes, 1945 to the 1960s*

Legislation

Legal System

- Crown Proceedings Act (1947) – deprived the crown of certain immunities in civil litigation.
- Legal Aid and Advice Act (1949) – established a new system of legal aid for poor people.

Elections

- Redistribution Act (1944) – appointed impartial boundary commissions to make periodic revisions of constituency boundaries in accordance with statutory guidelines.
- Representation of the People Act (1948) – abolished 12 university seats; removed right of owners of businesses to vote twice (at place of residence and place of business).

Parliament

- Parliament Act (1949) – reduced the delaying power of the upper house from two years (spread over three sessions) to one year (spread over two sessions).
- Life Peerages Act (1958) – provided for the creation of life peers (peerage to cease upon the the death of holder); permitted women to enter the upper house for the first time.
- Peerage Act (1963) – allowed peers to renounce their peerages in order to stand for or remain in the House of Commons.

Other changes

Increased use of cabinet committees.

---

aimed at 'controlling rather than criticising' the department concerned, a remark that underlined the deferential attitude towards the executive that prevailed in the Commons in this period (Giddings, 1994).

The most frequently-touted reform, an industrial parliament subordinate to the House of Commons but providing representation for the trade unions and employers' associations (Amery, 1947, p. 67), came to nothing. However its advocacy was rather ironic in view of the failure of political writers to notice a vital trend in British politics since 1914 which had been confirmed by postwar developments: 'the elevation of trade unions and employers' associations to the status of "governing institutions" (Middlemas, 1979, p. 20). In practice, pressure groups had already achieved representation at the highest governing level.

Early 1960s to 1975: Growing Doubts and the Drive to Modernise British Institutions

After a brief postwar period of constitutional confidence, the 1960s represented a decade of disillusion about the effectiveness of Britain's political institutions. Doubts, and the calls for institutional modernisation that accompanied them, were prompted mainly by growing concern over the relatively lacklustre performance of the economy and the need for remedies. Typical works on the mounting concern about the British economy were books such as *The Establishment* (1959), *The Stagnant Society* (1961) and *A State of England* (1963).

They all pointed to a sense of malaise over the decline of Britain, but there was less agreement about its causes and the possible remedies for it. Frequent targets for political reformers were Britain's out-of-date class structure, anachronistic industrial relations and inadequate system of education (Thomas, 1959, pp. 20, 23–46; Shanks, 1961, pp. 59–64, 121, 170–4, 219–31; Hartley, 1963, pp. 110–14, 207–22). But renewal was also sought in Britain's political institutions. In the view of one leading reformer: 'We find outselves at one of those times of crisis in the life of a nation when . . . great and sudden doubts have arisen about whether our whole machinery of government . . . is adequate to deal with modern problems' (Crick, 1964, p. x).

In the decade following the mid 1960s the drive for reform encompassed all of Britain's main political institutions and spread across the political spectrum. Both major party leaders, Harold Wilson and Edward Heath, were technocratic modernisers with a keen interest in institutional reform, and both promised radical improvements in local and national government in the mid 1960s. Pressure for institutional modernisation also came from royal commissions and committees of inquiry, committees of the House of Commons, reforming academics and jurists, and, in the case of the machinery of government, Whitehall itself (Seldon and Ball, 1994, p. 393; Jones and Keating, 1985, pp. 141, 152; Stacey, 1975, pp. 211–12).

Reforms may be grouped into those concerned to enhance democracy and those intended to improve the efficiency of the machinery of government (Exhibit 6.2). Into the first category fall changes in the franchise and voting mechanisms, parliamentary reform and moves to improve the system of redress for citizens' grievances. In the second category were changes to the central machinery of government and civil service reform. Devolution (see Chapter 4) and local government reform contained both elements, being designed to produce not only more efficient but also more open and responsive local government. Some conflict was possible, although not inevitable, between the two aims of more responsive and more efficient government and between the two dominant models of reform: participatory and managerial.

EXHIBIT 6.2 *The constitution and political institutions: main changes: 1960s to 1975*

Legislation

Elections

- Representation of the People Act (1968) – lowered voting age to 18.

Administration

- Parliamentary Commissioner Act (1967) – established parliamentary commissioner (ombudsman) to investigate cases of maladministration. Further Acts established health service commissioners (1973) and commissioners for local government (1974).
- Tribunals and Inquiries Act (1958) – established Council on Tribunals, a watchdog body with the duty to keep under review the working of the tribunals listed in the act; provided for appeals from certain tribunals to the courts; required ministers to give reasons for their decisions after an inquiry.
- Tribunals and Inquiries Act (1966) – extended surveillance of the Council on Tribunals over a larger number of inquiries.

Local Government

- Local Government Act (1972) – replaced former system of 81 county boroughs, 61 counties and 1356 county districts with new system of 53 counties (six metropolitan, 47 non-metropolitan) and 369 districts (36 metropolitan, 333 non-metropolitan) in England and Wales. Scotland was divided into nine regions and 53 districts.

Other changes

Referendum

- Referendum held on 5 June 1975 on Britain's continuing membership of the EEC.

Parliament

- New select committees established: Parliamentary Commissioner for Administration (1967), Science and Technology (1966), Race Relations and Immigration (1968), Scottish Affairs (1969), Agriculture (1967–9), Overseas Aid (1969–70), Education and Science (1969–70).
- European Community Secondary Legislation (1972).
- Expenditure Committee replaced Estimates Committee (1971).

Machinery of Government

- Cabinet committees – no appeal to cabinet without backing of committee chairman.
- Amalgamation of departments, for example Department of Health and Social Security (DHSS, 1968).
- Civil Service reform: Fulton Report (1968) made many recommendations, which were only partly implemented (see Exhibit 6.3).
- Prime minister's Policy Unit (1974) – established to improve advice to prime minister on key policy areas.

Enhancing Democracy and Accountability

There were two significant changes in this period. First, against the background of considerable student unrest on college and university campuses and following the recommendation of the Latey Committee, the voting age was lowered to 18. Second, the referendum on 5 June 1975 on whether Britain should remain in the Common Market represented a constitutional innovation as the first nationwide referendum in British history. Referendums had been held previously on issues such as Sunday pub opening in Wales and, in 1970, on whether Northern Ireland should remain in the UK, but never on matters concerning the whole of the UK. The idea of holding a referendum on entry to the EEC originated with two Conservative anti-marketeers, Enoch Powell and Neil Marten. Their proposal of a pre-entry consultative referendum was defeated in the House of Commons on 18 April 1972, but not before it had been taken up by the Labour Party, a decision that prompted the resignation of the deputy leader, Roy Jenkins. Jenkins opposed the referendum on the principled constitutional grounds that, as a mechanism of direct democracy, it was alien to the British parliamentary system. It was a populist device which was likely to produce adverse results for liberal progressive causes. As a keen pro-Marketeer, he feared commitment to a referendum would throw into doubt the recent favourable Commons vote on the second reading of the European Communities Bill. Finally, he forsaw the divisive effects of a referendum campaign on the Labour Party (Jenkins, 1991, p. 323). However, coupled with a commitment to renegotiate the terms of entry to the EEC, the referendum appealed to the Labour leadership as a means of holding together a seriously divided party; it was attractive to other Labour MPs because it offered hope of pulling Britain out of the Common Market; and to left-wingers such as Tony Benn it restored the British people's power of decision on profound issues.

Although the referendum formed an important precedent, especially for matters of fundamental constitutional importance, it remains uncertain whether this device has become permanently grafted on to the parliamentary system. Opponents contend that it is incompatible with British constitutional practice, first because it constitutes an abdication of responsibility by the government, second because a complex issue such as membership of a common market is inherently one for the judgement of experts not the relatively ill-informed average person, and third because on the dominant Burkean interpretation of the role of MPs, it is up to individual MPs to make decisions after consulting both conscience and constituents and taking into account the public interest.

Parliamentary reform in this period focused mainly on the establishment of select committees in the House of Commons and the attempt to reform the House of Lords. Advocates of select committees sought to increase the effectiveness of the Commons in holding governments to account and some gains were made: the meetings of the new select committees were held in public, and by 1970 it had become accepted practice that they could take evidence from ministers, not solely from civil servants as before. But reformers were disappointed with the limited coverage of the committees and the muted impact of their reports both in the Commons and on public opinion. For one critic the episode exposed the permanent dilemma of parliamentary reform aimed at strengthening the House of Commons against the executive, which was that 'fundamentally the Executive does not want this' and consequently 'it could take place only if there were . . . some diminution in the prerogatives of party leadership and the Executive' (Johnson, 1970, p. 247).

In an attempt to gain bipartisan agreement on reform of the House of Lords, the Labour government of 1966–70 held talks with the Conservative opposition but broke these off when the House of Lords, with its in-built Conservative majority, rejected the 1968 Rhodesia Sanctions Order. It then decided to introduce the proposals already agreed at the inter-party talks as a unilateral measure, but in doing so lost the support of many its own backbenchers. The main provisions of the 1969 Parliament (No.2) Bill (abolition of the right of hereditary peers to vote, but not to speak, in debates; limitation of the right to vote by life peers, bishops and law lords (the government of the day should be able to secure a working majority in the House of Lords by appointing sufficient peers for the purpose); and reduction of the House of Lords' power of delay to six months) were filibustered out in the Commons by an alliance between the Labour left, which wanted to abolish the House of Lords and feared that reform would only strengthen the institution, and the anti-reformist right, which believed that reform would weaken the Lords. Conservatives feared that limiting voting to life peers would enhance the prime minister's power of patronage, perhaps facilitating the 'flooding' of the Lords with politically sympathetic peers in order to pass radical legislation. With Enoch Powell leading the opposition of Conservative backbenchers and Michael Foot at the head of Labour backbench opponents of the bill, and with neither front bench enthusiastic, the legislation was dropped in April 1970.

Administrative law developed in three main ways. First, the Labour government redeemed an electoral pledge to introduce a parliamentary commissioner for administration (ombudsman), whose role would be to investigate public complaints of maladministration by government departments. However some critics consider that, although potentially a radical step, the Ombudsman was introduced 'in the most constitutionally conservative way possible. He was to be approachable only through an MP, so as to preserve the MP's role as mediator with the administration. His decisions were to be advisory, so as to preserve the doctrine of ministerial responsibility. He was even forbidden, in the pursuit of the same principle, to name civil servants, though this proved impossible to sustain in practice' (Jones and Keating, 1985, p. 155). The ombudsman was given access to all departmental files and ministers lacked the power to veto an investigation. But the ombudsman's actual brief – to investigate cases of maladministration, that is those where a fault in procedure had led to an error of judgement – was a rather narrow one and seemed to eliminate the possibility of considering 'unreasonable' decisions by the departments. The health service commissioners in 1973 were given slightly broader powers: the public had direct access to them, and although, like the ombudsman, they were unable to question the merits of a decision, they were empowered to report on 'failure of the service' and 'failure to provide a service' as well as investigating complaints of maladministration (Stacey, 1975, p. 192). Local commissioners (1974) were limited to cases of maladministration but, as with the health commissioners, public access to them was direct and their power of publicity was greater in that local authorities were required to hand over copies of their reports.

Second, following widespread concern in the 1950s about the lack of order and consistency in the operation of adminstrative tribunals, legislation in 1958 established a council on tribunals, whose surveillance was further extended in 1966. However the operation of tribunals was still being criticised in the mid 1970s, first with regard to their independence, and second for the inadequate representation of and lack of assistance for individuals in certain tribunals, and the fact that no appeals were allowed against their decisions (Thornhill, 1975, pp. 120–4; Stacey, 1975, pp. 176–82). The recommendation of the Law Commission in 1969 that a royal commission be appointed to consider citizens' rights and remedies against the state was not adopted.

Third, a considerable expansion in the judicial review of administrative actions began: a new 'judicial activism' that contrasted sharply with earlier judicial deference to executive discretion. In a series of cases the courts revealed a willingness to find against public authorities on the grounds that they had exceeded their powers, misused – that is, failed to to exercise reasonably – a discretionary power, or behaved contrary to the dictates of natural justice (the right to a fair hearing and the rule against bias) (de Smith *et al.*, 1983, pp. 558–607; Thornhill, 1975, pp. 124–7).

Improving the Efficiency of Government

In seeking to make government more efficient and effective, reforming administrations focused on improving the coordination of the machinery of government and improving the government's capacity for forward policy planning. L. S. Amery had recommended a small cabinet of non-departmental ministers to improve coordination and planning at cabinet level, but Churchill's small-scale experiment with non-departmental ministers, or 'Overlords', in 1951–3 failed, a major problem being the divorce of policy planning from administration. Thereafter prime ministers continued to operate with large cabinets (normally of 18–21 ministers), seeking coordination and forward planning through cabinet committees and non-departmental ministers such as the chancellor of the Duchy of Lancaster. But such non-departmental ministers were not, as in the Churchill experiment, given control over departmental ministers. By the late 1960s, however, the problem of policy coordination had intensified, with too many items on which cabinet committees could not agree being pushed up to cabinet. One response to this was Harold Wilson's decision to allow no appeal to cabinet without the backing of the chairman of the cabinet committee (James, 1992, p. 69; Madgwick, 1991, p. 76). Another response was to amalgamate departments. This assisted high-level coordination by enabling decisions to be taken within departments rather than between them, thereby reducing the need for so many interdepartmental committees, limiting appeals to cabinet and enabling all the heads of major departments to be included in the cabinet (Jones, 1975, pp. 42–3).

Numerous attempts were made to improve the quality of advice available to prime ministers and cabinets and their capacity to plan policy and resources effectively. Three measures were aimed specifically at improving economic planning and coordination: the Public Expenditure Survey Committee (PESC, 1962); the Department of Economic Affairs (DEA, 1965); and Programme Analysis and Review (PAR, 1970). The PESC emerged within the Treasury in the late 1950s out of the need to improve decision making on public expenditure, whilst the DEA, which originated out of dissatisfaction with the flagging performance of Britain's economy in the 1960s, was designed to act as 'an expansionist counterweight to the Treasury' (Thornhill, 1975, p. 70). However the difficulty of establishing a workable division of labour between the two departments led to the failure of the experiment and the winding up of the DEA in 1969. The PAR was set up by Heath to supplement the PESC by reviewing departmental spending programmes, but since the departments themselves chose which of their policies to submit for PAR review, the system was inherently limited and gradually faded during the 1970s before being abolished by Margaret Thatcher (Pliatzky, 1982, pp. 103–5; Drewry and Butcher, 1991, p. 89).

As well as the PAR, the Heath government also established the Central Policy Review Staff (1970), a think-tank intended to provide independent appraisals of the effectiveness of government policies. Its tasks included helping ministers to analyse the underlying implication of alternative courses of action and to establish the relative priorities to be given to the different sectors of their programmes. Potentially useful in providing the cabinet with a 'counter-brief' to the departmental view, the CPRS needed the support of the prime minister in order to function effectively. It had this for several years, producing several high-quality reports before being wound up in 1983 by Margaret Thatcher, who considered she had no need of such an organisation to inject fresh thinking or enforce a collective strategy (Blackstone and Plowden, 1988; Madgwick, 1991, pp. 215–18).

A more long-lived initiative that also imported outside advisers into the heart of government was the prime minister's Policy Unit (1974). This was established by Harold Wilson, who had long held the ambition of strengthening the policy advice available to the prime minister. The Policy Unit remained a permanent feature of the core executive, valued by successive prime ministers not only for its briefings on departmental policies but also because it dealt with ideas not covered by the departments and with those involving political difficulties (Madgwick, 1991, pp. 112–15).

The Civil Service was widely indicted for elitism, incompetence, lack of relevant expertise and excessive caution, and was considered by some to be one of the causes of Britain's decline. Accordingly the Wilson government set up the Fulton Committee (1966–8) to examine and make recommendations on its structure, recruitment and management, including training (Exhibit 6.3). Only a few of its recommendations received early implementation, a common view being that the Civil Service itself blocked many of the proposed reforms. Many contemporaries held that the committee's narrow terms of reference restricted its ability to examine the work of the Civil Service in the context of the machinery of government, and in particular the convention of ministerial responsibility. But later observers tended to view the committee's report as setting the agenda for continuous discussion of the role of the Civil Service and as the forerunner of the Thatcher reforms (Drewry and Butcher, 1991, p. 54; Hennessy, 1990, p. 206).

From 1960 to 1975 there was a considerable expansion and modernisation of local government. Local authority expenditure more than doubled, and by 1972 local government employed over 2.5 million workers. Underlying the expansion were the range of welfare responsibilities that had been acquired in the late 1940s, together with the new powers of planning and environmental control added in the 1950s and 1960s. However the structure of local government in the 1960s remained virtually unchanged since the late nineteenth century and was generally perceived as in need of reform, its variegated pattern of numerous very small authorities being regarded as incapable of dealing effectively with modern needs. Plans in the 1940s to replace the existing system with 240 all-purpose authorities had come to nothing.

Change began with the reorganisation of local government in London between 1963 and 1965. An enlarged Greater London Council (GLC) and 32 boroughs, together with the Inner London Education Authority (ILEA) and the City of London Corporation, replaced 87 authorities. Next the Local Government Act (1972) transformed the local government structure in England and Wales. The Redcliffe–Maud Report (1969) had recommended the establishment of 58 unitary, all-purpose authorities in England, plus metropolitan councils with a lower tier of metropolitan districts for the three

EXHIBIT 6.3 *The Fulton Report on the Civil Service (1968): recommendations and implementation*

- The Civil Service was still essentially based on 'the philosophy of the amateur' (or 'generalist' or 'all-rounder'). The recommendation that preference should be given to 'relevant' degrees was not implemented, the government believing that the best graduates should be recruited whatever their degree subjects.
- There was insufficient scope for specialists, e.g. scientists, engineers. The recommendation that specialists should be given more training in management and opportunities for greater responsibility and broader careers had not been implemented by the early 1990s, when the dominance of the generalist in the departmental hierarchy had not really changed and policy making remained almost exclusively the preserve of the generalist administrator.
- Too few civil servants received training in management. The recommendation that a Civil Service College be established to train civil servants in management skills was implemented in 1970.
- The overall management of the Civil Service was inadequate. Moves between one department or post and another tended to be too frequent, there was insufficient career planning and promotion was too dependent on seniority. The Treasury was incapable of performing an effective 'central management role'. The recommendation that a Civil Service Department be established, under the control of the prime minister and with the permanent secretary of the Civil Service Department designated as Head of the Home Civil Service was implemented immediately. However this arrangement came to an end in 1981, when the Civil Service Department was disbanded. The Treasury regained responsibility for manpower, pay, allowances and pensions, a new unit within the Cabinet Office, the Management and Personnel Office, was put in charge of personnel management, recruitment and training, and (from 1983) the cabinet secretary became head of the Home Civil Service.
- The system of 'classes' in the Civil Service, with 'rigid and prolific compartmentalism' arising from the number and variety of classes, seriously impeded its work. The recommendation was that all classes should be abolished and replaced by a single unified grading system covering all civil servants. Some rationalisation took place, the main changes being the establishment of the open structure (begun in 1972 and covering the top seven grades by 1986) and the formation of the administration group in 1971 by merging the lower rung of the administrative class with the clerical and executive classes. However the single unified grading structure recommended by Fulton had not appeared by the early 1990s.
- The Service was excessively secretive. An inquiry into the provisions and operation of the Officials Secrets Act was recommended. The Franks Report (1972) advocated the repeal of Section 2 of the Official Secrets Act (1911) and this was eventually done by the Official Secrets Act (1989). However this act was criticised as an illiberal measure because it tightened the law of secrecy for the categories of information protected against disclosure by the criminal law which remained.
- The Civil Service was socially exclusive and rather isolated from the rest of the community. Fulton recommended recruitment changes to broaden the social basis of top civil servants (three fifths of whom were private sector and Oxbridge-educated in 1968), and also by an expansion of late entry to allow

Exhibit 6.3 cont. overleaf

Exhibit 6.3 continued

people from other occupations such as business and the professions to become civil servants. It also recommended greater mobility and the capacity for two-way transfers on a temporary basis between the civil service and other employment. Partial success had been achieved in implementing these recommendations by the 1990s. Oxbridge was only slightly less dominant in entry to the top (AT/HEO) grades of the Service, but efforts to broaden the basis of recruitment were continuing. Expansion of late entry had disappointing results, but by the mid 1980s a significant increase in two-way secondments between Whitehall and outside professions had taken place.
- There were weaknesses in aspects of departmental structure relating to accountability and policy planning. Fulton saw 'no reason to believe that the dividing line between activities for which Ministers are directly responsible and those for which they are not, is necessarily drawn in the right place today', and suggested that hiving off some departmental functions was worth consideration. Hiving off did not begin in earnest until the late 1980s.

Source: Drewry and Butcher, 1991, pp. 51–4, 143; Greenwood and Wilson, 1989, pp. 102–20; Hennessy, 1990, pp. 194–208

major conurbations of Birmingham, Liverpool and Manchester. But this advice was rejected and the reorganisation of 1972 to some extent strengthened the two-tier nature of the system while also streamlining it by reducing the overall number of authorities from 1500 to roughly 500.

However, despite these and other reforms, problems remained for local government. One problem was financial. With central grants increasing and the rates, a local property-based tax, declining as a source of local revenue in these years, local government became more vulnerable to central intervention after 1975. Second, local government became increasingly politicised in the late 1960s and 1970s: the proportion of councils under party control (a mere 50 per cent in 1965) increased and the ideological climate surrounding councils became more intense as the localities felt the impact of new social and political movements such as feminism, environmentalism, the urban left and the drive for racial equality. Meanwhile the national importance of locally delivered services ensured that local government remained the focus of public attention. With some Conservative councils resisting Labour comprehensive education policy after 1965 and some Labour councils struggling against Conservative housing legislation in the early 1970s, central–local relations deteriorated (Stoker, 1990, pp. 3–31).

A rage for institutional reform possessed Britain during this period, but it had modest effects. The central principles of the constitution – its unitary nature, executive dominance in parliament and ministerial responsibility – remained untouched. The most powerful agencies of constitutional change need to be sought elsewhere than in the consciously engineered reforms of political institutions. These were twofold: the dominant position attained by 'corporatist government', and membership of the EEC (1973).

First, corporatist government involved the determination of economic and industrial policy by negotiations between government and the major producer groups. During the 1970s the formalisation of corporatism through such institutions as the National Economic Development Council (NEDC, 1961) and the practice of regular meetings between prime ministers and the Confederation of British Industry and Trades Union Congress led to concern being expressed about its constitutional consequences. The main worry was that national economic policy was being made secretly by the government and the affected interests, with the elected parliamentary representatives being shut out from the decision-making process. When taken into the heart of government, sectional representation, by ignoring the interests of the large number of citizens that were not represented in the process, might lead to a crisis of legitimacy for the British state.

Second, the momentous constitutional consequences of joining the EEC were more clearly expressed at the time by opponents of entry than by Euro-enthusiasts, who emphasised the economic benefits of joining, or by the governments concerned, which, insofar as they mentioned constitutional matters, stressed the possibility of withdrawal. The Heath government's 1971 white paper explicitly stated that membership presented 'no question of any erosion of essential sovereignty' and that 'our courts will continue to operate as they do at present'. Critics of entry on the Labour left (Tony Benn) and right (Douglas Jay and Peter Shore), and on the Conservative right (Enoch Powell), focused their campaigns on the enduring loss of British parliamentary sovereignty that EEC membership would entail. Their predictions, although less obvious in the 1970s than later, proved correct. By becoming a member of the EEC the United Kingdom accepted that, in the areas it covered, EC law took priority over UK law and in practice became another source of the British constitution (Mount, 1992, pp. 218–25; Jones and Keating, 1985, pp. 181–92; *The Economist*, 14 October 1995, p. 26).

1975 to the Present: Radical Discontent and the Written Constitution Debate

A new phase of the postwar constitutional debate began in the late 1970s. Discussion of the constitution in terms of fundamental principles replaced the more limited, piecemeal approach of the preceding phase. Compared with the general satisfaction with British constitutional arrangements expressed on both the left and the right in the 1940s and 1950s and with the relatively modest reform proposals of the 1960s, the new mood was critical and radical. Greater scepticism about the virtues of the British constitution began on the right in the late 1970s but passed to the centre and left in the 1980s. Whereas the watchwords of earlier reformers were efficiency and participation, the new concern became the coherence of the constitution itself. By the late 1980s the previous orthodoxy that all was well with the

British constitution, or that at worst it required only judicious modernisation, had been overthrown by 'a new orthodoxy that insisted that there was a fundamental disorder' (Wright, 1989, p. 199). With the right still adhering to the traditional view of the constitution, the stage was set for vigorous debate. This section examines the constitutional implications of the institutional changes of the 1980s before turning to the debate about constitutional reform.

The Europeanisation of British Politics

Glossed over by governments in the 1970s, the constitutional impact of British membership of the European Community became clearer to elite and popular opinion during this period and also intensified as a result of legislation and legal judgements that tied the UK ever more tightly into European institutions. Two major treaties transferred power away from the UK to the European Community. The Single European Act (1986) extended the principle of weighted majority voting in the Council of Ministers while the Treaty of Maastricht (1993) established a European Union with the goal of 'an ever closer union between the peoples of Europe', involving a common currency, a common foreign and security policy, and European citizenship (see Chapter 5). In the Factortame case (1991), the European Court of Justice ruled that UK courts had the power to suspend an act of parliament (the Merchant Shipping Act, 1988) that appeared to break EC law. Thereby it explicitly underlined the clause in the European Communities Act (1972) that stipulated that acts of parliament should take effect subject to Community law (Exhibit 6.4). Opponents of British membership of the European Community could still cling to the possibility of withdrawal, but this prospect was remote, and the doctrine of the 'sovereignty of parliament' – once called 'the fundamental law' of the British constitution – had been breached. All the major British political institutions had become increasingly enmeshed in European Union law and decision making by the 1990s. This had profound consequences for the executive, upon which Brussels was a much more powerful constraint than parliament, for the judiciary, which had been accorded a vital new constitutional role in the interpretation and application of Community law, and for parliament itself, which, having failed to develop effective procedures to curb the executive, found its influence even further reduced by its inability to maintain adequate surveillance of EC law. As Madgwick and Woodhouse sum up: 'Membership of the European Community (Union) incorporates Britain into the Constitution of the Community, a largely-written constitution of a quasi-federal character, interpreted and enforced by a constitutional court. In the perspective of British constitutional development and traditions, this is a radical departure, more radical than most of the early enthusiasts for a common market intended, or knew about' (Madgwick and Woodhouse, 1995, pp. 61–2).

EXHIBIT 6.4 *The constitution and political institutions: main changes, 1975 to the 1990s*

Legislation

Europe

Parliamentary sovereignty was further undermined by:

- the European Communities Act (1972), which transferred certain areas of policy making to EC institutions;
- the Single European Act (1986), which extended weighted majority voting on the Council of Ministers;
- the Treaty of Maastricht (1992), which provided for ever-closer union.

Local Government

Further centralisation of the British system of government:

- Finance: central government control increased through the 'capping' of local authority spending and the replacement of rates by the poll tax (1990) and then the council tax (1993).
- Structure: abolition of Greater London Council and six English metropolitan counties (1985); unitary authorities replaced the two-tier system in Scotland and Wales and in a limited number of areas in England (1996).
- Role: changed from service provider, responsible for direct delivery of services in education, social services and housing to service enabler, ensuring that services were provided rather than providing them itself.

Other Changes

Administration

- Civil Service reform: civil service reduced by 200 000 (1979–95); changes designed to strengthen budgetary control and accountable management introduced in 1980s; following the Ibbs Report (1988), service delivery functions hived off into executive agencies (108 by early 1995, containing two thirds of civil servants). The 1990s also saw the introduction of market testing to ensure value for money and the privatisation of some central government activities.
- Quangos: quasi-autonomous non-governmental public bodies became increasingly influential in British politics – by 1995, they disposed of about one fifth of all public spending. Examples are NHS trusts, training and enterprise councils, urban development corporations, Housing action trusts, further and higher education funding councils. Many assumed responsibilities formerly exercised by local government. Generally they were appointive, non-accountable bodies taking their decisions in secret.

Exhibit 6.4 cont. overleaf

Exhibit 6.4 continued

Parliament

- New select committees covering all major departments of state except the Lord Chancellor's Department. There were 14 select committees in 1980 (including one, Scottish Affairs, from an earlier period) and 17 by 1995.
- Nolan Committee on Standards in Public Life: its recommendations included (1) prohibition of MPs from working for lobbying companies and (2) appointment of an independent parliamentary commissioner for standards.

The Rule of Law

- Numerous episodes and cases led many to question the security of this fundamental principle of British public life. These included several national security cases involving crown immunity, a series of serious miscarriages of justice, and many cases in which the 'rights' of British citizens were upheld by the European Court of Human Rights.

Legal System

- A large increase in judicial review of administrative action occurred, with annual applications for judicial review increasing fourfold in the 1980s to over 2000 in 1990 and ministerial decisions continuing to be struck down by adverse court rulings in the 1990s.

Constitutional Monarchy

Of the three roles of the British monarchy – symbol of the nation, provider of advice to governments and guardian of the constitution – the first weakened in this period, the second came to be seen as of little significance, and the circumstances in which the third function might apply were perceived as much reduced. The symbolic role of the monarch survived intact the postwar transformation of Britain from an imperial, religious and deferential society to a non-imperial, secular, multi-ethnic and non-deferential one. But during the late 1980s and 1990s the adverse publicity surrounding the collapse of the royal marriages, revelations of the extent of the queen's fortune in the context of the fact that she did not pay tax, and an ill-advised offer of public money by the heritage secretary to help pay for the restoration of the fire-damaged Windsor Castle, led to a partial collapse in the popularity of the monarchy, and in December 1992 24 per cent favoured its abolition. There was open discussion of republican ideas for the first time since the 1860s, with some writers suggesting the transfer of the remaining prerogative powers of the monarch to the speaker of the House of Commons. A passive monarchy, deeply entwined with the peak institutions and groups of an archaic class structure, seemed ill-placed to regain the popularity upon which a large part of its effectiveness as symbol of the nation depended.

Second, it became clear in this period that the monarchical role invented by Bagehot in the 1860s (to be consulted, to encourage, to warn) had not been carried out since the time of George V (1865–1936). According to Ferdinand Mount, 'there is little evidence that the Prime Minister of the day . . . takes the slightest notice of the royal advice' (Cannadine, *TLS*, 3 November 1995; Mount, 1992, pp. 95–6). Third, the monarchy's remaining powers in the formation and dissolution of governments were reduced in 1965 by the adoption of a procedure for the election of its leader by the Conservative Party, which eliminated the possibility of the monarch exercising influence when the leadership of a majority party was uncertain, as in 1957 and 1963. However the possibility remained that the sovereign would need to play a part in the resolution of situations in which there was a hung parliament (that is, no majority party) or when a prime minister without a majority or with an uncertain one requested a dissolution of parliament. In such or other, at present unpredictable, circumstances the monarch's constitutional guardianship role of 'upholding the law' would come into play.

Parliamentary Government

There were four significant trends in parliamentary government in this period, although these did not point uniformly in one direction. First, an already centralised system of government became more centralised as the functions of local government were progressively stripped away and handed over to quangos (quasi-autonomous non-governmental organisations), with members appointed by ministers, or to commercial enterprises. The political and constitutional consequences of these developments were twofold. First, domineering central intervention on such a large scale definitively ended the 'dual polity' situation that characterised central–local relations between the 1920s and the 1960s, in which a central government preoccupied with external affairs and a comparatively 'unpolitical' local government operated in considerable independence of each other. Second, the transfer of powers to non-elective quangos in many areas created a severe problem of democratic control and political accountability – the 'democratic deficit'.

Second, the representativeness of the House of Commons became a matter of concern for several reasons. First, the four successive general election victories by the Conservatives just over two fifths of the electoral vote meant that for eighteen years government was in the hands of a party that was supported by only a minority of the electorate. Second, the disproportion between the large number of votes and the small number of seats won by the Liberal/Social Democrat Alliance in 1983 and 1987 raised the question of the fairness of the electoral system. Third, the social representativeness of the House of Commons became an issue, especially with regard to the low proportion of women MPs.

Third, despite some strengthening of the role of parliament in national affairs, this was more than offset by failure to reinforce procedures for parliamentary surveillance of the executive. Positive moves included the ending of corporatist bargaining with peak business and labour organisations by the Thatcher government; the establishment of fourteen departmental select committees in 1979 to examine the expenditure, administration and policy in the principal government departments; the greater vitality of the House of Lords, whose rejuvenation began in the 1960s; and the occasional surge of vigour in the House of Commons, as exemplified by the toppling of Prime Minister Margaret Thatcher in 1990 and the considerable difficulties the Major government had with Euro-sceptic Conservative backbenchers after 1992.

However the ending of corporatism probably strengthened the authority of government more than that of parliament. Moreover, although the new departmental select committees represented 'one of the most significant constitutional developments of the century' and, in the words of the Commons Procedure Committee in 1990, provided 'an improved framework for the sustained scrutiny of government departments', they did not produce 'any transformative effect on the relationship between MPs and parties, or between MPs and government' (Adonis, 1993, pp. 264, 173–4). In addition, despite the growth of backbench dissent from the 1970s, the strength of the government whips normally ensures that even governments with small majorities achieve their legislative aims on controversial issues, no matter what 'sound and fury' they encounter on the way. Witness the success of the Labour government (1974–6) on nationalisation and the Conservative Government (1992–7) on the Maastricht Treaty and railway privatisation. Governments with large or even decent majorities (and these were twice as frequent as those with a small or no majority postwar) can afford to treat opposition from their official opponents or from within their own party with contempt, as the Thatcher government of 1987–90 did over the poll tax and water privatisation. An authoritative study concludes that the poll tax was 'a public policy failure of the first magnitude' for which 'system failure' was to blame as well as human error. The 'fundamental weakness' in it was 'the "elective dictatorship" which gave the government an almost free rein to carry through its poll tax plans . . . . Parliament was a rubber stamp' (Butler *et al.*, 1994, pp. 302–3). During the almost 300 hours of parliamentary time occupied by water privatisation, '*not one* amendment of any substance was made by either House' (Adonis, 1993, p. 102). Meanwhile the upper house remained a quaint anachronism that, despite its greater activity compared with the 1950s, was incapable of offering more than feeble resistance to the government of the day. In the 1990s moreover, following growing public concern about such matters as MPs accepting payment for asking parliamentary questions and MPs' failure to declare outside interests, the Nolan

Committee (1995) made a large number of recommendations designed to improve standards in public life.

The other major Thatcherite reform of institutions (in addition to that of local government) involved the restructuring of the civil service, and this had important implications for the central constitutional convention of minister-ial responsibility. Ministerial responsibility is fundamental in linking execu-tive to legislature and has been described as 'the organising principle of British government' and as, in effect, constituting the British 'conception of the State' (Madgwick and Woodhouse, 1995, p. 132; Beattie, 1995, p. 158). It requires, first, ministerial answerability to parliament in the sense of the obligation to reveal explain and justify decisions, and second, accountability to parliament in the sense that when mistakes are made, ministers are considered responsible and may bc blamed and criticised, reshuffled, sacked or forced to resign.

The expectation of ministerial resignation for policy failure or the mistakes of departmental civil servants came to be recognised as a myth in the postwar period. Between 1962 and 1992, of sixteen ministerial resignations only one was for policy failure (and that involved reshuffle rather than leaving the government) and there were no resignations for the errors of officials. Most were for personal misconduct or political misjudgement. Already weakened, the convention was further blurred as a result of the Civil Service reforms. These were aimed at reducing its size, cutting its cost, improving its efficiency, curbing its privileges and transforming its culture from negative and fault-finding to positive, cooperative and action-orientated. Hiving off much of the Civil Service into executive agencies in the 1980s was followed by the market reforms and privatisation of the 1990s. The Ibbs Report (1988) wanted chief executives of the agencies to be directly accountable to parliament, but the government preferred to retain the formal parliamentary accountability of ministers. However, with Ministers soon adopting the practice of referring MPs' questions to chief executives, it became apparent that political accountability had become further confused and was in danger of falling into a 'no man's land' between ministers, supposedly accountable for policy, and chief executives, responsible for operational matters.

Fourth, procedures to redress citizens' grievances improved during this period as a complex but rather incoherent and still far from comprehensive system took shape. There were five main ways of protecting individual rights (through members of parliament, administrative tribunals and inquiries, the ombudsman, the European Court of Human Rights, and judicial review) and important developments occurred in the last two of these. A growing number of Britons took their cases to the European Court of Human Rights and received favourable judgments, with which the government generally com-plied, although the European Convention on Human Rights (1951) had not by 1996 been incorporated into British law. In addition the willingness of the courts to review administrative action on the grounds of illegality, irrationality, procedural impropriety and proportionality continued to grow, with applications for judicial review increasing nearly fourfold between1980 and 1990. According to one legal commentator, 'the great legal success story of the past thirty years has been the remorseless march of administrative law calling governments to account in courts'. In his view judges' 'enthusiasm for checking government has been reinforced by the twin streams of European law . . . flowing from the Luxembourg Court of Justice and the Strasbourg Court of Human Rights' (Lee, 1994, p. 138). A gradual but still incomplete reversal had occurred in the immediate postwar British dismissal of the European Convention of Human Rights as meaningless abstractions incapable of being fitted into the concrete Anglo-Saxon legal system. The underlying aim of the Citizens' Charters introduced by the Major governments was to offer simple remedies for people aggrieved at a failure to meet published standards in public services. Derided initially, the charters made some progress with public opinion but remained more a consumerist expression of a depoliticised citizenship than a genuine legal guarantee of the rights and entitlements of individuals against the state (Oliver, 1993, pp. 26–7).

However, despite some improvements, the British system of redress remained fallible in the 1990s. As well as many serious miscarriages of justice, this period saw the legislature restrict accused people's right to silence, extend police powers, impose wide-ranging curbs on freedom of assembly and public protest, and curtail the freedom of the press. It also witnessed a series of national security cases involving the prosecution of civil servants and journalists for leaking information that, critics alleged, far from being prejudicial to national security, was simply politically embarrassing to the government and should have been in the public domain anyway. These cases fuelled the campaign for a Freedom of Information Act. In addition, judicial review of government action under its prerogative powers remained minimal (Carroll, 1994, pp. 54–8). In the view of two academics writing in 1990, civil liberties in Britain were 'in a state of crisis' (Ewing and Gearty, 1990, p. 255).

The Debate on Constitutional Reform

Public confidence in the British constitution and British political institutions, which was still fairly high in the 1970s, fell during the 1980s and plunged even lower in the 1990s. In an ICM poll in March 1994, only 32 per cent expressed trust in the monarchy, and even smaller proportions of the sample avowed confidence in the Civil Service (21 per cent), parliament (13 per cent) and government (11 per cent). In a MORI opinion poll conducted for the Joseph Rowntree Trust in May 1995, 79 per cent of respondents were in favour of a written constitution, a similar percentage were in favour of a bill of rights, 77 per cent wanted more frequent referendums and 81 per cent supported a freedom of information bill (*Independent*, 30 May 1995). This declining public confidence formed the background to the growing interest in constitutional reform.

Major dissatisfaction with Britain's constitution was first expressed at the elite level in the late 1970s, most notably by Lord Hailsham (1978), who argued that Britain was abandoning limited government and moving towards 'elective dictatorship'. To him, 'the political apparatus consists of an omnipotent Parliament virtually consisting of a single chamber dominated by a vastly-powerful executive and completely uncontrolled by an effective judicial machinery'. This concern was taken up by political analysts and by politicians on the centre and left in the 1980s, when some extremely radical commentaries appeared. For the political scientist F. F. Ridley the emperor really did have no clothes, and 'the term British constitution is near meaningless'. Whereas writers on the constitution in the 1950s had believed in its effortless superiority to foreign constitutions, Ridley saw it as markedly inferior. Earlier experts had seen the rest of the world as out of step with Britain, but Ridley considered Britain was out of step with the rest of the world, to its detriment. The British constitution lacked the legitimating authority of the written, codified, single-document constitutions of other countries. Unlike them it was neither formed by an authority outside itself, such as a popular constitutional convention, nor was it a higher form of law than other law, nor was it entrenched and only changeable by special procedures (Ridley, 1988, pp. 340–4). The critics were mainly concerned about two fundamental weaknesses in the British constitution: the feebleness of checks upon a very powerful executive, and the lack of concrete protection of civil rights. *The Economist* summed up these criticisms as follows.

> The key concepts pioneered by Britain which have so influenced the growth of democracy elsewhere – the separation of the executive, legislative and judicial branches of government to provide institutional checks and balances, and the guarantee of fundamental rights protected from the encroachments of an overmighty government – were born of Parliament's battle to restrain the monarch in the seventeenth and eighteenth centuries; *but they were never firmly established in Britain itself* (*The Economist*, 14 October 1995, p. 24, emphasis added).

Serious debate about constitutional reform began in the late 1980s, and by the mid 1990s it had taken shape as an argument between liberal reformers and defenders of the constitutional status quo. Although there was considerable overlap between their specific proposals, the reformers could be subdivided into advocates of piecemeal reform and supporters of a written constitution. The novelty about the situation was the support that radical reform received from the Labour Party, which for most of its history had been constitutionally conservative. Another new element in a campaign for piecemeal reform, which despite public support in the opinion polls was far from being a truly popular one, was the support of individuals and groups from all parts of the constitutional spectrum, including Liberal Democrats, the mainland nationalist parties and prominent right of centre sources such as *The Economist* weekly newspaper, the Conservative intellectual Ferdinand Mount and the right-wing 'think-tank', the Institute of Economic Affairs. Leading proponents of a written constitution were Charter 88, the left of centre Institute for Public Policy Research, and the Labour left-winger Tony Benn.

The considerable amount of common ground between the proposals of the piecemeal and radical reformers was not surprising given the similarity of their political analyses. Thus concern about an overpowerful executive led to a desire to strengthen parliament by, for example, introducing fixed-term parliaments, extending the role of select committees and reforming the House of Lords. The perception that the system was overcentralised led to proposals for regional devolution and enhanced powers for local government. A wish to reinforce the political centre, together with indignation at the unfairness of the first past the post system, lay behind the demand for electoral reform. Anxiety about the fragility of individual rights resulted in calls for a bill of rights, and the belief that British political debate was less well-informed than it should be owing to government secrecy underpinned the advocacy of a freedom of information act. If enacted piecemeal by ordinary legislation, these proposals would make a significant difference to the nature of the British constitution, but they would not transform it completely. Parliamentary sovereignty would remain its cardinal principle, even if further eroded by a bill of rights and EU membership; and the UK would still be a unitary rather than a federal state, albeit one with the federalist elements strengthened. However, if the constitution were written in codified form in a single document, parliamentary sovereignty would no longer be the basic principle of the British constitution. Rather the constitution itself would be the supreme principle. Constitutional amendment would be more difficult to achieve than under the present flexible constitution. If, in addition, the UK were restructured along federal lines, the unitary nature of the British state would disappear too.

A traditionalist case in defence of the constitutional status quo was made by the Conservative Party. The Conservatives were prepared to concede minor reforms of parliamentary procedure and some greater openness with regard to certain government information, but the party resolutely opposed devolution (as likely to lead to the break-up of Britain) and defended the existing electoral system (as producing stable, effective government) and the existing House of Lords (as superior to alternative models). It was supported in its resistance to a bill of rights and a written constitution by the political scientist Philip Norton, who stressed the continuing coherence, accountability, flexibility and effectiveness of the Westminster model. In practice the

Conservative agenda in the 1980s and 1990s, which involved reducing the scope of government and making it more efficient and economical, had unlooked-for constitutional consequences in terms of strengthening the executive and centralising political power. Conservative institutional reform of the civil service and local government, along with the allocation of increased power to quangos in the 'patronage state', also had significant consequences for political and constitutional accountability. But in their evident unconcern about these developments, the Conservatives remained faithful to their traditional position which allocated pride of place to 'strong' government above 'representative' or 'responsible' government in their order of constitutional priorities.

Further Reading

Amery, L., *Thoughts on the Constitution* (Oxford: Oxford University Press, 1947).

Beer, S. H., *Modern British Politics* (London: Faber, 1965).

Birch, A. H., *Representative and Responsible Government* (London: Allen and Unwin, 1964).

Hailsham, Lord, *The Dilemma of Democracy* (Glasgow: Collins, 1978).

Johnson, N., *In Search of the Constitution* (Oxford: Pergamon, 1977).

Jones, B. and M. Keating, *Labour and the British State* (Oxford: Clarendon Press, 1989).

Jowell, J. and D. Oliver (eds), *The Changing Constitution*, 2nd edn (Oxford: Clarendon Press, 1989).

Laski, H., *Reflections on the Constitution* (Manchester: Manchester University Press, 1951).

Madgwick, P. and D. Woodhouse, *The Law and Politics of the Constitution* (London, Harvester Wheatsheaf, 1995).

Morrison, Lord, *Government and Parliament* (Oxford: Oxford University Press, 1964).

Mount, F., *The British Constitution Now* (London: Heinemann, 1992).

Norton, P., *The Constitution in Flux* (Oxford: Martin Robertson, 1982).

Norton, P., 'The Impact of Europe on the British Constitution, pre-Maastricht', *Talking Politics*, vol. 6, no. 3 (1994).

Oliver, D., 'Citizenship in the 1990s', *Politics Review*, vol. 3, no. 1 (1993).

Peele, G., 'The Constitution' in P. Dunleavy, A. Gamble, I. Holliday and G. Peele (eds), *Developments in British Politics 4* (London: Macmillan, 1993).

Ridley, F., 'There is no constitution: a dangerous case of the Emperor's clothes', Parliamentary Affairs, vol. 41, no. 3 (1988).

Smith, T., 'The British Constitution: Unwritten and unravelled', in J. Hayward and P. Norton (eds), *The Political Science of British Politics* (London: Wheatsheaf, 1986).

Stacey, F., *British Government 1966–1975: The Years of Reform* (Oxford: Oxford University Press, 1975).

Thornhill, W. (ed.), *The Modernisation of British Government* (London: Pitman, 1975).

Wright, A., 'The Constitution', in L. Tivey and A. Wright (eds), *Party Ideology in Britain* (London: Routledge, 1989).

7
The Political Parties

With the postwar political influence of the extreme left and extreme right remaining negligible, this chapter focuses primarily on mainstream political groups – the Conservative, Labour and centre parties.

The Conservative Party

By far the most successful party of modern times, the Conservatives were in power for 35 of the 52 years between 1945 and 1997, twice as long as their main political opponents. The party won eight of the fourteen general elections, gaining either a working majority (1951, 1970, 1992) or, more often, a respectable (1955, 1979) or very large (1959, 1983, 1987) majority. Its success stemmed from a variety of factors.

First, for much of the period the Conservative Party gained both from its own political unity and from divisions within the Labour Party, its main opponent, and between Labour and the centre parties for all of the period. Second, the Conservatives' rhetoric and policies, notably their nationalism and patriotism, reputation for economic competence, populism on crime and immigration, anti-socialism and support for a property-owning democracy, had a strong electoral appeal. The Conservatives gained most of their support from the working class, even in the heyday of class voting between 1945 and the 1960s (Waller, 1994, pp. 390, 393); indeed manual worker support actually increased from 23 per cent to 34 per cent between 1950 and 1992. The Conservatives benefited more than Labour from partisan dealignment. Thus whilst 45 per cent of voters identified with Labour and only 36 per cent with the Conservatives in 1966, the Conservatives held a narrow advantage (38 per cent to Labour's 36 per cent) in 1979 and a sizeable lead (43 per cent to Labour's 31 per cent) in 1992 (Margetts and Smyth, 1994, p. 15). More controversially, the Conservatives appeared to have gained from class dealignment as – with almost all the predominantly Conservative groups in the electorate expanding and almost all the predominantly Labour groups contracting from the early 1960s – 'the embourgeoisement of British society has undoubtedly tilted the balance of partisanship in the Conservatives' favour' (Crewe, 1993, p. 103). Finally, the way in which the electoral system discriminates against parties such as the Alliance proved 'indispensable to the Conservatives' ability to keep on winning elections' (Margetts and Smyth, 1994, pp. 16–17).

TABLE 7.1 *The political parties: total votes, share of votes and seats, 1945–97*

General election	Conservative			Labour			Liberal		
	Seats	% share of total vote	Votes (in millions)	Seats	% share of total vote	Votes (in millions)	Seats	% share of total vote	Votes (in millions)
1945	213	39.8	9.9	393	47.8	11.9	12	9.0	2.25
1950	298	43.5	12.5	315	46.1	13.2	9	9.1	2.6
1951	321	48.0	13.7	295	48.8	13.9	6	2.6	0.7
1955	344	49.7	13.2	277	46.4	12.4	6	2.7	0.7
1959	365	49.4	13.7	258	43.8	12.2	6	5.9	1.6
1964	304	43.4	12.0	317	44.1	12.2	9	11.2	3.1
1966	253	41.9	11.4	363	47.9	13.0	12	8.5	2.3
1970	330	46.4	13.1	287	43.0	12.1	6	7.5	2.1
1974 (Feb.)	297	37.9	11.8	301	37.1	11.6	14	19.3	6.1
1974 (Oct.)	277	35.8	10.4	319	39.2	11.4	13	18.3	5.35
1979	339	43.9	13.6	268	36.9	11.5	11	13.8	4.3
1983	397	42.4	13.0	209	27.6	8.4	23	25.4	7.8
1985	375	42.3	13.7	229	30.8	10.0	22	22.6	7.3
1992	336	41.9	14.1	271	34.4	11.5	20	17.8	6.0
1997	165	31.4	9.6	419	44.4	13.5	46	17.2	5.2

Under Liberal are included
Liberal-Social Democrat Alliance (1983–87)
and Liberal Democrats (1992 and 1997).

Third, the Conservatives enjoyed the good fortune to win two key postwar elections, those in 1951 and 1979, success in which gave the victorious party a good chance of remaining in power for a long time. These advantages were conferred in the first case by entering office at the start of the long postwar economic boom and in the second by North Sea oil reinforced by the Falklands victory (1983) and a booming economy (1987) (Seldon, 1994, p. 55; Butler and Kavanagh, 1992, p. 274). In both, the Conservatives benefited from the timing of the election, with Attlee making a tactical mistake in 1951 by calling an election despite a large Conservative lead in the polls (Morgan, 1989, p. 480), and the Commons defeat on devolution forcing Callaghan to hold an immediate election rather than deferring it for several months to the autumn, when public memories of the industrial chaos of the winter might have faded.

Fourth, the Conservative bias exhibited by the British press became more pronounced in the postwar period, and by the 1990s it was suggested that it was 'worth a swing of about 1 per cent to the Conservatives at each election' and that this formed 'a not insignificant advantage when cumulated over the long-term' (Crewe, 1993, p. 96) Finally, the Conservative Party was generally superior when it came to organisation, except in 1945, and party finances. The professionalism and expertise of its agents remained the party's greatest campaigning asset, and although their number fell from over 500 in the 1950s to 230 by the end of 1993, the Conservatives still had three times as many agents as Labour in the 1992 general election (Butler and Kavanagh, 1992, p. 272). Whilst its organisational advantage could neither prevent a landslide defeat nor generate an overwhelming victory, it could 'help to exaggerate the scale of the party's triumphs or to stem the tide of its defeats'. Thus organisational superiority made the defeats of 1966 and 1974 much less sweeping and recovery from them swifter. In elections where the result was close or unexpected, such as in 1950, 1951, 1964, 1970 and 1992, 'the outcome might have been crucially different for the Conservatives had they not had the organisational edge' (Ball, 1994, pp. 308–9). Conservative superiority in financial resources was even more pronounced, its central campaign spending in the 1983, 1987 and 1992 general elections totalling £22.7 million compared with Labour's £13.5 million and the Alliance/Liberal Democrats' £5.9 million.

A Changing Party

The main characteristics of Conservative organisation reflect its total dedication to the achievement of political power. The first dominant feature is concentration of power in the leadership in order to achieve maximum speed of response, flexibility and decisiveness. The second is the considerable discipline exhibited by the party's MPs, professional administrators and ordinary members, much of it self-imposed. Thus key appointments, including the shadow cabinet and party chairman, are in the hands of the leader, as is the determination of policy. However the loyalty the leader receives from the party is conditional upon the achievement or probable achievement of electoral success. The leader leads by consent, which can be and often has been withdrawn. 'If the leader is no good', said Churchill, 'he must be poleaxed'. A third important feature is the subordination of the party in the country to the party in parliament, the mass organisation, the National Union of Conservative Associations, having been formed in 1867 to support the parliamentary party. Against this background of certain continuities in Conservative affairs we now examine changes since 1945, focusing on four main areas.

The Conservative Leader

In the immediate postwar era a considerable social and psychological gulf separated the leader from the party. This was symbolised by the fact that the leader did not attend the party conference until he addressed it on the final day. From the mid 1960s, however, leaders were middle class rather than upper class: state-educated, first-generation achievers supplanted a leadership drawn from or closely related to the aristocracy. Symptomatic of the changing relationship between leader and led in a less deferential society was Conservative leaders' attendance at the conference for its entire duration and their deliberate cultivation of a meritocratic or populist image.

The change from a process of selection to one of election of the leader was another indication of the Conservatives' need to respond to democratic pressures. Before 1965 new leaders were appointed after various types of consultation. For example in 1957, following Eden's resignation, a consultation of the cabinet and MPs by two Tory notables showed that the majority favoured Macmillan over Butler. In 1963, when the leadership fell vacant because of Macmillan's ill-health, an unprecedentedly detailed canvass of MPs, peers and leading Conservatives outside parliament took place, designed, it seems, to favour Home and disadvantage the other candidates, especially Butler. But it backfired when Home proved unable to unite the party. Two ministers, Macleod and Powell, refused to serve, and Macleod wrote a famous critique of the selection process in *The Spectator*. The process also saddled the party with a leader who was unable to reflect the public mood of the day, which demanded economic expertise rather than an aristocratic, grouse-moor image (Bogdanor, 1994, pp. 74–80).

Accordingly, in 1965 the party adopted a new system for choosing its leader, consisting of multiple ballots of the parliamentary party (Exhibit 7.2). The provision for a possible three ballots enabled new compromise candidates to emerge if it seemed probable that the early front-runners would be incapable of securing the consent of the whole party – a particularly important consideration for a party that set such store on unity. There was also provision for the consultation of Conservative peers, the party outside parliament and, from 1990, Conservative MEPs.

"THANK GOODNESS, WE EVOLVE OUR LEADER IN OUR OWN WAY AND DON'T ELECT HIM DEMOCRATICALLY LIKE THOSE SOCIALISTS!"

Source: Vicky (Victor Weisz), *Evening Standard*, 14 October 1963

EXHIBIT 7.1   *Rules for the election of the Conservative leader from 1965*

Each candidate requires a proposer and a seconder. Since 1991, for a contest to take place, 10 per cent of the parliamentary party must write to the chairman of the 1922 Committee calling for an election.

- First ballot: to win, a candidate needs an overall majority of all Conservative MPs (1965–74, a majority only of those voting) plus a 15 per cent lead over the nearest rival. If not achieved the contest goes to a second ballot, for which new nominations are needed and new candidates may stand.
- Second ballot: to win, a candidate requires an overall majority; if not achieved, the three leading candidates go forward to a third and final ballot.
- Third ballot: unlike the first two ballots, this ballot uses a preferential procedure, in which each voter records a first and second choice. If no candidate gains an overall majority, the candidate with the fewest first-choice votes is eliminated and the second choices on his or her ballot papers are redistributed among the other two candidates. The winning candidate is presented to a party meeting consisting of Conservative MPs, peers, parliamentary candidates and members of the Executive Committee of the National Union for confirmation.

Before the balloting, soundings are taken of the views of Conservative peers, Conservative constituency associations and (from 1990) Conservative MEPs, and reported to the 1922 Committee.

Between 1975 and 1990 the rules provided for an annual election to take place within three to six months of the opening of a new parliament and after that, within 28 days of the opening of each new session. In 1991 these periods were reduced to three months and fourteen days respectively.

The system was modified twice after 1965, as new circumstances revealed flaws. Designed to operate only when a vacancy occurred, it was changed first in 1975 in order to permit a challenge to Edward Heath, who had refused to stand down after losing three out of four general elections. The new rules allowed an annual leadership election, and increased the size of the overall majority needed by the successful candidate on the first ballot from 15 per cent of the votes cast to 15 per cent of those entitled to vote. Second, the rule permitting an annual leadership election had never been intended to allow an incumbent prime minister to be challenged, as occurred in 1989 and 1990. A rule change in 1991 made such a challenge more difficult by stipulating that for an election to take place, not only must the challenger have a proposer and a seconder, but 10 per cent of the parliamentary party must write privately to the chairman of the 1922 Committee to call for an election.

The impact of the change from selection to election of the Conservative leader gave power to the majority of the parliamentary party (that is, the backbenchers) rather than the influential sections of the party, whilst the provision for an annual election increased the necessity for the leader to be sensitive to this powerful electorate (Norton, 1994, p. 112). This backbench power was seen first in 1975, when withdrawal of consent by Conservative MPs brought down Heath, and demonstrated even more forcibly in 1990, when – against the prevalent view that peacetime prime ministers were virtually immovable if they had a Commons majority, were in good health and willing to continue – Thatcher was deposed after a protracted struggle involving challenges in successive years. On both occasions the new method also enabled public opinion to be brought to bear against a leader who had lost popular support whilst retaining the backing of the party establishment, and also made it harder for 'establishment' candidates such as Whitelaw in 1975 and Hurd in 1990 to beat populist opponents (Thatcher and Major). Finally, as before the new system allowed relatively little influence to be exerted by members of the party outside parliament, who were overwhelmingly for Heath in 1975 and Thatcher in 1990 (Bogdanor, 1994, pp. 83–4, 93). Table 7.2 outlines leadership contests under the new system.

The Conservative Party in Parliament

From the 1970s, expressions of dissent and rebellion against the leadership became more frequent and involved more backbenchers. Furthermore the party became more ideological and more prone to faction-fighting.

Between 1945 and 1970 there was little overt dissent by Conservative MPs in parliament: Tory backbenchers did little more than voice disapproval or abstain. On the relatively few occasions when dissenting votes were cast, they involved only one or two MPs. The only significant rebellion in the 1959–64 parliament (overall Conservative majority, 100) was over resale price maintenance, and the government's majority dropped to one when the issue was

TABLE 7.2 *Conservative leadership contests, 1965–95*

	Ballot	Comments
1965	**First ballot** Edward Heath, 150 Reginald Maudling, 133 Enoch Powell, 15 Abstentions, 6	Home resigned and the leadership became vacant. Heath won an overall majority but not 15 per cent more of the vote than any other candidate. However Maudling and Powell withdrew so a second ballot was not necessary.
1975	**First ballot** Margaret Thatcher, 130 Edward Heath, 119 Hugh Fraser, 16 Abstentions, 11	Heath's leadership was challenged. After first ballot Heath and Fraser withdrew; Whitelaw, Prior, Howe and Peyton came forward.
	Second ballot Margaret Thatcher, 146 William Whitelaw, 79 James Prior, 19 Sir Geoffrey Howe, 19 John Peyton, 11 Abstentions, 2	Thatcher had overall majority and became leader.
1989	**First ballot** Margaret Thatcher, 314 Sir Anthony Meyer, 33 Abstentions, 27	Sir Anthony Meyer challenged the leader. Thatcher reelected as leader.
1990	**First ballot** Margaret Thatcher, 204 Michael Heseltine, 152 Abstentions, 16	Michael Heseltine challenged the leader. Thatcher had an overall majority in the first ballot but failed by four votes to achieve the 56 vote (15 per cent) margin required for victory. Therefore a second ballot was required, but after individual interviews with members of the cabinet Thatcher decided to withdraw. New candidates Major and Hurd came forward.
	Second ballot John Major, 185 Michael Heseltine, 152 Douglas Hurd, 56 Abstentions, 0	Major was only just short of an overall majority; however the other candidates withdrew and there was no third ballot. Major became leader.
1995	**First ballot** John Major, 218 John Redwood, 89 Abstentions, 20	Faced with significant criticism of his leadership within the party, Major resigned as leader. John Redwood resigned his cabinet post to run for the leadership. John Major convincingly achieved the overall majority plus the 15 per cent lead required, and remained as leader.

voted upon. However between 1970 and 1974 under Heath (majority 30) Conservative cross-voting increased dramatically: no fewer than 160 Conservative MPs cast one or more votes against the whips, and in 64 divisions, compared with a mere eight divisions between 1959 and 1964, ten or more Conservatives voted against the party whips. Conservative cross-voting brought about government defeats on six occasions, three times on a three-line whip. Even though it was a confidence vote, 15 Conservatives cross-voted and a further five abstained on the second reading of the European Communities bill (1972), leaving the government with a majority of only eight (Norton, 1995–6, pp. 108–9). This greater rebelliousness has been attributed to Heath's brusque style of leadership, notably his insistence that major legislation be passed unchanged and his unwillingness to listen to backbenchers' concerns (Norton, 1978, pp. 221–244).

Between 1979 and 1992 backbench dissent continued at similar levels to 1970–4, with approximately one fifth of all divisions witnessing dissenting votes. Whilst their large majorities generally immunised the Thatcher governments against defeat by such rebellions, they did suffer occasional defeats – for example over the tightening of the immigration rules (1982), the second reading of the Sunday Trading Bill (1986) and social security benefits for the elderly (1990). Seventy-two Conservatives voted with the opposition to defeat the Sunday Trading Bill, which was the first time in the century that a government with a working majority had been beaten on the second reading of a bill. However only 17 Conservatives cross-voted on the second reading of the Poll Tax Bill (1987) (Butler *et al.*, 1994, p. 114).

Backbench assertiveness continued under Major after 1992, and because of the government's small and diminishing majority it had to be taken more seriously. From the late 1980s, encouraged by Thatcher's populist anti-Europeanism, Europe became the central dividing issue within the party. During the drawn-out passage of the Maastricht Bill (1992–3), an alliance between Labour (generally pro-Maastricht but opposed to the Social Chapter and monetary union opt-outs) and Tory backbench rebels put the government in continuous danger of defeat and actually did produce defeat on two occasions. Later, on a vote of confidence on the European Communities (Finance) Bill (1994), eight backbench rebels had the Conservative whip withdrawn (Ludlam, 1996, pp. 98–120). Tory backbenchers also forced their views on the government with regard to pit closures (1992), the extension of VAT to domestic fuel (1994) and post office privatisation (1995), and helped press several ministers, including the chancellor of the exchequer, Norman Lamont, into resigning (Riddell, 1994, pp. 53–5).

The party's lack of ideological cohesion, from which in large part flowed its increasing divisions, dated from Margaret Thatcher's election as leader in 1975 (Seldon, 1994, p. 42). Ideological divisions proliferated in the 1980s and 1990s and the party that had traditionally been perceived as one of 'tendencies' rather than factions moved towards factionalisation, especially on Europe and the role of government. The more intense struggle within the party was marked by a large increase in the number of party groups. Between 1945 and 1975 a mere handful of groups existed, the main ones being One Nation (1950), the Bow Group (1951), the Monday Club (1961), the Selsdon Group (1973) and the Tory Reform Group (1975). During the 1980s and 1990s, as divisions opened up over the Thatcher legacy and Europe, new groups appeared. Thus No Turning Back (1985), Conservative Way Forward (1991), the Bruges Group (1988) and the 92 Group emerged on the neo-liberal Thatcherite right of the party and were opposed by the Lollards and other groups on the left, wet or damp wing of the party. To one academic this ideological in-fighting was nothing new since 'factionalism has been endemic in the party' (Barnes, 1994, p. 343). But it is doubtful whether the postwar party was ever so divided as it became after 1975, and especially in the late 1980s and 1990s.

Conservative Ideology

Conservative ideology went through two major phases between the 1940s and 1990s, with the dominant tendency in each phase representing one aspect of the dual Conservative tradition of collectivism and libertarianism (Greenleaf, 1973). The progressive right gained the ascendancy soon after the war and remained dominant until the mid 1970s. The 'new conservatism' of this phase, also described as 'one nation conservatism', 'progressive conservatism', Tory paternalism and liberal conservatism, believed in government intervention in the economy and the welfare state. Its leading exponents were R. A. Butler and Harold Macmillan and the Industrial Charter (1947) was the main policy document, which embodied, in Butler's words, Conservative accommodation to the 'major social revolution' implemented by the coalition and Labour governments. Progressive conservatism repudiated *laissez faire* economics and accepted the maintenance of full employment and the social services, the need for strategic control of the economy by government, and the irreversibility of key nationalisations such as coal, the railways and the Bank of England (Macmillan, 1969, cited in O'Gorman, 1986, p. 204). One-nation Tories also accepted that trade unions played an important role in the economy.

However progressive conservatism did contain a libertarian element. For Butler, a second purpose of the Industrial Charter was 'to present a recognizeable alternative to the reigning orthodoxies of Socialism'. Accordingly the collectivist theme of contemporary Conservative policy statements was balanced by a liberal emphasis, stressing the importance of the role of individual initiative and private enterprise in the mixed and managed economy. Progressive Conservatives also favoured some denationalisation where practicable, and encouraged a high level of personal savings and voluntary alongside state provision of welfare. They believed in private property, the maintenance of capitalism and equality of opportunity rather than social equality (levelling up rather than levelling down). As Smith and Ludlam point out, progressive conservatism was a 'very historically specific' attempt to combine acceptance of the new statist social and economic policies with elements of traditional conservativism, a pragmatic adaptation to changed circumstances in order to prove the party's fitness to rule (Smith and Ludlam, 1996, p. 8; O'Gorman, 1986, pp. 47–52; Barnes, 1994, pp. 330–35; Eccleshall, 1984, pp. 104–7; Willetts, 1992, pp. 37–8).

Two subordinate Conservative ideologies during the phase in which progressive conservatism was dominant were nationalism/neo-imperialism and neo-liberalism. Both tendencies were to be found in the ideas of Enoch Powell. The main focus for the discontent of the neo-imperialist old right in the 1950s and 1960s was the speed of decolonisation and immigration from the Commonwealth. However it was defeated on all the issues it contested at the time, including decolonisation, withdrawal from Suez, sanctions against the white regime in Rhodesia, entry into Europe and stronger support for the Northern Ireland Protestants (Seldon, 1991, p. 253). But the nationalist preoccupation with the assertion of British power in the world, the defence of British sovereignty and the preservation of traditional moral standards resurfaced powerfully in Thatcherism in the 1980s.

Neo-liberal economics was subordinate in old-right thinking, but in Powellism belief in free enterprise had equal status with a vigorously expressed patriotism. Although originally associated with progressive conservatism, in the 1960s Powell began to advocate free market economics and oppose interventionist government. For him, as for Friedrich von Hayek, the mentor of other postwar, neo-liberal Conservatives, economic freedom was organically linked to political freedom and a free way of life, but it was his populist nationalism that attracted attention in the late 1960s and early 1970s. Powell believed that, with the ending of the empire, Britain needed to protect its national identity by cherishing its own unique institutions and traditions. From this basic position flowed all his characteristic political interventions, including his emotional call for the repatriation of black and other Commonwealth immigrants in his 1968 'River of blood' speech and his vehement opposition to Britain joining the Common Market, the latter in the name of the sovereignty of parliament.

Conservative one-nation ideology enjoyed its last phase of postwar dominance under Edward Heath. Controversy has since arisen, however, over Heath's real ideology because of the apparent contrast between the neo-liberal Heath of 1965–72, whose policies seemingly contrasted with progressive conservatism, and the one-nation Heath of 1972–4, who conducted a policy U-turn by reverting to economic interventionism. One interpretation sees Heath in his first 'Selsdon man' phase as a genuine forerunner of Thatcher's neo-liberalism, committed to reversing the postwar consensus in all aspects except the welfare state and prevented only by a loss of nerve in

1972 from accomplishing his intentions (Blake, 1985, pp. 300–1; Seldon, 1991, pp. 245–6; Willetts, 1992, pp. 42–4). For others, Heath's commitment to full employment and the welfare state, and his liberal views on immigration and capital punishment place him in the one-nation tradition, within which he was primarily a technocrat whose dominating ideas were a strongly felt Europeanism and reform of Britain's institutions and industrial relations along rational lines (Dunleavy, 1993, p. 128). According to this view, rather than 'a dogmatic attachment to free market economics', his 'Selsdon Man' project represented 'a pragmatic attempt to modernise the British economy', in which neoliberal policies were dropped as soon as they seemed not to be working (Campbell, 1993, cited in Ludlam and Smith, 1996, p. 9; Dorey, 1995, p. 114; Garner and Kelly, 1993, pp. 85–6; Pugh, 1994, p. 288).

Under Margaret Thatcher the progressive one-nation Toryism that had supported the centrist postwar consensus was repudiated and the neo-liberal new right achieved ideological supremacy. For each tenet of progressive, consensual conservatism the new right proposed a libertarian alternative, advocating the control of inflation rather than the maintenance of full employment, the free market instead of the mixed economy, the reduction of union power and the liberalisation of the labour market against corporatist economic management and privileged unions, a limited state rather than a welfare state with high public expenditure, and a reversal of the modest egalitarianism of postwar fiscal policy in favour of the incentive effect of reducing the burden of direct taxation (see Chapters 2, 9, 10 and 12). The main idea underlying neo-liberal new right thinking on social and economic issues was that individuals making rational choices in free markets always produce superior results to collective solutions applied by the state. Market liberalism of this kind constituted the heart of Thatcherism (Dunleavy, 1993, p. 128). But Thatcherism also contained more traditional Conservative concerns such as a firm belief in the conventional two-parent family, a commitment to the reassertion of law and order, strong discipline and respect for authority, and a concern to maintain the integrity of the British state against devolutionists and regain its former former high world standing. Table 7.3 compares progressive and Thatcherite conservatism.

Party Organisation and Membership

Several significant changes were made in party organisation between 1945 and 1995. First, after the wartime decline of the party's popularity, culminating in the electoral disaster of 1945, far-reaching reforms of the constituency associations encouraged a massive increase in membership and stimulated the party to far exceed its main rivals in raising small political donations at the local level. Party membership declined after the 1950s but still remained larger than Labour's. Moreover, although Conservative associations in the 1980s played a smaller role in their local communities than thirty years

TABLE 7.3 *Progressive and Thatcherite conservatism*

	Progressive	Thatcherite
Change	Gradual	Rapid
Economy	Mixed	Free Market
State	Interventionist	Limited
Trade unions	Legitimate/constructive	Undemocratic/destructive
Welfare State	Universal right	Safety net
Morality	Liberal/social obligation	Conservative/private self-help
Europe	Integration/pool sovereignty	Assert independence/preserve sovereignty
Civil society	Pluralistic	Individualistic

Sources: derived from Smith and Ludlam, 1996, p. 12 and Smith, 1995, p. 2.

earlier, they were not necessarily any less effective politically or any less able to get out the Tory vote (Ball, 1994, p. 265).

Second, there were important developments in the central party organisation. First, until the 1970s Conservative policy making relied heavily on the Conservative Research Department (established in 1929), but from Thatcher's time the leadership turned increasingly for policy advice to agencies outside the party organisation such as the Centre for Policy Studies, the Adam Smith Institute and the Institute for Economic Affairs. Second, although the party continued to raise and spend more than its political rivals, finance became a difficult problem from the 1980s, with weak financial control leading to the emergence of a £19 million debt in 1993 and, as local fundraising declined, increasing dependence on donations from companies and wealthy individuals. Also, the sources of its funding became more politically sensitive in the 1980s as the party launched a legislative attack on the basis of Labour Party funds whilst continuing to refuse to publish its own accounts.

What model of power best describes the Conservative Party organisation? Writing in 1955 the political scientist R. T. McKenzie found in the top-down structure of the Conservative Party 'a tight-knit system of oligarchical control' (McKenzie, 1964, p. 291). He was particularly impressed by 'the enormous power which appears to be concentrated in the hands of the Leader' (ibid., p. 21). This power, he noted, ran through the party: the leader appointed his cabinet and even shadow cabinet colleagues, had 'the ultimate responsibility for policy' and, because of his appointment of the party chairman, the central office was in effect the leader's 'personal machine'. The absence in the party of 'any sense of formal accountability of the leadership to the individual members' and its organisation upon 'the historic values of hierarchy and deference' was underlined in the 1990s (Seyd and Whiteley, 1996, p. 68). This lack of a formal system of internal accountability is a valid description of the party's mode of operation throughout its entire history, not just of the postwar period. It was to campaign for greater formal accountability and more internal democracy that the Charter Movement (1981) was formed, its demands including the election of the party chairman, control of conference agendas and debates by an elected committee, and publication of party accounts. However, despite the absence of constitutional provision for internal accountability and democracy, it has been argued that the party structure is better described by models of power that allow for the diffusion of influence, however limited, than by simple command–obedience ones. Alternatives include a 'baronial' model (Rose, 1974, p. 214) and, because the leader–led relationship is 'one of mutual confidence and constant two-way communication', a 'family' model (Norton and Aughey, 1981, pp. 241–2). In addition to the constant dialogue between leaders and close associates, advocates of such models have been impressed by the vulnerability of leaders to challengers (especially since 1965), imperviousness to central advice of local associations and the occasional evidence of policy influence by the main conference and its linked area and functional meetings (Garner and Kelly, 1993, p. 114; Kelly, 1994, p. 256; cf. Seyd and Whiteley, 1996, pp. 67–8). The phrase 'autocracy tempered by consent' may be the most apt description of a party whose internal affairs became more turbulent, divided and ideological in the postwar period.

The Labour Party

In contrast to its main rival, the Labour Party enjoyed much less success, winning only six of the fourteen general elections and forming the government for a mere 17 of the 52 years between 1945 and 1997. Moreover Labour held office with a sizeable majority on only two occasions (1945–50 and 1966–70), ruling with tiny majorities for five years and as a minority government for two years. Second, whereas both major parties' share of the vote declined after 1970, the fall in the Labour vote over the subsequent six elections was more marked. While its average share of the vote between 1945 and 1970 was slightly ahead of the Conservatives at 46.05 per cent compared with 45.25 per cent, its average vote between February 1974 and 1992 dropped to a mere 34.3 per cent, compared with the Conservatives' 40.06 per cent. Between its postwar peak in 1951 and 1992, Labour's vote fell by 2.4 million. An important concern of recent historians has been to explain this 'strange death of Labour Britain' (Jefferys, 1993, p. 134).

Explanations of Labour's decline can be grouped into the long-term structural and the short-term contingent. The structural explanation focuses on the way class and sectoral trends operated against Labour. The contraction of the working class and trade unionism and the expansion of the middle class and of the home-owning sector resulted in an approximate 6 per cent reduction of the Labour vote and an increase in the Conservative vote by about 4 per cent between 1964 and 1987 (Crewe, 1993, pp. 103–4). The social class effect was reinforced by a changing economic geography in the 1980s.

With the south-east enjoying a prolonged boom and the north sunk in recession, skilled workers in the south-east became more likely than in the 1970s to vote Conservative and Labour was 'driven back to its Northern redoubts' (Pattie and Johnston, 1996, p. 51). Among the new working class living in the south, the Conservatives enjoyed a 46 per cent to 28 per cent lead over Labour in 1987. Labour remained dominant over Conservative only in the traditional working class of the north of England and Scotland, which voted 57 per cent to 29 per cent in its favour (*Guardian*, 15 June 1987).

The contingent explanation relates to public perceptions of the party's behaviour in office and its internal divisions. Whereas the Attlee governments were adjudged a success by Labour supporters, the record of the Wilson and Callaghan governments proved disappointing to them, especially to those on the party left (see pp. 182–4). Already handicapped by adverse judgements of its record in office, Labour's failure between 1979 and 1992 also rested on perceptions of its disunity, fostered by its 1981 split and the bitter internal warfare of the early 1980s. Underlying these political weaknesses was Labour's ideological failure to evolve a new version of its social democratic creed in line with the changed realities of British society (Jefferys, 1993, pp. 130–5). By 1979 the social democratic dream of constant increments of social welfare based on steady economic growth was in eclipse. 'The road to Jerusalem, it seemed was not open after all; perhaps it did not even exist. History had turned traitor. The left and centre were no longer in the van of political change' (Marquand, 1991, p. 158)

Party Leadership, Organisation and Ideology

The historical origins and evolution of the Labour Party until 1940 provide significant clues to post-1945 developments. First, unlike the Conservative Party, the Labour Party originated outside parliament when certain trade unions and Socialist societies decided to sponsor working men candidates for parliament, and the numerical and financial backing of affiliated trade unions remained the party's central feature. Second, Labour is a pluralist – or confederalist – party in which power is divided between the conference, the National Executive Committee (NEC), constituency Labour Parties (CLPs), the parliamentary Labour Party (PLP), the shadow cabinet and the leader. Its extra-parliamentary origin combined with its pluralist constitution made the relationship between the parliamentary leadership and the extraparliamentary party problematic from the first few decades. Whereas the 1918 constitution appeared to make the conference sovereign by according it 'direction and control of the work of the party', the PLP, in conformity with the norms of the parliamentary system that MPs are accountable solely to the electorate, developed a considerable measure of independence from the extra-parliamentary party. In practice the leadership was able to establish command over the party because of 'a pattern of institutional interlock' that bound together the main centres of power: the PLP, the NEC and the majority of the unions (Shaw, 1996, p. 17). Leading Labour MPs were usually the most influential members of the NEC and conference decisions were determined by the block votes of unions sympathetic to the party leadership. However the ideal of intraparty democracy remained powerful and capable of inspiring a considerable minority of the mass membership that resented its lack of control of the PLP (McKenzie, 1964, pp. 396, 407). Third, these internal tensions were exacerbated by ideology, with the party adopting a socialist objective in its 1918 constitution (clause 4) that committed it to the public ownership of the means of production, distribution and exchange.

Post-1945 the social democratic wing of the party adopted fully fledged Keynesianism whilst the left remained committed to public ownership, thereby setting the scene for the left–right struggle that became a leading feature of party history after 1945. Until the 1970s disagreements focused mainly on ideology, and on organisation and ideology after that. Broadly, the right were in the ascendant for the bulk of the postwar period, either as 'consolidators' (1948–56) revisionists (1956 to the 1970s) or modernisers (mid 1980s to the present); while the left, whose influence grew in both the PLP and the extraparliamentary organisation during the 1970s, achieved a brief supremacy in the aftermath of the 1979 election defeat. Underlying the coexistence in one party of two such distinct segments of opinion is the single-member, simple-plurality electoral system, which encourages parties to be broad coalitions. By marginalising the parties of the centre (Liberals/ Social Democrats/Liberal Democrats) and far left (Communists), the British electoral system forced Labour to live with both a left pledged to fundamental change and a right concerned to offer a viable reforming alternative to the Conservatives. In a more proportional system the two wings might have split into two different parties, but in Britain this proved impossible, as shown by the failure of the Social Democratic Party, composed largely of former Labour right wingers, in the 1980s (Ceadel, 1991, pp. 263–4). The party's internal differences forced Labour leaders to place a heavy emphasis on party management.

Party Concord, 1945–50

The first reason for the comparative harmony of this period was the party's sweeping electoral victory in 1945 and the Attlee government's record of reform. With minor revolts on the American loan (1945) and the inadequacy of maintenance allowances for the sick and unemployed in the National Insurance Bill (1946), plus some dissatisfaction over the failure to advance comprehensive education, dissent did occur in the PLP, but usually on too small a scale to embarrass the leadership. More serious dissent involving pacifists, pro-Soviet fellow travellers and anticommunist left wingers such as

Michael Foot and Richard Crossman surfaced over the pro-American bias of Labour foreign policy. Foot and Crossman helped form the 'Keep Left' group of 15 MPs in 1947 to press for a new foreign policy based on the creation of a neutral third force between the superpowers, but the group had largely broken up by 1949, by which date several far-left, pro-Soviet MPs had been expelled from the party.

Organisational reasons for party accord included, first, the steady support the government received from the trade unions. In part this derived from the real community of outlook shared by the political and industrial wings of the movement; in part from the immense authority throughout the movement possessed by Ernest Bevin, foreign secretary and former leader of the Transport Workers; and in part from its endorsement by the 'big three' union leaders, Arthur Deakin (Transport Workers), Tom Williamson (General and Municipal Workers) and Will Lawther (Mineworkers), all of whom were politically right-wing and strongly anti-communist. Second, Herbert Morrison, the leader of the house, took vital steps to ensure good relations between cabinet and backbenchers, such as setting up a liaison committee between backbenchers and cabinet and suspending standing orders to encourage tolerance and self-discipline within the PLP. Third, close control of the party organisation was maintained by Morgan Phillips, who has been described as 'the most authoritative general secretary Labour had known since the early days of Arthur Henderson in 1911' (Morgan, 1985, pp. 51, 59–81).

The Revolt of the Bevanites, 1950–7

Serious left–right disagreement first surfaced over public ownership. From about 1948, when most of the manifesto had been implemented, Labour faced a decision over what to do next. Morrison, on the party right, campaigned for 'consolidation' rather than further radical reforms such as further nationalisation, which might offend the middle classes. But while the Bevanites on the left saw public ownership as transferring 'the mainsprings of economic power' to the whole community, and believed that a willingness to extend it on a significant scale was a symbol of the party's continuing socialist commitment. However Morrison's view caught the party mood, and although the 1950 manifesto contained the famous 'shopping list' of nationalisation proposals (cement, water supply, meat wholesaling, sugar refining), these promises were dropped in the 1951 manifesto, which offered only a vague commitment to create new public enterprises when this served the public interest.

The left acquired its front-ranking leader Aneuran Bevan as a result of a major cabinet dispute: following a massive increase in the defence budget triggered by the Korean War, Bevan as health minister clashed with the chancellor of the exchequer, Hugh Gaitskell, over his proposal to introduce charges on optical services and dentures. Having lost the battle in cabinet, Bevan resigned both over the departure from the principle of a free national health service and out of disagreement with the huge rearmament programme, which he regarded as unjustified by the circumstances and potentially damaging to the economy. Bevan's move to the backbenches gave the left a leading socialist as spokesman and revitalised the old 'Keep Left' group, which quickly expanded into a force of about 40 Bevanites. According to Gaitskell, 'a fight for the soul of the Labour Party' had begun.

Neither the 'consolidators' nor the Bevanites had a new or a particularly coherent ideology on domestic affairs. As in the late 1940s, the main left-wing targets in the early 1950s were defence and foreign policy issues such as national service, German rearmament and nuclear weapons (Jefferys, 1993, p. 40). Although the Bevanites were no more than a severe irritant, the leadership, strongly backed by the trade unions, clamped down, imposing a formal ban on unofficial groups in the PLP and reviving standing orders, which meant that MPs could receive the party whip only if they stood by the majority decisions of the PLP. In 1955, after attacking Attlee in a defence debate, Bevan narrowly escaped expulsion from the party. A strong undercurrent in the left–right struggle in these years was the personal rivalry between Bevan and Gaitskell, which was finally resolved in 1955 when Gaitskell defeated his rival for the leadership after Attlee's resignation (Table 7.4).

TABLE 7.4 *Labour leadership contests 1955–80*

Year	Candidate	Votes	Year	Candidate	Votes
1955	H. Gaitskell	157	1976		
	A. Bevan	70	**First ballot**	J. Callaghan	84
	H. Morrison	40		M. Foot	90
				R. Jenkins	56
1960	H. Gaitskell	166		T. Benn	37
	H. Wilson	88		D. Healey	30
				A. Crosland	17
1961	H. Gaitskell	171			
	A. Greenwood	59	**Second ballot**	J. Callaghan	141
				M. Foot	133
1963				D. Healey	38
First ballot	H. Wilson	115			
	G. Brown	88	**Third ballot**	J. Callaghan	176
	J. Callaghan	41		M. Foot	137
			1980		
Second ballot	H. Wilson	144	**First ballot**	M. Foot	83
	G. Brown	103		D. Healey	112
				J. Silkin	38
				P. Shore	32
			Second ballot	M. Foot	139
				D. Healey	129

The Revisionist Ascendancy, 1957–70

The ascendancy of the Labour right continued, and a new revisionist ideology, which redefined socialism as social democracy, replaced the rather negative doctrine of 'consolidation' (Marquand, 1991, p. 120). This philosophy, which guided the policies of Labour governments for the next two decades, was formulated by Anthony Crosland in *The Future of Socialism* (1956). Crosland argued that, as postwar management by the state and industry had solved the major economic problems by delivering economic growth with full employment, socialists should concentrate on the ethical goal of achieving a more equal society by such means as redistributive taxation, comprehensive education and improvements in health and housing through high levels of public expenditure. The Bevanites posed little intellectual challenge to the new doctrine.

The Bevanites' political challenge soon faded also, as Bevan, made shadow foreign secretary by Gaitskell, helped the leadership defeat calls at the 1957 conference for unilateral nuclear disarmament. He claimed that unilateral abandonment of the H-bomb would be tantamount to sending a British foreign secretary 'naked into the conference chamber' and would constitute not statesmanship but 'an emotional spasm'. The same conference also saw the defeat of the left on domestic policy, with the party abandoning all but a commitment to renationalise steel and road haulage.

However left–right conflict flared up again after the 1959 general election defeat, when Gaitskell's proposal to remove Clause 4 from the party constitution provoked passionate opposition. In his view the commitment to public ownership gave a misleading impression of the party's intentions and was exploitable by the Conservatives for electoral purposes. A fervent revisionist, he believed that public ownership was only one of many means of reaching the socialist goal and did not warrant its privileged position in the party constitution. But Gaitskell's move foundered on the combined opposition of the left and the unions, for whom Clause 4 was a vital expression of the party's socialism (Drucker, 1979, pp. 44–53).

The 1960 conference brought another defeat for the leadership when a unilateralist position gained majority assent, a key factor being the emergence of a left winger, Frank Cousins, as general secretary of the Transport Workers Union. With Gaitskell vowing 'to fight and fight and fight again' to reverse the vote, the right mobilised the constituencies and unions and overturned the decision at the 1961 conference. The long-term consequence of the leadership's victory was to shatter 'the psychological bonds of the traditional view of Conference authority' (Minkin, 1978, p. 287). In the short term Gaitskell, backed by the Bevanites, whose own leader had died in 1960, faced and overcame a leadership challenge by Harold Wilson, who stood on a unity platform against the divisiveness of Gaitskell's leadership. However within two years, after Gaitskell's unexpected death, Wilson, who overlaid revisionism with scientific rhetoric to attract the middle class whilst drawing upon his leftist background to appeal to Labour traditionalists, had become leader (Table 7.4).

But the social democrat/socialist tensions within Labour had been shelved rather than resolved and conflict between the two traditions erupted again in the late 1960s, when dissent increased at all levels of the party. In parliament 20 or more Labour MPs voted against the party line on 31 occasions, although on only one of these occasions did Labour backbenchers enter a whipped opposition lobby (Norton, 1995/6, p. 108). Meanwhile, as the government made significant departures from its manifesto, its policies were repudiated with increasing frequency by the Labour Party conference (Shaw, 1996, p. 108). Wilson's large majority enabled him to shrug off dissent in parliament, and when faced by conference defeats he insisted that 'the Government must govern'. But he was forced to back down on trade union reform by vigorous opposition from Labour backbenchers (57 voted against the white paper 'In Place of Strife', with 30 more abstaining), the trade unions and the cabinet minister James Callaghan. By 1970, when Wilson insisted on placing his own personal stamp on the manifesto, the circumstances that had sustained the revisionist leadership against the rest of the party had almost disappeared. The grip of a solid block of right-wing unions had been broken by the rise of a powerful left within the unions that was able to command 30 per cent of the conference vote; and rank and file trust in the leadership, which had given leaders much latitude in managing the Conference agenda, was in decline.

The Right in Retreat, 1970–9

This phase saw the right in steady retreat but just retaining control (through its exercise of the prerogatives of government and the last-minute fiat of the leader) over the increasingly left-influenced manifesto. However revisionism lost credibility as a philosophy of government (Crosland, 1974), being undermined by the inability of Labour governments in the 1960s to achieve the high economic growth that was necessary to justify redistributive taxation and high levels of public spending. The revisionists had failed to give sufficient attention to the mechanisms of growth and the likelihood of external constraints, and revisionist-led governments had prioritised the balance of payments and defence of an unrealistic exchange rate above economic growth. By 1974 Labour had become 'a party without a doctrine', and the 1974–9 Labour governments stood at best for 'a kind of mitigated monetarism; for a slow, reluctant and humane retreat from post-war Keynesianism as opposed to a fast, enthusiastic and callous one' (Marquand, 1991, pp. 172–3, 199). Many Labour right-wingers became increasingly alienated from the party. The right was also divided over Europe, with Roy Jenkins, the shadow chancellor, resigning in 1972 over Wilson's decision to renegotiate Heath's terms of entry and call a referendum on British membership of the EEC in order to hold the party together.

Second, inspired by Tony Benn and assisted by the right's apathetic attitude to work on key NEC subcommittees, the left gained substantive control over policy. It largely shaped the NEC document *Labour's Programme 1973*, which proposed large-scale state intervention in industry through planning agreements and a National Enterprise Board, as well as the nationalisation of a leading firm in 25 industrial sectors. Wilson vetoed the nationalisation proposal, but Labour's February 1974 manifesto was still its most radical since the war. The left had pushed through these policies despite the lack of an overall majority on the NEC or at conference, largely because of the aid of right-wing anti-Marketeers. In order to contain the left's advance, the leadership was reduced to a desperate strategy of toning down what it considered the most damaging policies, employing the referendum tactic to hold the party together over Europe, and, in government, using the excuse of its narrow majority or lack of majority to avoid implementing the remaining left-inspired commitments.

Because of what it perceived as leadership sabotage of socialist manifesto commitments, the left pressed for organisational changes designed to subordinate the PLP and leadership to extraparliamentary activists. The Campaign for Labour Party Democracy (CLPD) was founded in 1973 to coordinate constituency and trade union activists behind demands for mandatory reselection of MPs, election of the leader by all sections of the party, not just MPs, and NEC control of the manifesto, then normally decided by a joint clause-5 meeting of the shadow cabinet and the NEC. The abolition in 1973 of the list of proscribed organisations by the NEC facilitated far left infiltration of run-down constituency Labour Parties (CLPs).

However, with Labour in government again from 1974, the left suffered defeats over the EEC referendum vote and the ousting of Benn from the Department of Industry, thereby ending its hope of a key role for the National Enterprise Board. After Wilson's unexpected resignation as PM in 1976, neither of the left-wing candidates, Foot and Benn, was able to defeat Callaghan in the leadership contest (Table 7.4). Nonetheless the large tax increases and spending cuts of 1975, followed by the even greater disappointment of the 1976 IMF-imposed package (involving large cuts in public expenditure), finally shattered the credibility of the revisionist right. The 1974–9 Labour governments' not unsuccessful struggles with a poor economic inheritance and early legislation benefiting disadvantaged groups were soon forgotten as the left sought reforms of the party constitution that would ensure that 'Socialism' was never 'betrayed' again. The cuts in real wages and social spending, failure to reduce unemployment, the shift to monetarism, leadership elimination of left-wing proposals in the 1979 manifesto and electoral defeat in 1979 left a bitter legacy in the party.

The Dominance of the Left, 1979–87

The left used its ascendancy to drive through radical constitutional and policy changes. Left strongholds in parliament were an expanded Tribune Group and the hard left Campaign Group (1982) whilst leading left-wing groups outside parliament were the Labour Coordinating Committee (1978), the Rank-and-File Mobilising Committee (1980) and the CLPD. Between 1979 and 1981 the Labour Party conference assented to broadening the system for election of the leader and the mandatory reselection of MPs, but not NEC control of the manifesto. A special conference at Wembley in 1981 decided the rules for election of the leader based on an electoral college divided 40 per cent trade unions, 30 per cent PLP and 30 per cent CLPs. Callaghan resigned the leadership in 1980 in the hope that the leading right-winger, Denis Healey, would be elected leader by the old system before an electoral college was introduced. But Foot won, having gained the support of many right-wingers, in part on the ground that he was more likely to hold the party together than his abrasive opponent. Eight MPs were deselected by the new reselection procedure, and several of those in danger of deselection joined the SDP.

The 1980 conference adopted a raft of left-wing policies such as nuclear disarmament, withdrawal from the EEC, and the alternative economic strategy. Underlying left-wing economic policy was the theory propounded by technocratic socialist Stuart Holland that the growth of the large multi-national companies invalidated Keynesian economics because such world companies could not be controlled by the nation-state. They could frustrate its fiscal policies by declaring their profits in low-tax countries, and because their investment decisions were taken over a long time scale they were impervious to national governments' short-term efforts to stimulate their economies by Keynesian 'pump-priming'. The optimum answer, therefore, was a socialist economy based on planning, large-scale public ownership, import controls and industrial democracy (Marquand, 1991, p. 199).

After virtually becoming two parties, social democrat and socialist, the party suffered its worst split for fifty years in 1981, when the 'Gang of Three' seceded to form the SDP and were soon joined by other Labour right-wingers (see pp. 190–1). Next Benn challenged Healey for the deputy leadership, the contest provoking a further embitterment of internal relationships and ending in victory for Healey by the extremely narrow margin of less than 1 per cent, largely because of abstentions by some soft-left MPs (Shaw, 1996, p. 165).

With the unions now concerned about the damaging internal feuding, the leadership began to fight back in 1982, defeating proposals for NEC control of the manifesto and beginning moves to expel members of the Trotskyite Militant Tendency from the party. But despite a right-wing majority, the clause 5 shadow cabinet–NEC meeting agreed a very left-wing manifesto, which was dubbed 'the longest suicide note in history' by the single dissentient, Peter Shore. After Labour's worst electoral defeat since 1931 Foot resigned, and Neil Kinnock, from the party's soft left, decisively defeated Roy Hattersley of the centre right for the leadership under the new rules (Table 7.5). Kinnock immediately began the task of modernising the party, calling for a new revisionism. This meant destroying Bennism, moving the party ideologically to the centre or centre left by acquiring a more individualist and less collectivist philosophy, and distancing Labour from its past by forcing it to shed its outworn cloth-cap image and its association with declining groups and regions.

This process was far from complete by 1987. Initially Kinnock lacked a power base. Left influence remained strong in the NEC, the unions and local government, where powerful left-wing leaders engaged in 'non-compliance' with Conservative 'rate-capping' in 1984 by refusing to set a rate. On non-compliance and the miners' strike (1984–5) Kinnock had to stand to the side, but he subsequently benefited from the failure of both these left-inspired episodes. Meanwhile he continued the drive to eject the members of Militant Tendency and also persuaded the party to drop its opposition to council house sales, modify its support for nationalisation in favour of the vaguer social ownership, and accept British membership of the EC. But Labour's continuing unilateralist commitment and public spending commitments were exploited by the Conservatives at the 1987 general election.

The Emergence of New Labour, 1987–95

This phase saw the triumph of the modernising leadership under Neil Kinnock, John Smith and Tony Blair. Labour revisionism was shaped by four main factors: the recasting of British social and economic policy by Thatcherism, which shifted the centre ground of politics sharply to the right; the party's need to dissociate itself from its own failures in government in the 1970s; opinion poll surveys that helped identify the changes required if the party were to appeal to new social groups; and changes in global economic conditions. Sweeping changes in ideology and organisation were needed.

Labour's ideological reorientation involved, first, the downgrading of nationalisation, culminating in 1995 when Blair persuaded the party to abandon its Clause 4 public ownership commitment in favour of a new clause making less specific pledges. Second, Labour repudiated its former Keynesian belief that government could promote growth and employment by demand management, and adopted a more modest role for government: controlling inflation and seeking supply-side improvements in education and training. It was assumed that changing global circumstances, including the removal of exchange and other capital controls, the huge growth in speculative currency flows and the vastly increased power of international financial markets, made 'Keynesianism in one country' no longer feasible

TABLE 7.5 *Labour leadership contests under the elctoral college, 1981–94*

	TU	CLP	PLP	Total
Leader				
1983				
N. Kinnock	29.04	27.45	14.77	71.27
R. Hattersley	10.87	0.57	7.83	19.28
E. Heffer	0.04	1.97	4.28	6.32
P. Shore	0.03	0.0	3.10	3.13
1988*				
N. Kinnock	38.96	24.36	24.90	88.64
T. Benn	1.04	5.64	5.10	11.76
1992				
J. Smith	38.51	29.31	23.16	91.02
B. Gould	1.48	0.69	6.82	8.98
Deputy Leader				
1981*				
First ballot				
D. Healey	24.69	5.36	15.30	45.36
T. Benn	6.41	23.48	6.37	36.64
J. Silkin	8.09	1.15	7.95	18.00
Second ballot				
D. Healey	24.99	5.67	19.75	50.43
T. Benn	15.00	24.32	10.24	49.57
1983				
R. Hattersley	35.23	15.31	16.71	67.26
M. Meacher	4.73	14.35	8.80	27.88
D. Davies	0.00	0.24	3.28	3.54
G. Dunwoody	0.03	0.09	1.19	1.32
1988*				
R. Hattersley	29.20	13.8	22.80	66.8
J. Prescott	12.70	8.4	2.60	23.7
E. Heffer	0.07	7.2	2.30	9.5
1992				
M. Beckett	0.00	0.00	0.00	0.00
J. Prescott	0.00	0.00	0.00	0.00
B. Gould	0.00	0.00	0.00	0.00
Leader				
1994				
T. Blair	52.30	58.20	60.50	57.00
J. Prescott	28.40	24.40	19.60	24.10
M. Beckett	19.30	17.40	19.90	18.90
Deputy leader				
J. Prescott	56.60	59.40	53.70	56.50
M. Beckett	43.40	40.60	46.30	43.50

* denotes challenge to incumbent. The electoral college gave trade unions 40 per cent and CLPs and the PLP 30 per cent each between 1983 and 1992, but thereafter one third of the votes to each section.

(Shaw, 1996, pp. 201–2, 223–4). Third, the party dropped its traditional 'tax, spend and borrow' policy in favour of firm control of public spending and minimal pledges that were limited to what could be financed by economic growth and higher taxes on the wealthy. The New Labour view was that, as a net cost to the economy, social spending should not be funded by borrowing nor, for both electoral and economic reasons, could it be paid for by increased taxes. Together with Labour's acceptance of many Thatcherite reforms in health and education, this marked a displacement of the welfare state from its former central role in the party's ideology. Fourth, anxious to demonstrate that it was not in hock to the unions, Labour moved away from its pre-1987 commitment to repeal Conservative trade union legislation, combining acceptance of most of the new labour code with advocacy of social partnership and support for statutory rights for individual workers embodied in the the EU Social Chapter (Shaw, 1996, p. 187; Rosamund, 1996, p. 198). Finally, electoral defeat in 1987 cleared the way to the party's abandonment of unilateralism in favour of a multilateralist position accepting Britain's possession of nuclear weapons.

On party organisation, in order to achieve maximum strategic flexibility the leadership first aimed to concentrate power in itself by stripping power and influence from the NEC and the conference. Second, for electoral reasons it sought to reduce the role of the trade unions at all levels of the party. Usefully for the leadership, this aim fitted in with the unions' wish from about 1985 to return to a more traditional relationship with the party, in which politics was left to the parliamentary wing and the unions confined themselves to industrial matters (Marsh, 1992, p. 162).

These goals involved reversing the left-inspired constitutional changes of the early 1980s. The general tactic employed by the leadership was to empower the entire party membership, considered moderate in opinion, against party activists. By 1995 the following changes had been agreed:

- Abandonment of the mandatory reselection of MPs (1992), and adoption of one member one vote (OMOV) in reselection by CLPs (1993).
- Electoral college reform, with OMOV introduced in the CLP section (1988). The union share was reduced to one third and the shares of the PLP (and from 1988 MEPs) and CLPs increased slightly to one third each (1993). Instead of block voting the unions were required to ballot all Labour-supporting political levy-payers in their section (1993).
- Conference: the voting power of the unions was reduced from 90 per cent to 70 per cent (1991), with plans for a further reduction to 50 per cent, and the unions were required to divide their votes among their delegations rather than cast them as a block. The CLPs were required to ballot their members in voting for their section of the NEC (1993).
- Manifesto: final authority remained with the Clause 5 shadow cabinet– NEC joint meeting, but the leadership downgraded the role of NEC

subcommittees as sources of policy advice, relied more heavily on policy forums and experts such as the Commission on Social Justice, and in 1996 announced plans to ballot the entire party membership on a pre-manifesto programme, which, because it could not be amended at conference, represented a further reduction in the policy-making role of the unions.

The Liberal Party (1945–88)

The Liberal Party survived the near-death experience of the immediate postwar period but proved unable to achieve a realignment of the left by uniting the country's progressive forces in a coalition capable of defeating the Conservatives. The nearest this project came to success was in 1983, when the Liberal–Social Democrat Alliance polled 7. 78 million votes but failed to break through as a governing party.

Until 1955 the Liberals seemed to be in a remorseless decline that could end only in extinction (Table 7.1). With 'a ramshackle and underfunded' organisation (Wallace, 1983) and lacking a distinctive political identity, the party fielded candidates in only about one fifth of constituencies in 1951 and 1955, and half of these regularly forfeited their deposits. The party had been pressed back to a residual core in its pre-1914 heartlands – the Celtic fringe and rural areas – retaining an urban presence only in old centres of radicalism and Nonconformity such as West Yorkshire.

As a campaigning organisation it was handicapped by the widely held belief that canvassing was a slightly disreputable activity and that advocating the 'right' policies was enough to attract voters. When the campaign in the highly marginal Bristol North-East began in 1955, the Liberals '*stopped canvassing*' (Milne and Mackenzie, 1955, cited in Stevenson, 1993, p. 37; emphasis in original).

The party was torn ideologically at this time between radical individualists, who stressed free trade (an old Liberal rallying cry), minimal government and individual liberty, and the Radical Reform Group, which believed in the social liberalism of Beveridge and Keynes.

Distinctive Liberal issues were few – electoral reform, regional matters and internationalism – and insufficient to recommend the party electorally. This decade represented the lowest point of Liberal fortunes. The reasons for its survival included the residual strength left in its regional and municipal bases; electoral pacts with the Conservatives; its retention of sufficient talented people to provide it with leaders and candidates; its structure as a loose grouping of mainly middle-class individuals motivated by a desire to assert moral principles in politics, which although a handicap in campaigning, was well adapted to 'survival and resisting take-over'; and, somewhat paradoxically, its very weakness, which meant that, for the main parties, absorption of a party so obviously in its last throes was hardly worth the effort (Stevenson, 1993, pp. 41–2).

The period 1956 to 1981 saw a steady Liberal revival. Between 1955 and 1979 the Liberal vote increased sixfold and its representation in parliament doubled. Liberal fortunes improved, first, because the party leaders, Jo Grimond (1956–67), Jeremy Thorpe (1967–76) and David Steel (1976–88) were able to project the party nationally in the new media age. Second, with a revitalised social liberalism displacing the old Liberal libertarian strand, the party acquired an ideology that was appropriate for the era of collectivist consensus and well-adapted to its position as the non-socialist alternative to Conservatism. Third, from a weak campaigning organisation, the party became a powerful one at all levels, especially in by-elections where it could concentrate its resources, its revival being punctuated by victories at, for example, Torrington (1958), Orpington (1962) and Rochdale, Sutton, Ely, Rippon and Berwick (1972–3). The party also became very effective in local elections, acquiring a presence in local government that formed the basis of its national campaigns. Both the Young Liberals, who pioneered 'community politics' in the late 1960s by focusing on local issues, and the Association of Liberal Councillors, another radical force, gave a harder edge to Liberal campaigning. With their emphasis on the values of participation, experimentation and diversity, the Young Liberal communitarians also provided a further strand to Liberal ideology (Behrens, 1989, p. 85).

The Liberal revival peaked in the general elections of 1974, bringing power closer in the 'hung parliament' situation of February 1974, when Heath offered the Liberal leader a seat in the cabinet but no more than a speaker's conference on electoral reform. However a coalition to 'prop up' a minority government was deeply unpopular with the party's members, and nothing materialised. In 1977, after the Labour majority had disappeared, the Liberals formed a pact with Labour and agreed to support the government, but it was given no cabinet seats or firm promises of electoral reform. The government did promise to press ahead with devolution legislation and make additional time available for a Liberal housing bill. For many Liberals, these concessions were insufficient and many wanted to withdraw when the vote for proportional representation (PR) in European elections was lost, but Steel succeeded in imposing his strategy of increasing the party's credibility through political coalitions, and the pact survived until May 1978.

Underlying the Liberal revival was growing voter dissatisfaction with the two major parties, greater electoral volatility and a greater willingness among voters to register their dissatisfaction in protest votes for a third party and engage in tactical voting. The Liberals also benefited after 1960 from class dealignment and from the trend for media campaigns, in which leader personality and party image mattered more than before. But volatility worked against the Liberals too: only 50 per cent of Liberal voters stayed loyal between October 1974 and 1979 compared with 75 per cent of Labour voters and 87 per cent of Conservative voters (Stevenson, 1993, p. 69).

The Social Democratic Party

The Social Democratic Party (SDP) was formed in March 1981, and by the end of its first year it had recruited 25 secessionists from Labour and one former Conservative. Its leaders – the 'Gang of Four': David Owen, Shirley Williams, Bill Rodgers and Roy Jenkins – were former Labour right-wingers who were disillusioned with Labour over Europe and its drift towards the left. With the Conservatives moving sharply to the right, this seemed an opportune moment for a mould-breaking centre party. Almost immediately the SDP moved into alliance with the Liberals, the two parties issuing a statement affirming their support for constitutional reform, including PR and devolution, a freedom of information act, industrial partnership, continuing EC membership and support for NATO. However, despite a huge vote in both 1983 and 1987, the Alliance failed to break the mould of British politics. The 1987 general election showed that rather than destroying the hegemony of the two major parties, respectively in hock to business and the unions, the SDP had itself been broken by these two parties operating within a simple plurality electoral system.

The Liberals and the SDP moved to full-scale merger in 1988, the majority of both parties approving the formation of the Social and Liberal Democrats, soon shortened to the Liberal Democrats. Minorities in each party resisted merger, but the groupings they formed proved politically unviable; all but Michael Meadowcroft of the 73 'old Liberal' candidates forfeited their deposits in 1992 and the 'continuing SDP' under David Owen folded in June 1990. The tensions within the Alliance were thus fully exposed at its end, in particular its inability to agree on a coherent political strategy. The main divisions, never resolved and probably unresolvable, were between the social market ideology and charismatic leadership of Owen (a junior Thatcherite option); the Jenkinsite package of electoral reform, a mixed economy, a developmental state and internationalism (the Liberal–Labour right option); and the grass roots, participatory, more gradualist strategy offered by many Liberals. Unlike the Scottish Nationalists, who benefited from a regional concentration of support, the Alliance suffered from the even spread of its vote.

Answers to the question of what the Alliance achieved range from the modest but significant (encouraging Labour to move back to the moderate centre, moving PR up the political agenda) to the totally negative – the argument that Labour would have moved back to the political centre anyway, and that after four successive election defeats it would have been forced to show some interest in electoral reform. Crewe and King even reject the Alliance's main, if rather negative, claim to influence: splitting the anti-

Conservative vote, thereby keeping the Conservatives in power. They also argue that the Liberal Democrats offered the same programme as the Liberal Party would have done if the SDP had never existed (Stevenson, 1993, pp. 98–100; Crewe and King, 1996).

The Liberal Democrats

The new merged party consisted of 19 MPs (17 former Liberals), 3500 councillors and about 80 000 members. It immediately elected Paddy Ashdown leader by a large majority. Its performance in the 1992 general election underlined the progress made by Liberalism since the dismal postwar decade. However there were certain bleaker continuities with the 1950s, the main one being the lack of proportionality between votes and seats and between share of the vote and share of the seats. Under a more proportional system, even the Alternative Vote (AV), the Liberal Democrats would have fared appreciably better; under the single transferable vote (STV), they would have had 102 MPs. Second, the party's lack of financial support meant a continuing disadvantage at elections: in the 1992 campaign, the Liberal Democrats, with £2.1 million to spend, had less than a third of Labour's and approximately one fifth of the Conservatives' resources. Third, the Liberal Democrats continued to draw a disproportionate number of its MPs from rural areas and the Celtic fringe. Fourth, the partys' success depended more on the fortunes of the major parties, especially the party in government, than on its own qualities. Its vote tended to be 'soft', with seats won in by-elections often reverting back to one of the main parties at general elections. Finally, the Liberal Democrats, like their Liberal predecessors, found it difficult to form a distinctive identity and were prone to suffer from a policy as well as an electoral 'squeeze' as the big parties took over their ideas.

The Green Party

Apart from the nationalist parties (Chapter 4), no small party has proved capable of winning parliamentary seats on a sustained basis. As a single-issue party, the Green Party (founded in 1985, formerly the Ecology Party, 1973) was at a particular disadvantage in parliamentary elections, and attracted just 1–1.5 per cent of the votes in the four general elections between 1979 and 1992 (Butler and Kavanagh, 1988, p. 344; Butler and Kavanagh, 1992, p. 343). Its peak moment to date (1996) occurred in the 1989 Euro elections, when it polled 2. 3 million votes (15 per cent of the total). However its failure to build on that success led to a search for explanations of the result itself and of the subsequent decline.

Factors relevant to the 1989 success include the high public profile of environmental issues at that time, ranging from concern about the consequences of the the Chernobyl nuclear power station disaster (1986) and the pollution of drinking water at Camelford, Cornwall (1988), to a more general awareness of global warming and ozone layer depletion. A political explanation is that at the mid-term point of an unpopular Conservative government, with the modernisation of Labour far from complete and the recently formed Liberal Democrats in confusion, the electorate expressed its protest by voting Green. The economic recession of the early 1990s may account in part for the party's failure to 'take off' from that high point: voting for a non-growth economy became more difficult when the 'feelgood' factor was missing. Political reasons included the recovery of the Liberal Democrats; internal feuding within the Green Party itself, with pragmatists at loggerheads with fundamentalists, and two of its leading figures, Sara Parkin and Jonathan Porritt, withdrawing from active roles in the party; and the nature of Green support, which came particularly from the conservation-minded in the rural south, just the constituency to be drawn away when the major parties adopted environmental policies and the Liberal Democrats, who had a long-term interest in environmental policies, made a political recovery (Pattie *et al.*, 1995, pp. 21, 25). But 'asset-stripping' of their more moderate ideas by the main parties showed that within the context of the wider environmental movement (Chapter 3) the Green Party had influenced the political agenda.

The party itself encompasses a wide range of ideas on the environmental spectrum, from 'pale greens' seeking the wiser use of resources and sustainable growth within the system to 'dark greens' opposed to all interference with the natural world, and from right-wing preservationists to left-wing 'red-greens' advocating an alternative society.

The Far Left

The Communist Party of Great Britain (CPGB) emerged from the war as the only significant Marxist-Leninist party, with two MPs, 100 000 votes, 256 councillors and 45 000 members. However it lost its two MPs in 1950 and by 1983 its vote had declined to 11 000. Support for it was undermined by many factors, including Soviet brutality in Eastern Europe and the revelation of Stalinist crimes in the 1950s, internal feuding between pro-Soviet hardliners and Eurocommunists from the late 1970s, the collapse of communism in the Soviet Union and Eastern Europe after 1989 and the revelation in 1991 that the party had received £100 000 per annum from Moscow between 1958 and 1979. The party relaunched itself in 1991 as the Democratic Left in an attempt to create a more pluralist, radical and democratic party.

Other far-left groups increased in importance, with the Trotskyist Militant Tendency (1964) successfully infiltrating the Labour Party after 1973, and the Leninist Socialist Workers Party (1976) attempting to build a revolutionary movement outside Labour by focusing on right-to-work and anti-racism campaigns and exploiting issues such as the poll tax. Other small Trotskyist groupings included the Workers Revolutionary Party (1973), whose 60 parliamentary candidates in 1979 gained a mere 13 500 votes and which soon afterwards broke up into many factions after the expulsion of its leader Gerry Healy and best-known members Corin and Vanessa Redgrave; and the Socialist League (formerly the International Marxist Group), which engaged in entryism in the early 1980s, when it backed the Benn campaign to democratise the Labour Party and became heavily involved in CND. In 1993, having been expelled from the Labour Party, Militant Tendency relaunched itself as Militant Labour (Callaghan, 1987, p. 159; Crick, 1984, pp. 206–8).

The Extreme Right

Mosley's British Union of Fascists (1932) had no effective successor in postwar Britain until the formation of the National Front (1967), an overtly racist party, that called for the repatriation of blacks and, especially in local elections, demanded the removal of coloured immigrants from council house waiting lists and the segregation of the children of immigrants in schools. Having displaced the CPGB as Britain's fourth party in 1974, the National Front gained its highest vote (191 000) in 1979 but failed to win a seat in parliament. With the Conservatives' tough stance on immigration drawing off its support, the party declined in the early 1980s and split in 1983. Its leader, John Tyndall, left to form the British National Party, which by 1992 had become the leading extreme right party. However, BNP and NF candidates combined numbered only 26 and gained only a tiny proportion of the vote. Extreme right candidates achieved higher shares of the poll at local elections but, apart from the two seats won by the NF in Blackburn (1976) and the BNP seat on Tower Hamlets Council (1993) usually failed to win any seats.

As well as standing for election, extreme right groups pursued a parallel strategy of street marches and attacks on ethnic communities. NF demonstrations and marches deliberately targeted areas with large ethnic populations in West Yorkshire, the West Midlands and East London, and it frequently clashed with the Anti-Nazi League (1977, relaunched 1992). The violent anti-black and anti-Jewish propaganda of the extreme right was an important factor in the rising tide of racial violence in the late 1980s, with reported racial attacks nearly doubling between 1988 and 1991.

Further Reading

Bogdanor, V. (ed.), *Liberal Party Politics* (Oxford: Clarendon Press, 1983).
Callaghan, J., *The Far Left in British Politics* (Oxford: Blackwell, 1987).
Ceadel, M., 'Labour as a Governing Party: Balancing Right and Left', in T. Gourvish and A. O'Day (eds), *Britain since 1945* (London: Macmillan, 1991).
Hunt, S., 'Fascism and the "Race Issue" in Britain', *Talking Politics*, vol. 5, no. 1 (Autumn 1992).

Hunt, S., 'The Far Left in British Politics', *Talking Politics*, vol. 8, no. 2 (Winter 1995–6).

Jefferys, K., *The Labour Party since 1945* (London: Macmillan, 1993).

Kavanagh, D. and A. Seldon, A. (eds), *The Major Effect* (London: Macmillan, 1994).

Ludlam, S. and M. Smith, *Contemporary British Conservatism* (London: Macmillan, 1996).

Norton, P. and A. Aughey, *Conservatives and Conservatism* (London: Temple Smith, 1981).

O'Gorman, F., *Conservative Thought from Burke to Thatcher* (London: Longman, 1986).

Pattie, C., R. Johnston and A. Russell, A. 'The Stalled Greening of British Politics', *Politics Review*, vol. 4, no. 3 (February 1995).

Rasmussen, J., 'They Also Serve: Small Parties in the British Political System' in F. Muller-Rommel and G. Pridham (eds), *Small Parties in Western Europe* (London: Sage, 1991).

Seldon, A. (ed.) *UK Political Parties since 1945* (Hemel Hempstead: Philip Allan, 1990).

Seldon, A. and S. Ball (eds), *The Conservative Party since 1900* (Oxford: Oxford University Press, 1994).

Seyd, P., *The Rise and Fall of the Labour Left* (London: Macmillan, 1987).

Shaw, E., *The Labour Party since 1945* (Oxford: Blackwell, 1996).

Stevenson, J., *Third Party Politics since 1945* (Oxford: Blackwell, 1993).

Tivey, L. and A. Wright (eds), *Party Ideology in Britain* (London: Routledge, 1989).

8
Voters and Elections

The analysis of voting behaviour in Britain remains a controversial issue. On the one hand there has been much disagreement between political scientists over which particular methodology and which particular set of findings is the most appropriate and accurate in describing political realities (see Denver and Hands, 1992). On the other hand the combined research of all psephologists has been dismissed as being at best, overtechnical, and at worst, trivial (see Crewe *et al.*, 1992, pp. 5–25). Some of these controversial issues will be touched upon in the discussion below, which makes reference to the appropriate literature on the topics as they arise. Reflecting the literature, the focus of this chapter is on elections to the House of Commons, particularly on general elections. Little attention is devoted to either local authority elections or elections to the European Parliament. Whilst this is appropriate in a review of the past fifty years, it is worth noting that within the next decade or so it may become appropriate to give greater academic attention to sub- and supranational elections should the twin processes of subsidiarity and federalism render general elections less significant in political life. Again following the literature, the focus of this chapter is on voting behaviour rather than broader electoral behaviour. In other words the focus is on the behaviour of those citizens who turn out to vote. Non-voters tend to be overlooked in the literature on voting studies, as indeed may be their fate in wider society. In the 1950s American political scientists argued that political apathy was good for democracy (Berelson *et al.*, 1954, p. 314) and could be considered as a barometer of public contentment. This assumption may or may not be valid. The point is that voting behaviour monopolises the attention of British political scientists, and there is no tradition of explaining the behaviour of the 25 per cent of the electorate who fail to participate.

Britain's Changing Party System

A statistical snapshot of the 1945 general election shows that 1683 candidates contested 640 seats. If the twelve university seats are excluded from calculation, then 35 members were elected in Britain for third parties. In terms of the popular vote, Labour won 47.8 per cent and Conservatives 39.8 per cent, giving a combined two-party total of 87.6 per cent. A similar snapshot of the 1992 general election, nearly half a century later, shows 2946 candidates contesting 651 seats. In the new parliament, 32 MPs were returned for third

TABLE 8.1 *Two-party support and domination, 1945–97*

General election	Percentage of votes cast for Conservatives and Labour	Percentage of electorate supporting Conservatives and Labour	Percentage of seats in the House of Commons won by the two main parties
1945	87.6	64.6	94.1
1950	89.5	75.3	98.1
1951	96.8	79.9	98.6
1955	96.1	73.8	98.6
1959	93.2	73.3	98.4
1964	87.5	67.5	98.6
1966	89.9	68.1	97.8
1970	89.4	64.4	97.9
1974 (Feb.)	75.0	58.5	94.2
1974 (Oct.)	75.1	54.6	94.0
1979	80.8	61.4	95.6
1983	70.0	50.9	93.2
1987	73.1	55.2	93.0
1992	76.3	59.3	93.2
1997	75.8	53.1	88.5

Source: based on Sarlvik and Crewe.

parties. Labour secured 34.4 per cent of the popular vote and the Conservatives 41.9 per cent, giving a total of 76.3 per cent. Careful selection of other years, say 1951 compared with 1983, would have given a sharper contrast, but even with the first and last general election in this review, the overall situation is clear. Whilst the two-party system has survived in the House of Commons and is as alive and well in 1992 as it was in 1945, a multiparty system has emerged among voters. What converts a multiparty electorate into a predominantly two-party parliament is, of course, Britain's much discussed first-past-the-post electoral system.

Decline in support for the two main political parties touched a low point in the general election of 1983, when the combined vote for Labour and the Conservatives was 70 per cent (Table 8.1). This combined support should, perhaps, be put into context and compared with the electorate as a whole and not just with those who voted. It is then revealed that only a half of the electorate supported the two parties which, despite this weak endorsement, went on to dominate the backbenches of the Commons. Less than one third of the electorate supported the party which formed the government.

The Dominant Party, Two-Party and Multiparty System

The numerical domination of the House of Commons by Conservative and Labour MPs has hardly been challenged over the last half century. Table 8.1 shows that from 1945–92 over 90 per cent of MPs belonged to either of the two major parties. Indeed in some ways the statistics even underestimate the two-party domination of the Commons since at certain times each party was at the centre of a parliamentary bloc. For example in the 1945 parliament, National and Liberal National MPs were Conservatives in all but name, whilst on the left Labour could generally count on the support of MPs from the Independent Labour Party, the Communist Party and the Common Wealth Party. MPs representing the two opposing blocs occupied 97.4 per cent of all seats. It is the break-up of one of these blocs – occasioned in particular by the Ulster Unionists organising as a distinct party rather than taking the Conservative whip – that conveys the impression in Table 8.1 of a slight weakening of the two-party grip from the mid 1970s onwards.

From time to time, however, third parties played a less marginal role in parliamentary affairs both in terms of public attention and political substance. The Liberals and nationalist parties made parliamentary advances as a result of by-election victories, and these are not recorded in Table 8.1. Nationalist advances in the mid to late 1960s, the mid 1970s (for the SNP) and late 1980s onwards were invariably reversed in the subsequent general elections. For example advances by Plaid Cymru collapsed in 1970 when '25 of its 36 candidates lost their deposits' (Norris, 1990, p. 29), and despite its improving pre-election position in opinion polls, 'the SNP's election slogan of "Free in '93"' turned into the embarrassing reality of 'Three (MPs) in '93' (Robins *et al.*, 1994, p. 162).

In the early 1980s many political commentators believed that they were witnessing the collapse of the two-party system in parliament as well as in the country. The Conservative and Labour Parties had moved towards their respective ideological extremes, thus opening up the centre and providing the opportunity for a third party to 'break the mould' of two-party politics. After 1981, the new Liberal-SDP 'centre party' captured media attention through skilfully timed defections from Labour as well as a run of spectacular by-election victories. Even in defeat, at the Warrington by-election, there was great media excitement when the voting trends were extrapolated to show that had there been a general election '501 SDP/Liberals, 113 Labour and one Conservative' would have been returned (Robins, 1982, p. 80). The Alliance eventually had more than 40 MPs, a solid base from which party strategists expected to advance, supported by an increasingly volatile electorate. However the Falklands victory transformed the electoral position of the Conservatives and the Alliance returned only 23 MPs in 1983. The two-party system seemed to be restored in Westminster, albeit in the face of a multiparty electorate that supported the Alliance only 2.3 per cent less than Labour.

The state of parliamentary arithmetic is an important factor in determining the political influence of third parties. If the two main parties are finely balanced, then a third party or grouping may be able to wield a degree of influence that is disproportionate to its numbers. Should any third party hold the balance of power then, reflecting its ability to 'make or break' government, its influence may be very great; even if it is not in this position its numbers could reduce the minority of the party in office, which bestows considerable influence. The general election of February 1974 produced a hung parliament with the Conservatives winning 301 seats, eight short of a majority, and Labour winning 296. The Liberals, with 14 MPs, could only have contributed to a Conservative-led majority and so did not hold the true balance of power. Having, for political reasons, rejected a pact with the Conservatives in 1974, the Liberals soon threw their parliamentary weight behind Labour in a pact that resembled a very loose form of coalition.

A minority Labour government assumed office and its Prime Minister Harold Wilson called another general election for October. Labour was returned with a slender majority, but this was soon eroded by by-election losses and defections. The Lib–Lab pact of March 1977 – formed to fend off the danger of no confidence votes – was not a formal coalition, but an agreement in which the Liberals won policy concessions from Labour in exchange for their support of Labour in the lobbies. The Liberals eventually felt they had failed to gain sufficient political benefit from the pact, and it was therefore terminated in May 1978. Labour then had to rely on the nationalists for survival, but the government fell the following year on a vote of no confidence.

After the 1992 general election John Major's Conservative government was described by an ex-chancellor as 'in office, but not in power'. By-election defeats, defections to both Labour and the Liberal Democrats, as well as the behaviour of a group of Conservative 'whipless rebels' brought the government close to a minority position. On this occasion, however, the 'third party' precipitating the Conservative crisis was a 'party within a party'. In an attempt to control his own backbenchers the prime minister took the remarkable action of resigning as party leader and putting himself up for re-election. What ensured his government's survival was crucial support from the Ulster Unionists as well as a tougher policy on the EU which placated his Eurosceptic rebels.

Minority, coalition and national governments were familiar occurrences in the first half of the twentieth century, but much rarer during the fifty years under review here. Whilst parliamentary arithmetic, in the form of small majorities, did precipitate early general elections after 1950 and 1964, and cause discomfort for the post-1992 Conservative government, authentic minority and coalition-like government existed only from the mid to the late 1970s. In other words, from 1945 onwards the two-party system providing majority government was the general rule in the Commons, and exceptions to this rule lasted little more than two years.

The Distortion of Voters' Preferences

In the first of the Nuffield election studies, McCallum and Readman questioned the fairness of an electoral system that delivered Labour and other socialists victory on the basis of winning only 65 000 more of the popular vote than the combined total of their opponents. 'How', they queried, 'does the support of 48 per cent of the electors for one party entitle it to nearly two-thirds of the membership of Parliament?' (McCallum and Readman, 1947, p. 253). This question grew more pressing as the electorate began to give increasing support to third parties, and as a consequence governments were based on a much smaller share of the popular vote. For example the consecutive Conservative governments from 1979 to 1992 were supported by little over 40 per cent of all voters.

In order to illuminate the distorting effect of the electoral system in translating votes into seats, political commentators have speculated about what the general election results would have been had other electoral systems been in place. For example, using electoral and public opinion data it was possible to make reasonable judgments about what would have been the parliamentary outcomes had the single transferable vote (STV) or additional member system been in operation. Such exercises illustrated the extent to which the Conservative hegemony of the 1980s and 1990s was based on the workings of the electoral system rather than on the collective choice of voters. Had Britain's electoral system been STV, as in Ireland, D'Honte, as in Belgium, the Netherlands, Portugal and Spain; Hagenbach-Bischoff, as in Greece; Panachage, as in Luxembourg; or Sainte-Lague as in Denmark, in all likelihood the 'Thatcher revolution' would not have taken place.

The postwar years have seen an increasing interest in electoral reform, particularly in the context of a new constitutional settlement. Enlightened self-interest alone would justify Liberal interest in promoting electoral reform. Whilst the Liberals/Liberal Democrats have performed well in local authority elections, their breakthrough into national politics as a credible alternative is still frustrated by the perception of a Liberal vote as a protest vote, a tactical vote or, at worst, a wasted vote. In the February and October 1974 general elections the Liberals won 19.3 per cent and 18.3 per cent of the popular vote respectively. Yet with the support of nearly one in five of all voters they returned only 14 and 13 MPs respectively. When the Liberal–SDP Alliance trailed Labour by just two per cent in 1983, 186 fewer seats were won by the Alliance. Even the public was amazed that Labour's 8.4 million votes gained 209 seats whilst the Alliance's 7.8 million votes secured only 23 (17 Liberals and six SDP). The ongoing conundrum faced by Liberals was that their party needed to be in power in order to implement electoral reform, yet it needed a reformed electoral system in order to get into power.

Similar self-interest put the issue of electoral reform onto Labour's agenda during the 1980s. With the party fearing it was in terminal decline and seemingly unelectable, some members felt that electoral reform was the surest way of reducing the scale of Margaret Thatcher's election triumphs. A party commission, chaired by Professor Raymond Plant, explored alternative electoral systems and the ramifications of reform for Britain. Whilst recommending reform, the commission did not go as far as the Liberals in advocating replacement of the existing system with one of proportional representation. Some political commentators have speculated that should Labour and the Liberal Democrats cooperate possibly in a future hung parliament, some form of electoral reform would result from bargaining between these two parties in order to improve their chances of forming future governments.

One-Party Dominance?

From the birth of the Labour Party in 1900 until the mid 1990s the British electorate returned only two Labour governments, both during the postwar years. Whilst a two-party system exists in the Commons, a dominant-party system has existed on the government front bench. Many political commentators believe that Britain's electoral system is the fundamental cause of what has been described as 'the slow death of pluralism in our democracy'. Although the swing of the two-party pendulum produced decisive victories for Labour in 1945 and 1966, when the pendulum swung back it appeared to get stuck, providing the Conservatives with prolonged periods in office. Unlike the Conservatives, Labour has never managed to serve two consecutive full terms in office. Much of Britain's political history is of a similar one-party dominance: the Tories were in power for all but a year between 1783 and 1830; and between 1830 and 1886 the Whigs and later the Liberals were dominant. The advent of a universal franchise, facilitated through the machinery of first-past-the-post, appeared to make only a small dent in the dominant-party system of government. As Heywood has argued, 'in the seventy years leading up to 1992, the Conservatives had been in government, either alone or as the dominant member of a coalition, for fifty of them' (Robins *et al.*, 1994, p. 15).

Some feel that the apparent stranglehold on government by the Conservatives became critical when the party became more ideological under Margaret Thatcher. Whilst one-party dominance was based on consensual politics, as during the 1950s, it did not result in a radical reshaping of the political agenda. However this ceased to be the case during the 1980s and 1990s, when the 'Thatcher revolution' increasingly affected areas such as the economy and nationalised industries, the welfare state and local government. It was argued that this prolonged period of ideologically driven government broke down long-established boundaries between the party and the state. There was great concern that Thatcherite values and procedures from the world of commerce had resulted in politicisation of the administration of large areas of the public sector, resulting in dominant-party government becoming one-party government.

Others felt that the dominance of the one-party in government was not necessarily sinister since opposition continued to flourish. It was argued, for example, that Thatcher's lengthy period in Number Ten had not resulted in a value shift amongst the electorate. Whilst some Thatcherite policies were popular, such as the sale of council houses, public opinion polls on issues such as managing the economy or the welfare state showed that the values of Keynes and Beveridge still held sway over and above the values of Thatcher. Thatcher's successive general election victories were won on little more than 40 per cent of popular support. The crucial factor in securing her victories, it was argued, was the fact that the anti-Thatcher vote was split deeply between the opposition parties.

Finally, it was argued, that the prolonged periods of Conservative government were secured by the skill of party leaders in judging the precise time when general elections should be held. Opinion polls have revealed an increasingly volatile public in terms of party support. We noted above that, had a general election been called before the Falklands War, it would have resulted in a Conservative wipe-out at the polls. Similarly, in the mid 1990s, with a rejuvenated Labour Party enjoying record levels of support in opinion polls, had a general election been called at any time during 1995 there would have been a greater Labour landslide than in 1945 (indeed this is precisely what eventually happened in 1997). But no general elections were called in these critical years and what actually occurred was a period of uninterrupted Conservative rule from 1979 to 1997. Some political scientists have argued that Conservative support has been just as volatile as Labour's, and that the string of Conservative victories has been the result of good timing rather than of any long-term dynamic in British politics. They conclude that

Mrs Thatcher has done a masterful job teetering on the volatile balance of public support between the parties, exploiting the opportunities provided by the leadership problems in the Labour party, public reaction to the Falklands war, the formation of the SDP, and an improving economy. She called the elections in 1983 and 1987 at what in retrospect appear to have been almost optimal times. Had she called either election from six months to a year earlier, the balance of party support would have been far less advantageous to the Conservatives. The same would have been true had the 1983 election been postponed six months. (Mishler *et al.*, 1989, p. 234).

The previous Labour prime minister, James Callaghan, had none of Thatcher's skill when it came to the timing of his general election. By waiting until the spring of 1979 instead of going to the country in the autumn of 1978, Labour suffered the political consequences of the 'winter of discontent'. This error of political judgment lost Labour between four and six percentage points of electoral support. The argument put forward is that there was nothing inevitable about Labour's defeats and the four consecutive Conservative election victories. Had a Labour government been returned in 1978 and weathered the public sector strikes of the 'winter of discontent' early in its administration, the Labour leader might have timed subsequent elections to his advantage, as Thatcher was able to do in reality.

Voting Behaviour in Postwar Britain

In their analysis of political change, Butler and Stokes note that there are three principal sources of change in electoral behaviour. First, there is the physical replacement of the electorate, since 'even in a few short years, some millions of electors die and others come of age' (Butler and Stokes, 1974, p. 4). To adapt this point made by Butler and Stokes about the passage of generations through the electorate, a voter who died aged 75 after voting in the 1945 general election would have been born when Gladstone was prime minister. A voter aged eighteen who voted for the first time in the 1997 general election, and who also lived to 75, would be able to vote in general elections stretching over half-way into the twenty-first century. Thus in half a century, the time span examined in this book, the composition of the electorate in terms of different generations changes on a massive scale.

Second, a process of partisan dealignment can occur in which the traditional loyalties of voters decline. Some political scientists argue that the electorate has become increasingly dealigned since the 1960s. Dealigned voting, it is argued, has resulted in increased volatility in voting behaviour. The weakening of party ties between voting behaviour and social class is part of this dealignment process which, on balance, is claimed to have worked to the electoral disadvantage of Labour. Other patterns of dealignment may have involved factors such as ethnic minority status and party choice and rural residence and party choice. Other political scientists identify dealignment as an unstable process that 'has occurred in fits and starts. The balance of power has fluctuated dramatically in a way that favours one party then the other without apparent long-term trend' (Mishler *et al.*, 1989, p. 219).

Finally, in the short run electoral change can reflect 'the electors' response to the immediate issues and events of politics' (Butler and Stokes, 1974, p. 5). A relatively unimportant political event can, in the context of an election campaign, take on disproportional significance in influencing voting.

Social Class and Voting Behaviour

The voting behaviour of the early postwar electorate was 'aligned' insofar as voters from the middle and working classes broadly supported differing parties (Figure 8.1). An analysis of the 1950 general election by Benney, Gray and Pear (1956) found that social class membership explained voting behaviour far more than other social characteristics such as age, gender or religion. Butler and Stokes (1974, p. 77) agreed that the preeminent role of social class in party choice was beyond question. The general picture of alignment between class and party is shown in Tapper and Bowles'

TABLE 8.2 *Voting by social class, 1945–58 (per cent)*

	AB	C1	C2	DE
Conservative	85	70	35	30
Labour	10	25	60	65

Source: Robins, 1982, p. 175.

reaggregation of voting behaviour in the general elections between 1945 and 1958 (Table 8.2).

From the 1970s, however, political scientists began to monitor changing patterns in voting behaviour. Not only did the link between class and party weaken, but so too did the link between voters and parties. In a major study of voting behaviour, Crewe and Sarlvik explored the weakening attachment of voters to the political parties. Tracing voters' loyalty patterns was an extremely complex research exercise, but it revealed that the degree of constant support for the two main parties was not as great as commonly supposed, and in this sense the trend shown in Figure 8.1 is deceptive. They found, for example, that only half of the Conservative voters lost prior to the 1979 general election returned to vote Conservative, whilst only a third of Labour's defectors returned to vote Labour in 1979. They concluded that 'in a typical election of the 1960s and 1970s under half (47 per cent) of the

FIGURE 8.1   *Class-based voting in general elections, 1959–79*

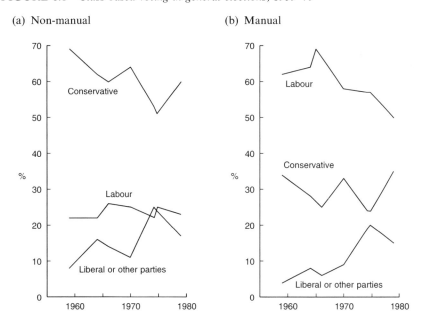

(a) Non-manual   (b) Manual

Source: Adapted from Sarlvik and Crewe, 1983.

British electorate, excluding new electors, voted for one or other major party twice running' (Sarlvik and Crewe, 1983, p. 63).

What contribution did the weakening ties between social class and voting behaviour make to the dealignment trend? In the immediate postwar decades class alignment was understood in terms of socialisation, whereby a variety of cultural class factors such as home, school and peer group reinforced class voting patterns. This appeared to explain why around two thirds of the working class supported their natural class party, Labour, and why around four fifths of the middle class supported the Conservatives. Class-based voting was seen as 'normal', so much so that political scientists focused their research effort on the minority of 'deviants' who did not vote along class lines, particularly working-class Tories.

Crewe and Sarlvik cautiously concluded that class–party links had weakened during the 1970s. Between the general elections of October 1974 and 1979, 'among manual workers the swing to the Conservatives was 9 per cent; among non-manual workers 5.5 per cent' (ibid., p. 83). Thus the pattern of decline was obscured because the Conservative vote increased across all social classes, sometimes at the cost of the Liberals rather than Labour. Within the working-class vote, for example, Conservative gains 'were at the expense of both, but of Labour more than of the Liberals' (ibid). Nevertheless the 1979 general election 'was only the latest instalment in a series of elections at which class voting has fitfully but gradually declined' (ibid., p. 86).

The topic of class voting has proved a controversial one among political journalists and academics; for example the electoral role of the C2s – which include the so-called 'Essex Man' – has been interpreted in differing ways. Some have argued that, as the largest social class, the vote of the C2s has been decisive in making or breaking governments. For example in 1979 there was a swing of 9 per cent to the Conservatives among the C2s whilst the rest of the electorate swung by only 3.5 per cent, which gained the C2s their reputation as the 'shock troops of Thatcherism'. Others disagree with this opinion and argue that whilst the C2s are an influential group, they are not an all-important one. In terms of swinging the result of an election, the support of the DE grouping is seen as of equal importance to the C2s. Among academics there has been disagreement about the main causes of changing voting patterns; rather than identifying the process of dealignment as eroding Labour support, changes in the class structure has been seen by some as the principal cause of the party's electoral decline until 1997. It is argued that in focusing on class dealignment 'political scientists have concentrated on minor rearrangements of the furniture while failing to notice a major change in the structure of the house. . . . Britain has been transformed from a blue-collar society into a white-collar one'. The impact of this change upon the electoral fortunes of the parties 'has probably been far greater than that of any class dealignment which may or may not have occurred' (Heath *et al.*, 1985, pp. 35–36).

Whether changes in voting patterns have resulted primarily from the class structure as old classes fragmented and new ones emerged, or from changes in voters' values as individual affluence assumed a higher priority than class solidarity, or from the relative appeal of existing and new political parties, many political scientists agree that 'the decline of class voting in Britain has permitted a more or less equivalent rise in issue-based voting choice' (Franklin, 1985, p. 150). The strongest expression of this argument comes in the form of a 'consumer' explanation of voting behaviour in Britain; the portrait of the voter that emerged from a major longitudinal study from 1959–74 was of

> Someone who is not simply conforming to his or her own past or follows other people's example, but makes up his own mind. While little interested in politics and fairly unsophisticated in his or her political thinking, the voter is nevertheless quite aware of the parties' major policy proposals and has views about the parties' ability or willingness to implement them; he also has fairly definite views on a variety of political issues, particularly those which have a bearing on his or her own life (Himmelweit *et al.*, 1981, pp. 202–3).

Labour's electoral decline during the 1970s and 1980s has been explained in terms of its unpopular policies: traditional voters simply stopped 'buying' what has been described as the party's 'collectivist trinity' of public ownership, trade union power and social welfare. Many 'shopped around' and found that other parties offered policies and issues that they found more attractive.

The implications of political change to a less stable and more volatile electorate for political parties and the party system are considerable. As Rose and McAllister have noted, 'the electorate today is wide open to change; three-quarters of voters are no longer anchored by a stable party loyalty determined by family and class. More voters float between parties – or are wobbling in their commitment to one party – than show a lifetime loyalty to a particular party' (Rose and McAllister, 1990, p. 1). Their research survey suggested that the electorate could be summarised in terms of nine groupings holding distinctive clusters of political values. At one extreme was what they termed the 'Victorian right', comprising 7 per cent of the electorate and favouring cuts in social benefits and greater control of trade unions; at the other was the 'hard left', the 5 per cent of the electorate that was pro-welfare, pro-union and against nuclear arms. Between were seven groupings, the largest of which comprised 18 per cent of the electorate. With a dealigned electorate, parties were less able to appeal to class interests. Party managers faced a complex task in identifying and targeting potential political support since no one cluster was large enough or homogeneous enough in its support for a single party to guarantee it electoral victory: 'to win an election, a party must put together a coalition of voters with different values and priorities' (Rose and McAllister,

1990, p. 179). If these arguments are accepted, then in fifty years British politics has moved from the certainties of class appeal, which in the past guaranteed a large degree of loyal support for the main parties, to a complex situation where parties have a wider and inevitably patchier appeal, with success depending on maximal rainbow-coalition building.

The Voting Behaviour of Men and Women

Political scientists have made the point that had women voted for Labour in the same proportion as men, Labour would have been continuously in government from 1945 to at least 1979. Certainly the 1992 general election would have resulted in a hung parliament and the possibility of Labour forming a minority government. However this was not the case and voting studies have shown that women were more Conservatively inclined than men during the 1950s, 1960s and into the 1970s. However, as Table 8.3 shows, by the late 1980s the gender gap in voting had largely disappeared, only to return in the voting behaviour of the 1992 general election. What factors might account for the ebb and flow of gender voting?

Greater Conservative support from women during the early postwar elections was assumed to result from women's role in the traditional family

TABLE 8.3 *Gender and party choice in general elections, 1964–97 (per cent)*

		Conservative	Labour	Liberal or other parties
1964	Men	40	48	11
	Women	46	42	12
1966	Men	38	53	8
	Women	45	46	9
1970	Men	44	49	8
	Women	51	41	8
1974 (Feb.)	Men	40	41	19
	Women	40	38	22
1974 (Oct.)	Men	34	46	19
	Women	40	39	21
1979	Men	47	39	13
	Women	46	39	14
1983	Men	46	30	24
	Women	43	28	28
1987	Men	44	33	22
	Women	44	31	25
1992	Men	38	36	19
	Women	44	34	16
1997	Men	31	44	17
	Women	32	44	17

Source: Coxall and Robins, 1994, p. 263.

structure. It was argued that, for a variety of social reasons, women were more socially aspiring than men, more religious, more deferential and more fatalistic – all factors that gravitated towards greater Conservative support. As few were in paid employment, it was argued, most women never experienced industrial conflict in the workplace and so did not value the role of trade unions – factors that would have increased Labour support.

The 1970s and 1980s brought changes that promised to lead to the disappearance of the gender gap. The steady increase in the number of women employed outside the home, the influence of feminism, the increasing interest among political parties in the 'women's vote' and the feminisation of poverty seemed to offer plausible explanations for the decline in gender voting. However the pattern of decline, with men and women voting for the parties in roughly similar proportions, may have been more apparent than real. What the overall statistics were in fact averaging out were distinctive age-related patterns. For some political scientists found that during the 1980s a gender gap existed amongst young people, but it was the reversal of the traditional picture. Young men gave more support (50 per cent) to the Conservatives than did young women (35 per cent). Denver and Hands (1990) suggested that young males were attracted by Margaret Thatcher's 'macho' image, whereas young females were attracted more by Labour's caring image on health, education and welfare. Once, however, the Conservative Party was led by 'caring' John Major the reasons for young people to vote as they did had gone and the traditional gender gap reemerged.

Key General Elections: 1945 and 1979

Are some general elections historically more significant than others because they represent the expression of social movement, the handing of power to a new political class, the ushering in of a new age, or the handing of power to individuals who stamp their personality on government policy and even seem able to shape events? In this context two general elections are examined below in terms of marking important changes in Britain's political culture. The choices are not straightforward or self-evident insofar as the 1950 general election was the first 'normal' postwar election – the 1945 general election was held whilst Britain was still at war with Japan. Nevertheless the 1945 election heralded what amounted to a peaceful revolution in British society. The 1945 general election was almost part and parcel of the victory celebrations following the defeat of Germany, and the public mood favoured continued state intervention in the economy and welfare provision. Labour, representing the popular face of socialism, enjoyed a landslide victory, supported by the millions who wanted their lives improved through public policy rather than private provision.

In retrospect the 1979 general election marked the end of the already weakened consensus on the role of government in society, although there is a case for identifying the 1983 general election as the one that consolidated Thatcherism's supremacy over divided opposition. However, in terms of a battle of political ideas rather than simply a battle for voters, 1979 was a watershed in British politics. Successive events in the 1970s seemed to prove that 'big government' had failed. Margaret Thatcher, Britain's first female prime minister, did not entirely win the hearts and minds of the electorate with her emphasis on reduced government and the greater play of free market forces; nevertheless changes in the economy, public administration and the welfare state, both in practice and expectation, amounted to what many saw as the 'Thatcher revolution'. Her crusade for 'popular capitalism' and the 'enterprise culture' was not totally successful since the electorate remained doggedly attached to public sector services, particularly the NHS. Nevertheless the political changes she introduced, and which were pursued as a management strategy by her successor, pervaded most aspects of everyday life and reshaped Britain's political agenda. Even New Labour, led by Tony Blair, was seen by many political commentators as a Thatcherite creation.

Dancing in the Street

The 1945 general election was held against the background of Germany's defeat and the end of the war in Europe (Exhibit 8.1). Britain and the other allied powers had crushed the Nazi military machine, victory was celebrated, although the world war was not entirely over – lives were still being lost in the Far East in the war against Japan. Churchill, Britain's respected wartime leader of the Conservatives, was ejected from office in a landslide Labour victory. This general election was a 'realigning' election in which Labour's campaign issues struck a chord with a war-weary electorate.

The authors of the first Nuffield election study felt that Labour's campaign harked back to the past with its constant warnings about what had happened at the end of the First World War, when victory had brought few if any benefits to the masses. Labour's message was that 'the Tories defaulted in 1918 and would do so again if given the chance' (McCallum and Readman, 1947, p. 45). Labour focused its campaign on domestic issues – decent homes, good schools, more jobs – and argued that this time everyone should benefit from Britain's victory, not just the rich. The few opinion polls that were conducted during the election campaign suggested that Labour was closely in tune with public opinion. For example a Gallup poll published in the *News Chronicle* indicated that 41 per cent of respondents felt that housing was the principal election issue, 15 per cent identified full employment as the top issue, and 7 per cent social security. A later poll showed that 42 per cent thought that Labour was the party best able to handle the housing crisis, whereas only 25 per cent felt that the Conservatives would do better. Thus, as the Nuffield authors concluded, 'Labour was highly favoured on the most canvassed election issue' (ibid, p. 242).

EXHIBIT 8.1   *The break-up of the coalition*

During the first three months of 1945 public interest was absorbed in the progress of military events. On 17 January the Russians entered Warsaw. Thence they drove westward unchecked until a fortnight later they drew up at the Oder within 50 miles of Berlin. Early in February the British forces began their attacks on the Rhine from the neighbourhood of Nijmegen. On the 23rd the United States 9th Army launched the offensive which one week later reached the Rhine at Dusseldorf. . . . The Rhine was crossed, first by the Americans at Remagen in a surprise attack. Then on 23 March the British armies under Field-Marshal Montgomery began their crossings between Rees and Wesel, in a combined air and land operation of tremendous magnitude. . . .

It thus appeared that the long-awaited election might soon be expected. The issues were already clear. They would be primarily domestic, and by far the most important would be Private Enterprise versus Nationalization. In the last days of March Mr Morrison made a speech to the London Labour parties in which he said that there was no longer adequate agreement on economic and industrial issues between the Conservative and Labour parties; and that it would require diplomacy and tact to carry on with the degree of unity necessary for the prosecution of the war. On 9 April Mr Bevin, at a Labour conference at Leeds, made an undisguised attack on the Conservative party, and reproached them bitterly for the record of their pre-war Government. . . .

In the first days of May there took place that fateful sequence of events, which began with the announcement of the death of Hitler on 1 May, and led up, day by day, to the unconditional surrender of all German fighting forces on 7 May. The nation received this news in a mood of profound solemnity. In unison they acclaimed Mr Churchill and praised him for this mighty deliverance. Never was his prestige higher, nor that of his Government, than in this moment of victory.

There followed a bewildering pause in the sequence of political events. . . . It was rumoured that all three parties were considering the whole question of the election and the timing thereof.The choice seemed to lie between an election in July or postponement till the autumn. . . .

On Wednesday 23 May Mr Churchill took the final step. At noon he sought an audience with the King, at which he tendered his resignation as Prime Minister, First Lord of the Treasury, and Minister of Defence. Four hours later he was summoned again to Buckingham Palace, and granted a further audience at which His Majesty . . . invited him to form a new administration. Mr Churchill accepted His Majesty's offer to hold the post of Prime Minister, and kissed hands on the appointment. He then asked the King for a dissolution of Parliament. . . .

Thus the ending of the Government was accomplished by Mr Churchill. He resigned on behalf of his Administration, thereby rendering unnecessary the resignation of individual Ministers. Immediately he set about constructing a new Ministry, known from its inception as the Caretaker Government. It was to consist primarily of members of the Conservative party reinforced by the National Liberals. It would also include a few non-party men and any Sinclair Liberals who should decide to remain. It was not yet known how many. The one thing that was known was that there would be no Labour Ministers. . . .

Yet while the greater mass of the public recoiled from the prospects of party struggles, that smaller but more influential section which finds in political argument and dispute the primary activity of leisure hours and thought, began to warm to the fray . . . the most ardent and enthusiastic of all were the rank and file political workers of the Labour party who felt for the first time that power was near or within their grasp.

Source: R. B. McCallum and A. Readman, *The British General Election of 1945*, Oxford, 1947, pp. 10–13, 21–3.

Source: David Low, *Evening Standard*, 27 January 1950

Conservative campaign messages were differently focused; they looked forward and put greater stress than did Labour on international politics, particularly the war with Japan. This enabled the Conservatives to emphasise the need for 'experienced leadership' and thereby capitalise on their greatest electoral asset, Churchill's reputation. The electorate, however, seemed able to distinguish between the qualities needed to lead Britain through war and those required for leadership in times of peace. Churchill's successful wartime record was not questioned, nor was his undoubted skill in foreign affairs, yet there was widespread doubt about his ability to lead once the war had ended. This doubt was reinforced by his misjudged attack on Labour, in which he claimed that socialism would produce a British version of the Gestapo.

A large 12 per cent swing resulted in a Labour landslide. Left-wing representation included an additional six MPs: two Communists, three for the Independent Labour Party and one for the Common Wealth Party. The Conservatives won 189 seats, to which can be added nine Ulster Unionists, two National and 13 Liberal National MPs. The Conservatives suffered a net loss of 185 seats. The Liberal Party won 12 seats. The first Labour government to hold real power had been elected in triumph; for Labour, this was its finest hour.

Dancing with Dogma

The Labour government was returned to office in the second general election of 1974 with a parliamentary majority of just three seats. These had disappeared by April 1976 and the government survived through pacts and deals made first with the Liberals and later the nationalist parties. Forty-two

MPs were members of neither the Labour nor the Conservative Party, and the minority Labour government was able to draw sufficient third-party support until the Scottish Nationalists joined the Conservatives and Liberals in a vote of no confidence, which the government lost by one vote on 23 March 1979.

Reflecting the impact of global adjustments on Britain's economy, crisis had become a familiar aspect of normality. Inflation, unemployment and a balance of payments crisis made contradictory policy demands on the government. A policy of continuing pay restraint, designed to tackle infla-tion, led to much discontent among low-paid workers in public sector unions. A series of strikes – dubbed by newspapers as the 'winter of discontent' – provided some unfortunate incidents and adverse publicity as far as the government was concerned, for the government, which prided itself on having a special understanding with the trade unions, clearly had an industrial relations problem.

The 1979 general election was not exactly a triumph for Margaret Thatcher and the Conservatives in terms of parliamentary majority or popular vote. Indeed by postwar standards Thatcher's government was close to the bottom in terms of electoral support; 56 per cent of all votes cast had gone to candidates opposed to Conservatism. There was no enthusiasm for the Conservative manifesto; indeed the Nuffield study concluded that 'the events of 1979 offer a good example of a government losing an election rather than of an opposition winning it' (Butler and Kavanagh, 1980, p. 340). The Conservative majority of 43 in the Commons was substantial, but dwarfed by the 144 seat parliamentary majority they were to obtain in the 1983 general election. The scale of Labour's defeat in 1979 in terms of the popular vote was the worst since 1931, and in terms of core support 'Labour now held only half (50%) of the trade union vote and less than half (45%) of the working class vote' (ibid, p. 350). Yet for Labour worse was to come in the general election of 1983. So in what sense can it be argued that 1979 was a watershed election?

The 1979 general election was critical insofar as the Conservative victory opened the door of Number Ten to a prime minister who was to become its longest resident this century. It was also critical in that Margaret Thatcher formally ended what remained of the postwar consensus; in public she scorned the idea of consensus politics and projected herself as a convic-tion-led politician. Thatcher was a radical politician, at times just as likely to attack previous Conservative governments as Labour ones (see Chapters 2 and 12). Finally, 1979 was critical in terms of the policies that were to develop subsequently from ideas either tested or voiced in the early Thatcher years. It can be argued that many aspects of British society have been transformed since 1979. For this reason 1979 was a watershed general election that facilitated the many changes that added up to the 'Thatcher revolution'.

Further Reading

Benney, M., A. P. Gray, and R. H. Pear, *How People Vote* (London: Routledge and Kegan Paul, 1956).

Berelson, B. R., P. F. Lazarsfield and W. N. McPhee, *Voting: A Study of Opinion Formation in a Presidential Campaign* (Chicago: University of Chicago Press, 1954).

Butler, D. and D. Kavanagh, *The British General Election of 1979* (London: Macmillan, 1980).

Butler, D. and D Stokes, *Political Change in Britain: The Evolution of Electoral Choice* (London: Macmillan, 1974).

Conley, F., *General Elections Today* (Manchester: Manchester University Press, 1990).

Crewe, I., P. Norris, D. Denver and D. Broughton (eds), *British Elections and Parties Yearbook 1991* (London: Harvester Wheatsheaf, 1992).

Denver, D. and G. Hands (eds), *Issues and Controversies in British Electoral Behaviour* (London: Harvester Wheatsheaf, 1992).

Franklin, M. N., *The Decline of Class Voting in Britain* (Oxford: Clarendon Press, 1985).

Heath, A., R. Jowell and J. Curtice, *How Britain Votes* (Oxford: Pergamon Press, 1985).

Himmelweit, H., P. Humphreys, M. Jaeger and M. Katz, *How Voters Decide* (London: Academic Press, 1981).

McCallum, R. B. and A. Readman, *The British General Election of 1945* (London: Oxford University Press, 1947).

Mishler, W., M. Hoskin and R. Fitzgerald, 'British parties in the balance: a time-series analysis of long-term trends in Labour and Conservative support', *British Journal of Political Science*, vol. 19, no. 2 (1989), pp. 211–36.

Robins, L. (ed.), *Topics in British Politics* (London: Politics Association, 1982).

Robins, L., H. Blackmore and R. Pyper (eds), *Britain's Changing Party System* (London: Leicester University Press, 1994).

Rose, R. and I. McAllister, *Voters Begin to Choose* (London: Sage, 1986).

Rose, R. and I. McAllister, *The Loyalties of Voters* (London: Sage, 1990).

Sarlvik, B. and I. Crewe, *Decade of Dealignment: The Conservative Victory of 1979 and Electoral Trends in the 1970s* (Cambridge: Cambridge University Press, 1983).

9
Managing Britain's Economy

Britain's modern history is of a manufacturing country that has had to export goods and services in order to import raw materials and sufficient food to feed its population. Britain and its empire dominated the world economy during the nineteenth century, but its position had weakened by the early years of the twentieth century as other industrial nations increased their output and trade. By the second half of the twentieth century both Labour and Conservative governments became preoccupied with the pressing question of how to stop, and then reverse, Britain's relative economic decline. The problem was that Britain's economy grew too slowly compared with its trading rivals (Figure 9.1). For example, whilst the economy grew on average by 2.25 per cent per capita a year between 1950–1979, the equivalent figure for Germany was 4.75 per cent, for France 4 per cent and for Italy 4.4 per cent (Maynard, 1988, p. 27). The special problem for Britain was that high economic growth seemed to cause other problems, for instance higher inflation and a balance of payments deficit, whose only cure was government policies that deflated the economy at the cost of rising unemployment.

How did successive postwar governments tackle this seeming dilemma? A large number of strategies, policies and other innovations were put into practice in an attempt to bring permanent improvement to the British economy, but most were derived from two basic and contrasting ideas about how the economy should be managed. The first idea was that capitalism sometimes worked in an unreliable way and that much government intervention was required both to make the system work more efficiently and to remedy some of capitalism's undesirable side effects. For many people the

FIGURE 9.1 *Comparative economic growth rates, 1938–64*

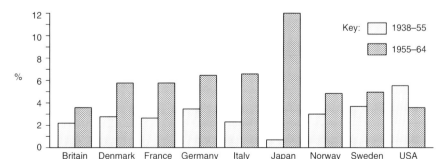

213

validity of this idea was confirmed by the experience of government direction and control of the economy during two world wars, particularly the second. The war effort seemed to solve many of the economic problems Britain had endured during the 1930s: full employment returned and the traditional industries – coal mining, steel and ship building – became busy once again, lifting regions such as Wales and the north out of long-lasting depression. Intellectual weight was given to the idea that governments should intervene in the economy by the work and writings of John Maynard Keynes, particularly his *General Theory of Employment, Interest and Money* (1936). Many of the policies pursued by postwar governments were 'Keynesian' in the sense that they were based on his ideas or on developments of his ideas by economists who considered themselves as 'Keynesians'. The era of Keynesian-inspired policies, which aimed at achieving economic growth in the context of high employment, lasted from the immediate postwar years until the 1970s, when they came under increasing attack from the Conservative new right.

The second idea was that capitalism was generally best left to run itself and that attempts by governments to intervene were doomed to failure. Indeed government intervention was perceived as a political threat to people's liberty as well as being an inferior economic approach to reliance on the workings of free market forces. The argument for giving free markets a bigger role and government a smaller role was supported in Friedrich von Hayek's book *The Road to Serfdom* (1944), and in Karl Popper's *The Open Society and its Enemies* (1945). Both these books were at odds with orthodox thinking during the postwar decades but became essential reading for the Conservative new right during the 1970s, when Keynesian policies seemed unable to cope with the crises faced by Western economies. In particular Keynesians were in disarray when it came to solving the problem of high inflation, which was in contrast to new right economists, who argued that their monetarist approach would cure inflation once and for all. For them, and for the new Conservative leader, Margaret Thatcher, high growth would be secured by liberating entrepreneurial energy, which previous governments had stifled, in the context of low inflation. This approach, known in Britain as 'Thatcherism', dominated policy making during the 1980s and 1990s, although it became increasingly challenged by new Keynesian-inspired policies.

By the end of the Second World War, Britain was facing two inescapable demands on its limited resources. First, its war-weary population was anticipating a generous explosion of welfare provision, ranging from improved housing to better health, education and social security services (see Chapter 10). Second, to finance the war effort Britain had sold or used up much of its overseas assets and incurred much debt, and therefore had to make massive effort to raise output to pay for crucial imports. Yet much of Britain's infrastructure and industrial plants were in need of new investment and many factories were struggling to meet the increased demand from consumers at home, who were anxious to break away from the austerity of the war years. Were important mistakes made in these early postwar years that led to Britain's economic distress from the 1960s onwards?

Corelli Barnett (1986) has argued that the war provided Britain with a temporary respite from its economic problems, all of which were to return during the peace. The Attlee government, Barnett argues, constructed Labour's 'New Jerusalem' welfare state on the foundations of an economy that was too weak to support it. As a result, resources that should have gone into reconstructing the economy went into fulfilling social policy. This, he argues, must be seen as a missed opportunity. At a critical point Britain failed to tackle fundamental problems related to its lack of competitiveness and as a consequence it experienced severe difficulties from that point onwards. Will Hutton, possibly more sensitive to electoral demands on government, disagrees with this view and argues that from a poor starting point Britain made immense scientific and productive progress throughout the 1940s: 'it out-produced Germany during the Second World War and narrowed the gap with the US – a remarkable achievement' (Hutton, 1995, p. 129). As far as Hutton is concerned, the roots of Britain's economic malaise lay not in one big missed opportunity but in the thinking and expectations of those who operated the British version of capitalism. Unlike the communitarian capitalist cultures of Germany and Japan, where a long-term view is taken of the need to invest in order to produce profits, the direction of British capitalism is more influenced by the stock market's demand for profits in the short term.

The Era of State Intervention

What the public expects of governments can vary over time. After years of tight governmental regulation and control during the war years, the electorate of 1945 expected the government to be responsible for maintaining full employment as well as raising living standards. Generally speaking, governments can meet public expectations by intervening in the economy in a variety of ways and by using a number of instruments to shape economic developments. First, governments can intervene directly by owning and running parts of the economy, by planning for economic growth or regional development; or through indirect controls such as controls on prices and incomes. Second, governments can use monetary policy to determine the volume of money in circulation, and through changes in the interest rate they can influence the amount of purchasing power in the economy and thereby the level of inflation. Finally, governments can use fiscal policy tools, such as the level of taxation on incomes, goods and services, or the amount of government spending and borrowing in order to control the amount of demand in the economy, which is reflected in the level of employment. It was primarily through use of the latter instruments that Keynesians intended to achieve growth and full employment.

Demand Management

It must be borne in mind that those at the peak of their political careers during the 1940s and 1950s had seen the devastation caused by the great slump of the 1930s, with its mass unemployment, social unrest and poverty. Much of their thinking was shaped by a determination never to allow such conditions again. Keynes believed that the deprivations of the 1930s could be avoided by maintaining a high level of demand in the economy, which would stimulate growth and increase the number of workers needed to increase output. In 1944, before the election of the Labour government, the 'Employment Policy' white paper accepted a commitment to demand management 'in order to maintain the highest possible level of employment' (Robins, 1987, p. 13). In other words Keynes' ideas had encroached on the thinking of the major parties and, although the term had not yet been coined, the era of 'Butskellism' had begun.[1]

Keynes recognised that Treasury decision makers had to handle fiscal controls with great care; for if they created too little demand there would be unemployment, too much and there would be inflation and a problem with the balance of payments. The latter situation would develop if there was already full employment yet still a demand for more workers, encouraging workers to squeeze higher wages from their employers under threat of changing jobs. At the same time excessive wage increases would create a

The era of state intervention: Britain's John Maynard Keynes at the UN Monetary and Financial Conference, Bretton Woods, USA, 1944.

demand for goods that British factories might find hard to satisfy; fewer goods would be available for export and more would have to be imported to meet domestic demand. The same economic instruments could be used to reduce inflation and cure the balance of payments problem by deflating the economy. Measures such as increasing taxes, restricting credit and cutting public spending would have the effect of reducing aggregate demand, causing a fall in output, a drop in inflation, a surplus in the balance of payments and the probability of a rise in unemployment.

The political temptation with demand management of the economy was for governments to coincide this 'stop–go' cycle with the timing of general elections (Figure 9.2). In particular the 1950s saw governments moving to the 'go' phase by stimulating demand before a general election. This created a 'feel-good' factor in terms of better incomes, increased affluence and reduced unemployment. After reelection by grateful voters, the cycle moved rapidly to the 'stop' phase, with falling output and rising unemployment. To the frustration of the opposition, it seemed that the cycle could be repeated successfully at the next general election, the electorate seemingly having a short political memory.

Did 'stop–go' policies, with their underlying boom and bust cycles, inflict actual harm on Britain's economy? Certainly 'stop–go' created a climate of uncertainty that undermined business confidence, for during the 'go' phase business found it hard to cope with the high level of consumer demand, and during the 'stop' deflationary phase it was difficult to raise money for investment since the risks seemed too great. Firms that had been planning new investment abandoned their plans and the low investment that resulted has been identified as a major cause of Britain's long-term economic decline.

FIGURE 9.2   *The stop–go cycle*

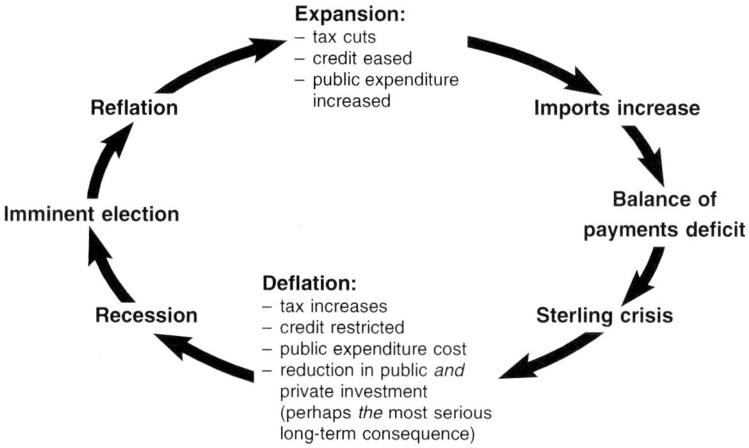

Expansion:
– tax cuts
– credit eased
– public expenditure increased

Reflation

Imports increase

Imminent election

Balance of payments deficit

Recession

Deflation:
– tax increases
– credit restricted
– public expenditure cost
– reduction in public *and* private investment (perhaps *the* most serious long-term consequence)

Sterling crisis

Source: based on Thomas, 1992, p. 55.

Placing on one side reservations about the effect of stop–go on the long-term performance of the economy, demand management policies were generally successful, raising output in the immediate postwar years (1946–52), by almost one third. Many people did not, however, feel correspondingly better off since much of this newly created wealth went into correcting the balance of payments rather than into domestic consumption. In other words, although the war was over the climate of austerity continued well into peacetime, and it was reinforced by continued rationing of some foodstuffs and other goods. However under the stewardship of Labour Chancellor Sir Stafford Cripps – a minister so mean that he had the reputation of living off cress that he grew on his blotting paper in the Treasury – the economy began to regenerate, despite potential hazards on the road to recovery such as the dreadful winter of 1947 and the Korean War of 1950.

The Conservatives were elected to power in 1951 and, with a manifesto slogan of 'Set the People Free', promptly ended all remaining controls, including rationing. The 1950s was a period in which the 'age of austerity' slipped quickly into an 'age of affluence'. By 1956 Harold Macmillan felt able to claim that in Britain 'we have the second highest standard of living in the world and have never been so prosperous', or, as later paraphrased by newspaper journalists, 'you've never had it so good'. But whilst the absolute standard of living in Britain had risen impressively, the higher rates of growth enjoyed by other industrial nations meant that their living standards were fast catching up and would soon overtake Britain's (Figure 9.1).

During the 1960s the Conservative government, and then more markedly Labour governments, began to put greater emphasis on other forms of intervention, particularly planning and wage controls. The Keynesian era, during which British people had enjoyed more than two decades of near full employment and rising living standards, finally ended in disarray in the early 1970s. In a period of severe economic crisis, which was to test the durability of capitalism, Keynesian policies appeared increasingly irrelevant as solutions to the new problems faced by Western governments.

Briefly, the development of Western economies had been highly dependent on the supply of cheap oil, particularly from the Middle East. However political and economic events brought an abrupt end to cheap oil, resulting in what is sometimes referred to as 'the energy crisis', although in many ways the crisis stretched beyond energy to embrace the survival of Western lifestyles. The Organisation of Petroleum Exporting Countries (OPEC) – an Arab-dominated oil producers' cartel – began to increase the price of crude oil for economic, profit-maximising reasons. The Arab–Israeli conflict of 1973, when the United States gave its traditional backing to Israel, led to a reduction in oil extraction for political reasons. In 1974 the price of oil quadrupled, injecting massive inflation into the economy (Table 9.1); but counter to Keynesian logic, as inflation soared and the balance of payments worsened, so unemployment rose sharply. Thus 'Stagflation' hit Britain's

TABLE 9.1 *Inflation, unemployment and industrial action, 1970–94*

	Inflation (%)	Unemployment (%)	Days lost through strikes (millions)
1970	6	2.6	11.0
1971	9	2.6	14.0
1972	7	2.9	24.0
1973	9	2.0	7.0
1974	16	2.1	15.0
1975	24	3.1	6.0
1976	17	4.2	3.0
1977	16	4.4	10.0
1978	8	4.4	9.0
1979	13	4.1	29.0
1980	18	5.1	12.0
1981	12	8.1	4.0
1982	9	9.6	5.0
1983	5	10.5	4.0
1984	5	10.7	27.0
1985	6	10.9	6.0
1986	3	11.1	2.0
1987	4	10.0	4.0
1988	5	8.4	4.0
1989	8	6.3	4.0
1990	9	5.8	2.0
1991	6	8.1	1.0
1992	5	9.7	0.5
1993	2	10.3	0.6
1994	3	9.4	0.4

economy, and monetarist economists from the new right began to argue that it was they, not Keynesians, who had the solution to economic recovery.

Nationalisation

The rhetoric of the Labour Party, particularly during the 1930s, was explicitly socialist in nature. Although the term 'socialism' was not used in the party's constitution, clause four committed Labour to 'the common ownership of the means of production, distribution and exchange'. Socialism is a political concept with many potential meanings, but Labour made common ownership – nationalisation in policy terms – its defining principle. Thus when Attlee's Labour government embarked on a massive programme of nationalisation, it was easy to interpret this as socialist dogma being put into practice. This, however, may be an over generous interpretation of the influence of socialists in Labour policy making.

Public ownership and the direct control of economic activity existed outside the world of socialism. For example both world wars had seen stringent government control over critical industries and services, and public corporations were created long before the arrival of Attlee in Number Ten, such as the Port of London Authority (1908) and the Central Electricity Board (1927). There were, in other words, non-socialist reasons for public ownership and control. Indeed the Conservative government elected in 1951 denationalised surprisingly little: just road haulage and steel (both industries were subsequently renationalised by Labour, and then privatised by the Conservatives). Also, Edward Heath's Conservative government nationalised the aero-engine company Rolls-Royce. Rolls-Royce was in financial difficulties because inflation had made its fixed-price contracts uneconomic, and when government subsidies failed to save the company it was nationalised. It is safe to assume that socialist motives were entirely absent from Heath's decision to nationalise the company.

Much the same might have been said of Attlee and his ministers when it came to the principal reason for nationalising the 'commanding heights' of British industry. Crucial industries such as coal, iron and steel, and the railways were fragmented, clapped out by the war effort and in the hands of private owners who lacked the resources needed for new investment to modernise and contribute to Britain's economic recovery. Nationalisation provided the moral justification for using public money to reinvest and reorganise these vast undertakings. At the same time, control of these 'commanding heights' of the economy would assist the government to plan for growth and recovery. Postwar nationalisation was seen in different ways by Labour: the left wing saw it in terms of fulfilling a socialist commitment, whilst the right wing believed it a necessary mix for the recovery of Britain's capitalist economy.

From the outset, the lack of political independence of the nationalised industries was recognised as a problem and there was considerable discussion about how government influence could be curtailed. The political temptation for governments was to use the nationalised industries for electoral purposes. They could be overmanned and used as a tool to help control unemployment; commercially based price increases could be postponed until after general elections had taken place; price increases over what was commercially justified could be used as a hidden form of taxation after elections had been held.

In addition to the impact that political interference had on the public's image of the nationalised industries, there were other reasons that led to their increasing unpopularity. The nationalised industries were generally perceived as inefficient in comparison with private sector companies. There were also fears, exploited by Conservative politicians, that since the nationalised industries were monopolies that automatically received a government subsidy if they made a loss, there was no competition or threat of bankruptcy and job loss to improve efficiency. Because public sector trade unions felt that jobs were safe in the nationalised industries, free from the discipline of market forces, industrial practices remained outmoded and labour relations were generally poor. Whilst the public attitude remained positive towards state involvement in the welfare state, particularly the NHS, state intervention in the form of nationalised industries became seen as overbureaucratic, wasteful and inefficient.

There was also an argument that the public sector, including the nationalised industries, was holding back growth in the private sector, and money that went into public sector enterprises could have been used more productively in the private sector. Since resources were limited, public sector investment 'crowded out' private sector investment. Hence it was argued that a smaller commitment to the wealth-consuming public sector would release more resources for the wealth-creating private sector.

Both Conservative and Labour governments disposed of state assets during the 1970s; but the process of denationalisation, or privatisation, did not begin in earnest until the 1980s. The Conservative election manifesto of 1979 pledged to privatise ship building and the aerospace industries, to sell off the National Freight Corporation, and to allow council tenants to buy the houses they occupied. There followed a massive transfer of assets to the private sector, some being sold to the public and others directly to private sector concerns. Policies that would have seemed extreme and even reckless during the 1950s and 1960s appeared as normal in the 1980s, perception of them having been altered by the arrival of a new economic orthodoxy that expected government now to play a far smaller role in society.

Planning for Growth

Contrary to the expectations of many Labour Party members, the nationalised industries were never used as instruments for planning the economy. During the 1960s both Conservative and Labour governments showed considerable interest in planning, but none of their experiments proved successful in solving Britain's low growth problem. Conservative interest resulted from the success of French 'indicative planning', whereby interested parties set targets for growth, employment and so on, which were feasible if all parties voluntarily complied with the agreed policies. In 1961 the Conservative chancellor proposed to set up a National Economic Development Council (NEDC, – immediately nicknamed 'Neddy' by journalists) which would bring together trade union leaders, employers, ministers, chairmen of key nationalised industries and independent experts to consider the long-term growth of the economy. The Conservatives were anxious to avoid centralised planning from inside Whitehall. Through its wide membership – essentially a tripartite membership comprising unions, employers and government – Neddy was able to build consensual policies about what could be achieved in the future. Neddy first met in 1962 and set what was described as an 'ambitious but realistic' growth target of 4 per cent a year over the next five years (compared with the actual average growth of 2.7 per cent a year over the previous five years). Unfortunately this ambitious target proved unrealistic, but nevertheless all parties agreed that the Neddy experience was useful and should be developed.

The new Labour government of 1964 retained the Neddy system – the NEDC itself, subcommittees (so-called 'little Neddies') that focused on particular industries, and the secretariat in the shape of the National Economic Development Office – although its precise purpose and functions remained somewhat unclear. This may have been the result of wilful obstruction by employers, who were later said to have undermined every constructive approach to industry made within the context of Neddy (Hutton, 1995, p. 40).

The Thatcher governments saw Neddy as an unwanted leftover from a bygone corporatist age. Hence Neddy became increasingly marginalised during the Thatcher administrations, meeting less frequently, and it was finally wound up by the second Conservative government of John Major.

When it came to planning for economic growth, Labour's plans were more ambitious than reliance on Neddy. A new government department, the Department of Economic Affairs (DEA), was established to counterbalance the influence of the Treasury in shaping economic policy. Labour Prime Minister Harold Wilson believed that beneficial 'creative tension' would result from the DEA's long-term view on the economy, challenging the Treasury's short-term, day-to-day perspective. The first casualty, it was anticipated, would be the end of destructive stop–go policies.

The DEA, headed by George Brown, had the responsibility of formulating a national plan. This, it was hoped, would provide a greater national focus on growth and result in a more sustained effort to remove the ancient obstacles to growth. The national plan, published in 1965, included an assessment of British industry, consideration of prices and incomes issues, and a growth target of 25 per cent in national output over the following six years, which represented an annual growth target of 3.8 per cent a year.

Was the national plan little more than a useful party political propaganda tool in the run-up to the next general election? Some Labour ministers feared that the national plan would fail unless it was accompanied by devaluation to improve competitiveness, secure a surplus on the balance of payments, and thereby kick-start growth. Wilson resisted demands for devaluation since the last devaluation had been under a Labour government in 1949 and he feared that Labour would be labelled the 'party of devaluation' if he took similar action. (Little did he know that devaluation would be forced upon his government in any case in a year's time.) As it was, Labour took deflationary measures – the 'July measures' – to protect sterling and at the same time abandoned the national plan.

Industrial Policy

Many in the Labour Party saw the achievements of the Conservative governments from 1951–64 in terms of 'thirteen wasted years': the economy had underperformed and Labour was confident that more efficient management would improve the productivity of British industry. As it was, British industry did not attract the high level of investment enjoyed by some rivals – for example Germany and Japan – and unlike these countries Britain could only dream about export-led growth rather than actually achieve it.

Britain was not paying its way in the world, and part of the problem was diagnosed as uncompetitiveness resulting from too little investment. A report revealed that, for example, whilst 62 per cent of machine tools used in Japanese factories and 56 per cent in German factories were less than ten years old, in Britain the equivalent figure was only 38 per cent. There was also concern and disappointment that British finance would not invest in British inventions, leaving the way clear for rival countries to profit from them.

The resulting situation was reflected in Britain's annual balance of payments, which at the time were believed to be worse than the revised figures shown in Table 9.2.

Improving the balance of payments became a central aim of Harold Wilson's Labour governments. A Neddy report concluded that the structure of industry was a major obstacle to higher economic growth and increased manufacturing exports. It was argued that many British companies were too small to compete effectively, and that they needed to be rationalised into larger, more efficient units. In response Labour set up the Industrial Reorganisation Corporation (IRC), 'a statutory body equipped with state funds to help promote rationalisation, mergers and restructuring of industries and firms, where this was needed to help exports or to pool resources for new technological advance' (Wilson, 1971, p. 202). The IRC intervened in a number of areas, most notably to facilitate the merger of British Motor Holdings with Leyland Motors to become British Leyland (now BMW-owned Rover). The IRC was the responsibility of a newly created Ministry of Technology, another agency concerned with encouraging technological

TABLE 9.2 *Britain's balance of payments, 1964–9*

	Surplus/deficit (£ million)
1964	−355
1965	−27
1966	+101
1967	−298
1968	−270
1969	+460

advance. Finally, Labour initiated a new selective employment tax (SET), paid by some employers but not others and designed to squeeze workers out of service industries into manufacturing. The SET was controversial but clearly part of Labour's industrial policy.

Edward Heath's Conservative government, which came into office in 1970, was opposed to Labour's interventionist industrial strategy. The Conservatives believed that reduced government intervention would result in a more competitive climate, which in itself would make industry more efficient. To this end, the Conservatives decided that no public money would be used to support 'lame duck' industries and accordingly the IRC was stripped of its powers. However, events were to force a policy U-turn on the Heath government, the foremost of which was the collapse of Rolls-Royce (referred to above). The government could not put its rhetoric into practice and allow Rolls-Royce to collapse since the company played a crucial role in keeping the RAF airborne. In the national interest, therefore, public money was poured into Rolls-Royce.

The Thatcher governments presided over an acceleration of deindustrialisation, and for the first time since the industrial revolution Britain imported more manufactured goods than it exported. Critics of Thatcherism argued that the vast revenues from North Sea oil were squandered during the 1980s, and that resources that could have been devoted to making industry more competitive were used to support unnecessary mass unemployment and unjustified consumer spending. In 1985 a House of Lords Committee on Overseas Trade published a controversial report, which concluded that Britain's poor prospects posed 'a grave threat to the standard of living and to the economic and political stability of the nation'. The report foresaw the economy stagnating as North Sea oil ran out and revenues fell, with the value of sterling collapsing and import costs rising, leading to rapid inflation. The chancellor, Nigel Lawson, dismissed the report as a 'mixture of special pleading dressed up as analysis and assertion masquerading as evidence which led the committee to its doom-laden conclusion'. The Thatcher government was determined to pursue the path of non-intervention and, unlike Heath's Conservative government, avoid policy U-turns. Put simply, the Thatcherite approach was that the government of business was no longer the business of government.

Prices and Incomes Policies

Government economic policy has frequently been directed towards correcting the consequences of its previous policy decisions. For example in the 1950s, the 'go' phase of stop–go economic management created a climate in which incomes were encouraged to rise rapidly. But this prompted a chain reaction in which rising wages pushed up the cost of goods, making exports uncompetitive. Hence the 'stop' phase (see Figure 9.2). Also, the government's pursuit of full employment gave trade unions increased power to bargain higher wage rises, as companies were desperate not to lose workers to other companies that were willing to pay more. Once again, increased wages pushed up prices, which in turn led to another round of wage increases. Incomes policies represented attempts to replace the spiral of higher wages and higher prices of the market place with government-imposed moderation and stability.

Since the central purpose of trade unions is to improve the standard of living of their members, they have traditionally been suspicious of incomes policies and reluctant partners in bargaining over wage restraint. This was the case when Labour Chancellor Sir Stafford Cripps operated a voluntary policy of wage restraint in the late 1940s: the trade unions voiced opposition but nevertheless acquiesced. In the early 1960s the Conservative government set up the National Incomes Commission to review incomes policy issues, and on this occasion the unions refused to participate. Nevertheless, various incomes policies were pursued, including a nine-month 'pay pause' for public sector workers.

Many trade unionists felt that incomes policies were unfair since emphasis was placed on the restraint of wages. They believed that if wage increases were held back, then price increases and company profits ought also to be restrained. It was argued that workers felt exploited when they saw big increases in company profits and dividends paid to shareholders whilst their wages remained more or less the same. The Labour government that was elected in 1964 was prepared to apply 'moderation' across the board in terms of a comprehensive prices and incomes policy. A Statement of Intent (Exhibit 9.1) preceded the establishment of the National Board for Prices and Incomes (NBPI). Initially the NBPI operated a voluntary policy, having no other sanction than the force of moral argument as it monitored price changes and wage increases. The NBPI was criticised for being overly bureaucratic, for focusing more on incomes than on prices, and for lacking authority as implementation of its judgments was voluntary in nature rather than compulsory. Arguing in support of the NBPI, others pointed out that it produced a great deal of valuable information and research, that the emphasis was bound to be on incomes since there were millions of price changes every year, many of them seasonal, and its actions finally became compulsory when a six month wage freeze was ultimately implemented (Moonman, 1971, p. 12).

The NBPI was a highly interventionist body. Prices and incomes issues were referred to it by the relevant minister, and after a time it enjoyed additional 'early warning' procedures regarding forthcoming increases. Typical of price recommendations, for example, was that there should be a freeze on all prices in the baking industry. On the incomes side of its work, even the prime minister was impressed by the determination of the NBPI to moderate wage increases. Recounting the first case referred to it – involving

EXHIBIT 9.1   *The Statement of Intent*

1. The government's economic objective is to achieve and maintain a rapid increase in output and real income combined with full employment. The social objective is to ensure that the benefits of faster growth are distributed in a way that satisfies the claims of social need and justice. In this way general confidence will be created in the purpose of the national plan and individuals will be willing to make the utmost contribution towards its implementation.

2. Essential conditions for the achievement of these objectives are a strong currency and a healthy balance of payments.

3. The economic situation, while potentially strong, is at present extremely unsatisfactory. Drastic temporary measures have been taken to meet a situation in which the balance of payments was in serious deficit, with exports falling behind imports. But these measures can provide only a breathing-space.

4. To achieve a more permanent solution we must improve the balance of payments, encourage exports and sharpen our competitive ability. Our longer-term interests lie in reducing the barriers to international trade. We must take urgent and vigorous action to raise productivity throughout industry and commerce to keep increases in total money incomes in line with increases in real national output and to maintain a stable general price level. Unless we do this we shall have a slower rate of growth and a lower level of employment.

5. We, government, management and unions, are resolved to take the following action in our respective spheres of responsibility.

6. The government will prepare and implement a general plan for economic development, in consultation with both sides of industry through the National Economic Development Council. This will provide higher investment: for improving our industrial skills; for modernisation of industry; for balanced regional development; for higher exports; and for the largest possible sustained expansion of production and real incomes.

7. Much greater emphasis will be given to increasing productivity. Government will encourage and develop policies designed to promote technical advance in industry, and to get rid of restrictive practices and prevent the abuse of monopoly power and so improve efficiency, cut out waste, and reduce excessive prices. More vigorous policies will be pursued designed to facilitate mobility of labour and generally to make more effective use of scarce manpower resources, and to give workers a greater sense of security in the face of economic change. The government also intend to introduce essential social improvements such as a system of earnings-related benefits in addition to the improvements in national insurance benefits already announced.

8. The Government will set up machinery to keep a constant watch on the general movement of prices and of money incomes of all kinds and to carry out the other functions described in paragraph ten below. They will also use their fiscal powers or other appropriate measures to correct any excessive growth in aggregate profits as compared with the growth of total wages and salaries, after allowing for short-term fluctuations.

9. We, the representatives of the TUC, the Federation of British Industries, the British Employers' Confederation, the National Association of British Manufacturers, and the Association of British Chambers of Commerce accept that major objectives of national policy must be:
    (i)   to ensure that British industry is dynamic and that its prices are competitive;
    (ii) to raise productivity and efficiency so that real national output can increase, and to keep increases in wages, salaries and other forms of income in line with this increase; to keep the general level of prices stable.
10. We therefore undertake, on behalf of our members, to encourage and lead a sustained attack on the obstacles to efficiency, whether on the part of management or of workers and to strive for the achievement of more rigorous standards of performance at all levels; and to co-operate with the government in endeavouring in the face of practical problems, to give effective shape to the machinery that the government intends to establish for the following purposes:
    (i)   to keep under review the general movement of prices and of money incomes of all kinds;
    (ii) to examine particular cases in order to advise whether or not the behaviour of prices or wages, salaries or other money incomes is in the national interest as defined by the government after consultation with management and unions.
11. We stress that close attention must be paid to easing the difficulties of those affected by changing circumstances in their employment. We therefore support, in principle, the government's proposals for earnings-related benefits and will examine sympathetically proposals for severance payments.
12. We, government, management and unions, are confident that by co-operating in a spirit of mutual confidence to give effect to the principles and policies described above, we and those whom we represent will be able to achieve a faster growth of real incomes and generally to promote the economic and social well-being of the country.

low-paid railwaymen, for whom the prime minister had some sympathy – he commented that the NBPI 'was interpreting its terms of reference tightly and applying the most severe of norms in this case, which covered some of the lowest-paid workers in Britain. On the other hand, to yield incontinently to strike threats would mean the end of any meaningful prices and incomes policy, with serious effects abroad' (Wilson, 1971, p. 199).

Subsequent governments pursued both compulsory and voluntary policies to regulate wage movements. The Conservative government of 1970–4 moved from voluntary restraint to a compulsory freeze before adopting a wage increase formula tied to cost-of-living increases. The Labour governments that followed regulated wage increases through a voluntary 'social contract' with the trade unions. The arrangement between the government and the unions was based on a complex bargain: in exchange for unions relating wage increases to price increases the government would first restore union rights that had been lost during the previous Conservative administration, and then improve the 'social wages' of workers through the welfare system. The social contract met with increasing union opposition as it slowly developed into a policy solely concerned with wage restraint.

Settlement of wage levels through government intervention rather than the free play of market forces was invariably difficult to achieve. In implementing an incomes policy for anything other than a brief period, governments encountered a number of problems based on four basic causes. First, once an incomes policy came to an end many unions lodged big claims in a 'catching up' exercise. This was exacerbated by some unions having traditionally higher-paid workers who were determined to maintain pay differentials between themselves and lower-paid workers. Second, having agreed to an incomes policy with the government, trade union leaders frequently found that they could not 'deliver' the agreement of their members. In other words, what might have seemed a reasonable settlement to trade union executive committees was unacceptable to shop stewards on the factory floor. Third, incomes policies frequently caused frustration and opposition, which resulted in industrial action. Harold Wilson's government endured a damaging seamen's strike which was caused in large part by Labour's prices and incomes policy; a national miners' strike for pay in excess of the pay policy award resulted in the 'three-day week' and led to Edward Heath calling a general election on the issue of 'who governs: the unions or a democratically elected Conservative government?'; and James Callaghan's social contract between the Labour government and the unions collapsed in the 'winter of discontent' public sector strikes. Finally, such strikes were directed not at employers but 'against the government' (Mitchell, 1972, p. 18).

The Thatcher governments had no formal incomes policy although there was a policy for incomes. Public spending was capped, so public sector wage settlements above the levels allowed for by the government were paid for by the redundancy of workers who could no longer 'be afforded'. Regarding the private sector, the chancellor argued that Britain's 'unemployment' problem was really a 'high wages' problem. Nigel Lawson believed there was a direct link between wages and jobs; the cheaper jobs were in terms of wages, the more would be demanded by employers. He told parliament that 200 000 new jobs would be created for every 1 per cent cut in the real income of those in employment. Consistent with this view, Conservative governments scrapped the wages councils, which until then had decided the wages of nearly three million low-paid workers, on the ground that wages councils pushed up wages too rapidly. The outcome of this deregulation will be that by the end of the century a remarkable revolution will have occurred in the labour market, with women then forming the majority of workers, mostly in low-paid, part-time or temporary jobs. What were seen in 1945 as 'real jobs', that is 'men's jobs', have been the principal casualty of this revolution.

The Era of Retreat

The 1970s was a decade of crisis for the British economy. The shockwaves from the oil crisis which swept through the economy were intensified, rather than calmed, by the policies of various governments. For example, in order to avoid the crippling balance of payments problems that had bedevilled previous Labour governments, the Conservative government removed fixed exchange rates in 1972 and allowed sterling to float on the foreign exchanges. Edward Heath's government did not fully realise the implications of this move, which, accompanied by a relaxation of credit controls, fuelled inflation. Excess demand in the economy tended to push down the international value of sterling and thereby stimulate inflation rather than, as had been the case under fixed exchange rates, result in rising imports and a balance of payments problem.

Some economists were concerned that the rapid expansion of the money supply – which rose by 30 per cent in the year after the flotation of sterling and by another 20 per cent in the following year (Maynard, 1988, p. 12) – was the principal cause of the subsequent high inflation. To them the problem was made even worse by the high level of government spending, financed by borrowing, which was intended to curb rapidly rising unemployment but in reality provided another boost to the already high inflation.

By the end of the 1970s any assessment of Britain's economy made gloomy reading: unemployment had doubled; inflation had risen by an average of 12 per cent each year; on average economic growth was a derisory 2 per cent a year; and Britain had incurred large debts to the International Monetary Fund. Faced with this dismal view of the economy, policy makers made a subtle change in their priorities. Rather than attempting to maintain full employment, their first priority was now to curb inflation.

A Loss of Faith in Government Intervention

The twin approaches associated with Keynes and Beveridge, which had brought full employment and the welfare state, were once seen as crucial to the survival of capitalism in a democracy where the biggest share of the vote was in the hands of the working classes. The economic crisis of the mid 1970s weakened faith in the efficacy of the policies of Keynes and Beveridge, which now seemed to endanger rather than guarantee the survival of capitalism. The opportunity was created for new ideas and approaches to challenge the old orthodoxies.

A small minority of politicians had always doubted the wisdom of demand management. Even during the years of 'Butskellism' they had criticised the management of the economy and argued that growing state intervention would inevitably end in failure. A Conservative chancellor, Peter Thorneycroft, resigned in 1958 over the insistence of his cabinet colleagues for public spending to be maintained at what he believed was too high a level. Enoch

Powell was an articulate opponent of government intervention and represented other economic liberals within the Conservative leadership, until he was sacked from the shadow cabinet in 1968 over his controversial and outspoken views on immigration.

The Conservative government elected in 1970 began with the firm intention of reducing government intervention in the economy in order to create a more competitive climate in which British industry would become more efficient. This was the approach of so-called 'Selsdon Man' – named after a Conservative seminar at the Selsdon Park Hotel in Croydon – which reached some tough conclusions about the need to reform trade unions, reduce the size of the welfare state and end state subsidies for loss-making companies, all to be achieved, if necessary, at a much higher level of unemployment. But as we have seen, events were to push this Conservative government off-course and force a number of policy U-turns on Prime Minister Edward Heath that resulted in more, not less, intervention.

After the general elections of 1974 the new Labour government took some steps away from traditional interventionist techniques. Chancellor Denis Healey tightened monetary controls in 1976; he sold off part of the government's shareholding in British Petroleum (BP); and Prime Minister James Callaghan informed a Labour conference that his government was now challenging basic Keynesian assumptions (see page 249).

Significantly, Anthony Crosland also informed conference delegates that the era of high government spending had come to an end. Addressing his remarks to Labour councillors, he announced that as far as government spending was concerned 'the party's over' and that local government could expect much financially leaner times ahead. There seemed little doubt that even Labour was abandoning Keynesian policies for their lack of relevance regarding the problems Britain faced in the 1970s.

Rolling Back the State

The election of the first Thatcher government in 1979 marked a further movement towards 'supply side' economics and away from reliance on 'demand management'. It was argued that economic efficiency was being hampered by the distorting effects of government intervention and trade union activity. The role of government ought to be one of constructing an environment within which free market forces could operate efficiently through policies such as deregulation, trade union reform, the removal of government controls and improving the skills of the workforce. What government should not do, it was argued, was replace the free market with interventionist policies.

Margaret Thatcher drew on many ideas that originated on the new right, an ideological grouping based around a number of key individuals and think tanks. Briefly, the new right rejected all policies of postwar governments, both Conservative and Labour, that worked to produce a more egalitarian society. The new right valued liberty above and beyond measures designed to increase equality, and for the new right liberty was best protected through the workings of a free market and most threatened by restrictions on market forces. Since 1945 the biggest restrictions had come from government intervention and trade union restrictive practices. Whilst promoting free markets was central to new right thinkers, some emphasised the need for greater managerial efficiency, some were more nationalistic, some were moralistic, and some were more interested in monetarist economic policy.

Monetarism

Monetarism is an elaborate economic theory (see Walters, 1986), but at its heart is the simple idea that inflation is caused by 'too much money chasing too few goods'. Previous governments had pursued interventionist policies in an attempt to increase economic growth and thereby produce more goods. Monetarists focused on the other side of the equation and their policies were aimed at reducing the amount of money in the economy, which would put a squeeze on inflation.

The Thatcher government put monetarism into practice by means of the medium-term financial strategy (MTFS), a step-by-step approach to reducing inflation by reducing the growth of the money supply (in terms of a measure known as sterling M3). Consistent with the new right's belief in reduced government, monetarists argued that the most effective way of controlling the money supply was for the government to control its own spending. The policies of previous governments, particularly that of Edward Heath's referred to above, suggested there was a time lag of around two years in the relationship between movements in the money supply and the inflation rate. The MTFS was designed to banish inflation from the economy over a course of years by keeping the growth of sterling M3 within agreed targets. Getting rid of inflation was seen by monetarists as a crucial precondition for Britain's economic revival.

The strict discipline of targets for the money supply quickly collapsed. Once targets had been overshot, the chancellor set new, higher targets, but eventually these too were exceeded. By 1985 many commentators thought that the money supply was out of control; the MTFS growth target of 5–9 per cent was overshot by an actual growth of 19 per cent in the money supply. Yet despite monetarist theory, inflation fell sharply. Not surprisingly the MTFS was abandoned.

If the MTFS did not reduce inflation, what did? Economists believed that the high interest rates set to control credit attracted foreign speculators to invest their money in Britain. The inflow of this money drove up the international value of sterling, which was already strong because of its new status as a petro-currency backed by North Sea oil. This situation reduced the competitiveness of British companies, which were undercut at home by cheaper imports and whose exports were now too expensive in overseas markets. Firms that had taken out loans were also hit by the higher interest charges. The combination of high interest rates and high exchange rates was disastrous for many British companies, and within two years one in five manufacturing jobs had been lost. It was commonly believed that deep recession accompanied by mass unemployment had resulted in falling inflation. Monetarist theory, like Keynesian theory, was in tatters.

Public Spending

Public spending is generally financed through taxation and government borrowing. The new right was opposed to 'big government'; taxation was seen as a denial of liberty, since individuals could not exercise choice in how their income was spent; and increased government borrowing in the form of a higher public sector borrowing requirement (PSBR) was seen as fuelling further inflation.

Monetarist policy was aimed at reducing public spending both absolutely and as a proportion of the national income. However, the recession of the early 1980s resulted in the need for increased spending, not less. In real terms public spending rose from £77 billion in 1979 to £132 billion in 1985.

A study by Sir Leo Pliatsky, *Paying and Choosing* (1985), examined changes in public spending between 1978–9 and 1983–4. He found that the pattern of spending had changed, with some areas receiving less whilst others received more, but the total had risen relentlessly. It was argued that governments had relatively little scope to reduce public spending. It was calculated that around a fifth of public spending was fixed because of long-term commitments; around two thirds was determined by 'demand' in terms of the numbers of unemployed, patients for treatment, pupils for schooling and so on., leaving around 10 per cent where the government could make cuts and save money. But even here, cuts in public spending could bring hardship to some and have significant political consequences.

The Thatcher government's rhetoric changed from 'cutting' public spending to 'controlling' public spending. This latter process was assisted by the sale of nationalised industries: money gained from selling state assets was counted as 'negative spending', which allowed public spending to increase whilst appearing to keep spending totals within strict targets.

Privatisation

By 1979 around 10 per cent of the nation's wealth was being created by public sector industries. In terms of new right thinking, the investment that went into these industries 'crowded out' investment that could have gone into the private sector. As far as the new right was concerned, the nationalised industries represented unnecessary government involvement as too often they were supported by subsidies rather than by profits. It was argued that enterprises that were inefficient in the public sector would be transformed into successful, profit-making companies responsive to customer needs if they experienced the discipline of market forces. This could be achieved by moving ownership from the public to the private sector. At the same time it was argued that moving the nationalised industries into the private sector would make it easier for them to raise finances as well as help to create an enterprise culture through wider share ownership, especially among employees of the privatised industries. As well as denationalising, or privatising, public sector enterprises, the Thatcher governments also encouraged the sale of council houses to tenants through the 'Right to Buy' legislation. Both policies were intended to create a share/property owning democracy as a bulwark against socialism.

Privatisation involved a number of new approaches alongside the transfer of public assets to the private sector. First, public services previously provided by public sector employees were *contracted out* to private firms. Second, *market testing* and *competitive tendering* ensured that those services which remained in the public sector did so because they offered the best value for money. Finally, *deregulation* removed restrictions and opened up new areas of public provision to competition from the private sector.

By the final year of Margaret Thatcher's residence in Number Ten, privatisation sales had generated nearly £20 000 million (excluding proceeds from council house sales). However fears were expressed that privatisation was bringing short-term benefits at the cost of long-term disadvantages: 'The sale of public assets is limited – once the best of the family silver is sold the financial benefits of continuing sales is limited. . . . Recession, the expected decline in oil tax revenue . . . and a substantial reduction in privatisation receipts, could cause fiscal instability, if not crisis' (Whitfield, 1992, p. 10). Critics of privatisation also pointed out that many public sector enterprises, for example Amersham International, Cable and Wireless and Rolls-Royce, had been competing with private sector rivals before they were privatised. Furthermore some privatised organisations were still not subject to competition, for instance public utilities had merely changed from public sector monopolies into private sector monopolies and many were providing a lower level of service. The government was frequently criticised for selling off public assets much too cheaply, thereby giving taxpayers a poor deal. Finally, there was much public dismay at the personal greed exhibited by what were seen as mediocre businessmen who happened to be in the right place at the right time to profit from privatisation.

Some political commentators disagreed over the impact of the three Thatcher governments. Some saw Thatcherite policies as basically pragmatic but heavily disguised by political rhetoric, whilst others saw Thatcherism as representing a radical and ideological break in the policies pursued by previous governments. The latter cited the massive privatisation programme as evidence for their viewpoint since it would never have taken place had Labour been reelected in 1979.

The Decline of the Trade Unions

During the 1970s trade unions were generally recognised as powerful institutions, and the general secretary of the Trades Union Congress (TUC) and the leaders of large unions were as familiar to the public as Britain's leading politicians. Poor industrial relations were a problem (see Table 9.1) and previous governments had attempted trade union reform. A Labour white paper, 'In Place of Strife' was published in 1969, but plans to introduce legislation were abandoned in face of mounting opposition from the trade union movement. The subsequent Conservative government passed the Industrial Relations Act in 1971, which resulted in workers being imprisoned and industrial chaos, and thus marked the second failed attempt to 'put the unions on a legal footing'. The dilemma for both Labour and Conservative governments that wanted to reform unions on the one hand and pursue a prices and incomes policy on the other, was that they needed the goodwill and compliance of the unions with regard to wage restraint. Antagonising the unions on the question of reform risked losing their cooperation on prices and incomes.

The new right was hostile towards trade unions, which were seen as collectivist, socialist organisations that were severely hampering the free working of market forces. Unlike prices and incomes policies, monetarist policies designed to control inflation did not rely on the cooperation of the trade unions. Monetarism consigned trade unions to a marginal role, representing a major break in the corporatist tradition of economic management. In other words the days of 'beer and sandwiches' at Number Ten had ended. Furthermore, various privatisations had also distanced government from the unions since the new employers were in the private sector and no longer represented an arm of 'big government'.

The recession of the early 1980s resulted in mass unemployment (see Table 9.1), the hardest hit being in basic industries where trade unionism had traditionally been strong. The effect of unemployment was disastrous for the old manual trade unions; for example the Transport and General Workers Union, Britain's largest trade union, had a membership of 2 086 281 in 1979 but this dropped to 1 270 776 over the following ten years. The National Union of Mineworkers, which fought a year-long battle over pit closures in the mid 1980s, shrunk from 372 122 members in 1979 to 123 479 over the ten-year period and continued its membership plunge into the 1990s.

Marginalised in policy making and now weakened by recession, trade unions were in no position to resist government reforms. Even so the government exercised caution and tackled reform through step-by-step legislation, with each act building on the previous legislation in order further to restrict traditional union freedoms. By the end of the Thatcher years, union members were restricted by limitations on secondary picketing, the closed shop and eligibility for social security, as well as new protection for non-strikers. At the same time unions were obliged to hold secret ballots for strike action, executive elections and ballots to hold political funds.

Whilst some traditional trade unionists still looked to a future Labour government to reverse the Conservative reforms, others accepted there could be no return to the days of wildcat strike action, abuses of democracy and unpopularity with the general public. These 'new realists' accepted that trade unions had to survive in a more market-oriented environment and that old forms of industrial relations were no longer appropriate. By the 1990s trade unions had become 'depoliticised' to a considerable degree, focusing more on their immediate concerns of pay and conditions, and playing an even smaller role within the politics of New Labour.

The Impact of Change

What impact did changing from interventionist policies to ones based on market solutions have on the performance of the economy? In other words, how successful were the radical economic policies pursued by the Thatcher governments? The indicators presented in Table 9.3 portray the Thatcher era as one that was not particularly distinguished by economic performance. It might be argued, however, that it is too early to assess the impact of the Thatcher reforms since her governments simply established the framework that would provide success for future governments. In this respect, defenders of the Thatcher revolution argue that the 1980s set the scene for the resurgence of Britain's economy: an enterprise culture had been distilled in both managers and workers and this was reflected in improved industrial relations and rising productivity; inflation had been reduced to a permanently low level; Britain was now attracting record levels of foreign investment; and unemployment was falling in line with increased demand for labour in a more flexible job market.

TABLE 9.3 *The economic record of achievement of postwar governments, 1951–88 (per cent)*

	Growth of GDP	Inflation	Unemployment
Conservatives: 1951–64	3.2	3.5	1.7
Labour: 1964–70	2.4	5.2	2.0
Conservatives: 1970–74	2.4	11.7	3.1
Labour: 1974–79	1.8	21.2	4.7
Conservatives: 1979–88	2.0	8.4	9.5

Source: *The Guardian*, 26 April 1989.

Critics of the Thatcherite economic policy argue that a high price was paid in the form of mass unemployment, low wages, reduced social benefits, the creation of an underclass and greater job insecurity, in exchange for few, if any, long-term benefits. For far from modernising the economy, it is argued, the Thatcher reforms simply hastened the pace of deindustrialisation and quickened Britain's relative economic decline. Studies by academics such as Ken Coutts and Wynne Godley (1989) focus on Britain's performance in terms of economic growth, productivity, inflation and the money supply. They conclude that in most cases the record was poor in relation to Britain's past performance or to the contemporary performance of competitor economies, or both. They criticise Thatcherite economic policies for their lack of productivity and consequent adverse impact on the balance of payments. Furthermore, economists such as William Keegan (1989) argue that North Sea oil revenues were squandered, that privatisation generally resulted in poorer management and reduced public satisfaction, and that no attempt was made to tackle the fundamental weaknesses in the British economy.

Note

1. The term 'Butskellism' was coined by journalists to describe the similarity between the policy approaches of Chancellor 'Rab' *But*ler and his Labour opposite, Hugh Gait*skell*. Forty years later policy similarities between Tory leader John Major and Labour leader Tony Blair led journalists to recreate the term in their talk of 'Blaijorism'.

Further Reading

Barnett, C., *The Audit of War* (London: Macmillan, 1986).
Coutts, K. and W. Godley, 'The British Economy under Mrs Thatcher', *Political Quarterley*, vol. 60, no. 2 (1989).
Gamble, A., *Britain in Decline* (London: Macmillan, 1990).
Grant, W., *Business and Politics in Britain* (London: Macmillan, 1993).
Hutton, W., *The State We're In* (London: Jonathan Cape, 1995).
Maynard, G., *The Economy Under Mrs Thatcher* (Oxford: Blackwell, 1988).
Mitchell, J., *The National Board for Prices and Incomes* (London: Secker and Warburg, 1972).
Moonman, E., *Reluctant Partnership: a critical study of the relationship between government and industry* (London: Gallancz, 1971).
Robins, L., *Politics and Policy-Making in Britain* (London: Longman, 1987).
Shanks, M., *Planning and Politics: the British experience 1960–76* (London: PEP/ Allen and Unwin, 1977).
Thomas, G., *Government and the Economy Today* (Manchester: Manchester University Press, 1992).
Walters, A., *Britain's Economic Renaissance: Margaret Thatcher's Reforms 1979–1984* (Oxford: Oxford University Press, 1986).
Whitfield, D., *The welfare state: privatisation, deregulation, commercialisation of public services* (London: Pluto Press, 1992).
Wilson, H., *The Labour Government 1964–1970* (London: Weidenfeld and Nicolson/ Michael Joseph, 1971).

10
Social Policy and the Welfare State

By the end of the Second World War there was a broad agreement between main political parties that Britain should develop a welfare system. However, although it has become commonplace to talk of the 'postwar consensus' on social policy, there was not a consensus of opinion on the need for increased welfare in the strictest sense of the term since politicians from different parties had their own distinctive reasons for supporting greater social provision. Also, within the parties some were opposed to the welfare state for a variety of reasons. Some on the political right opposed welfare policies on the grounds of both cost and the bad effect that increased welfare would have on those who would receive. On the political left were those who took a much greater interest in public ownership policies than in welfare policies, while others feared that a successful welfare state would make capitalism acceptable and thereby undermine the chance of creating a truly socialist society in Britain. The broad centre ground of politics, however, did support the establishment of a welfare state and this was in line with the mood of the electorate of the 1940s; most people were not prepared to return to the harsh times of the 1930s after making sacrifices for the war effort.

Pragmatic Conservatives and Liberals were willing to follow and even direct the new public mood, with its rising expectations, as victory approached. Described as 'reluctant collectivists' (Lowe, 1993, p. 16) these politicians accepted that in practice capitalism as they knew it was not working out as classical theory had predicted, and they conceded that the state must assume a greater role in alleviating social distress, deprivation and lives going to waste. Hence they supported the welfare state as a means of correcting the worst aspects of capitalism. This was in contrast to Labour's progressive socialists, who believed that a welfare state would bring a fairer and more egalitarian 'New Jerusalem' to Britain. Thus for different reasons there was a general agreement on what sort of Britain should emerge after the end of the war, so that 'when Labour came to power in 1945 the main battle over the development of the welfare state was more or less over' (Hill, 1993, p. 8). In summary, what amounted to a 'great debate on welfare' took place during the time of the wartime coalition government, and this resulted in a tripartite agreement on large areas of social policy, including education, social security and health care.

The new Labour government, led by Clement Attlee, neither introduced British people to welfare benefits nor had sole responsibility for setting up the welfare state. Firstly, as already noted in the introduction, there had been considerable development in welfare since the early years of the century, so that by the time of the war 'most low-income male earners were contributors to a social insurance scheme which provided limited flat-rate pensions, sickness benefits and unemployment benefits, together with primary medical care for themselves' (ibid., p. 12). In this sense postwar welfare was simply an extension of prewar welfare. Secondly, had Churchill been returned to office in 1945 there is no doubt that there would have been a large-scale advance in welfare, since much had been agreed before the war ended, and in the case of education the necessary legislation had already been passed. These points are not raised in order to deny Labour's role in implementing and resourcing welfare provision, but to place Labour's considerable achievement into context.

Did Britain Get a Welfare State?

Some academics have argued that the talk of the postwar 'welfare state' in Britain is 'a useful shorthand' but a misleading one (Klein, in Jones, 1993, p. 14). Neither in 1945 nor since, it is argued, has the provision of welfare been extensive enough to shape people's lives in a more egalitarian society to merit use of the term 'welfare state'. Rather, it is suggested, it is more accurate to describe Britain as a 'social security state', which only requires the state 'to guarantee its citizens a national minimum of civilised life' (Lowe, 1993, p. 12). These terms are difficult to define, but Asa Briggs captured what many agree is meant by the term 'welfare state' when he argued that

> A 'Welfare State' is a state in which organised power is deliberately used (through politics and administration) in an effort to modify the play of market forces in at least three directions – first, by guaranteeing individuals and families a minimum income irrespective of the market value of their work or property; second, by narrowing the extent of insecurity by enabling individuals and families to meet certain social contingencies (for example, sickness, old age and unemployment) which lead otherwise to individual and family crises; and third, by ensuring that all citizens without distinction of status or class are offered the best standards available in relation to a certain agreed range of social services (Briggs, quoted in ibid., 1993, pp. 13–14).

This definition can be interpreted as embracing the two basic visions of welfare that existed through the postwar decades and lingered on in the 1990s debate on the future of welfare. The former directions for welfare can be accommodated more easily within the Conservative notion of welfare providing a temporary 'safety net' during periods of personal or family difficulty, whilst the latter direction lends itself more to the Labour vision of a universal welfare system that brings personal and family benefits in good times as well as bad.

Labour's vision of the welfare state included all members of society: although wealth from the better-off members of society would be redistributed to help poorer members, the better-off would also help the better-off; thus, notionally, a millionaire without dependents would contribute to the system in order to provide support for others, which might include a millionaire with a family. Labour argued that a universal system of welfare would remove any stigma that might be attached to receiving a benefit. In other words Labour reasoned that a poor family need feel no shame in receiving a particular benefit as more affluent families would be receiving similar benefits. At the same time, if a benefit was universal, such as health care, it was accepted by all that the best level of treatment should be made available. Finally, if benefits were universal there would be no need for means testing – an undignified process – in order to find out whether people were poor enough to qualify.

During the 1950s many members of the Labour Party began to rethink and redefine the meaning of socialism. These so-called 'revisionists' argued that society had developed beyond the point where a Marxist analysis made any sense and that socialism was no longer about the state owning capital. Rather, in the modern postwar world socialism was about providing all members of society with the opportunity to develop whatever potential talents or skills they possessed. The revisionists redefined socialism in terms of building a welfare state that would include all social classes in an integrated and increasingly egalitarian society. Such a universal welfare state could not be financed by redistribution alone but would need the resources resulting from a high rate of growth in a well-managed economy. Labour's revisionists saw in economic growth the means of achieving greater relative equality without reducing the standard of living of the better-off.

Reluctant collectivists such as one-nation Tories did not share Labour's vision, and were much more at ease with the concept of 'equality of opportunity' than 'equality' of all citizens. Many Conservatives adhered to the idea of a more limited welfare state in which benefits would be targeted and paid only during times of hardship (Exhibit 10.1). In this sense welfare was a temporary state that would only continue until an individual or family recovered from illness or found employment. Some Conservatives feared that a welfare state that provided benefits 'from the cradle to the grave' would be too costly, and financing it would impede the recovery of Britain's war-damaged economy. They preferred the vision of the welfare state as a safety net to protect people against hardship, and they saw little point in well-off people receiving state benefits they did not really need. Furthermore, it was argued within Conservative circles that the welfare system should be limited because too much welfare would weaken what was then referred to as

EXHIBIT 10.1 *The welfare state in transition*

'The principles which underpinned the welfare state for most of the period after 1945 were essentially universalistic and statist. Both elements of this set are important. On the one hand, welfare provision was to be distributed to all on the central basis of need. On the other hand, it was to be planned by state or state-sponsored agencies. Thatcherism objected to both of the principles, preferring targeted provision to universalism, and the market to the state. Yet, in the field of welfare, so great was public support that no fundamental shift to fully-targeted individual provision within a market system could be made. Reform had to be introduced gradually.

The shift from universal to targeted modes of provision has often been piecemeal and in many areas is even now insignificant. At the margins of most welfare services, individuals have been encouraged to take more responsibility for their own needs. Within many services attempts to increase the element of targeted provision have also been made. Yet overall the impact of change has been slight. At no point has the state-funded safety net been fully removed from any area of welfare. Far more central to the Conservatives' reform programme has been marketisation. Here, however, it is important again to stress that what has been sought is marketisation of the state sector, not outright shift to private sector markets. Convinced that markets are more efficient resource allocators than the state is or ever can be, Conservative governments in recent years have sought to introduce market principles to core parts of the welfare state.

Internal markets are therefore being introduced in education, health and personal social services. Old principles of strategic planning within a unified service are being changed to new principles of market relations. This is a vast and ambitious programme of change. It depends on clear separation of purchasers and providers, for no market system can operate unless a distinction of this kind is made. . . .

Welfare markets, like all others, are however regulated by government. The extent of regulation within the welfare state is substantial. In tandem with marketisation of the base of Britain's welfare services, Conservative governments have created all sorts of mechanisms whereby welfare markets can be managed. In education, the national curriculum and regular testing throughout a child's school life are just two new aspects of the regulatory framework created in recent years. In health, a new Management Executive now supervises operation of internal NHS markets, and issues detailed supervisory guidelines to health authorities. Welfare markets are thus tightly controlled.

Real state spending on welfare services 1979–93 (£bn 1991–2)

	1978–79	*1991–92*	*1992–93 (est.)*
Social security	46.0	70.0	75.9
Health	21.2	31.5	33.2
Education	24.7	29.6	31.0
Housing	12.4	5.8	5.9
Personal social services	3.7	5.9	6.2
Total	108.0	142.8	152.2

Source: HM Treasury, *Public Expenditure Analyses to 1995–96: Statistical Supplement to the 1992 Autumn Statement*, Cm 2219 (London: HMSO, 1993).

The twin aims of the reform programme are efficiency and choice. However, for the government the first of these two themes is certainly more important than the second. Despite the rhetoric of choice, diversity and freedom which has accompanied much of the reform programme, the central objective has been to squeeze more value for money out of the welfare state. Marketisation, in the opinion of government ministers, is the best way to do this. The fact that markets are also said to extend choice is a welcome, but nevertheless secondary, aspect. . . .

Perhaps most fundamental to the reform programme is, however, the government's attempt to change British welfare culture. This attempt really has two dimensions. On the one hand, the general public is to be made more responsible and self-reliant by the reforms currently being enacted. What is sought here is a shift from the 'dependency culture' to the 'enterprise culture': people are to look more to their own resources, and less to the state's, in the welfare sphere (and others). On the other, welfare workers are to be made more efficient and productive by reform. What is sought here is a shift from professional codes to business modes of operation'.

Source: Extract from Ian Holliday, 'The Welfare State 1979–93: Safe in Conservative Hands?', *Talking Politics*, vol. 6, No. 2, 1994, pp. 88–92.

'the moral backbone of the country'. It was argued that a welfare state with numerous benefits would undermine the will to work as well as erode people's determination to lead independent lives and take responsibility for looking after themselves and their families. This argument, which was at times voiced in opposition to the principle as well as the scope of welfare, found expression once again in the views of the new right some three decades after the end of the war.

The Liberal Inheritance: Keynes and Beveridge

John Maynard Keynes and William Beveridge are frequently portrayed as the intellectual founding fathers of Britain's welfare state. Basically, Keynes had developed an economic theory that he thought would enable governments to prevent the sort of economic depression experienced in the 1930s. Through 'demand management' a government could stimulate growth in the economy, and thus generate increased taxation just when it was needed for increased social expenditure. In other words, governments could invest and spend in order to replace a decline in private consumption and investment. Keynes's theory was accepted as the new orthodoxy by all political parties and was reflected in the 1944 'Employment Policy' white paper, which stated that:

'The Government accept as one of their primary aims and responsibilities the maintenance of a high and stable level of employment after the war. . . . A country will not suffer from mass unemployment so long as the total demand for its goods and services is maintained at a high level' (quoted in Lowe, 1993, p. 100).

William Beveridge

Basically, it was various forms of Keynesian-inspired economic management that led to the relatively high levels of employment from 1945 to the mid 1970s.

It was a central assumption of Beveridge's plan that full employment would help slay the five giant evils – want, disease, ignorance, squalor and idleness – on the road to Britain's postwar reconstruction. The Beveridge Report, *Social Insurance and Allied Services*, formed the blueprint for welfare services. He recognised that successful social insurance depended on 'the introduction of a system of family allowances, the setting up of a comprehensive health and rehabilitation service and the maintenance of full employment' (Hill, 1993, p. 15). The coalition government enacted the family allowance proposal, but it was not implemented until Labour was in power.

Constructing the Welfare State

Labour inherited a war-ravaged economy in which an estimated quarter of the nation's wealth had been consumed. Nevertheless the government anticipated a 'peace dividend', which along with Marshall Aid from the United States would enable the establishment of a British-style welfare state by 1950 and formally end the Poor Law. The high wartime taxation remained in place, as did rationing, which increased during the bleak winter of 1947, and these combined to dampen consumer demand.

Providing Social Security

Attlee's Labour government ushered in social benefits legislation with the Family Allowances Act, the National Insurance Act and a National Assistance Act for individuals who did not qualify for National Insurance benefits. The political right voiced some oppoistion to these measures as they feared that friendly societies and private sector insurance companies would be put out of business, while the political left argued that the reforms did not go far enough.

Members of the public may well have been misled by the language used to describe many of these benefits. Perhaps the term 'insurance' was most confusing since it implied that contributions were invested in a fund for future pay-outs, whereas in many ways national insurance was simply an additional form of taxation in which revenues were used immediately to fund various benefits. This has led to problems today because, having contributed to 'insurance' all their working lives in the mistaken belief that this would guarantee their future security, many elderly people are being forced to sell their homes in order to pay for care.

Although the Beveridge proposals were very popular with the wartime electorate and were at the heart of the welfare state concept, 'social security policy attracted little popular or political enthusiasm after 1945' (Lowe, 1993, p. 123). Subsequent Conservative administrations led by Churchill, Eden, Macmillan and Douglas-Home were dominated by the one-nation tendency and resisted attacks on welfare from the party's right wing. The cabinet refused to accept what were seen at the time as stiff cuts in public expenditure in order to combat inflation, which led to the resignation of the chancellor (Thorneycroft) and his two ministers (Powell and Birch) in 1958. Although welfare was defended, in many ways the emphasis of the 1951–64 Conservative regime was on private affluence rather than on the 'social wage', as summed up by Macmillan's alleged remark that the British people had 'never had it so good'.

Wilson's Labour governments (1964–70) introduced a number of limited measures, but social policy fell victim to the economic problems that were besetting Britain. A redundancy pay scheme was introduced, as were income-related supplements to certain existing benefits. Labour undertook a number of administrative reforms, including the merger of the Department of Health and the Department of Social Security into a new 'super-ministry'.

When Heath's Conservative government entered office in 1970 it was widely expected that it would adopt a tough attitude towards the working class in general and the welfare state in particular. This expectation arose as a result of a pre-election conference held at the Selsdon Park Hotel, Croydon, where a rightward shift in policies was proposed. 'Selsdon Man' appeared to mark the arrival of more politically abrasive Conservatives alongside the remaining Butskellites. However, after some spectacular policy reversals the Heath government was characterised by continuity with preceding adminis-trations rather than change. Indeed the minister for social services, Sir Keith Joseph, who later converted to new right thinking, pressed the Treasury for a greater share of public spending.

Source: Vicky (Victor Weisz), *Evening Standard*, 5 August 1965

The Labour governments of 1974–9 came to office with the aspiration to introduce large increases in benefits, but in reality had to cope with cuts in public expenditure as part of the tight controls insisted upon by the IMF in 1976 as pre-conditions for a loan. However, some reforms were made: child benefits, payable directly to mothers, replaced family allowances in tax bills, which generally went to fathers; and a radical new state earnings-related pension scheme (SERPS), designed to benefit women in particular, was introduced.

Housing Policy

End-of-war Britain was in need of much new housing, but the house-building record of Attlee's Labour government was not particularly good (Figure 10.1) and this made it vulnerable to attack from the opposition. First, Labour underestimated the number of new homes that needed to be built, but even when this was recognised and attempts were made to speed up the process, a lack of skilled builders and building materials held back progress. Second, the minister of health, who at the time was also responsible for housing, insisted that council houses be built to higher standards than in the past. In part this was because Bevan 'had a vision of council housing as provision for *all*' and not just for less well-off families (Hill, 1993, p. 37). His vision was of socially mixed communities, much like a village society 'where the doctor, the grocer, the butcher and the farm labourer all lived in the same street' (quoted in ibid., p. 37).

The resulting housing shortage gave the Conservatives a stick with which to beat Labour. An opinion poll conducted in 1946 suggested that 41 per

FIGURE 10.1 *House building in England and Wales, 1945–93*

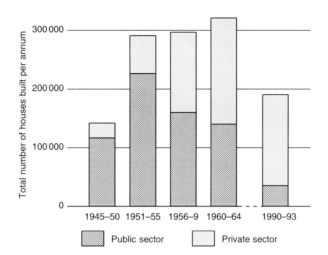

cent of the electorate identified housing as their most important concern. Labour's discomfort was made worse by the competing demands on the housing budget; as Lowe has argued, should the government's priority be given 'to industrial workers in order to increase labour mobility and thereby economic growth? Should it be given to the returning soldiers . . . or should it be given, in accordance with traditional Labour policy, to the most needy?' (Lowe, 1993, p. 245). Since all the demands could not be met, disillusionment was inevitable. The Housing Act 1946 emphasised provision of high-standard homes for working people at rents they could afford. Subsidies would be financed by the Exchequer and local authority rates so that the standard rent could be set at ten shillings (50 pence) per week: 'In the context of 1946, 10s per week net rent represented less than 8 per cent of average income and was probably well within the grasp of the great majority of households. Certainly in real terms it was less than many council tenants had been paying in the years before the war' (Malpass, 1990, p. 75).

The Conservatives, returned to office in 1951, did not share Labour's housing policy and were guided by their own vision of Britain as a property-owning democracy. The Conservatives had always seen the right to own property as an absolute right, and in this context home ownership had special importance since it conferred rights and duties that resulted in a fuller form of citizenship. In this sense, the Conservatives believed that the right to own property resulted in a more ordered and stable society.

Some three and a half million homes had been destroyed or damaged beyond repair during the war, and so an obvious election pledge by the Conservatives was to built more homes than Labour. The Conservative target of 300 000 new homes a year depended initially upon local authority building, but in 1954 the government 'brought about a major change of policy by restricting local authority production and expanding the private sector' (Malpass and Murie, 1982, p. 49). Some sections of the electorate expressed their disapproval of affluent working-class people living in sub-sidised council houses. Consequently the Housing Act 1961 introduced a new rents policy in which subsidies were targeted at the most needy and others experienced rent rises as their subsidy was reduced. It was assumed that without generous rent subsidies, well-off council tenants would increasingly move into the private sector. Growth in owner occupation was further encouraged by fiscal changes in 1963, which resulted in a mortgage subsidy in the form of tax relief.

The race to build new homes, with a consequent emphasis on quantity rather than quality, was to store up problems for future administrations. The war-time loss in the housing stock had been tackled and many slums had been cleared and replaced, but 'By the early 1990s some of the public sector houses built during this era have deteriorated or become so unpopular that they are unlettable. A particular problem sector has been high-rise houses' (Hill, 1993, p. 51).

One aspect of housing policy – the exploitation of poor tenants by private landlords – became a scandal in its own right when it emerged during the Profumo Affair (which involved the war minister sharing the same mistress as the military attaché at the Soviet embassy). One of the characters in the scandal, Mandy Rice Davies, was linked to a property dealer called Peter Rachman who ruthlessly intimidated and exploited his tenants, and the term 'Rachmanism' entered the British political vocabulary.

Labour policy under Wilson reflected private sector values associated with the 'age of affluence' rather than those of Attlee's 'age of austerity' and preference for the public sector. As Malpass comments:

> The Labour governments of the 1960s had none of the confidence in, and commitment to, council housing that had been such a feature of the early post-war years. The 1965 White Paper proposed only that the public sector would provide up to half of the annual output of 500,000 dwellings per year that was the target of 1970. The increase in local authority building was excused in terms of the severity of the contemporary housing problem, rather than being advocated as a desirable development in itself. In this respect Labour's policy was similar to that of the Conservatives in the early 1950s ... subsidies were increased in 1967, but, interestingly, the increase was accompanied by exhortations to local authorities to extend their provision of rent rebates. ... In this respect, too, Labour was converging on positions previously associated with the Conservative Party (Malpass, 1990, pp. 51–2).

Public expenditure cutbacks following economic crises led the Wilson government to reduce the planned number of council homes by 16 500 a year, saving £55 million in 1969–70. Wilson explained that 'this meant going back on our election pledge on house-building, due to the overriding need in the new situation to swing £500 millions of real resources from home demand to exports' (Wilson, 1971, p. 485).

Consistent with its Selsdon image, the Heath Conservative government required council rents to move upwards to a 'fair' or market level and replaced existing subsidies with a new deficit subsidy system. The 1972 Housing Finance Act was ignored by Labour councillors in Clay Cross in Derbyshire and Bedwas in South Wales, to the political embarrassment of the opposition. In 1975 a Labour government repealed the fair rents legislation, and the 1975 Housing Rents and Subsidies Act gave back to local authorities responsibility for setting rents.

Educating the Nation's Children

Postwar secondary education was reorganised by the 1944 Education Act – the so-called Butler Act – bringing, according to its slogan, 'education for all'. Butler was a Conservative in the coalition government, became the first minister of education, and was responsible for replacing the pre-1944 diversity with a common framework for school provision. The Act recognised a clear break between the primary and secondary stages, thus abolishing all-age elementary schools; raised the school leaving age to 15, to be further raised to 16 as soon as possible; made secondary education free; and made religious education the only compulsory subject in the school curriculum.

The Act and the manner in which it was implemented were criticised for a variety of shortcomings. First, the way in which the Act was implemented was socially conservative and out of tune with the radical and optimistic public mood of 1945. Most authorities established a bipartite system of prestigious grammar schools for the minority of pupils who passed the 11 plus 'scholarship' examination and secondary modern schools for the 80 per cent who failed. Furthermore, a result of the selection process was that middle-class pupils populated grammar schools alongside a small proportion of working-class pupils, whilst most working-class pupils found themselves consigned to secondary moderns. Second, technical schools, which were expected to come into existence alongside secondary modern and grammar schools, failed to materialise in substantial numbers, nor did the planned part-time technical education for those who left school at 15. In this sense the 1944 Act failed to provide the 'technical and further education system, that Britain so desperately needed' (Barnett, 1986, p. 291).

A number of government reports on education showed how social class factors influenced individual success at school, with many working-class pupils underachieving. Whilst the Conservatives always supported the existence of a private sector, providing parental choice for those who could afford it, some liberal Tories also supported comprehensive education.

Despite this, comprehensive education soon became a partisan issue with Labour supporting comprehensives as a means of achieving a more egalitarian society. Many on the left also supported progressive teaching methods on the ground that 'open schools would lead to an open society'. The Labour minister Tony Crosland was committed to egalitarianism in education and required direct grant grammar schools either to move into the state sector or to become entirely independent. He also issued a circular, '10/65', inviting local authorities to submit proposals for comprehensive education. This was subsequently revoked by Margaret Thatcher when she was minister for education in Heath's administration in Heath's administration, and made mandatory by a later Labour government in the 1976 Education Act.

A growing chorus of industrialists, parents and academics expressed anxiety about falling education standards, and the findings of the Bullock Report confirmed these fears in terms of a small drop in primary reading standards. Right-wing academics attacked progressive education from 1969 onwards in a series of 'black papers'. Labour Prime Minister James Callaghan responded to these concerns in a speech at Ruskin College, Oxford, raising his own doubts and fears over some modern teaching methods, initiating what came to be known as the 'great education debate'.

Postwar governments also expanded provision in higher education. The Robbins Committee, set up in 1961, recommended that more students should enter university, in particular to study the sciences. A number of technical colleges developed into colleges of advanced technology, and in 1965 these became fully fledged universities. The first of 30 new polytechnics was established in 1969. In the same year Labour's specific contribution, first known as the University of the Air but officially named the Open University, received its charter.

The National Health Service

The National Health Service is frequently seen as Labour's greatest achievement in the construction of the postwar welfare state, and probably the most enduringly popular welfare service with the public. The reasons for its popularity are not hard to understand; as Lowe argues 'Poor health and the inability to pay for adequate medical treatment have traditionally been amongst people's greatest fears' (Lowe, 1993, p. 163). A health care service that provides comprehensive and free treatment for all eliminates such fears.

Establishing the NHS involved lengthy and frequently bitter negotiations between the minister of health, Nye Bevan, not noted for his tact, and the medical profession. Doctors feared becoming salaried civil servants, but Bevan eventually won over the profession by 'buying off' consultants with the concession that they could continue to treat private patients within the structure of the NHS.

The NHS was established in 1948, but within a few years concern was voiced about rising costs. At the same time Britain's rearmament costs meant that more resources had to be devoted to the defence budget. Charges were introduced for dental and ophthalmic services and Bevan resigned from the cabinet in protest. This issue was to recur in later Labour governments. Charges, particularly prescription charges, were a self-imposed litmus test for Labour's good intentions on health care. Wilson's government abolished prescription charges in 1965 only to reinstate them in 1968.

Much debate on the NHS has concerned structural reform with a view to making the service less expensive. Conservative reforms in 1974 reorganised the service with new area health authorities and regional health authorities but the resulting structure was highly bureaucratic and failed to produce the anticipated benefits. Labour tinkering involved attempts in 1975 to phase out pay beds from NHS hospitals, a move that was opposed by the medical profession.

The Retreat from Welfare

A number of events converged in the 1970s to change the political climate and give political ideas that had been discredited in the past a new acceptability. In the first place the door was opened to a major onslaught on the policies based on the theories of Beveridge and Keynes by the unwitting cooperation of the political left. For it was the left that argued that the welfare state had failed because poverty was still widespread; it was the left that declared that comprehensive schools had failed to integrate society, and it was the left that complained that the NHS was failing because of under-resourcing. Whilst the left thought that the solution to each of these 'failures' lay in a further leftward drive of Beveridge principles, others, including the new right, were beginning to formulate alternative solutions.

At the same time the Keynesian component of the postwar settlement was seen as failing in terms of economic management. Basically, Keynesian-based policies were aimed at maintaining high levels of employment, whereas the biggest problem of the 1970s was inflation, and Keynesian policies appeared to have little relevance as far as beating inflation was concerned. In 1976 Labour Prime Minister Callaghan acknowledged that the Keynesian era was over when he told conference delegates that

> We used to think you could spend your way out of recession and increase employment by cutting taxes and boosting government spending. I tell you in all candour that that option no longer exists and that in as far as it ever did exist, it only worked by injecting a bigger dose of inflation into the economy, followed by a higher level of unemployment as the next step (Callaghan, 1987, p. 426).

Whilst the Labour Government's response to the problems of the 1970s was to increase monetarist controls – to use monetarism as an economic tactic –

there were others on the political right who favoured monetarism as an economic strategy within a philosophy that favoured free markets over government intervention. Collectively this tendency was known as the new right. Friedrich von Hayek's *The Road to Serfdom* (1943) and Karl Popper's *The Open Society and its Enemies* (1945) were rediscovered by many Conservatives and caused them to reject their party's 'Butskellite' past. The new right – which comprised individuals and groups sharing a similar basic outlook, although different priorities were discernible in terms of the 'free marketeers', 'the monetarists', the 'new moralisers' and the 'managerialists' – accepted that a strong yet minimal state was necessary to maintain a framework within which society could be organised through the free play of market forces. This, it was argued, would maximise liberty (but not equality), which was defined as the fundamental value of a civilised society. Individual liberty was seen by the new right as best protected by the free market, thus anything that limited the free working of the market was identified as an enemy of freedom. According to this logic, government spending and taxation, collectivist organisations such as trade unions and other bodies such as monopolies with the power to distort markets, central planning and the welfare state were all seen as inconsistent with the maximisation of liberty. During the 1970s the new right was able to capitalise on economic crises of the time:

> The New Right theorists used the economic problems to argue for the changes that they had long wished to see. The reduction of public expenditure, they urged, was not only desirable but absolutely essential if Britain's economic ills were to be remedied. They were particularly anxious to see a reduction in social expenditure, which could be achieved by transferring responsibility for the provision of education, health and other social services to private markets (Johnson, 1990, p. 4).

Right-wing economists argued that public investment, such as that in welfare, 'crowded out' private investment. This was seen as doubly harmful since it made it even harder for the private sector to pay the taxes that funded the public sector. In the words of Sir John Hoskyns, a new right managerialist, 'a population of about 17 million currently in work in the private sector must pay for some 5 million people working in local and central government' (quoted in Hutton *et al.*, 1991, p. 7). It followed that less government, lower taxes and a smaller welfare state would release the entrepreneurial energies and resources currently sapped by a parasitic public sector. This new orthodoxy facilitated the rearticulation of long-held Conservative prejudice that there were two competing cultures: an undesirable culture of dependency, created and sustained by the experience of living in a welfare state; and a desirable culture of enterprise that created wealth for the benefit of all. Even the poorest, it was argued, would benefit from an enterprise culture since increased wealth would 'trickle down' from the richest. The Conservative secretary of state for social security, John Moore, argued in 1987 that

> A climate of dependence can in time corrupt the human spirit. Everyone knows the sullen apathy of dependence and can compare it with the sheer delight of personal achievement. To deliberately set up a system that creates the former instead of the latter is to act directly against the best interests and indeed the welfare of individuals and of society (quoted in ibid., 1991, p. 21).

This argument was in tune with the increasingly held view that 'problems cannot be solved by throwing money at them', but went one step further by suggesting that government expenditure caused the problem in the first place, and that there was a moral case for governments to spend less. It was also in tune with the changing Conservative moral climate, which demanded a retreat from the permissive values of the 1960s and reinstatement of 'old fashioned Victorian values': independence, thrift, hard work, saving, religion, country, fidelity and family, all of which reemerged in the 'Back-to-Basics' campaign in the 1990s.

The 'Perverse Incentive'

New right moralists argued that the dependency culture and its perverse incentives had actually resulted in the welfare state creating poverty. A perverse incentive was defined as any welfare measure designed to help individuals in need but which actually encouraged others to put themselves in the position of needing help. It was argued, for example, that giving unmarried teenage mothers priority on council house waiting lists encouraged other girls to get pregnant in order to leave home and get a council house. It was argued that this perverse incentive could be removed by making absent fathers rather than councils responsible for supporting the young mothers and their children. Another perverse incentive, it was argued, undermined adult family life: welfare benefits paid to divorced wives bringing up children made it more likely that families would break up. If there were no such benefits, according to the new right, then parents might not separate so readily. Legislation passed in the 1990s, with considerable parliamentary support for the principles involved, did much to eliminate these particular perverse incentives. Others on the right, however, argued that the entire welfare state represented one massive perverse incentive. In *The End of the Welfare State* (Bell *et al.*, 1994), published by the Adam Smith Institute, it was argued that the welfare state had caused moral decay, condemned people to living in squalor and destroyed traditional family life, and only by abolishing the welfare state could individuals and families be saved from such degradation. Some Conservatives were influenced by the social analysis of Charles Murray, an American sociologist, and saw Britain's emerging underclass in terms of the 'feckless poor' who refused to work, were poor parents, were troublesome neighbours and frequently criminal, and who exploited welfare benefits without benefiting from them. The underclass was seen as representing a distinctive form of poverty that destroyed communities as a result of violent crime, casual violence, drug abuse, males dropping out of the labour market and a large number of births outside marriage. In particular Murray stressed the link between crime and births outside marriage, which attracted the attention of many Conservatives who, mistakenly or not, correlated Britain's rising crime rates with increasing single motherhood. With these and other related arguments in mind, some on the right were prepared to wind up costly welfare altogether for an underclass that was seemingly impervious to Butskellite policies designed to improve their lives.

The political left dismissed Murray's ideas and countered that the underclass were victims of Thatcherite policies, which had brought about mass unemployment, the casualisation of labour and resulting low pay, the failure of skills training, the collapse of public housing provision and growth of homelessness, and the collapse of other public services. Nevertheless the left conceded that the postwar welfare state, founded on the intellectual contributions of Keynes and Beveridge, could not be reinvented by a future Labour government. The Social Justice Commission, a centre-left think tank that served the Labour Party, recommended the withdrawal of traditional universal benefits, greater targeting, the ending of tax relief on mortgage interest payments, retention of a reformed Child Support Agency, and that students should contribute financially to their university education. The Commission reflected US Democrats' preference for 'a hand-up rather than a hand-out'. The only significant recommendations that offended the new right involved the establishment of a minimum wage and a somewhat higher top tax rate for high earners.

Across the political spectrum from the 'no turning back' group of right-wing Conservative MPs to New Labour, it is now accepted that the welfare state cannot exist unchanged in the future. However, as in 1945, the agreement between parliamentary rivals falls far short of a consensus of why welfare has to change and, in important areas, how it should be reformed.

Market-Led Reforms

The faith of the new right in the workings of market forces stretched beyond the confines of the economy. Market forces were seen as an efficient means of managing other relationships, particularly within the welfare state. Rather than a monopoly supplying a service – such as local authorities or the NHS – many Conservatives preferred the idea of numerous smaller units providing the service in an environment shaped by market forces. It was believed that competition between these smaller welfare-providing units would improve efficiency by driving up standards whilst pushing down costs. Through the process of competing for customers, new market-orientated welfare services were seen as a means of achieving improved value for money in public spending. What customers should expect of particular welfare-providing units, and the means by which one unit could be compared with another, were provided by citizen's charters and a variety of performance league tables respectively. Finally, specific functions of welfare-providing units were seen as subject to improvement through the involvement of the private sector in one form or another, ranging from market testing and compulsory competitive tendering to privatisation.

Savings in social security were actually achieved by reducing the number of applicants entitled to claim specific benefits; devising tougher tests of eligibility for certain benefits; restricting increases in the value of future benefits, such as pensions; abolishing income-related supplements; providing loans from a budget-capped social fund in place of emergency payments, and putting more resources into uncovering fraudulent claims. The Thatcher and Major governments also became increasingly concerned about the future welfare cost of Britain's ageing and dependent population. The Fowler Review of 1983 was particularly concerned about the affordability of the state earnings-related pension scheme, (SERPS) and reduced the overall cost of the scheme. Deregulation enabled the private sector to play a greater role, with some unfortunate consequences. In the first place, private insurance companies showed little or no interest in providing pensions for the less well-off, and secondly their representatives mis-sold up to one and a half million private pensions to individuals who were already in superior schemes. Finally, the government took a significant step towards abdicating responsibility for the elderly as part of its Care in the Community programme. Local authorities, private residential homes and, in the opinion of feminists, women, will be the providers of affordable care in the future.

Housing was another area of welfare in which the private sector and increased customer choice were intended to play a major role. Consistent with the traditional Conservative 'property owning democracy' ideal, the 1980 Housing Act gave council tenants the right to buy their homes at a substantial discount on market values. This marked the largest of all privatisations in terms of the total value of these former public sector assets. The Act also favoured one time *bête noire* of housing, private landlords, by making it easier for them to evict tenants. Subsequently the 1986 Housing and Planning Act allowed councils to transfer their properties to other landlords, such as housing associations, and the 1988 Housing Act offered tenants the right to 'pick a landlord' (Tenants' Choice) and established Housing Action Trusts to take over running the most deprived estates. Finally, the 1993 Housing and Urban Development Act gave some lease-holders the right to buy, a move that was opposed by many private sector landlords.

In many ways removing the 'nanny state' has had disastrous consequences for housing policy. Homelessness has risen, and previously unknown 'cardboard cities', in which people sleep rough, have sprung up in many town centres. Many owner-occupiers have been unable to maintain their mortgage repayments and consequently their homes have been repossessed. Many others are unable to sell because the value of their properties has fallen below what is still owed on their mortgages (negative equity). Many of the 'good' council estates have been sold off, leaving councils with crime-ridden vandalised 'sink' estates that have become the dumping grounds for problem families. And finally, by abusing Conservative legislation, Westminster City Council, one of the Conservatives' flagship London councils, operated a 'homes for votes' policy, which became Britain's biggest local government scandal.

The Thatcher governments made fundamental changes to the education system. In order to increase parental choice the 1980 Education (No. 2) Act introduced the Assisted Places Scheme, which enabled a small number of parents on modest incomes to send their children to private schools. In many ways this Act recreated the sort of opportunities provided by the old direct grant schools. The Act also gave other parents greater choice over which state school their children attended. Later the 1986 Education (No. 2) Act required all state schools to have a body of governors that included parents.

The 1988 Education Reform Act replaced the Butler Act in terms of shaping not just the framework but also the content of school education, for the Act specified that a national curriculum be taught to all pupils under the age of sixteen, with national testing of pupils at four key stages. In line with increasing parental choice, the act also introduced 'open enrolment', together with the possibility of schools opting out of local authority control by assuming centrally funded grant-maintained status. The Education Reform Act added to the responsibilities of governing bodies by introducing local management of schools, a move designed to ensure that schools were effectively managed and more responsive to 'customer' needs.

This legislation was enacted in response to the new right argument that during the 1960s education had become subverted to the cause of social engineering rather than the pursuit of high academic standards. To repair the situation, it was argued, the influence of those responsible for causing the 'damage', those with professional vested interests, had to be reduced. At the same time the influence of those with the greatest interest in raising education standards, parents and employers, should be increased. In other words, it was argued that education had fallen under the control of producers (teachers, unions and local education authorities) and needed to be put under the control of consumers (parents, pupils and employers). The new right therefore proposed policies that would reduce the influence of producers, such as opting out, whilst increasing the role played by consumers, such as greater choice and responsibility. Ideally consumers should be transformed into customers. It was argued that a market-led system in education would mean that schools would have to compete with each other for customers and that this competition would lead to a general rise in standards. Parents would choose to send their children to good schools, which would prosper. Poor schools would then be forced to improve so as to attract more pupils, or face the prospect of further decline and eventual closure. The right argued that the use of vouchers, with which parents could purchase an education for their children, would create something akin to a real marketplace in education. Parents who wanted their children to attend private schools would be able to 'top up' their vouchers with cash to the fee levels charged. In this way the new right envisaged a market that would stretch across the state and private sectors of education. The Major government introduced a voucher scheme for nursery education that spanned state, voluntary and private provision.

Critics of the reforms argued that parental choice was often misinformed and frequently non-existent. Firstly, it was argued that the information contained in league tables showing the relative performance of local schools was crude and misleading. Secondly, in practice popular schools were in a position to select which pupils they would accept. Many parents who chose such schools for their children were disappointed and had to send them to second- or third-choice schools. In this sense, measures aimed to increase parental choice frequently recreated the selective system of the immediate postwar decades.

Many of the arguments raised in the 'great education debate' were applied to the NHS. It was argued that the NHS was working to serve the needs of producers (the medical profession) rather than the needs of consumers (patients). Again it was argued that the grip of the professionals on the service could be broken by the introduction of market forces. A white paper, 'Working for Patients', argued that although the NHS was one large organisation, it played two distinctive roles. On the one hand it *provided* health care to the public, but this health care had to be paid for, so on the other hand the NHS was also a *purchaser* of health care. On the purchaser side were added newly created fund-holding GPs: on the provider side new self-governing NHS trust hospitals existed alongside private and directly managed institutions. In the new system hundreds of providers would compete for business and draw up contracts with thousands of purchasers. It was argued that the resulting competition would increase efficiency and drive down the cost of health care.

'Working for Patients' created expectations that the market reforms would result in patients being referred to the specialists and hospitals of their choice. This politically embarrassing misperception had to be corrected in haste, for it was mainly doctors who would be making choices on behalf of their patients. In this sense the internal market of the NHS would be more akin to a quasi-market. Critics, particularly in the Labour Party, argued that the internal market would divert scarce resources into a new bureaucracy to administer that market. They also feared that the health reforms would result in a two-tier system of care, with fund-holding GPs able to buy immediate treatment for their patients whilst the patients of non-fund-holding GPs joined lengthy waiting lists.

Further Reading

Barnett, C., *The Audit of War* (London: Macmillan, 1986).

Hill, M., *The Welfare State in Britain* (Aldershot: Edward Elgar, 1993).

Hutton, J. *et al.* (eds), *Dependency to Enterprise* (London: Routledge, 1991).

Johnson, N., *Reconstructing the Welfare State* (London: Harvester/Wheatsheaf, 1990).

Jones, C. (ed.), *New Perspectives on the Welfare State in Europe* (London: Routledge, 1993).

Lowe, R., *The Welfare State in Britain since 1945* (London: Macmillan, 1993).

Malpass, P., *Reshaping Housing Policy* (London: Routledge, 1990).

Malpass, P. and A. Murie, *Housing Policy and Practice* (London: Macmillan, 1982).

Wilson, H., *The Labour Government 1964–1970* (London: Weidenfeld and Nicolson/Michael Joseph, 1971).

11
Foreign and Defence Policies

The Basis of Britain's Foreign and Defence Policies

Have Britain's foreign and defence policies changed as a result of different parties being elected to government, or have they been relatively constant because of factors such as Britain's geography and national interests? Certainly Clement Attlee expected that Labour policies on foreign affairs and defence would be very different from Conservative or Liberal policies. Before he became prime minister he argued that 'there is a deep difference of opinions on foreign as well as home policy, because the two cannot be separated' (Attlee, 1937, p. 226). However, three out of four foreign policy studies of the 1945–51 period of Labour government concluded that continuity rather than change characterised Labour's approach to the wider world. From his study of the period, Fitzsimons (1953) concluded that there was a basic continuity in British foreign policy since Britain's interests remained the same whatever party happened to form the government. In his academic study, Rose (1959) analysed the relationship between the socialist principles developed by Labour before 1945 (at the time Attlee made his statement) and the principles that guided Labour policy in the postwar years. Like Fitzsimons, he concluded that Labour's foreign policy was based on the same principles as previous governments and that there was nothing 'socialist' about them. Gordon's book, *Conflict and Consensus in Labour's Foreign Policy* (1969), made the point that Labour leaders frequently used socialist rhetoric to disguise their policies. He gave the example of a later Labour Prime Minister, Harold Wilson, who justified 'a costly and ill-conceived East of Suez engagement as Britain's socialist contribution to collective security', only to justify a hasty British withdrawal from East of Suez as 'at long last opening the road to vigorous socialism at home' (Gordon, 1969, p. 248). Finally, in *British Labour's Foreign Policy* (1952) Windrich concluded that Labour's postwar foreign policy was distinctive from that of all previous governments because it was socialist in nature. It has been argued that she reached this mistaken conclusion because the focus of her research was on policy statements and party documents rather than on policy itself. Some academics feel that her interpretation of Labour policy was overly influenced by socialist rhetoric, as referred to by Gordon, and not by the reality of what policy was actually accomplishing.

If we accept the majority opinion of these researchers that Britain's foreign and defence policies are pragmatic and non-ideological, then what sort of principles are they based upon? In answering this question, two related 'doctrines' are frequently mentioned. The first is a memorandum written by a senior Foreign Office official, Sir Eyre Crowe, in 1907:

> The general character of England's foreign policy is determined by the immutable conditions of her geographical situation on the ocean flank of Europe as an island state with vast overseas colonies and dependencies, whose existence and survival as an independent community are inseparably bound up with the possession of preponderant sea power (quoted in Frankel, 1975, pp. 117–18).

In other words, the immutable fact that Britain is an island, situated where it is, meant that Britain became a maritime nation and governments made far-flung imperial commitments, which resulted in the British having a global rather than a continental outlook. With respect to continental Europe, Sir Eyre Crowe defined Britain's natural role as maintaining the balance of power and, it was to be hoped, peace, so that Britain could devote maximum resources to pursuing its global interests. His memorandum stated:

> It has become almost an historical truism to identify England's secular policy with the maintenance of this balance by throwing her weight now in this scale and now in that but ever on the side opposed to the political dictatorship of the strongest single state or group at any given time (quoted in Richard *et al.*, 1971, p. 20).

The doctrine outlined in the Crowe memorandum explains in large part Britain's opposition to German domination of Europe during the first half of the twentieth century and, with the cooperation of the United States, opposition to Soviet domination throughout most of the second half. Some might even argue that the ghost of this doctrine is still haunting Britain and making it difficult to adjust to life inside the EU (see Chapter 5). Certainly in the early postwar years there was a political gulf between Britain's maritime Atlanticist NATO strategy in containing Soviet ambitions and the European Defence Community (EDC) strategy favoured by Britain's neighbours in continental Europe.

The second expression of British foreign policy doctrine, again with Britain's island status being central, was Winston Churchill's 'three circles' conception:

> The first circle for us is naturally the British Commonwealth and Empire, with all that that comprises. Then there is also the English-speaking world in which we, Canada and the other British Dominions, and the United States play so important a part. And finally, there is United Europe. . . . Now if you think of the three inter-linked circles you will see that we are

the only country which has a great part in every one of them. We stand in fact at the very point of junction and here is this island at the very centre of the seaways and perhaps of the airways also; we have the opportunity of joining them all together   (quoted in Frankel, 1975, p. 157).

These 'three majestic circles' were not of equal importance. Charles de Gaulle recorded in his memoirs that Churchill once told him, 'Here is something you should know; whenever we have to choose between Europe and the open sea, we shall always choose the open sea' (Richard *et al.*, 1971, p. 26). This unique position qualified Britain as a world power. British policy was outward-looking, having a 'special relationship' with the United States based on the usefulness of British influence in many important areas of the world, and in bringing that special relationship to assist in the defence of Western Europe. Postwar Britain has seen a change in the diplomatic priority of Churchill's three circles. The relative decline of Britain's power resulted in withdrawal from global commitments and a loosening of the special relationship with the United States. Europe, at Britain's back door, increased in importance as Britain declined from a world power to a regional power.

Great-Power Britain

The perception of Britain's policy makers as well as the wider public was that Britain emerged from the Second World War as a great power. The assumptions of Sir Eyre Crowe and Winston Churchill underpinned Britain's role in the world. Together with the United States and the Soviet Union, Britain was treated as one of the Big Three. Certainly Britain had a moral claim to great power status for its stand against Hitler's fascist war machine. For this reason the defeated countries of Western Europe expected Britain to take the leading role in reconstructing the peace. Britain was also a great power in terms of diplomatic skills, having gained experience from administering an empire that spanned a quarter of the globe. It was felt that in terms of mediating between the other two members of the Big Three – the capitalist United States and the communist USSR – Britain's diplomatic skills could influence the course of world affairs. When it came to the strength of Britain's economy, however, the claim to great-power status was flimsy. The war had seriously weakened Britain's economy, and unless there was a miraculous recovery the 'writing was on the wall' for Britain's inevitable diplomatic decline, but few at the time wished to read it. The illusion of lasting great power status was easily conjured up by policy makers for the following reasons.

First, Britain was a global power in terms of its military presence in 40 countries: Austria, Belgium, France, Germany, Gibraltar, Greece, Italy, Netherlands, Burma, Hong Kong, India, Indonesia, Japan, Malaysia/Singapore, Aden, Cyprus, Egypt, Jordan, Libya, Oman, Palestine, Trucial States,

Bermuda, British Guyana, British Honduras, the Falklands, Jamaica, British Somalia, Ethiopia, Gambia, Ghana, Kenya, Mauritius, Nigeria, Northern and Southern Rhodesia, Sierra Leone, South Africa, Tanganyika and Uganda (Saunders, 1990, p. 50). British forces were involved in 85 military operations between 1950 and 1966 in the increasingly difficult task of maintaining *Pax Britannica* (Reed and Williams, 1971, p. 152).

Second, Britain acquired nuclear weapons, as had the other two great powers. A blow to Britain's special relationship with the United States was dealt by the McMahon Act, which brought an end to Anglo-American collaboration in nuclear research. However Attlee decided that Britain would press on with its own nuclear programme. Britain's independent deterrent force was based on its V-bombers (Vulcans, Victors and Valiants) which carried British nuclear bombs. This, along with the global deployment of conventional forces, was seen as giving Britain a continuing right to sit at the 'top table'.

The Commonwealth and World Role

The British Empire was the largest empire the world had ever known. Yet the cost of bringing order and stability, *Pax Britannica*, to a quarter of the world's population was modest. At the height of Britain's imperial history in the 1860s the cost of policing and defending the empire was no more than 2 per cent of GNP (Frankel, 1975, p. 289). Frequently unrest could be quelled merely by a small show of force – so-called 'gunboat diplomacy' – which served as a symbol of the much greater military force that Britain could bring to bear if necessary. Furthermore Britain's economy benefited from the large, protected market that the empire provided However, a century later defence costs had risen more than fourfold to 9 per cent of GNP, and arguments about the benefits of Commonwealth trade to Britain were much less forceful. In addition there was a growing feeling that protected markets had disadvantaged British industry by making it less competitive.

Nevertheless in the early postwar years warm sentiment was still being expressed towards the Commonwealth by politicians from all parties and the public. The British dominions – self-governing countries of white settlement, the most important being Canada, Australia, New Zealand and South Africa – remained loyal to Britain in both the First and Second World War. Many people in Britain had 'kith and kin' who had settled in these countries, and these relatives stayed in touch and still looked to Britain as 'home'. Whilst Conservatives took pride in the 'old' Commonwealth, Labour was highly supportive of the 'new' Commonwealth, which offered emerging countries membership of a non-aligned alternative to the Cold War power blocs.

Not all went well with the Commonwealth in the early postwar years, however. Some countries left; there was disagreement over the granting of independence to India and Pakistan; and British pride was hurt when

Australia and New Zealand formed a treaty with the United States in 1951 (ANZUS), which excluded Britain. However in other respects the Commonwealth was regarded with affection and seen as a source of British influence in the world. With hindsight, it can be said that British people saw the Commonwealth as something it was not. Its substance was exaggerated, its strength was overestimated and its influence on world politics was magnified. In this sense the Commonwealth was a myth. It was, however, an important myth insofar as it gave Britain a world role that, whilst not as large as America's, qualified Britain as a junior partner in policing the world. The existence of the Commonwealth also meant that Britain was not 'merely' a European power. Geographically Britain was *of* Europe but politically it was not confined *to* Europe.

Britain's world role was performed through a network of military bases, a number of naval patrols and numerous treaty commitments including, in the Middle East, CENTO (formerly the Baghdad Pact) and in South-East Asia, SEATO. Britain also contributed troops to UN military activities, as well as enjoying a number of military successes in the containment of communism. In addition to fighting alongside the United States under the UN flag in Korea when communist North Korea invaded South Korea (1950–3), British troops waged a successful jungle war against communist guerillas in Malaya (1948–53).

The Suez Fiasco

Many historians look back to 1956 and see it as a turning point for Britain's role in the world. The Middle East was seen as an important area of strategic interest for Britain, particularly after the 'loss' of India. Likewise the Suez canal was important for Britain's overseas trade – over a quarter of the cargoes that passed through were British, and Britain owned nearly half of the shares in the Suez Canal Company. Earlier, negotiations had taken place with Egypt over running the canal and the British began to withdraw its troops from the Suez Canal Zone in 1954. In 1956, in the context of Cold War politics and Egypt's willingness to play one superpower off against the other, the United States and Britain withdrew their offer of financial aid for the construction of the Aswan Dam. Egypt's new leader, Colonel Nasser, promptly responded by nationalising the Suez Canal, but did agree to pay compensation to the shareholders.

Prime Minister Anthony Eden, who was ill and subject to violent mood changes, misread the situation. On the one hand he appeared to misapply the lessons learnt from appeasing Hitler in the 1930s; Eden saw Nasser, a nationalist and socialist dictator, as another Hitler who must be stopped in his tracks. On the other hand he reacted like a nineteenth-century imperialist and resorted to gunboat diplomacy in the belief that he had passive support from the United States, which, as it turned out, he did not.

Secret plans were hatched to invade Egypt, regain the canal and topple Nasser. The conspiracy, codenamed 'Operation Musketeer', was worthy of a good spy film. In highly secret talks, Israel agreed to cross the Sinai Desert and invade Egypt, giving Britain and France a pretext to launch their own invasion in order to reestablish peace and protect the canal. Britain calculated that the United States might condemn the Anglo-French invasion in public whilst supporting it in private. It was felt that the United States would be happy to see Nasser removed, since he was forging closer links between Egypt and the Soviet Union. In addition the US President, Dwight Eisenhower, was facing election and it was thought that he would not risk upsetting the Jewish vote by criticising Israel, and hence France and Britain. Hence the plan went into action, with Britain deploying 80 000 troops, 150 warships (including seven aircraft carriers) and 80 merchant ships carrying 20 000 military vehicles. Cairo was bombed and the Egyptian airforce was destroyed. In spite of the time it had taken to organise the invasion, Britain pulled out of the operation when only twenty miles or so short of its military objective of reaching the canal. French troops continued for a short period, but then they too withdrew.

Why did Britain pull out of 'Musketeer', abandon its French ally and accept what amounted to a defeat? For a start, world opinion condemned the invasion, and criticism was voiced by the United States, the USSR, the United Nations and the Commonwealth. Furthermore support at home slumped, and Eden's political opponents became increasingly critical of his actions as suspicion grew that there had been an international conspiracy. It was, however, pressure on the pound sterling, then an important reserve currency, that proved critical in changing policy: the United States would only support sterling if Britain abandoned its military adventure in Egypt. Britain complied.

Britain got the worst of all worlds from the Suez operation. It upset international opinion by invading Egypt, and upset France by pulling out. It gave the Soviets a propaganda gift whilst turning world attention away from the Soviet's brutal invasion of Hungary. Nasser, far from being toppled from power, became a political hero for nationalist movements since he showed that Britain could be humiliated by a much smaller power. On top of all this, the canal was put out of use as it was blocked by sunken vessels.

Some academics have argued that Suez was an aberration and that Britain's international relations soon returned to normal. Northedge (1967), for example, has argued that none of the Suez after-effects was as serious as feared or prophesied by Eden's critics. This overlooks, however, what the Suez war symbolised in connection with Britain's international position. Britain's power had been in relative decline throughout the twentieth century, but in just six days Britain's military failure proved that it no longer qualified as a great power alongside the United States and the Soviet Union. Britain may have enjoyed a glorious imperial past and the empire had, perhaps surprisingly, been successfully converted into a British-led Commonwealth, but after 1956 nothing would ever be quite the same again for Britain.

The Wind of Change

Britain's military failure in Suez was initially seen in terms of its armed forces being overstretched. The immediate solution was to put greater emphasis on nuclear deterrence, thus releasing conventional forces for operational rather than strategic ends. In other words the thinking was that the Soviets and their Warsaw Pact allies would be contained by the knowledge that any invasion of Western Europe would be countered by nuclear weapons rather than conventional armed force in West Germany.

In the medium term, Suez impinged on the thinking of Britain's policy makers in terms of reassessing the 'three circles' doctrine. Prime Minister Harold Macmillan began to realign foreign policy. He rebuilt the Anglo-American special relationship in order to maintain Britain's nuclear status but also to shift many responsibilities to the United States, which enabled Britain to withdraw from its global commitments and focus on Europe. As Frankel has argued, the special relationship had become 'a learning process in which the United States was assuming British responsibilities and was learning from British experience' (Frankel, 1975, p. 207). The United States – influenced by the domino theory, whereby the fall of one country to communism was likely to 'knock over' the neighbouring countries like a row of dominoes – accepted that *Pax Americana* should replace *Pax Britannica*. At the same time the United States supported Britain's application for membership of the EEC, thus maintaining harmony between the fundamental elements of the circles.

In 1960 in Cape Town, Harold Macmillan spoke of 'a wind of change' blowing through the continent of Africa. Although this wind was to be resisted by the apartheid regime in South Africa for a further thirty years, Britain did respond to indigenous demands elsewhere for independence and political self-determination. Britain had, post-Suez, lost the will to govern Commonwealth countries in the face of local opposition. Much rethinking took place about the true nature of the Commonwealth, and a new orthodoxy accepted that the Commonwealth was a fragile organisation whose usefulness to Britain was now limited. In political terms this view was confirmed by the failure to export democracy to the newly independent nations, by the emergence of corrupt regimes that were frequently inclined to abuse Britain, and by occasional armed conflicts between Commonwealth members. In economic terms the Commonwealth was not capable of being transformed into any viable form of trading organisation. Within a dozen years of Suez, over thirty colonies and dependencies were granted independence around the globe, stretching from Jamaica, Trinidad and Tobago in

FIGURE 11.1   *The retreat from empire, 1947–80: Africa*

Source: *The Oxford History of Britain: The Modern Age*, 1992, ed. by H. C. G. Matthew and
K. O. Morgan (Oxford University Press).

the West Indies, through Nigeria, Uganda, Nyasland and Northern Rhodesia in West and Central Africa, Kenya in East Africa, Aden and Somaliland
in the Middle East, to Singapore and Malaya in the Far East.

Harold Wilson's Labour government came into office in 1964 convinced
that the Commonwealth, neglected by the Conservatives, could be revived,
thus enabling Britain to continue to play a world role. Labour saw in the
Commonwealth an alternative to Britain's membership of the EEC. Views,
however, were to change. Wilson recounted the problems his government
experienced in trying to strengthen the Commonwealth:

The developing countries were more concerned with aid programmes. The
developed – particularly Australia but, to a small extent, Canada, too –

FIGURE 11.2 *The retreat from empire, 1947–80: the Far East and the West Indies*

Source: *The Oxford History of Britain: The Modern Age*, 1992, ed. by H. C. G. Matthew and K. O. Morgan (Oxford University Press).

were resistant to closer trading relations. For while they welcome the continuation, and encouragement, of their long established agricultural exports to Britain, they were not disposed to adopt arrangements which put their own domestic manufacturers at risk. There was the fact, too, that long years of neglect of Commonwealth trade had led to the development of strong non-Commonwealth ties . . . There is in fact nothing under the sun more laissez-faire than Commonwealth trade (Wilson, 1971, p. 117).

In military matters Labour soon found that domestic economic problems forced the pace of policy change. The 1965 defence white paper reflected changes in strategic thinking. Less reliance would be placed on nuclear weapons, and it was acknowledged that conventional forces had an important role to play in the Cold War defence strategy. Naturally this put a strain on the resources devoted to military commitments outside Europe. Other commitments had to be shared. The white paper stated that 'We cannot be the permanent policeman for the whole of Africa and Asia. Whatever might have been possible in the nineteenth century the days of *Pax Britannica* are over. We must share our responsibilities with our friends and allies' (quoted in Reed and Williams, 1971, p. 181). Relentless economic problems led to the cancellation of the TSR-2, a tactical strike reconnaissance aircraft, which was replaced by the cheaper American F-111 until that order too was cancelled, and to the cancellation of a new aircraft carrier – the combined loss of which had implications for Britain's remaining global responsibilities.

Britain no longer had the resources to maintain a presence east of Suez. In simple terms, the Labour government had become obsessed with Britain's balance of payments problem, which could be addressed in large part by withdrawing troops from overseas and thus making a saving of £500 million a year. The United States, now with troops bogged down in Vietnam, was dismayed by Britain's decision to withdraw from east of Suez. But the government insisted that 'Britain's defence effort will in future be concentrated mainly in Europe and the North Atlantic'. Accordingly it was announced that Britain's withdrawal from Singapore, Malaysia and the Arabian Gulf would be completed by 1971.

The Rhodesian Rebellion

In the 'scramble for Africa' by European countries determined to secure colonies in the 1880s, British imperialist Cecil Rhodes obtained a charter to govern areas to the north of the Limpopo, the river that marked South Africa's northern frontier. Rhodes had an ambition that one day a railway would stretch from Cairo to the Cape, passing through British-controlled territory for its entire length. His British South Africa Company flew the union jack over the territories that were to become Northern and Southern Rhodesia. In 1923 the white settler population of Southern Rhodesia decided not to join South Africa and accepted responsibility for self-government, with Britain retaining minimum reserve powers. In the postwar years Britain wanted to avoid any of its colonies following the path of apartheid chosen by South Africa. In 1953 Britain created the multiracial Federation of Central Africa from the Rhodesias and Nyasaland. Federation was a success for the white population, bringing growth to the economy of Southern Rhodesia and turning Salisbury, capital of both Southern Rhodesia and the Federation, into a booming modern city. Black opinion, particularly in Northern Rhodesia and Nyasaland, increasingly opposed federation, which collapsed in 1964 with Northern Rhodesia and Nyasaland seceding to become independent Zambia and Malawi respectively.

This left Southern Rhodesia, with a minority of a quarter of a million white Rhodesians governing four million black Africans, with an uncertain future. A new constitution had been negotiated with Britain, but it was viewed in differing perspectives by the colony and by Britain. The Rhodesians had established a modern thriving country from the African bush and wanted to maintain 'responsible government'. But as a condition for independence Britain insisted on there being progress towards 'democratic government' by the black majority.

Negotiations between Salisbury and London made no progress. Rhodesian politics moved to the right, and in 1964 Prime Minister Winston Field was removed to make way for Ian Smith. In the view of the Rhodesian Front, now the dominant white party, if Britain refused to recognise the reality of Rhodesian independence, then Rhodesia would have to declare its own independence and gain its freedom in much the same way as the Americans had done in 1775–6. Accordingly in 1965 the unilateral declaration of independence (UDI) was announced and Rhodesia became an illegal regime.

The Rhodesian rebellion provides an illuminating case study of Britain's retreat from its world role. In social terms, Britain's response reflected the close ties of kith and kin that bound Britain to the old dominions. In Rhodesia's case there was much 'pride in being "British"', in loyalty to the crown and the flag, in upholding the standards of an idealised homeland' (Barber, 1967, p. 4). Rhodesians rallied to Britain's side during the Second World War, and indeed Ian Smith was an RAF fighter pilot. When his plane was shot down he served with the Italian partisans. In the 1960s there were still many Rhodesian-born officers in the RAF, and cabinet papers revealed that the defence minister was concerned about the 'psychological problems' of setting British against Rhodesian troops. Other ministers agreed that in principle Britain should not contemplate taking military action against Smith's regime.

In political terms, therefore, military action to end the rebellion was ruled out, so Britain led the international response in applying economic sanctions against Rhodesia. Much diplomatic activity took place between Britain and Rhodesia in an attempt to return the regime to legality. Wilson met Smith for talks on HMS *Tiger* in 1966 and on HMS *Fearless* in 1968, neither time with any success. Significantly, the United States intervened in what was a British colonial problem when the US secretary of state, Henry Kissinger, attempted a diplomatic settlement in conjunction with the 'Front Line' states. This initiative, which was an assumption of Britain's responsibilities, failed on both the first and the second attempt.

Finally, economic considerations also played a part in Britain's response to UDI. Cabinet records show that Britain was most concerned that any policies concerning Rhodesia should not damage Britain's economy. Whilst

Source: Vicky (Victor Weisz), *Evening Standard*, 5 January 1966

military action against land-locked Rhodesia was logistically feasible, it would have been expensive. The Labour government was anxious that any sanctions against Rhodesia should not harm Zambian copper production since that would in turn harm Britain's economic interests.

The Rhodesian problem was eventually resolved locally, although Britain became involved in the final stages. After declaring itself a republic in 1969 Rhodesia began to encounter increasingly serious security problems. Portugal's withdrawal from its African colonies, particularly Mozambique, made it harder for Rhodesia to secure its borders. Guerilla activity increased, and the Smith regime was eventually forced into an internal settlement with 'moderate' Bishop Muzorewa that reduced white political domination. In June 1979 Smith stood down as prime minister and Rhodesia was renamed Zimbabwe Rhodesia. In August the Commonwealth heads of government approved the holding of a constitutional conference at Lancaster House in London, leading to a new constitution, a general election and the discharge of Britain's colonial responsibility with the creation of Zimbabwe. The Rhodesian guerilla war had claimed 30 000 victims in total. But in this colonial struggle, no British troops had been lost.

EXHIBIT 11.1 *The greatest empire ever known*

The following extract from a children's book by Harry Cooper, *How the Empire Grew*, is typical of descriptions of the empire before 1939. Note the romantic style and proud tone in which the Empire is described.

'Half this British Empire is in the northern hemisphere, and half in the southern. It is an empire whose summer never wanes and whose winter never yields. Some of its cities are always toiling under the sun, some of them sleeping under the stars. The Equator runs like a skewer through British possessions on the African continent and in the Indian Sea, while up in the Arctic regions there are three British islands any one of which is larger than Ireland; and in the far south, looking across to the polar snows where Scott perished, are the bleak and wind-swept Falklands, with an area altogether as large as Wales.

Within the British Empire the lion stalks the antelope, and the polar bear chases the seal; the brilliant flamingo wades in the shallow pools, the vulture hovers over the desert caravan, and the penguin toddles upon perpetual ice. Some of the tallest peaks in the world, among the Rockies to the west in the Himalayas to the east, look down upon ordered British territory, and its valleys are made fertile by some of the longest rivers, the Indus and the Ganges, the Nile and the Zambesi, the Mackenzie and the St. Lawrence.

Included in the British Empire are sandy wastes and tropical forests, waving prairies and frozen steppes, rainy hill slopes where the tea harvest is gathered, and desolate coasts where lamps are trimmed for the passing mariner, river beds where the diamond occasionally sparkles, and coral islands covered with the palm. Vast tracts in Canada, the Sudan, in Nigeria, and in northern India still await development.

Roughly, British soil bears one-third of the world's cane sugar, one-fourth of the world's cotton, one-fifth of the world's wheat. On its pastures nearly half of the world's cattle and more than half the world's sheep are fed. Half the gold that has glittered since the middle of the last century has come from a British reef, and half of the world's tin come from a British mine. As to those indispensable materials of modern civilisation, oil and rubber, wells are being drilled in British territory in three continents, and plantations actively developed in two.

Some of the most populous regions on the earth's surface are included in the British Empire, and some of the most sparsely populated. While in the United Kingdom there are forty-five millions of people, over the same area of Labrador there are only four thousand. In Canada or Australia there may not be one homestead to the square mile; in British India there may be fifty homesteads. Ancient Rome, including its suburbs, cannot have had a population of more than 650 000, so the archaeologists tell us; but there are nine cities in the British Empire which have a larger population than that to-day. And three of the nine are sunburnt cities of the East.'

Source: Harry Cooper, *How the Empire Grew*, Lutterworth Press, London, 1932.

The Falklands Conflict

The Falkland Islands lie in the South Atlantic, some 8000 miles from Britain and 400 miles off the coast of Argentina. In the early 1980s these remote and inhospitable islands had fewer than 2000 inhabitants, mostly of British stock, and an economy based on sheep farming (Exhibit 11.1). The Falklands have a chequered colonial history, having also been settled by the French and Spanish, and there were periods when the islands were abandoned by all. What was indisputable in the early 1980s, however, was that British people had lived continuously on the islands for the past 150 years.

The Falklands were involved in famous sea battles in both world wars, but they were of limited strategic importance to Britain as foreign and defence policies were focused more on Europe. Along with the even more remote island of South Georgia, the Falklands were an imperial leftover that now formed part of Britain's interests in Antarctica. Some Foreign Office officials doubted Britain's claims to sovereignty over the Falklands, and in the 1970s the government had appeared willing to reach a compromise with Argentina, which knew the Falklands as the Islas Malvinas and considered them an Argentine possession. From time to time political leaders in Argentina whipped up nationalistic feeling against British sovereignty of the islands as a way of diverting public opinion from domestic problems. Although not serious, in 1977 the Royal Navy made a show in the area in order to warn off Argentina. A small detachment of Royal Marines was committed to the Falklands, together with the lightly armed ice patrolship HMS *Endurance* and occasional naval patrols.

The logic of Britain's increased defence commitment to Europe was that savings could be made in areas outside NATO. It was decided that navy cuts would include withdrawing HMS *Endurance* from the South Atlantic. At the time there were protests in parliament that such a policy could convey the wrong message to Argentina, namely that Britain no longer claimed sovereignty over the Falklands. Indeed this turned out to be the case, and Argentina's military dictator, General Galtieri, believed that he now had the freedom to do as he wished regarding the Falklands. The first incident involved Argentina landing scrap metal merchants on South Georgia in March 1982 to remove a derelict whaling station. The Argentine flag was raised on the island and regulations ignored, and suddenly this commercial scrap metal contract looked more like an occupation of British territory. Britain protested but there was little that could be done in practical terms.

The Argentine navy was conducting manoeuvres when both the US and British intelligence services suddenly realised that these were a prelude to an invasion of the Falklands. This occurred on 2 April 1982, and after a short struggle against overwhelming forces, the British Marines stationed there surrendered. The news that the Falkland Islands had fallen to Argentina shocked the British public and made the British government look incompetent, having been outwitted by a 'tinpot' dictator. The government had no political alternative but to regain the Falklands, through diplomacy or by force.

A naval task force was quickly assembled, including a number of vessels that had been destined to be scrapped as a result of the recent navy cuts (Figure 11.1). Ascension Island, another leftover from British imperialism, provided a crucial staging post in the operation to regain the Falklands. British public opinion was whipped up by an extremely jingoistic tabloid press, and in a very crude way the impending Falklands War was seen as the last opportunity for Britain to set the records straight after the Suez fiasco, before Britain withdrew entirely from its global commitments. The United States, with others, hoped that the conflict could be settled diplomatically before the task force reached its destination. However attempts at mediation by Secretary of State Alexander Haig failed.

If the Falklands conflict had occurred in either of the two world wars, it would not have been so clearly remembered. Two large vessels were sunk, fewer than a thousand lives were lost and there was minimal civilian casualty. But so great was Britain's global withdrawal by 1982 that the very waging of the Falklands War was a risky venture, and the resulting victory truly spectacular. South Georgia was regained, and in May British troops landed at San Carlos in the Falklands engaging in fierce conflict with Argentinian

FIGURE 11.3 *Defence cuts, 1975–95*

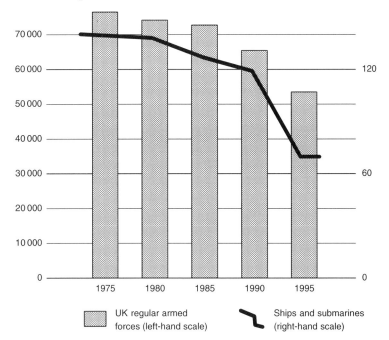

soldiers as they moved towards Port Stanley and total victory. The Conservative government had converted an error in political judgment into a British military victory. Margaret Thatcher's political image was transformed and the so-called 'Falklands factor' influenced the direction of British politics for a considerable time to come. But the Falklands War did not represent a reversal of British policy, rather an exception to the general rule of imperial retreat had been made in response to Argentina's aggression. As Sanders comments, Britain 'had indeed retreated from its world role and . . . no longer possessed the capability of sustaining it. . . . By the mid 1980s, British imperialism – both political and economic – was very largely a thing of the past: most of the action was concentrated in Europe' (Sanders, 1990, pp. 133–4).

The Special Relationship

There was a minority view within the British political elite in the late 1950s that Britain's and the United States' interests were so closely interwoven that constitutionally the two countries should be drawn together. Others believed that in trading terms Britain would prosper more within a 'North Atlantic Free Trade Area' than in European-oriented organisations such as EFTA or the EEC. This body of opinion saw the United States, with its common cultural roots, as Britain's 'natural' ally. Some of those who disagreed with this view, nevertheless agreed that there had always been a 'special relationship' between the two. Although the relationship may have been more special to Britain than to the United States, it was based on similar interests. The United States, newly emerged as a superpower in the postwar world, shared Britain's imperial interest in international stability. Both were naval powers, capable of patrolling the great oceans, and both were concerned about the expansion of Soviet naval forces. Both were capitalist countries, opposed to the communist-inspired ideology of the Soviet Union. Both had an interest in containing the Soviet threat globally and especially in Europe. Both were nuclear military powers, although Britain had come to depend on the United States for its sophisticated nuclear weaponry.

However in Britain and Europe there was scepticism about the special relationship. It was sometimes argued that in normal times the relationship was not special, and when it did exist it proved only temporary. It was argued, for example, that the United States only entered the Second World War because its own fleet had been attacked in Pearl Harbor by the Japanese, and that once it was at war alongside Britain it was no surprise that a special relationship developed. But, it was argued, the relationship weakened once peace returned, as shown by the United States abruptly ending its nuclear collaboration with Britain. At the end of the century the United States is seen as having a special interest in the nations of the Pacific Rim rather than with any single country in Europe.

The Cold War

In his famous speech in Fulton, Missouri, in 1946, Winston Churchill argued that 'From Stettin in the Baltic to Trieste in the Adriatic, an iron curtain has descended across the continent'. It was said at the time that all the Soviets needed to invade the nations of Western Europe and reach the English Channel was their boots. True or otherwise, this quip would not have amused many of those living in Western Europe during those uncertain years. It was anticipated that democracy would return to Poland, yet free elections never took place. Elections did take place in Hungary and the communists were defeated, yet they were able to subvert the government and gain control. There was a communist coup in Czechoslovakia. The Western powers were denied road access to the Western-controlled zone of Berlin, and a massive airlift was necessary to keep the population alive and free from need of communist 'rescue'. It is a matter of debate whether all these moves were examples of communist aggression – steps on the road to communist world domination – or whether they were defensive measures by the Soviet Union. For the Soviet population had suffered massive casualties at German hands, and controlling the countries of Eastern Europe could be seen as securing a buffer zone between Russia and the defeated but still feared Germans.

Sitting close to Churchill at Fulton was President Truman, who shared Churchill's fears about the dangers Europe was facing. The resulting Truman Doctrine – that it 'must be the policy of the United States to support free peoples who are resisting attempted subjugation by armed minorities or by outside pressures' – had the immediate aim of resisting communist influence in Greece and Turkey and the general aim of containing communism globally. It was followed by the Marshall Plan (see Chapter 5) for economic recovery and then by NATO, which formally signified the United States' commitment to the defence of Western Europe. The containment of communism outside Europe included the Korean War (1950–3), in which US and British forces under the UN flag repelled communist North Korea's invasion of capitalist South Korea, and British counter-insurgency activities in Malaya.

The Nuclear Age

In military terms the second half of the twentieth century was unlike any previous age. The invention of atomic, then hydrogen bombs with their huge destructive power, was a new factor in international politics. From the time of their invention nuclear weapons divided public opinion. Some believed that the power of these weapons was so appalling that using them in any conflict was unthinkable. It was also argued that the Soviets were rational people and common humanity meant that they would think in much the same way as people in the West. Since nuclear weapons were therefore never likely to be used, they should be viewed as 'diplomatic weapons' that had more to do with a country's international status than with its real defence needs. Others disagreed with this line of argument, arguing that nuclear weapons had already been used in anger against Japan, and that the new nuclear age was likely to be uncertain, unstable and dangerous.

Relatively few atomic weapons had been manufactured by the late 1940s and early 1950s. The Soviets exploded their first bomb in 1949, and Britain's independently produced bomb was first tested in 1952. The major strategic threat to the West was considered to be the Red Army marching across the plains of West Germany. During the 1950s a doctrine of 'massive retaliation' was articulated in order to deter the Soviets from any possible invasion, and American decision makers stressed that any Soviet incursion would unleash a full nuclear response by the West. It was believed that the possibility of its major cities and/or military capabilities being destroyed as a punishment would have a sobering effect on the Soviet Union's territorial ambitions. It would have been easy, for example, for Soviet forces to seize Soviet-encircled West Berlin whenever they wished, but the threat of massive nuclear retaliation was seen as the most credible way of deterring communist aggression and keeping freedom alive in Berlin. Britain subscribed to the doctrine of massive retaliation, particularly because nuclear deterrence was a cheaper way of defending Western Europe than the huge conventional armies that would be needed to deter invasion. In theory at least, all that was needed in West Germany was a small conventional army to act as a 'tripwire' to engage with the invading communist forces and signal that the conflict was serious enough to move to the nuclear stage.

Massive retaliation was based on the United States having a near mono-poly of nuclear weapons as well as on the role of bombers in a war between NATO and the Warsaw Pact. Technological advances, especially by the Soviet Union in space technology and its ability to shoot down high-flying spy planes, meant that massive retaliation was no longer a credible threat to the Soviets. This became clear during the Cuban missile crisis of 1962, when the United States and the Soviet Union were engaged in eyeball-to-eyeball confrontation. US intelligence discovered six Soviet-built missile sites in communist Cuba, only 90 miles from the US mainland. This situation was decidedly unacceptable to the United States. Rather than engaging in massive retaliation, however, the US president pursued the low-risk strategy of a naval blockade of Cuba. Soviet ships bound for Cuba were either stopped or turned back, and diplomacy resolved the conflict rather than military might. On the basis of negotiations, the Soviet Union removed its missiles from Cuba and NATO withdrew its missiles from Turkey.

US Secretary of State Robert McNamara developed a doctrine of 'flexible response' in the early 1960s to replace the now redundant concept of massive retaliation. The idea that a minor conflict between the United States and the Soviet Union should trigger a nuclear holocaust was now seen as a nonsensical doctrine. Rather the US response to any Soviet threat would be in direct proportion to that threat. Flexible response was particularly appropriate once the United States had developed a 'second strike' capacity. Whatever the moral arguments for or against, it would have made military sense in the early nuclear years for the United States to strike first in any superpower conflict. This was because whichever side delivered the first blow would have launched a bomber fleet to destroy the enemy's bombers, and hence reduced its ability to strike back. It was, perhaps, the logic of striking first and consequent uncertainty that made massive retaliation credible during the immediate postwar years.

New weapons systems brought greater stability to superpower relations, particularly the development of submarine-launched missiles. In the first place, submarines were hard to detect and therefore difficult to destroy. If, for any reason, the Soviets used nuclear weapons against the West it would be an act of suicide as submarine-launched Polaris missiles would be able to strike back immediately. In the second place Polaris missiles had multiple warheads, each of which could strike a separate Soviet target (multiple independently targetable reentry vehicles, or MIRVs). This meant that the US response to a Soviet first strike, would cause massive destruction. Hence by the 1960s the perverse logic of getting in the first strike was no longer appropriate. Greater political stability was reflected in superpower détente and by West Germany pursuing a policy of *Ostpolitik*, which contributed to a further relaxation of Cold War tensions through recognition of Germany's postwar frontiers.

Britain attempted to keep up with the changing technology and develop an intercontinental ballistic missile system to replace the vulnerable V-bombers. The British missile Blue Streak was not a success and it became clear that further development was beyond Britain's defence budget. Only US help could retain Britain's status as a credible nuclear power. The special relationship had nose-dived after the Suez fiasco, but it was remarkable how quickly it was reestablished around Britain's nuclear needs. The United States provided no other country with its nuclear weapons systems, but was willing to upgrade the V-bombers with Skybolt air-to-ground missiles. To Britain's dismay President Kennedy later cancelled the development of Skybolt, but after a crucial meeting in July 1962 between Kennedy and Prime Minister Macmillan at Nassau in the Bahamas it was agreed that Britain could purchase Polaris, the most advanced weapons system available.

Tensions within NATO

The existence of a common adversary, the Warsaw Pact, did not necessarily result in NATO members being bound together in a close union. Indeed it was commonplace for decision makers to be occupied with some or other crisis within NATO. For example there was a long-running disagreement about economic resources and political control, as well as about strategy and credibility. From the US point of view the European partners in NATO showed a constant unwillingness to make a fair contribution to their own defence. At the same time they were unhappy if the United States, which paid the lion's share, appeared to dominate NATO decision-making. From the US point of view it seemed quite reasonable that 'he who paid the piper called the tune' in NATO affairs.

From the European point of view, particularly the French, who withdrew from NATO's military structure in 1966, the Atlanticist orientation of NATO resulting from the special relationship was not in the best interests of the continental members. France doubted the US commitment to defending Europe against Soviet attack and did not believe that Americans would contemplate the destruction of their homeland to save Paris, Rome or Bonn. They feared that a nuclear exchange between United States-dominated NATO and the Soviet-dominated Warsaw Pact would be confined to a Western and central European battleground. For this reason some Europeans saw the need for their own independent nuclear capability to deter the Soviets.

From Vietnam to the Gulf

In 1964 the United States unwisely entered the conflict in Vietnam that had caused the French to abandon Indo China. Consistent with its policy of containment, the United States supported South Vietnam in its fight against Vietcong guerillas from communist North Vietnam. One dilemma for the United States was that had democracy run its course in South Vietnam, a communist government would have been elected. In order to contain communism, therefore, the United States had to prop up a right-wing dictator and ignore the political aspirations of the South Vietnamese. Another dilemma for the United States was that it was geared up to fight a conventional war in Vietnam, whereas the enemy's methods were far from conventional. Finally, the United States had never been defeated militarily, and this came to dominate the presidential mindset as more and more American troops were committed to this unwinnable war. Britain was anxious to act as a peacemaker in Vietnam, but despite American requests it was adamant about not involving British troops. Whilst it was true that British troops had been deployed to defend Malaysia against Indonesia, British public opinion failed to see how involvement in Vietnam would serve the national interest. It is probably true to say that some Britons had never forgiven the United States for failing to support Britain during the Suez crisis, and found pleasure in watching the US administration 'sweat a bit' as they struggled with their own version of Suez. Where Kennedy and Macmillan had been able to inject their friendship into the special relationship, Johnson and Wilson did not get on and the Vietnam question reduced the special relationship to a low point.

The health of the special relationship improved in the 1980s through both a hotting up of the Cold War and the close personal relations between the new right leaders of Britain and the United States. 'Reaganomics' and 'Thatcherism' were drawn from a philosophy in which communism was identified as a particularly evil enemy of freedom. Militarily, the introduction of new nuclear weapons – Pershing IIs and cruise missiles to counter Soviet SS-20s – increased superpower tensions. At the same time the United States embarked on an ambitious strategic defense initiative (SDI): the so-called 'Star Wars' research and development project, which pushed the arms race to a higher and very costly level. If successful the SDI would produce a new generation of space-based weapons that would defend the West against any Soviet nuclear strike. This would leave the Soviet Union without a credible nuclear deterrent since it would be defenceless against a US attack. As we shall see, this and other events were to trigger momentous political changes in Europe, and by 1987 the Cold War was over. The Warsaw Pact collapsed and the Soviet Union disappeared in a remarkable democratic revolution.

Hope that a 'new world order' of peace and stability would replace the military rivalry of the Cold War was soon dispelled. In 1990, President Saddam Hussein of Iraq ordered the invasion of Kuwait, a move that threatened Western oil supplies. A decade earlier this would have given pleasure to the Soviet Union, but now it was possible for a US-led alliance of 29 countries to remove Iraq by force without fear of the war spilling over and escalating along old Cold War divisions. The Gulf War illustrated how one-sided the special relationship had become in military terms. Compared with the huge US Navy the British fleet was already small and destined to get even smaller. Yet judged by the navies of other European countries the Royal Navy remained impressive. In essence the United States, the only remaining superpower, has now taken over almost all of the responsibilities that comprised Britain's junior partnership role in the 1950s.

The European Context

Along with the other big powers, Britain attended the Yalta Conference in February 1945 and the Potsdam Conference the following July to establish the frontiers of postwar Europe. From the outset Britain was suspicious of Soviet territorial intentions and Churchill put far less trust in Stalin than did Roosevelt and then Truman. (British policy towards the organisation of Western Europe during the Cold War years is discussed in Chapter 5, which considers the Maastricht Treaty, believed by some political commentators to be as critical in shaping the New Europe as Yalta and Potsdam were in shaping postwar Europe.)

Later, Poland, Czechoslovakia and Hungary all attempted to weaken their ties with the Soviet Union, but military force returned them to the communist fold. The flexibility required to construct a New Europe began in the

1980s, when the leadership of the Soviet Union fell to the relatively young Mikhail Gorbachev. (A succession of previous leaders – Leonid Brezhnev, Yuri Andropov and Konstantin Chenenko – had all been close to death during their periods in the Kremlin.) Along with others, Gorbachev felt that the Soviet system had failed at home and abroad. In many ways the Soviet Union could be seen as two countries: one that was capable of financing research into advanced nuclear and space technology, the other a vast area in which most people lived in almost Third World conditions. Gorbachev launched a programme to modernise and rebuild the Soviet Union ('per-estroika'), in a new, open, more democratic political climate of 'glasnost'. New thinking supported the idea of a 'common European home', stretching from the Atlantic to the Urals, based on international trust and a minimum military presence. In other words, from the Soviet point of view the Cold War was over. The democratic revolution engulfed all countries in the old communist bloc, including the previously very authoritarian East Germany, which re-united with West Germany in October 1990.

Attempts at arms control and arms limitation took on a new vigour. Gorbachev accepted the 'zero option', which saw the de-commissioning of Pershing II, cruise and SS-20 missiles. Further progress on the elimination of nuclear weapons was accompanied by progress in reducing the levels of conventional forces. The old Cold War adversaries agreed never again to use the threat of military force against each other.

NATO had its origins in the Cold War struggle, and the ending of the Cold War raised questions about its future role. Some saw the alliance developing into a crisis-management organisation, some as a peace-keeping force in troubled areas such as Bosnia, while others were keen to maintain the defence profile of NATO, albeit against an as yet unknown enemy. A minority view was that since NATO had been born out of the Cold War, like the Warsaw Pact it should wither and disappear now that the Cold War was over. It was argued that newer organisations, such as the 34-nation Conference (now Organisation) on Security and Cooperation in Europe, should shape the New Europe along with an enlarged EU.

Britain's Changing Role

The Second World War ended with Britain heading a proved-loyal empire, which brought with it a special relationship with the United States. The cost of Britain's 'finest hour' fighting alone against the forces of fascism left it in poor economic health. Within a few decades Britain changed from a world power with global commitments to a middle-sized power with increasingly regional interests. Once the Suez affair had revealed Britain's relative international decline, a message reinforced by its loss of nuclear independence, the accommodations and adjustments necessary for a reduced regional role were essential but problematic. Whilst withdrawal from its overseas commitments went relatively smoothly, Britain found it difficult to accommodate itself to the reality of membership of the European Community and its more federal successor.

Fifty or more years on from the end of the Second World War, in diplomatic terms Britain is still 'punching above its weight' in world affairs. It remains a permanent member of the UN Security Council; it is still a nuclear power; it is still the leading member of the Commonwealth, which, after being dominated by African affairs, now has a new relevance regarding the tiger economies of Asia. British culture is disseminated by the British Council and the BBC World Service. Britain's role in the wider Europe and the European Union is uncertain, but may be brought into some form of alignment through successful diplomacy in the future. In short, whilst Sir Eyre Crowe's famous memorandum has been thrown into reverse in terms of Britain's orientation, Winston Churchill's 'three circles' are still relevant to Britain's post Cold War foreign policy. However each circle has been redefined, and that which Churchill saw as least important for Britain's interests is now the most important.

Further Reading

Attlee, C. R., *The Labour Party in Perspective* (London: Gollancz, 1937).

Barber, J., *Rhodesia: the Road to Rebellion* (London: Oxford University Press, 1967).

Fitzsimons, M. A., *The Foreign Policy of the British Labour Government 1945–51* (Notre Dame: University of Notre Dame Press, 1953).

Frankel, J., *British Foreign Policy 1945–1973* (London: RIIA/Oxford University Press, 1975).

Gordon, M. R., *Conflict and Consensus in Labour's Foreign Policy 1914–1965* (Stanford, Stanford University Press, 1969).

Northedge, F. S., *Descent from Power* (London: Allen and Unwin, 1967).

Reed, B and G. Williams, *Denis Healey and the Policies of Power* (London: Sidgwick and Jackson, 1971).

Richard, I. *et al.*, *Europe or the Open Sea?* (London: Charles Knight, 1971).

Rose, C. R., *The Relation of Socialist Principles to British Labour Foreign Policy*, (Unpublished DPhil thesis, Nuffield College, Oxford, 1959).

Sanders, D., *Losing an Empire, Finding a Role* (London: Macmillan, 1990).

Wilson, H., *The Labour Government 1964–70* (London: Weidenfeld and Nicolson/ Michael Joseph, 1971).

Windrich, E., *British Labour's Foreign Policy* (Stanford, CA: Stanford University Press, 1952).

12
Ideological Perspectives on Postwar British Politics

There are many valid perspectives on postwar Britain. One important approach focuses on the decline of Britain from a leading imperial and world power – a clear third behind the two superpowers in 1945 – to a middle-ranking European one by the last quarter of the twentieth century. Accepting loss of empire as inevitable, proponents of this approach concentrate on comparative economic decline, offering varying cultural, political and economic interpretations of it (Weiner, 1981; Barnett, 1986; Coates and Hillard, 1986; Gamble, 1990; Coates, 1994). Another key approach views this period in terms of the emergence, breakdown and possible reformation of consensus (Dutton, 1991; Kavanagh and Morris, 1994; see also Chapter 2 above). The consensus perspective has been challenged by those who consider it underestimates the degree of party and ideological conflict between the 1940s and 1970s, and is therefore a 'myth' (Pimlott, 1988; Jones and Kandiah, 1996).

Other more limited perspectives have appeared in this book. Whilst the decline of social class both as an influence on people's lives and as an influence on politics, especially voting behaviour, is a contested one (Denver and Hands, 1992; Margetts and Smyth, 1994, pp. 9–10; see also Chapters 3, 7 and 8 above), there is no doubt that other group and ideological cleavages have increased in significance. Black immigration turned Britain into a multicultural society in which the political impact of race as an issue was seen in such phenomena as Powellism and the rise of the extreme right, as well as in the behaviour of the mainstream political parties. Second-wave feminism intensified public awareness of gender and led to marked advances for women in the worlds of work and politics. The environmental movement, working through pressure groups and the Green Party gave politics a pale green fringe, although it encountered government resistance when it came to economic growth and nuclear power, and progress on removing the causes of marine, riverine and airborne pollution has remained extremely slow (Chapters 3 and 7). Nationalism, present in 1945 almost wholly as national rejoicing for victory in war, assumed increasingly divisive forms, including public disenchantment with government by Westminster and a desire for greater independence in Wales and Scotland, a ferocious internal war against the British government by the IRA and an insular, chauvinist resistance to integration in Europe by some members of both major parties, especially the Conservatives in more recent times (Chapters 4, 5, 7, 8 and 11). The constitution itself became a contested issue, although some people's desire for change exceeded the capacity to achieve it. Such change as occurred came towards the end of the period as a consequence mainly of the Conservatives' 'reinvention of the state' in the 1980s and 1990s and of Britain's membership of the European Union (Chapters 5 and 6).

All these categories – class, race, feminism, environmentalism, nationalism and constitutional change – offer relevant if partial perspectives on postwar British history. This final chapter, however, seeks a comprehensive picture of the period in terms of the roles of party and state, government policy on wealth and welfare, and relations between the individual and the state. Accordingly it offers an overview from the sharply contrasted perspectives of the three major ideologies of the era: the Marxist left, the Conservative new right and the social democratic centre.

The Marxist Left

Like the new right, the Marxist left see the first three postwar decades in terms of the collapse of social democracy, but whereas the extreme right perceives social democracy as a species of socialism, the extreme left sees it as a modified form of capitalism: capitalist democracy. For the Marxist left, the Labour Party is not a socialist party at all but a social democratic or 'labourist' party dedicated to the moderate reform – and thereby, in effect, the strengthening – of capitalism rather than its abolition. It therefore competes with the Conservatives only in terms of the more effective management of capitalism, seeking to advance the material interests of the working class within capitalist society. In the 1950s the Labour leadership abandoned even the rhetorical pretence of being a socialist party by adopting Croslandite 'revisionism' as its guiding philosophy. The Beveridgean welfare state and Keynesian managed economy administered by the Labour governments of Attlee and Wilson made little difference to the inequalities and injustices of the British class system. The middle class benefited more than the working class from the welfare state, and when the postwar social democratic state was undermined by crisis in the 1970s, massive social inequality remained.

Marxists believe that the Labour Party missed its greatest 'historical opportunity' after 1945, when a sweeping electoral victory and a radical public mood presented a golden chance for social and political transformation. Half a revolution had already been accomplished by the war and capitalism had been discredited by the prewar slump and unemployment. In Nairn's view, 'Not one of the obstacles that have blocked or distorted the rise of Socialism everywhere else was present. The chance was unique' (Nairn,

1964, pp. 354–5; see also Coates, 1975; Miliband, 1972, 1984). The chance to create a socialist society may not have existed, but the possibility of radical change certainly did (Saville, 1988, p. 142). But far from accomplishing the social revolution with which it was credited by Labour intellectuals such as Anthony Crosland in the 1950s (Crosland, 1956), the Attlee government actually carried out very limited reforms, achieving only a 'marginal' alteration in the distribution of social power, wealth and opportunity and leaving the basic structure of capitalist society unchanged. Its record on nationalisation was particularly disappointing, the range of industries nationalised being 'almost the least Labour could do without violating its election pledges' (Coates, 1975). The changes left 80 per cent of the economy in capitalist hands, the much-lauded (by social democrats) 'mixed economy' being in practice a capitalist economy. The previous owners were greatly over-compensated and, more significantly, the Morrisonian model of public ownership retained the former managerial hierarchies, thereby leaving the power structure untouched. There was no serious consideration of the workers' control model, which could have achieved a real shift of power to the working class. The Labour government failed to introduce economic planning of national resources, and although much of its welfare policy was valuable it did little to remedy the grossly inequitable distribution of wealth and income in Britain. Finally, far from attempting to develop a third way in foreign policy between the two superpowers, the Labour government was content to act as a junior partner to the United States. Its fundamentally Conservative conduct of foreign affairs resulted in excessive concessions being made to the United States, especially with regard to the military use of British airfields, a defence expenditure beyond the means of a middling power and, with the major exception of the Indian subcontinent, an over-sluggish response to the legitimate independence claims of the colonies.

Out of power between 1951 and 1964, Labour intellectuals failed to develop a feasible theory for further Socialist advance. The revisionist right led by Gaitskell and Crosland, believing the social revolution had already occurred under Attlee, redefined Labour goals in terms of managed capitalism. Although the revisionists failed to remove the commitment to public ownership from the party constitution, their view that all that was now required was for Labour to deliver continued increments of moderate reform on the path set by Attlee prevailed. It was not seriously challenged by the Socialist left of the party.

According to the Marxist analysis, the disappointing performance of Labour governments in the 1960s and 1970s was inherent in the limitations of their objectives. Wilson was a revisionist social democrat who had no radical plans when he entered office in 1964. To him modernisation meant the more efficient operation of a capitalist economy. He rejected the idea of class antagonism and had no wish to extend public ownership. His major economic decisions were taken with the aim of establishing Labour's credibility with the international business community. He also persisted with 'unswerving support for the United States', in the hope of making Anglo-US cooperation the backbone of his foreign policy. In fact he merely chose 'a Labour way', that is, with 'heart-searching, qualifications, exceptions and so forth' of 'carrying out Tory policies'. His efforts at economic planning made those of the Attlee government, themselves meagre enough, appear 'positively heroic'. His incomes policy reflected little concern for social fairness: it involved 'people earning £1000 a month (or more) telling people earning £1000 a year (or less) that they must stop being greedy'. By the 1970s much of the radical consciousness of the Labour movement in the the 1940s had dissipated, the Labour leaders having demonstrated that they were not socialists who had 'lost their way' but merely 'bourgeois politicians with, at best, a certain bias towards social reform' (Miliband, 1972, pp. 350–77). Labour had used its power not to redistribute wealth, income and social privilege but rather to undermine the industrial power, job security and living standards of its own supporters (Coates, 1975, ch.5).

When it entered office in 1974 the Labour Party pledged to achieve 'a fundamental and irreversible shift in the balance of power and wealth in favour of working people and their families'. However, as before, it entered office with 'too inflated a sense of the power' it would be free to exercise and was 'too optimistic about the ease of reform and regeneration of a total society by a single parliamentary party'. On this occasion, it faced not only the usual constraints placed on a reforming government by the centres of private power but also a much-weakened national economy and 'a crisis rooted in capitalism as a world system'. For Marxists the 1970s economic 'crisis' occurred when a major international recession, generated by, among other things, intensifying world competition and falling profits, combined with the inflationary consequences of rising public expenditure. Judged by social democratic criteria, the 1974–9 Labour governments' response to the crisis of simultaneously rising unemployment and inflation was a success: it engineered and sustained 'a remarkable degree of working class industrial and political moderation', at least until the explosion of industrial conflict in 1978–9. But judged by Marxist criteria, Labour's record was once again disastrous since it failed to fulfil its radical programme and achieved political and economic stabilisation only by severely reducing working class living standards. Once again it subordinated working class aspirations and interests to 'the imperatives of capital accumulation' (Coates, 1975, pp. 2, 154, 200, 259, 261).

Marxist explanations of Labour's failure to transform the structures of power and class in Britain may be summarised in terms of the movement's inherent moderation and the strength of institutional and constitutional blockages.

Labour Movement Moderation

To Marxists, neither branch of the Labour movement is either radical or socialist. Labour Party ideology consists of a mild democratic reformism; when in power it is invariably too moderate, conciliatory and willing to compromise. Within the party the centre right dominated the minority of left wingers for all but a brief period in the early 1980s. The main bulwark of its power was the party constitution, which permitted an 'independent' parliamentary Labour Party to resist outside pressures. The adoption of Croslandite revisionism was a major ideological blunder. First, he defined socialism in terms of equality and social justice rather than in terms of ownership of the means of production. Accordingly he stressed that the benefits of economic growth would be redistributed by state welfare and graduated taxation rather than extending public ownership. This idea was based on the mistaken belief that capitalism had undergone fundamental change in the 1940s and 1950s so that managerial control had become more important than ownership and strong unions provided countervailing power to the owners of capital. Hence, rather than a cardinal socialist principle, public ownership had become simply one means to attain social justice, and moreover one that should be considered pragmatically on its merits. Second, with class antagonisms now tempered by state welfare in a mixed economy and fewer voters identifying themselves as working class, a socialist party, in his view, should seek to be a national party rather than a class party. To Marxists this idea greatly exaggerated the extent to which opposed class interests were becoming a thing of the past (Plant, 1983, pp. 20–3). Far from being a force for radical change, therefore, the Labour Party formed one of the conservative forces in British society, operating not for the promotion of working class interests but for 'the containment of class conflict and pressure from below' (Miliband, 1984, p. 15).

Second, Marxists contest the new right's view of trade unions as 'overmighty' institutions and perceive them instead as vehicles that contain working-class pressure. Far from being militant or aggressive, trade unions are defensive organisations that offer no challenge to private property, social hierarchy and massive inequalities of power and reward. To governments, they have been indispensable allies in the management of class conflict. Especially since the Second World War, Labour governments in particular have expected unions to play 'a major part in maintaining industrial discipline, curbing militancy, and persuading their members to reduce their demands for higher wages' (Ibid., p. 58). In return for collaborating over incomes policies, the unions were rewarded with some sympathetic legislation (for example in 1975), but for the most part gained no influence over national policy making. Their greater militancy made them less reliable allies of government in the 1970s, but despite their occasional ability to provoke a major crisis – as in the 'exceptional cases' of 1968–9, 1972–3 and 1978–9 – the media and political right generally exaggerated the power of the unions (Ibid., pp. 58–68).

Instititutional and Constitutional Blockages to Socialism

To the relatively minor extent to which Labour threatened the existing order, the 'conservative forces' of the main political institutions provided important bulwarks against grass-roots radicalism. Ostensibly neutral institutions of the British state – parliament, the civil service, the armed forces, the police, the judiciary, the monarchy and local government – all played their part in the co-option and thereby the taming of Labour. First, the 'parliamentary embrace' seduced Labour MPs into greater moderation through several means, including the intimidating influence of the venerable atmosphere, procedures and rituals of the House of Commons, the self-conceit generated by membership of the 'best club in Europe', and above all the strength of appeals to party loyalty and the power of Labour leaders to reward or punish through their control over patronage (Ibid., pp. 41–4). Second, the far left believed that the civil service was a conservative power bloc that obstructed radical reform (Sedgemore, 1980; Miliband, 1984, p. 104). Third, far from being impartial upholders of the law and defenders of the realm, the police and military were part of 'a system of class inequality and domination' that had 'profoundly "political" connotations'. Thus the police and sometimes the military were invariably far more zealous in enforcing the law against the left than against the fascist-style right, while judges also displayed conservative bias in consistently finding against the rights of trade unionists and the policies of radical Labour councils (Miliband, 1984, pp. 110, 118–19. Finally, the House of Lords and the monarchy were seen as part of 'the machinery of containment embedded in the British political system'. Although 'not vital', their political role was 'not negligible' and could in times of conflict and crisis become 'considerable': for example the setting up of a special commission on breaches of the oil sanction against Rhodesia was only one of several Labour measures voted down by the Conservative-dominated upper house in the 1970s (Ibid., pp. 123–30).

Two major approaches to Thatcherism appeared on the left: (1) a more traditional class politics analysis and (2) a broader theory of it as a new hegemonic project developed by the Gramsci-inspired writers of the *New Left Review* and *Marxism Today* (Exhibit 12.1).

Class politics analysts see Thatcherism as primarily the ruling class's response to the political and economic problems of the 1970s, which produced 'a crisis of legitimacy' for the British state. The crisis developed because the social democratic state proved unable to satisfy the demands of the business class for favourable conditions for capital 'accumulation' (that is, profitable enterprise) and of the people in general for good wages, welfare benefits and public services. The crisis was exacerbated by world economic recession and Britain's relative economic decline. The attempt to alleviate the

EXHIBIT 12.1   *New Left perspectives on postwar history*

From the 1960s, Perry Anderson, Tom Nairn and other *New Left Review* writers developed a left-wing perspective influenced by concepts drawn from the Italian Marxist Antonio Gramsci (1891–1937). They and subsequent analysts such as Andrew Gamble employ the Gramscian concept of hegemony to explain the failure of modernisation in Britain and the emergence of Thatcherism. Interested in ideas and culture, Gramsci developed the concept of hegemony to explain how a ruling class maintained its dominance not simply by physical force or economic control but by persuading other classes to accept its system of beliefs and share its values. Properly understood, according to Gamble (1988, 2nd edn, 1994) the idea of hegemony involves the successful interweaving of ideological, economic and political domination.

Nairn argues that the problems of post-1945 Britain have to be seen in the context of the failure of the bourgeois, modernising revolution of the nineteenth century, which meant that Britain never acquired an efficient manufacturing sector and never became a genuine democracy. Rather, bourgeois capitalism was contained within a patrician hegemony that 'never favoured the aggressive development of industrialism'. Rather than overthrowing the landowning aristocracy, the bourgeoisie formed an undynamic alliance with it, establishing a new hegemony based on conservative liberal values diffused via the intelligentsia and the public schools. In the twentieth century, by a strategy of welfare and other 'concessions', a defensive working class was yoked to this relatively immobile social order.

After 1945 the costs of the failure of bourgeois radicalism became apparent: Britain could now be seen to possess an obsolete economy embedded in a traditional constitutional order. The modernising social democratic egalitarianism of the 1940s was a myth and in the 1960s and 1970s Labour again proved incapable of giving Britain the social, economic and constitutional reforms necessary to transform it into a genuinely modern society. The political initiative thus passed to the right (Nairn, 1977).

problems by cutting public expenditure and reforming industrial relations merely provoked working-class militancy. According to this analysis, Thatcherism was a desperate last throw of a business class determined to restore the conditions for successful capitalist enterprise, by force if necessary. Accordingly the Thatcher governments conducted a fierce assault on the working class by cutting back the welfare state, privatising the nationalised industries and breaking the power of organised labour by permitting high long-term unemployment, curbing trade union powers by legislation and crushing strikes. To the objection that wiping out one fifth of the manufacturing industry in 1980–1 hardly represented a coherent strategy for industrial capital, class analysts reply either that industrialists were prepared to accept short-term losses in order to improve the climate for business in the long term or that such a strategy was a rational one for the dominant part of British capital, which has always been commercial and financial rather than industrial. To class analysts there was nothing new about Thatcherism; it was simply one more episode in the long war between capital and labour (Gamble, 1988, p. 175).

The Gramsci-inspired *Marxism Today* school, however, see Thatcherism as a novel development ('a new hegemonic project'). Like the class analysts, they believe that it originated in the 1970s crisis of the social democratic state and that it involved economic restructuring by the dominant class – the 'free economy'. But they believe it went further and that interwoven with the economic strand were equally important ideological and political ones. Thus in addition to 'the strategy of accumulation, to reverse decisively the decline of the British economy', Thatcherism involved 'a strategy for reorganising the State and civil society, both to make the accumulation strategy work and overcome resistance to it, and to re-establish the authority of the State with the Conservative party as its dominant political force' (Gamble, 1988, p. 223). Building ideological and political support for the reorganisation of the State entailed discrediting social democracy, welfare provision and the key institutions of the labour movement by playing upon populist themes such as rising crime, welfare 'scroungers' and union 'greed' and 'irresponsibility'. To this school of thought, right-wing populism was combined with authoritarianism since a strong state was necessary to police the market order, to uphold social and political authority and, in particular, to take on and defeat resistance from organised interests. The *Marxism Today* writer Stuart Hall called the Thatcherite hegemonic project 'authoritarian populism' and saw the tabloid press as playing a pivotal role in establishing the new right-wing 'commonsense' of the times (Hall and Jacques, 1983, pp. 9–39). To Andrew Gamble, it was best described in terms of its aim: the establishment of 'a free economy and a strong State'. In his view, by the late 1980s its main success had been in industrial relations, but it had proved more a formula for managing than for reversing Britain's economic decline (Gamble, 1988, pp. 23–6, 174–87, 222–3, 235–7).

The New Right

Like the Marxist left, the new right rejected the social democratic policies that had prevailed between 1945 and the 1970s. Statist policies based on the Keynesian managed economy, the Beveridgean welfare state and neo-corporatist relations with producer groups, had proved an economic disaster. They had produced a stagnant economy (characterised by high unemployment, escalating inflation and frequent, damaging strikes) which had been outclassed and overtaken by its main competitors. A fall in the international standing of the country had been an inevitable accompaniment of economic decline. In addition social welfare policies, allied with the 'permissive society' reforms of the 1960s, had undermined social authority and self-reliance and led to the 'dependency culture'. The new right thus developed a comprehensive indictment of all the major trends in postwar British history.

First, the new right offered an economic critique of postwar Keynesian demand management, its basic argument being that Keynesian policies had been discredited by recent historical experience. Designed to provide governments with fiscal and monetary levers to stimulate growth, they had in practice led to a 'black hole' of national uncompetitiveness, declining profits, rising unemployment, accelerating inflation, overmighty unions and a swollen public sector. State intervention was condemned (1) because it produced inferior results to market solutions and (2) because government bureaucracies were inherently inferior to markets as a mechanism for allocating economic resources (Exhibit 12.2).

EXHIBIT 12.2   *The right-wing assault on the postwar settlement: the attack on Keynesianism*

One of the leading intellectuals of the Thatcher counterrevolution was the Austrian-born economist and political philosopher, F. A. von Hayek. In *The Road to Serfdom* (1944) he argued in favour of a society based on the free market economy and individual freedom within the law. In 1980, writing of the economic theory underlying the postwar settlement, he maintained that:

'The final disaster we owe mainly to Lord Keynes. His erroneous conception that employment could be directly controlled by regulating aggregate demand through monetary policy shifted responsibility for employment from the trade unions to government. The error . . . misrepresented full employment entirely as a function of government monetary policy. For forty years it has thus made the price mechanism ineffective in the labour market by preventing wages from acting as a signal to workers and employers. . . . Inevitably the consequence is continuous and accelerating inflation' (Hayek, 1984 in Coates and Hillard, 1986, pp. 111–12).

As well as intervening too much in the economy, government in the social democratic state, as Margaret Thatcher argued in 1977, had grown 'far too big'. 'A Government that did less, and therefore did it better', she continued, 'would strengthen its authority' (cited in O'Gorman, 1986, pp. 220–1). The leading new right argument was that the excessive rise in state expenditure had crowded out the wealth-creating capacity of the private sector. It became commonplace in new right circles to deplore 'the excessive growth of the public sector for consuming well over half of everything produced in this country, mostly on activities which themselves consume wealth with no countervailing production' (Lord Keith, in Coates and Hillard, 1986, p. 75).

The detailed case for the 'crowding out' thesis espoused by the new right was succinctly stated by the Oxford economists Robert Bacon and Walter Eltis. They began from the basic proposition that 'the marketed output of industry and services taken together must supply the total private consumption, investment and export needs of the whole nation'. They then argued that Britain had suffered from three important difficulties between 1961 and 1974: a steady fall in the proportion of the labour force producing marketed output; a rise in the number who relied on others to produce marketed output for them, such as civil servants, social workers and most teachers and medical workers; and a 19 per cent rise in the entitlement of the non-market sector to buy marketed output. The results were damaging to the British economy. First, as taxes were increased to pay for the larger number of public sector workers, workers sought to offset the increased 'social wage' by raising their wage demands, leading to explosive wage inflation. Second, with both government and workers making exorbitant claims on the economic product, company profits and investment fell and there were severe balance of payments difficulties. The solution favoured by the right was to expand the market sector of the economy by cutting public spending, reducing nationalised industry losses and subsidies and eventually privatising the public corporations and much more of the public sector. Bacon and Eltis cite Margaret Thatcher as having already accepted this fundamental case in 1975 as she asserted the need not to 'overload' the private sector (Bacon and Eltis, 1976, pp. 21–3, 27–32, 92–116). An overblown public sector needed to be 'rolled back' because it was taking too large a share of productive resources and could not be trusted to use them as efficiently as the private sector.

'Overmighty unions' were also a target for the new right thinkers Sir Keith Joseph and F. A. von Hayek. First, the ability of the most powerful unions, through national collective bargaining, to gain settlements in line with or ahead of inflation had adverse consequences for weakly organised and non-unionised workers and businesses who paid the bill in higher taxes, fewer jobs and more bankruptcies. Second, political wage determination by corporatist-style bargains struck by governments with unions since the early 1960s had failed in that it had distorted the workings of the market and accelerated economic decline. Third, the law conferred too many privileges on unions, producing a 'militants' charter'. The result, according to Sir Keith Joseph, was that 'in a trade dispute most things seem permitted to the union side: breaking contracts, inducing others to break contracts, picketing of non-involved companies, secondary boycotts'. Fourth, the unions, working through the labour movement, had propagated the misguided myth that 'free enterprise is the "class enemy"'. In this mistaken belief 'they have taught workers to resist efficiency, obstruct management, insist on overmanning, resent profit and ignore consumers'. Finally, in Hayek's view certain trade union restrictive practices such as demarcation rules and the closed shop were inimical to a free society (Sir Keith Joseph and F. A. Hayek, cited in Coates and Hillard, 1986, pp. 98–114). The policy implications of this new right analysis for government action were clear: move to arms' length relationships with the unions; curb the unions' legal privileges; provide a legal framework that would encourage 'moderate' and 'responsible' unions and preclude swift, unofficial strikes; encourage a pro-business culture whilst attacking class-war attitudes to society; and finally, engage in a trial of strength with the strongest and most militant unions, and win. Thatcher and Sir Keith Joseph seized upon the industrial militancy of 1978–9 as 'a symbol of the bankruptcy of social democracy'. It provided them with final and conclusive confirmation that 'trade union power could not be appeased. It had to be destroyed if decline was to be reversed and the authority of the state restored' (Gamble, 1988, p. 94).

Finally, the new right criticised the entire trend of postwar history in its attack on the welfare state. First, collectively provided services were ineffi-cient in helping those whom they were designed to help. If individual consumers were given an equivalent amount of money to that spent by bureaucrats on their behalf, they could be guaranteed to spend it more effectively. Second, a universal system of benefits gave too little to the neediest in society whilst offering unnecessary amounts to the better-off. In addition to depriving people of choice, therefore, the system was unfair and inadequate. Third, instead of promoting self-reliance, state-provided benefits discouraged self-help and encouraged dependency. Finally, the welfare state had grown well beyond the intentions of its founders by extending existing commitments and adding new ones, many of which were justifiable at the time, such as payments to the disabled. But the overall result, according to the Thatcherite businessman Sir John Hoskyns, was that the welfare state had become 'Britain's biggest man-made disaster'. It was 'astronomically expensive compared with the economy that supports it'; for 'a fragile economy like Britain's' the spending and taxing burden had passed 'its tolerable limits' (cited in Hillard and Coates, 1986, pp. 127–33). Hoskyns's view that Britain had never recovered from the 'strategic error' made in 1945 of committing the country to the three fold burden of full employment, wholesale nationalisation and the creation of a welfare state before rebuild-ing its productive base was supported by the historian Corelli Barnett. His *The Audit of War* (1986) argued among other things that a group of high-minded intellectuals backed by leading members of the Labour and Liberal parties propelled Britain into establishing a welfare state that the country could not afford, against the better judgement of more cautious politicians such as Churchill and in defiance of the real national priority which should have been economic modernisation.

The perspective from which the new right launched its attack on the collectivist, full employment, egalitarian and corporatist priorities of the 1945 settlement was that of a *laissez faire* utopia, 'an economy without unions, markets without rigidities, a minimal public sector and private provision of almost all goods and services' (Gamble, 1988, p. 184). Its critique targeted social and cultural values as well as economic policy. It sought to overturn the value system that had been dominant since the 1950s, which identified the public sector with unselfish action for the well-being of the whole community and the private sector with selfish action that brought personal gratification at the expense of society at large. Its new cultural model emphasised the virtues of private activity in terms of entrepreneurial initiative and individual choice and freedom, and denigrated public-sphere activity in terms of being a burden on the rest of society.

New right thinking also contained an important traditional Conservative aspect that was antiliberal in morality and nationalist in ideology. Whereas the neoliberal new right focused on economic decline, new right conservatives emphasised moral and social decay and Britain's loss of international prestige. They called for a restoration of authority at all levels of British society from government to the family, and for a reassertion of national influence abroad and preparedness in the face of the communist threat. Like the economic neoliberals, they particularly admired the nineteenth century, and advocated a return to the Victorian values of thrift, self-help and personal responsibility. Like the neoliberals too, they considered that British history had taken a wrong turn after 1945, and that the excessive tasks assumed by governments had led eventually to the erosion of political authority.

The major fear of the Conservative new right was a total breakdown of political and social authority. It was a frequent contention among politicians and political commentators in the 1970s that Britain was becoming 'harder to govern', and that the problems facing the country seemed to be more numerous and more intractable. In addition the will of the authorities was frequently flouted by insubordinate elements such as strikers, demonstrators, vandals, criminals and football hooligans. Respect for authority in schools, places of work and on the streets appeared to be in decline (King, 1976, pp. 25–7, 92–4). Traditional Conservatives saw the increase in the divorce rate, the easy availability of abortion, the teaching of peace studies in schools, excessive sex and violence on television, rising crime and workers' flouting of authority in the workplace as symptoms of moral decay. They therefore called for a restoration of governmental authority, first by governments attempting to do less and doing it more successfully, and second by strengthening the forces of law and order. Traditional Conservatives gave priority to the restoration of social discipline over the neoliberal commitment to restoring economic liberty, blaming socialism for the moral decay at the heart of the nation (Exhibit 12.3).

Some Conservatives traced the origins of the moral rot to the 'permissive' reforms of the 1960s and the 'catastrophic' relaxation of moral standards with respect to divorce, abortion, homosexuality and the punishment of murderers, and the weakening of the rules of censorship in printed matter and the performing arts. According to them, it was then that misguided, child-centred theories of education and soft attitudes to criminality based on reformation rather than punishment had taken root. In 1982, Margaret Thatcher asserted her belief that permissive clap-trap in the 1960s had 'set

EXHIBIT 12.3 *The traditional New Right: the need to restore moral authority*

The right-wing political journalist Peregrine Worsthorne advanced the following argument (traditional conservatism but with a marked populist element):

'What people sense about British Socialism is not that it leads to an iron pattern of State tyranny but that it allows public affairs to run completely wild. The impression it leaves is not of power but of impotence, and of being one of the main causes of national and social disintegration. . . . Also associated in the public mind with British Socialism – and again in marked contrast with the Iron Curtain variety – is a lack of concern about crime, sexual morality, or the spread of pornography, and about discipline in schools, universities and the home. Parts of the Labour Party are against the police, the armed forces and corporal and capital punishment as well as spurning the economic disciplines of the market, the boss and the landlord. They are . . . against all the instruments and methods by which authority is maintained. . . . The spectre haunting most ordinary people in Britain is neither of a totalitarian State nor of Big Brother, but of other ordinary people being allowed to run wild. What they are worried about is crime, violence, disorder in the schools, promiscuity, idleness, pornography, football hooliganism, vandalism and urban terrorism'
(Worsthorne in Cowling, 1978, pp. 147–8, 150).

---

the scene for a society in which the old values of discipline and self-restraint were denigrated' and that the 1980s were 'reaping what was sown' twenty years before (quoted in Durham, 1994, p. 66). In 1985 the Conservative Party Chairman, Norman Tebbit, also traced the upsurge of crime and violence to the permissive 1960s. 'The permissives', he stated, 'scorned traditional standards. . . . Family life was derided as an outdated bourgeois concept. . . . Violence and soft pornography became accepted in the media' (Ibid., p. 66).

Finally, the conservative new right were concerned about the decline in Britain's international status. In the late 1970s, Thatcher combined calls for a military reinforcement of NATO and an ideological crusade against Soviet communism with an appeal to reassert British greatness as a world power. Britain's decline, she believed, had resulted partly from the rise of the superpowers and partly from the country's economic decline, which had been the consequence of 'processes that the Labour government has assisted'. It was a vital task for the Conservative Party to reassert the slumbering patriotism of the British.

The call by new right Conservatives in the 1970s for a reversal of postwar social democratic policies represented a rejection of the political work of their Conservative predecessors – namely the decisions and policies of the Churchill, Eden, Macmillan, Home and Heath governments between 1951 and 1974. The speeches of Sir Keith Joseph, published as *Reversing the Trend* (1975), 'constituted a sustained criticism of all postwar governments since

1945, Conservative as well as Labour' (Seldon, 1994, p. 58). Having served in three of those Conservative governments, Sir Keith accepted that he had to take his 'share of the blame for following too many of the fashions' (Cockett, 1995, p. 242). Not until 1974 had he been converted to the true faith – libertarian, rather than collectivist, Conservatism: 'I had thought that I was a Conservative but now I see that I was not really one at all' (Ibid.). Sir Alfred Sherman, who was closely involved with Margaret Thatcher and Sir Keith Joseph in the new right 'think-tank', the Centre for Policy Studies, espoused the need to reverse postwar 'middle way collectivism' even more bluntly in a memorandum to Sir Keith in June 1975: 'Conservatives cannot stand on the unworkable wish-wash inherited from Butler and Macmillan. They must offer something workable' (quoted in Cockett, 1995, pp. 242, 247).

The new right's view of the Thatcher governments is straightforward. According to them she was one of the greatest prime ministers the country has ever had and her record, although flawed, nevertheless constitutes a towering and unique achievement. Its major successes were first in economic policy, with privatisation, the taming of the unions and the tax-cutting stimulus to popular capitalism all constituting unequivocal triumphs. The emphasis of her macroeconomic policy on curbing inflation rather than maintaining full employment and her microeconomic stress on improving the operation of markets reversed decades of ineffective Keynesian attempts at demand management and incomes policies. These radical policies adminis-tered a profound and necessary shock to the British economy. Strikes declined in number and severity, managements became free to manage and productivity improved. Significant reforms were launched in education and the health service too but Thatcher's second great achievement was restoring British prestige in the world. Her tough anti-Soviet stance and emphasis on maintaining a large nuclear and conventional weapons establishment, to-gether with her close relationship with the United States, contributed to the collapse of communism in the USSR and its satellites. She successfully asserted British interests within the European Union and resisted closer European integration in the name of preservation of national sovereignty. The most potent symbol of her rule was the Falklands War, which, in the words of Nigel Lawson, 'finally laid the ghost of Suez. It showed the world – and, even more important, ourselves – that Britain still possessed a patri-otism and a moral fibre that many had thought had gone forever' (quoted in Riddell, 1991, p. 215).

Thatcher was also remarkable for her determined, resolute style of government, holding firm at crucial moments when others might have buckled. In 1981, with unemployment rising sharply, she backed her chancellor when he raised taxes to curb public sector borrowing, against conventional economic wisdom. In 1982, in defiance of the military experts, she took the huge risk of despatching a large armada to reclaim the Falklands. In 1984–5, she confronted and defeated the National Union of

Mineworkers in defiance of the traditional advice to governments to 'never take on the miners'.

Finally, Thatcherism moved the political agenda sharply to the right, providing a programme for her successor to complete and for her opponents to adjust to. In all important areas, Major continued the Thatcherite policies (Smith and Ludlam, 1996, pp. 273–81). Meanwhile a succession of Labour leaders pushed their party towards the centre-right, accepting the Thatcherite agenda on economic and welfare policy and competing over which party could best administer the market economy.

The Political Centre

Whereas the Marxist left includes the Labour left and far left groups outside the party, and the new right embraces Thatcherites within the Conservative Party and various think-tanks and media sympathisers outside it, the political centre is made up of a broad cross-party spectrum of opinion that straddles the Labour right and centre, the Liberal Democrats (and former Liberals and Social Democrats) and the Conservative left or 'wets'. This ideological stratum may be termed 'social democracy'. It signified the political forces supportive of the Keynesian–Beveridgean postwar settlement between the late 1940s and the 1970s, when it was politically dominant, with both the far left and the neoliberal right marginalised. It was the progressive ideology of the day, having been administered since 1945 by both parties when in power. Postwar history in the 1970s was written predominantly from the perspective of social democracy and generally with a favourable slant on the postwar consensus. The managed economy and welfare state were depicted as affording a politically acceptable, democratic way of combining economic efficiency and social justice. However social democrats in the mid 1990s confronted the different task of accounting for the collapse of this settlement in the late 1970s and offering a social democratic verdict on the Thatcher/Major years.

Two important interpretations of 'what went wrong with British social democracy' emerged in the political centre: the adversary politics thesis, and the developmental state theory. The adversary politics thesis achieved prominence after 1974 as first a Liberal and then a Liberal–Social Democrat argument and was given powerful support by the political scientist S. E. Finer in his book *Adversary Politics and Electoral Reform* (1975). The idea that Britain lacked a developmental state is associated with David Marquand, whose book *The Unprincipled Society* appeared in 1988. Marquand, a historian and political scientist, was a Jenkinsite right-wing Labour MP in the 1970s, a founder member of the SDP in 1981 and returned to New Labour in 1995. A version of the developmental state argument is also to be found in the work of the political scientists Ian Budge and David McKay (1993).

The Adversary Politics Thesis

The adversary politics thesis argues that Britain has suffered from excessive party competition, especially since the 1960s, with particularly damaging consequences for the continuity of economic and industrial policies (Exhibit 12.4)

If the monetarist thesis that a modern economy could be run simply by regulating the money supply was rejected, incomes policy was essential to combine reasonably full employment with price stability. But, argued, Michael Stewart, incomes policy, which always became unpopular after a time, could succeed only if 'consistently supported by both the main parties, and not regularly repudiated by the one in opposition in the hope of gleaning electoral dividends' (cited Coates and Holland eds, p. 192). However in the late 1960s and 1970s this did not happen. Conservative attacks in opposition forced Labour to abandon its incomes policy in 1969, leading to the 1969–70 wage explosion. Then the Conservatives rejected incomes policy on entering office in 1970, only to adopt a statutory incomes policy two years later, and Labour's attack on this contributed to the inflationary wage round of 1974–5. When in government itself, Labour replaced the Conservatives' statutory policy with a voluntary one. Stewart concludes: 'If the opposition had in each case refrained from making party capital out of the government's incomes policy, the rate of inflation during the 1970s would probably have been considerably lower, and the general performance of the economy better' (Ibid., pp. 192–3). Labour's incomes policy broke down in the 'Winter of Discontent' in 1978–9 but the incoming Conservative administration's dismantling of the policy led to a wage explosion that sent inflation soaring again.

EXHIBIT 12.4   *The adversary politics thesis*

Michael Stewart, an economist, contended in *The Jekyll and Hyde Years* (1977) that an important reason for Britain's poor economic performance after 1964 lay in its malfunctioning party system:

'Both Labour and Conservative Parties, while in opposition, have succumbed to the temptation to condemn a large proportion of the government's policies and have promised to reverse many of these policies when they themselves took office. The result has been *a fatal lack of continuity*. Incoming governments have spent their first year or two abolishing or drastically modifying the measures – often quite sensible – of their predecessors, and pressing ahead with the measures – often unrealistic or irrelevant – which they have formed in opposition. After a year or two they have come to closer terms with reality, and changed course, but *by that time much harm has been done*, and the benefits that would have accrued from continuing the policies they inherited have been lost' (Hillard and Coates, 1986, p. 190, emphasis added).

Similar chopping and changing occurred with policies on industry. Labour favoured investment grants, the Conservatives preferred investment allowances. Labour introduced selective employment tax, the Conservatives abolished it. Labour set up the Industrial Reorganisation Corporation, the Conservatives did away with it. Labour nationalised steel, the Conservatives returned it to the private sector, only for Labour to take it back into public ownership. The Conservatives agreed a long-term policy for the steel industry (in the public sector) in the early 1970s but Labour radically revised the plan in the mid 1970s. Party competition also subjected the economy to the exigencies of the electoral cycle, with the governing party manipulating the economy to produce pre-election booms in order to find favour with the voters, only for these to be followed by post-election deflationary 'squeezes'. This continued subjection of the economy to short-term party considerations produced a situation that was harmful to business confidence and to long-term investment and growth. As the Hansard report *Politics and Industry: the Great Mismatch* (1979) pointed out, party competition through the simple majority system precluded long-term planning of the kind required by industrialists.

The Liberal Party linked excessive party competition to another centrist bugbear: class-based politics. In its view, the fact that the two major parties represented the interests of capital and labour respectively made British politics too ideological, thereby promoting conflict at the expense of compromise and consensus (Exhibit 12.5).

The party believed that the only way to break the stranglehold of the two-party system, and the confrontational adversary class politics it generated, was to introduce electoral reform. A system of proportional representation

EXHIBIT 12.5   *The class politics thesis*

The Liberal Party manifesto of October 1974 stated:

'The Liberals are unashamedly committed to breaking the two-party system in which the Party of Management alternates with the Party of Trade Unionism, each committed to the reversal of their predecessors' policies. Both interest groups represent vital elements in our society. Neither should ever be allowed to dominate the thinking of the government of the day. Instant reversal has brought uncertainty over Europe, over pensions, in the future of industry and has undermined confidence and stability' (Craig, 1975, p. 468).

Shirley Williams, one of the four founders of the SDP, stated in 1981:

'We must end parties based on class . . . the fact that we are going to have a party which is not affiliated to interest groups, whether middle class and business, or so-called blue-collar and union, is in itself terribly important' (quoted Tracy, 1983, p. 42)

would strengthen the political centre – where the moderate majority of the electorate were to be found – against the political extremes. It would thereby provide a coherent basis for social democratic government to pursue the policies of the 'middle way'. After the formation of the SDP in 1981, this became the standard argument of the Liberal–SDP Alliance in the 1980s. Later, the Liberal Democrats also saw its outdated political system as the major cause of Britain's decline and advocated proportional representation to strengthen the political centre, thereby producing greater stability in government and ending the sudden swings in economic policy before and after elections (*The Times Guide to the House of Commons*, 1992, pp. 345, 350, 362–5).

Like the new right, the former Labour right wingers who became founder members of the SDP had become convinced by the late 1970s that the unions were too powerful both in the Labour Party and in national politics. But their response to excessive union power was to curb it by using electoral reform to strengthen the political centre rather than by launching a head-on legislative and political assault. Writing in 1980, Marquand contended that it was no longer possible to devise a workable non-Marxist economic policy that 'did not not entail conflict with the unions'. In his view the private sector needed to be strengthened and the share of national income going to profits increased, but Labour was incapable of carrying out such a policy because the right needed the political support of the unions to retain control against the left, and the unions were bound to block such moves (cited in Tracy, 1983, p. 41). Having exercised veto power over the industrial relations reforms of both Labour and Conservative governments in 1969 and 1971, the unions were too strong to be ignored but too weak to deliver their part in national wages bargains, which were the counter-inflationary alternative to huge rises in unemployment.

Political scientists were divided over the validity of the adversary politics thesis. Richard Rose argued that the political record from 1945 to 1979 demonstrated continuity rather than violent policy swings. Thus there was no division of principle on 80 per cent of the bills introduced by the 1970–4 Conservative administration and no division of principle on 77 per cent of the bills introduced by the 1974–9 Labour governments (Rose, 1984, p. 80). On key economic indicators such as the minimum lending rate, the public sector borrowing requirement and public expenditure as a proportion of GDP, there were long-term secular trends, that were seemingly unaffected by changes in government. Gamble also found a strong underlying continuity of economic policy postwar, with the parties agreeing on prioritising the integration of the British economy into the US-dominated world economy, on rectifying the balance of payments and maintaining exchange rates, and, with no adversary divisions appearing until 1983, on commitment to the EEC. The adversary thesis, Gamble believed, exaggerated the role of parties in policy formation and underestimated that of other bodies and institutions.

To the limited degree that adversary politics occurred, by concentrating attention excessively on such issues as nationalisation, it inhibited detailed examination of government policy and the exploration of alternatives by oppositions (Gamble and Walkland, 1983, part B).

Walkland, however, found 'considerable evidence' of the damaging effects of adversary politics on the management of the economy. He cited the economic cycles of pre-election boom and post-election deflation, together with nationalisation, taxation, social insurance and industrial relations policies, as cases in point. He criticised the neoliberal Conservative right and the Marxist left for their refusal to accept this evidence. Neither the neoliberal right's view of the 1945–79 period as 'a Keynesian inflationary swamp' that was totally responsible for contemporary economic ills, nor the Marxist left's view of right-wing Labour administrations as 'crypto-Tories' was in the least tenable. He also criticised Rose, whose 'moving consensus' argument was hardly relevant to the formation of economic policy. The adversary thesis accepted that there had been periods of 'good government' after 1945 – for example by the Conservatives from 1962–4, by Labour from 1967–70 and post-1976 – but maintained that these were all 'emergency administrations' that were having to come to terms with the indulgence of their predecessors; they were governments that did the right thing only after all other alternatives had been exhausted (Ibid., part A).

The adversary thesis gained further support after 1979, when Conservative privatisation, trade union reform, the rejection of corporatism and formal incomes policy, the emphasis on curbing inflation with unemployment at over three million, and far-reaching changes in local government and the welfare state constituted 'significant discontinuities' with the previous era (Kavanagh, 1990, p. 317)

The Developmental State

The developmental state thesis turns on its head the new right argument that postwar Britain suffered from too much government intervention, by arguing that it suffered from too little government intervention, or rather too little of the right kind. Its advocates maintain that historically 'British Governments . . . have played a more limited role in relation to their economy and society than have governments in comparable countries', and that 'as a result they have been poorly equipped to engage in the kind of highly positive interventions followed by most other governments in the European Community'. The high level of public spending that existed after 1945 does not contradict this point because public sector spending is only one indicator of government power. Another very important indicator is the extent to which the central government has managed, coerced or influenced social and economic forces or, as Marquand puts it, has been able 'to supplement, constrain, manipulate, or direct market forces to public ends' (Budge and McKay, 1993, p. 210; Marquand, 1991, p. 220).

According to its theorists, the developmental state is a state with the administrative capacity for detailed intervention in society and the economy, and, when required, the political will to undertake it. It is well-coordinated and cohesive at the top, with no important divisions between the central departments of state, for example the Treasury and spending departments, has strong vertical administrative links with the localities and regions, such as France possesses with its prefectures, and contains effective horizontal linkages between state administrators and politicians and major social groups such as business and trade unions at both central and local levels. Finally, it has a political culture that favours systematic and detailed intervention by government. The British state displays none of these features to any significant extent (Exhibit 12.6).

EXHIBIT 12.6   *The lack of a developmental State in Britain*

The University of Essex political scientists Ian Budge and David McKay provide the following example of the absence of a developmental State in Britain:

'[In] the late 1970s the government invested close to £100 million to set up a car-manufacturing firm (de Lorean) in Belfast. Having done this, total operational control was left in the hands of the American founder, so sponsoring ministries were taken completely by surprise by his bankruptcy and eventual disgrace in the 1980s. *The firm had not been monitored even to the extent that civil servants knew of its month by month prospects. Within the British administrative tradition there was of course no reason why they should: their job was to dispense money in terms of general criteria, not follow through delivery in detail*' (Budge and McKay, 1993, p. 213, emphasis added)

Several reasons, taken together, help explain the failure of a developmental state to emerge in Britain.

1. *The dual polity.* As noted in Chapter 6, from the eighteenth century to the early 1960s, a conceptual and practical division of responsibilities existed between 'high politics', which dealt with defence and foreign policy and was primarily the responsibility of the centre, and 'low politics', which involved matters such as health, welfare, transport and the maintenance of order and was handled at the local level. This was the 'dual polity' and it involved the centre and periphery operating in relative independence of each other (Bulpitt, 1983). For Britain's national political elites, this implicit division of spheres of responsibility had the inestimable advantage of allowing them to concentrate on the more prestigious sphere of international politics, involving, in Holland's phrase, 'the pursuit of greatness' through empire, victory in wars and, post-1945, the 'world role', an independent nuclear deterrent, and the 'East of Suez' strategy. This meant that until the late 1960s

'the essence of British public affairs – its central thrust – did not relate to the nurturing of commercial or productive efficiency' (Holland, 1991, p. 348).

2. '*Simple, general solutions to economic and social problems*'. Britain's early industrialisation, which gave it world economic leadership in the nineteenth century, validated the doctrine of economic liberalism, involving government non-intervention and free trade, which became the ruling orthodoxy of the time. The successor to this 'simple, general solution' to economic management was the Keynesian macroeconomic theory of demand management adopted by governments after 1945. The appeal of this economic theory to British political leaders was its relative simplicity, since it 'rested on central manipulation of finances without any detailed follow-up. . . . To reform the economy, detailed micro-economic intervention was unnecessary. All that was needed was a change in public expenditure or in fiscal and monetary policy and "all would be well"' (Budge and McKay, 1993, pp. 212–13). Keynesianism suited the 'official mind' of the centre because it gave it an instrument of control at a distance, a system of rule by automatic pilot, which enabled it to avoid much contact with the periphery (Bulpitt, 1983).

3. *The failure of administrative reform*. The greatly expanded reponsibilities assumed by the state after 1945 were not matched by equivalent changes in the machinery of government. During the Second World War, a 'state of the art' bureaucracy came into being as Whitehall was revolutionised. Detailed planning became the norm, with the power of the Ministry of Food extending into every larder in the land and few workers unaffected by the control of the Ministry of Supply over raw materials for industry. 'In terms of regional policy and State intervention in industry, Supply was the biggest and most successful department of industry Whitehall has ever possessed or ever will' (Hennessy, 1990, pp. 114, 117). However, despite the larger scope of the state, which demanded radical reform of the civil service after 1945, and despite the awareness of some leading civil servants that closer bureaucratic links with industry were required, no such reforms or changes took place. In Hennessy's view, 'This represents probably *the* greatest lost opportunity in the history of British public administration' (Ibid., pp. 120–4).

4. *The lack of a public philosophy of the interventionist state*. Another reason for the failure of the social democratic state to overcome the difficulties it encountered from the 1960s was its inability to develop an appropriate public philosophy. Marquand criticises postwar social democracy as a Fabian, elitist, top-down, bureaucratic, centralising, paternalist creed that, despite the humanity and generosity of its goals, gave too little attention to developing strong civic and democratic structures and institutions that would give people a voice in society. In his view the social democrats 'wanted to do good, but they were more anxious to do good to others than help others do good to themselves. As they saw it, the role of

public intervention was to provide, to manipulate, or to instruct, rather than to empower' (Marquand, 1991, p. 212). However as society became wealthier, better-educated and less deferential, it became less prepared simply to abide by decisions taken on its behalf by social democratic ministers. NHS patients, parents, DHSS clients, local authority tenants and many other groups wanted a voice, but lacked one because of the social democrat failure to draw upon a non-statist, participatory and decentralised form of public intervention. The result was chronic social discontent, 'a swelling chorus of complaint'.

Second, the revisionist social democrats sought social equality but neglected fraternity. They lacked a concept of citizenship, a sense of mutual obligation deriving from membership of a community, of a public interest that was more than the sum of private interests. Like British culture in general, their thinking was saturated with individualistic assumptions. During the Second World War, social democratic government could base its call for popular sacrifices on an appeal to patriotism, national survival being a public interest that was readily understood. But when governments had to persuade key social groups to sacrifice their interests in the difficult economic circumstances of the 1970s they lacked a viable language of civil morality, fraternal solidarity or communal loyalty with which to do so. In Marquand's view, 'Revisionist policies failed because they were not sustained by the communitarian ties upon which a social democratic political economy depends' (Ibid., p. 221).

In summary, the postwar social democratic settlement collapsed partly because social democratic governments had the misfortune to be in power when intensification of the long-term structural problems of the British economy combined with the world economic crisis of the 1970s. But it broke down also, first, because of the failure of the British state to develop institutions capable of mobilising political consent. When this was belatedly attempted from the 1960s in the tripartist relations between government, employers and unions, it collapsed partly because the main producer organisations were too narrow, fragmented and undisciplined to deliver the support of their members, partly because of the violence of the antagonisms between capital and labour, and partly because of governments' inability to appeal to any compelling idea of the general interest against sectional interests. In a still individualistic and market-orientated society, it was rational for business and the trade unions to prioritise their sectional interests. Second, despite the wave of participatory and decentralising sentiment in the 1960s and 1970s, there were no effective reforms to spread political influence and 'empower' people. Welfarism and Keynesianism increased both social demands and expectations and the bargaining power of labour, but neither their inventors nor Labour revisionists had developed a theory of the social democratic state by which these enhanced demands and interests could be accommodated and reconciled. Keynes had assumed that an enlightened technocracy of civil servants would be capable of taking decisions in the public interest, whilst Crosland and his followers assumed that political citizenship in the sense of a participatory political culture had been achieved. Neither assumption was tested in the two decades after the war, but when they were confronted by a serious challenge in the late 1960s and 1970s they broke down and the postwar social democratic consensus came to an end.

There are two main strands in the social democrat interpretation of the Thatcher/Major years. Analysts in the political centre believe that Thatcherism failed in many key areas. First, in the words of one Conservative 'wet', it represented 'a grim failure of economic management'. The Thatcher and Major governments presided over 'the two worst slumps and the most irresponsible boom since the war', all of which 'inflicted severe damage on the economy' (Gilmour, 1992, pp. 276–7). Hence the Conservatives' economic record constituted no improvement on their predecessors' achievements, the economic growth rate averaging a mere 1.8 per cent between 1979 and 1995 compared with 2.1 per cent between 1970 and 1979. In addition, the Conservatives failed to reduce the burden of public expenditure, and their income tax cuts were more than offset by increases in indirect taxes so that the total tax burden *rose* rather than fell. Although they acknowledge that Conservative trade union reforms and privatisation returned Britain to a free market economy, social democrats do not regard these as unqualified achievements. Trade union reforms diminished workers' rights, left them unprotected against cost-cutting managements and made the management–worker balance too one-sided. The privatisations too were flawed, with many public assets being sold too cheaply, too little concern about the creation of private monopolies and an insufficiently rigorous system by which to regulate the privatised utilities. The marketisation of British society by these and other measures such as financial deregulation reintroduced the kind of problem facing late-nineteenth-century market liberalism: the fairness of market outcomes (Marquand, 1988, p. 31). The social costs of marketisation were too high: the widening gulf between rich and poor, intensifying social polarisation, and above all the emergence of an underclass. This increase in inequality reversed the postwar trend and had the paradoxical consequence, when considered in the light of new right aims, of both increasing welfare dependency and minimising choice for millions more people. For, as social democrats point out, the allegedly greater choice provided by a market society is greater only for those with money: for the poor it does not exist as 'choice without access or entitlement is largely fraudulent' (Gilmour, 1992, p. 116). Not only did the worst-off groups not gain from 'trickle-down' economics, the economic effects of increasing poverty and inequality deprived the economy of at least £13 billion of spending by the poorest-off in the1980s (Hutton, 1996, pp. 172, 179).

Finally, for social democrats the long period of Conservative new right ascendancy had unacceptable constitutional consequences, provoking concern about 'elective dictatorship', the absence of political checks and balances and the emergence of a 'democratic deficit'. Pluralists criticised an electoral system that permitted the implementation of far-reaching changes on the basis of the support of a mere two fifths of voters and one third of the electorate. There was also widespread concern about the erosion of democratic institutions in a number of ways, including the undermining of elected local government, the decline of the public service ethic and the deterioration of standards in public life. A particular source of anxiety was the emergence of a patronage state based on the proliferation of unelected quangos filled with political appointees.

In concluding a chapter that has discussed such sharply opposed ideological perspectives on postwar British politics, it is worth drawing attention to sober academic analyses that bring out the continuities of policy in postwar Britain, even between governments of different ideological complexion (Rose, 1984; Riddell, 1991, pp. 222–3; Dorey, 1995, pp. 288–320). This is not to deny the significance or extent of the ideologically shaped changes that did take place. Rather it is to suggest that pragmatism has been influential as well as doctrine; that in general change has been gradual and incremental rather than radical; that much activity by governments has been reactive rather than creative – responding to events rather than shaping them; and above all, that all governments, whatever their political hue are severely constrained by external forces such as public opinion, foreign treaty obligations and the international economy.

Further Reading

Barnett, C., *The Audit of War* (London: Macmillan, 1986).

Budge, I. and D. McKay (eds), *The Developing British Political System: the 1990s* (London: Longman, 1993).

Coates, D. and J. Hillard (eds), *The Economic Decline of Modern Britain: The Debate between Left and Right* (London: Harvester Wheatsheaf, 1986).

Dorey, P., *British Politics since 1945* (Oxford, Blackwell, 1995).

Gamble, A. and S. Walkland, *The British Party System and Economic Policy, 1945–1983* (Oxford: Clarendon Press, 1984).

Gamble, A., *The Free Economy and the Strong State*, 2nd edn (1st edn, 1988) (London: Macmillan, 1994).

Hutton, W., *The State We're In*, new revised edn (London: Vintage, 1996).

Gilmour, I., *Dancing with Dogma* (London: Simon and Schuster, 1992).

Kavanagh, D., *Thatcherism and British Politics*, 2nd edn (Oxford: Oxford University Press, 1990).

Marquand *The Unprincipled Society* (London: Fontana, 1988).

Marquand, D., *The Progressive Dilemma* (London: Heinemann, 1991).

Miliband, R., *Parliamentary Socialism*, 2nd. ed. (London: Merlin Press, 1972).

Miliband, R., *Capitalist Democracy in Britain* (Oxford: Oxford University Press, 1984).

Pierson, C., *Socialism after Communism* (Oxford: Polity, 1995).

Riddell, P. *The Thatcher Era and its Legacy*, 2nd edn (London: Macmillan, 1991).

Rose, R., *Do Parties Make a Difference?*, 2nd edn (London: Macmillan, 1984).

Saville, J., *The Labour Movement in Britain* (London: Faber and Faber, 1988).

Bibliography

Addison, P., 'The Road from 1945' in P. Hennessy and A. Seldon (eds), *Ruling Performance* (Oxford: Blackwell, 1987).

Addison, P., *The Road to 1945*, 2nd edn (London: Pimlico, 1994; 1st edn, 1975).

Adonis, A., *Parliament Today*, 2nd edn (Manchester: Manchester University Press, 1993).

Alford, B. W. E., *Britain's Economic Performance, 1945–1975* (London: Macmillan, 1988).

Amery, L., *Thoughts on the Constitution* (Oxford: Oxford University Press, 1947).

Arthur, P. and K. Jeffery, *Northern Ireland since 1988* (Oxford: Blackwell, 1988).

Attlee, C. R., *The Labour Party in Perspective* (London: Gollancz, 1937).

Bacon, R. and W. Eltis, *Britain's Economic Problem: Too Few Producers* (London: Macmillan, 1976).

Baker, D., A. Gamble and S. Ludlam, 'More Classless and Less Thatcherite? Conservative Ministers and New Conservative MPs after the 1992 Election', *Parliamentary Affairs*, vol. 45, no. 4 (1992).

Ball, M., F. Gray and L. McDowell, *The Transformation of Britain* (London: Fontana, 1989).

Ball, S., 'The National and Regional Party Structure' in A. Seldon and S. Ball (eds), *Conservative Century The Conservative Party since 1900* (Oxford: Oxford University Press, 1994).

Barber, J., *Rhodesia: The Road to Rebellion* (Oxford: Oxford University Press, 1967).

Barnes, J., 'From Eden to Macmillan, 1955–59' in P. Hennessy and A. Seldon (eds), *Ruling Performance: British Governments from Attlee to Thatcher* (Oxford: Blackwell, 1987).

Barnes, J., 'Ideologies and Factions' in A. Seldon and S. Ball (eds), *Conservative Century The Conservative Party since 1900* (Oxford: Oxford University Press, 1994).

Barnett, C., *The Audit of War* (London: Macmillan, 1986).

Bealey, F., J. Blondel and W. P. McCann, *Constituency Politics* (London: Faber, 1965).

Beattie, A. 'Ministerial Responsibility and the Theory of the British State' in R. A. W. Rhodes and P. Dunleavy (eds), *Prime Minister, Cabinet and Core Executive* (London: Macmillan, 1995).

Beer, S., *Modern British Politics* (London: Faber and Faber, 1965).

Behrens, R., 'The Liberal Party' in L. Tivey and A. Wright (eds), *Party Ideology in Britain* (London: Routledge, 1989).

Bell, S. *et al.*, *The End of the Welfare State* (London: Adam Smith Institute, 1994)

Benn, A., 'What the Market Really Means', *Record* (February, 1973).

Benney, M., A. P. Gray and R. H. Pear, *How People Vote* (London: Routledge and Kegan Paul, 1956).

Berelson, B. R., P. F. Lazarfield and W. N. McPhee, *Voting: A Study of Opinion Formation in a Presidential Campaign* (Chicago: Chicago University Press, 1954).

Birch, A. H., *Representative and responsible Government* (London: Allen and Unwin, 1964).

Birch, A. H., *Political Integration and Disintegration in the British Isles* (London: Allen and Unwin, 1977).

305

Blackstone, T. and W. Plowden, *Inside the Think Tank* (London: Heinemann, 1988).

Blake, R., *The Conservative Party from Peel to Thatcher* (London: Fontana, 1985).

Bochel, J. and D. Denver, 'Candidate Selection in the Labour Party: What the Selectors Seek', *British Journal of Political Science*, vol. 13, no. 1 (January, 1983).

Bogdanor, V., *Devolution* (Oxford: Oxford University Press, 1979).

Bogdanor, V. (ed.), *Liberal Party Politics* (Oxford: Clarendon Press, 1983).

Bogdanor, V., 'The Selection of the Party Leader' in A. Seldon and S. Ball (eds), *Conservative Century The Conservative Party since 1900* (Oxford: Oxford University Press, 1994).

Boyle, K. and T. Hadden, *Ireland: A Positive Proposal* (London: Penguin, 1985).

Brivati, B. and H. Jones (eds), *What Difference did the War Make?* (Leicester: Leicester University Press, 1993).

Brooke, S., *Labour's War: the Labour Party during the Second World War* (Oxford: Clarendon Press, 1992).

Brown, A., D. McCrone and L. Paterson, *Politics and Society in Scotland* (London: Macmillan, 1996).

Budge, I. and D. McKay (eds), *The Developing British Political System: The 1990s*, 3rd edn (London: Longman, 1993).

Bulpitt, J., 'Conservatism, Unionism and Territorial Management' in P. Madgwick and R. Rose (eds), *The Territorial Dimension in United Kingdom Politics* (London: Macmillan, 1982)

Bulpitt, J., *Territory and Power in the United Kingdom* (Manchester: Manchester University Press, 1983).

Burch, M. and M. Moran, 'The Changing British Political Elite, 1945–1983: MPs and Cabinet Ministers', *Parliamentary Affairs*, vol. 38 (Winter, 1985).

Butler, D. and M. Pinto-Duschinsky, *The British General Election of 1970* (London: Macmillan, 1970).

Butler, D. and D. Stokes, *Political Change in Britain: The Evolution of Electoral Choice*, 2nd edn (London: Macmillan, 1974).

Butler, D. and D. Kavanagh, *The British General Election of 1979* (London: Macmillan, 1980).

Butler, D. and D. Kavanagh, *The British General Election of 1987* (London: Macmillan, 1988).

Butler, D. and D. Kavanagh, *The British General Election of 1992* (London: Macmillan, 1992).

Butler, D. and G. Butler (eds), *British Political Facts 1900–1986*, 6th edn (London: Macmillan, 1986).

Butler, D. and G. Butler (eds), *British Political Facts 1900–1994*, 7th edn (London: Macmillan, 1994).

Butler, J. 'Foreign and Defence Policy under Thatcher and Major' in S. Ludlam and M. J. Smith (eds), *Contemporary British Conservatism* (London: Macmillan, 1996).

Byrne, P., 'Pressure Groups and Popular Campaigns' in P. Johnson (ed.), *Twentieth Century Britain* (London: Longman, 1994).

Cairncross, A. K., *The British Economy since 1945* (Oxford: Blackwell, 1992).

Callaghan, J., *Time and Chance* (London: Fontana, 1987).

Callaghan, J., *The Far Left in British Politics* (Oxford: Blackwell, 1987).

Campbell, J., *Edward Heath* (London: Jonathan Cape, 1993).

Camps, M., *European Unification in the Sixties* (Oxford: Oxford University Press, 1967).

Cannadine, D., 'After the "annus horribilis"', *The Times Literary Supplement*, November 3 1995.

Carr, F. and S. Cope, 'Implementing Maastricht: the limits of European Union', *Talking Politics*, vol. 6, no. 3 (1994).

Carroll, A. J., 'Judicial Control of Prerogative Power', *Talking Politics*, vol. 7, no. 1 (1994).

Catterall, P. and S. MacDougall (eds), *The Northern Ireland Question in British Politics* (London: Macmillan, 1996).

Ceadel, M., 'Labour as a Governing Party: Balancing Right and Left' in T. Gourvish and A. O'Day (eds), *Britain since 1945* (London: Macmillan, 1991).

Childs, D., *Britain since 1939: Progress and Decline* (London: Macmillan, 1995).

Coates, D., *The Labour Party and the Struggle for Socialism* (Cambridge: Cambridge University Press, 1975).

Coates, D., *The Question of UK Decline* (London: Harvester Wheatsheaf, 1994).

Coates, D. and J. Hillard (eds), *The Economic Decline of Modern Britain: The Debate between Left and Right* (London: Harvester Wheatsheaf, 1986).

Cockett, R., *Thinking the Unthinkable Think Tanks and the Economic Counter-Revolution, 1931–1983* (London: HarperCollins, 1995).

Cooper, M-. P., 'Understanding subsidiarity as a political issue in the European Community', *Talking Politics*, vol. 7, no. 3 (1995).

Conley, F., *General Elections Today* (Manchester: Manchester University Press, 1990).

Coutts, K. and W. Godley, 'The British Economy under Mrs Thatcher', *Political Quarterly*, vol. 60, no. 2 (1989).

Cowling, M. (ed.), *Conservative Essays* (London: Cassell, 1978).

Coxall, B. and Robins, L., *Contemporary British Politics*, 2nd edn (London: Macmillan, 1994).

Coxall, B., 'The social context of British politics: class, gender and race in the two major parties, 1970–1990' in B. Jones and L. Robins (eds), *Two decades in British politics* (Manchester: Manchester University Press, 1992).

Craig, F. W. S. (ed.), *British General Election Manifestos 1900–1974* (London: Macmillan, 1975).

Craig, F. W. S. (ed.), *British Electoral Facts 1832–1987*, 5th edn (Aldershot: Gower, 1989).

Crewe, I., 'Parties and Electors' in I. Budge and D. McKay (eds), *The Developing British Political System: the 1990s* (London: Longman, 1993).

Crewe, I., P. Norris, D. Denver and B. Broughton (eds), *British General Elections and Parties Yearbook* (London: Harvester Wheatsheaf, 1992).

Crewe, I. and A. King, *SDP: the Birth, Life and Death of the Social Democratic Party* (Oxford: Oxford University Press, 1996).

Crick, B., *The Reform of Parliament* (London: Weidenfeld and Nicolson, 1974).

Crick, B. (ed.), *National Identities* (Oxford: Blackwell, 1991).

Crick, M., *Militant* (London: Faber and Faber, 1984).

Criddle, B., 'Candidates' in D. Butler and D. Kavanagh (eds), *The British General Election of 1987* (London: Macmillan, 1988).

Cronin, J. E., *Labour and Society in Britain, 1918–1979* (London: Batsford, 1984).

Crosland, A., *The Future of Socialism* (London: Jonathan Cape, 1956).

Crosland, A., *Socialism Now* (London: Jonathan Cape, 1974).

De Porte, A. W., *Europe between the Superpowers* (New Haven, CT: Yale University Press, 1979).

De Smith, S., H. Street and R. Brazier, *Constitutional and Administrative Law*, 4th edn (Harmondsworth: Penguin, 1983).

De Smith, S. and R. Brazier, *Constitutional and Administrative Law*, 6th edn (Harmondsworth: Penguin, 1990).

Denver, D. and G. Hands (eds), *Issues and Controversies in British Electoral Behaviour* (London: Harvester Wheatsheaf, 1992).

Digby, A., *British Welfare Policy* (London: Faber and Faber, 1989).

Dorey, P., *British Politics since 1945* (Oxford: Blackwell, 1995).

Drewry, G. and T. Butcher, *The Civil Service Today*, 2nd edn (Oxford: Blackwell, 1991).

Drucker, H., *Doctrine and Ethos in the Labour Party* (London: Allen and Unwin, 1979).

Dunbabin, J. P. D., 'British elections in the nineteenth and twentieth centuries: a regional approach', *English Historical Review* (April, 1980).

Dunleavy, P., 'The Political Parties' in P. Dunleavy, A. Gamble, I. Holliday and G. Peele (eds), *Developments in British Politics 4* (London: Macmillan, 1993).

Dunleavy, P., A. Gamble, I. Holliday and G. Peele (eds), *Developments in British Politics 4* (London: Macmillan, 1993).

Durham, M., 'The Conservative Party and the Family', *Talking Politics*, vol. 6, no. 2 (1994).

Dutton, D., *British Politics since 1945: The Rise and Fall of Consensus* (Oxford: Blackwell, 1991).

The Economist, 14 October 1995.

Eccleshall, R., *British Liberalism Liberal Thought from the 1640s to 1980s* (London: Longman, 1986).

Ewing, K. D. and C. Gearty, *Freedom under Thatcher: Civil Liberties in Modern Britain* (Oxford: Clarendon, 1990).

Field, F., C. Pond and M. Meacher, *To Him Who Hath: A Study of Poverty and Taxation* (Harmondsworth: Penguin, 1977).

Fielding, S., P. Thompson and N. Tiratsoo, *'England Arise!': The Labour Party and Popular Politics* (Manchester: Manchester University Press, 1995).

Finer, S. E. (ed.), *Adversary Politics and Political Reform* (London: Anthony Wigram, 1975).

Fitzsimons, M. A., *The Foreign Policy of the British Labour Government 1945–51* (Notre Dame: University of Notre Dame Press, 1953).

Foster, R., *Modern Ireland 1600–1972* (Harmondsworth: Penguin, 1989).

Frankel, J., *British Foreign Policy 1945–1973* (London: RIIA/Oxford University Press, 1975).

Franklin, M. N., *The Decline of Class Voting in Britain* (Oxford: Clarendon Press, 1985).

Fulford, R., *The Liberal Case* (London: Penguin, 1959).

Gamble, A., *Britain in Decline*, 3rd edn (London: Macmillan, 1990).

Gamble, A., 'Territorial Politics' in P. Dunleavy, A. Gamble, I. Holliday and G. Peele (eds), *Developments in British Politics 4* (London: Macmillan, 1993).

Gamble, A., *The Free Economy and the Strong State*, 2nd edn (1st edn, 1988) (London: Macmillan, 1994).

Gamble, A. and S. Walkland, *The British Party System and Economic Policy, 1945–1983* (Oxford: Clarendon Press, 1983).

Garner, R. and R. Kelly, *British Political Parties Today* (Manchester: Manchester University Press, 1993).

Garner, R., *Environmental Politics* (London: Harvester Wheatsheaf, 1996).

Gearty, C., *Terror* (London: Faber and Faber, 1991).

George, S., *An Awkward Partner: Britain and the European Community* (Oxford: Oxford University Press, 1990).

George, S. and M. Sowemimo, 'Conservative Foreign Policy towards the European Union' in S. Ludlam and M. J. Smith (eds), *Contemporary British Conservatism* (London: Macmillan, 1996).

Giddings, P., 'Select Committees and Parliamentary Scrutiny: Plus Ça Change', *Parliamentary Affairs,* Special Hansard Society 50th Anniversary edn, 1994.

Glennerster, H., *British Social Policy since 1945* (Oxford: Blackwell, 1992).

Goldthorpe, J. and C. Payne, 'Trends in Intergenerational Class Mobility in England and Wales, 1972–1983', *Sociology,* vol. 20, no. 1 (1986).

Gordon, M. R., *Conflict and Consensus in Labour's Foreign Policy 1914–1965* (Stanford: Stanford University Press, 1969).

Gorst, A., L. Johnman and W. Scott Lucas (eds), *Post-War Britain 1945–64: Themes and Perspectives* (London and New York: Pinter Publishers, 1989).

Gourvish, T. and A. O'Day (eds), *Britain since 1945* (London: Macmillan, 1991).

Grant, W., *Business and Politics in Britain,* 2nd edn (London: Macmillan, 1993).

Greenleaf, W. H., 'The Character of Modern British Conservatism' in R. Benewick and B. Parekh (eds), *Knowledge and Belief in Politics* (London: Allen and Unwin, 1973).

Greenwood, J., 'Promoting working class candidature in the Conservative Party: The limits of Central Office power', *Parliamentary Affairs,* no. 41, vol. 4 (October, 1988).

Greenwood, J. and D. Wilson, *Public Administration in Britain Today,* 2nd edn (London: Unwin Hyman, 1989).

Hadfield, B. (ed.), *Northern Ireland: Politics and the Constitution* (Buckingham: Open University Press, 1992).

Hailsham, Lord, *The Dilemma of Democracy* (Glasgow: Collins, 1978).

Hall, S. and M. Jacques (eds), *The Politics of Thatcherism* (London: Lawrence and Wishart, 1983).

Halsey, A. H., 'Trends since World War Two', *Social Trends,* 17, 1987.

Halsey, A. H. (ed.), *Trends in British Society since 1900,* 2nd edn (1st edn, 1972) (London: Macmillan, 1988).

Hanson, A. H. and B. Crick (eds), *The Commons in Transition* (London: Fontana/ Collins, 1970).

Hartley, A., *A State of England* (London: Hutchinson, 1963).

Hayward, J. and P. Norton (eds), *The Political Science of British Politics* (London: Wheatsheaf, 1986).

Heath, A., R. Jowell and J, Curtice, *How Britain Votes* (Oxford: Pergamon Press, 1985).

Heath, A., R. Jowell, J. Curtice, G. Evans, J. Field and S. Witherspoon, *Understanding Political Change* (Oxford: Pergamon Press, 1991).

Hennessy, P. and A. Seldon (eds), *Ruling Performance: British Government from Attlee to Thatcher* (Oxford: Blackwell, 1987).

Hennessy, P., *Whitehall* (London: Fontana, 1990).

Hill, M., *The Welfare State in Britain* (Aldershot: Edward Elgar, 1993).

Himmelweit, H., P. Humphreys, M. Jaeger and M. Katz, *How Voters Decide* (London: Academic Press, 1981).

Holland, R., *The Pursuit of Greatness Britain and the World Role, 1900–1970* (London: Fontana, 1991).

Hunt, S., 'Fascism and the "Race Issue" in Britain', *Talking Politics,* vol. 5, no. 1 (1992).

Hunt, S., 'The Far Left in British Politics', *Talking Politics,* vol. 8, no. 2 (1995–6).

Hutton, J. *et al.* (eds), *Dependency to Enterprise* (London: Routledge, 1991).

Hutton, W., *The State We're In,* new revised edn (1st edn, 1995) (London: Vintage, 1996).

Ingle, S., *The British Party System,* 2nd edn (Oxford: Blackwell, 1989).

Inglehart, R., *The Silent Revolution: Changing Values and Political Styles among Western Publics* (Princeton, NJ: Princeton University Press, 1977).

James, S., *British Cabinet Government* (London: Routledge, 1992).

James, S., 'The Cabinet System since 1945', *Parliamentary Affairs*, Special Hansard Society Fiftieth Anniversary edn (1994).

Janosik, E., *Constituency Labour Parties in Britain* (London: Pall Mall, 1968).

Jefferys, K. 'British Politics and Social Policy during the Second World war', *Historical Journal*, vol. 30 (1987)

Jefferys, K., *The Labour Party since 1945* (London: Macmillan, 1993).

Jenkins, R., *A Life at the Centre* (New York: Random House, 1991).

Johnson, N., 'Select Committees as Tools of Parliamentary Reform' in A. H. Hanson and B. Crick (eds), *The Commons in Transition* (London: Fontana/Collins, 1970).

Johnson, N., *In Search of the Constitution* (Oxford: Pergamon Press, 1977).

Johnson, N., *Reconstructing the Welfare State* (London: Harvester Wheatsheaf, 1990).

Johnson, P. (ed.), *Twentieth Century Britain* (London: Longman, 1994).

Jones, B. and M. Keating, *Labour and the British State* (Oxford: Clarendon Press, 1989).

Jones B. and L. Robins (eds), *Two Decades in British Politics* (Manchester: Manchester University Press)

Jones, C. (ed.), *New Perspectives on the Welfare State in Europe* (London: Routledge, 1993).

Jones, G. W., 'Development of the Cabinet' in W. Thornhill (ed.), *The Modernisation of British Government* (London: Pitman, 1975).

Jones, H. and M. Kandiah (eds), *The Myth of Consensus: New Views on British History, 1945–64)* (London: Macmillan, 1996).

Joseph, Sir K., *Reversing the Trend* (London: Conservative Political Centre, 1975).

Jowell, J. and D. Oliver (eds), *The Changing Constitution*, 2nd edn (Oxford: Clarendon Press, 1989).

Kavanagh, D., *Thatcherism and British Politics*, 2nd edn (Oxford: Oxford University Press, 1990).

Kavanagh, D. and P. Morris, *Consensus Politics from Attlee to Thatcher*, 2nd edn (1st edn, 1989) (Oxford: Blackwell, 1994).

Kavanagh, D. and A. Seldon (eds), *The Major Effect* (London: Macmillan, 1994).

Keegan, W., *Mr. Lawson's Gamble* (London: Hodder and Stoughton, 1989).

Kellas, J. G., *The Scottish Political System*, 4th edn (Cambridge: Cambridge University Press, 1989).

Kelly, R., 'The Party Conferences' in A. Seldon and S. Ball (eds), *Conservative Century The Conservative Party since 1900* (Oxford: Oxford University Press, 1994).

King, A. (ed.), *Why is Britain becoming harder to govern?* (London: BBC, 1976).

Kitzinger, U., *Diplomacy and Persuasion: how Britain joined the Common Market* (London: Thames and Hudson, 1973).

Laski, H., *Reflections on the Constitution* (Manchester: Manchester University Press, 1951).

Lee, S., 'Law and the Constitution' in D. Kavanagh and A. Seldon (eds), *The Major Effect* (London: Macmillan, 1994).

Levy, R., 'Governing Scotland, Wales and Northern Ireland' in R. Pyper and L. Robins (eds), *Governing the UK in the 1990s* (London: Macmillan, 1995).

Lovenduski, J. and V. Randall, *Contemporary Feminist Politics* (Oxford: Oxford University Press, 1993).

Lovenduski, J., P. Norris and C. Burgess, 'The Party and Women' in A. Seldon and S. Ball (eds), *Conservative Century: The Conservative Party since 1900* (Oxford: Oxford University Press, 1994).

Lowe, R., 'The Second World War, Consensus, and the Foundation of the Welfare State', *Twentieth Century British History,* vol. 1, no. 2 (1990).

Lowe, R., *The Welfare State in Britain since 1945* (London: Macmillan, 1993).

Lowe, R., 'Postwar Welfare' in P. Johnson (ed.), *Twentieth Century Britain* (London: Longman, 1994).

Lowe, R., interview with A. Seldon, 'The Influence of Ideas on Social Policy', *Contemporary British History,* vol. 10 (Summer, 1996, no. 1).

Ludlam, S. and M. J. Smith (eds), *Contemporary British Conservatism* (London: Macmillan, 1996).

Ludlam, S., 'The Spectre Haunting Conservatism: Europe and Backbench Rebellion' in S. Ludlam and M. J. Smith (eds), *Contemporary British Conservatism* (London: Macmillan, 1996).

McCallum, R. B. and A. Readman, *The British General Election of 1945* (Oxford: Oxford University Press, 1947).

McKenzie, R., *British Political Parties*, 2nd edn (London: Mercury Books, 1964).

McKibbin, R., *The Ideologies of Class* (Oxford: Oxford University Press, 1991).

Madgwick, P. and Rose, R. (eds), *The Territorial Dimension in United Kingdom Politics* (London: Macmillan, 1982).

Madgwick, P., *British Government: The Central Executive Territory* (London: Philip Allan, 1991).

Madgwick, P. and D. Woodhouse, *The Law and Politics of the Constitution* (London: Harvester Wheatsheaf, 1995).

Malpass, P., *Reshaping Housing Policy* (London: Routledge, 1990).

Malpass, P. and A. Murie, *Housing Policy and Practice*, 3rd edn (1st edn, 1982) (London: Macmillan, 1990).

Margetts, H. and Smyth, G. (eds), *Turning Japanese? Britain with a permanent party of government* (London: Lawrence and Wishart, 1994).

Marquand, D., *The Unprincipled Society* (London: Fontana, 1988).

Marquand, D., 'The decline of post-war consensus' in A. Gorst, L. Johnman and W. Scott Lucas (eds), *Britain 1945–64 Themes and Perspectives* (London and New York: Pinter Publishers, 1989).

Marquand, D., *The Progressive Dilemma* (London: Heinemann, 1991).

Marquand, D. and A. Seldon (eds), *The Ideas That Shaped Postwar Britain* (London: Fontana, 1996).

Marsh, D., *The New Politics of British Trade Unionism* (London: Macmillan, 1992).

Maynard, G., *The Economy under Mrs Thatcher* (Oxford: Blackwell, 1988).

Meehan, E. J., *The British Left Wing and Foreign Policy* (New Brunswick: Rutgers University Press, 1960).

Middlemas, K., *Politics in Industrial Society* (London: Andre Deutsch, 1979).

Middlemas, K., 'The Party, Industry, and the City' in A. Seldon and S. Ball (eds), *Conservative Century: The Conservative Party since 1900* (Oxford: Oxford University Press, 1994).

Midwinter, A., M. Keating and J. Mitchell, *Politics and Public Policy in Scotland* (London: Macmillan, 1991).

Miliband, R. *Parliamentary Socialism*, 2nd edn (London: Merlin Press, 1975).

Miliband, R., *Capitalist Democracy in Britain* (Oxford: Oxford University Press, 1984).

Minkin, L., *The Labour Party Conference* (Manchester: Manchester University Press).

Mishler, W., M. Hoskin and R. Fitzgerald, 'British Parties in the Balance: A Time Series Analysis of Long-Term Trends in Labour and Conservative Support', *British Journal of Political Science*, vol. 19, no. 2 (1989).

Moonman, E., *Reluctant Partnership: a critical study of the relationship between government and industry* (London: Gollancz, 1971).

Moran, M., *Politics and Society in Britain*, 2nd edn (London: Macmillan, 1989).

Morgan, K. O. *Rebirth of a Nation: Wales 1880–1980* (Oxford: Clarendon Press, 1981).

Morgan, K. O., *Labour in Power 1945–1951* (Oxford: Oxford University Press, 1985).

Morgan, K. O., *The People's Peace: British History 1945–1989* (Oxford: Oxford University Press, 1990).

Morgan, K. O., 'The Twentieth Century' in K. O. Morgan (ed.), *The Oxford History of Britain*, updated edition (Oxford: Oxford University Press, 1993).

Morrison, Lord, *Government and Parliament*, 3rd edn (Oxford: Oxford University Press, 1964).

Mount, F., *The British Constitution Now* (London: Heinemann, 1992).

Nairn, T., 'The Nature of the Labour Party', *New Left Review*, nos 27 and 28 (1964).

Nairn, T., *The Break-Up of Britain* (London: Verso, 1977).

Newton, K., 'Do People Read Everything They Believe in the Papers? Newspapers and Voters in the 1983 and 1987 Elections' in I. Crewe, P. Norris, D. Denver and D. Broughton (eds), *British Elections and Parties Yearbook 1991* (Hemel Hempstead: Simon and Schuster, 1992).

Newton, K., 'The Mass Media: Fourth Estate or Fifth Column?' in R. Pyper and L. Robins (eds), *Governing the UK in the 1990s* (London: Macmillan, 1995).

Norris, P., *British by-elections: the volatile electorate* (Oxford: Clarendon Press, 1990).

Norris, P. and J. Lovenduski, *Political Recruitment: Gender, Race and Class in the British Parliament* (Cambridge: Cambridge University Press, 1995).

Northedge, F. S., *Descent from Power* (London: Allen and Unwin, 1967).

Norton, P., *Conservative Dissidents* (London, Temple Smith, 1978).

Norton, P. and A. Aughey, *Conservatives and Conservatism* (London: Temple Smith, 1981).

Norton, P., *The Constitution in Flux* (Oxford: Martin Robertson, 1982).

Norton, P., 'The Impact of Europe on the British Constitution, Pre-Maastricht', *Talking Politics*, vol. 6, no. 3 (1994).

Norton, P., 'The Parliamentary Party and Parliamentary Committees' in A. Seldon and S. Ball (eds), *Conservative Century: The Conservative Party since 1900* (Oxford: Oxford University Press, 1994).

Norton, P., 'Parliamentary Behaviour since 1945', *Talking Politics*, vol. 8, no. 2 (1995–6).

O'Day, A., 'Britain and the Two Irelands' in T. Gourvish and A. O'Day (eds), *Britain since 1945* (London: Macmillan, 1991).

O'Gorman, F., *Conservative Thought from Burke to Thatcher* (London: Longman, 1986).

Oliver, D., 'Citizenship in the 1990s', *Politics Review*, vol. 3, no. 1 (1993).

Oliver, D., 'Parliament, Ministers and the Law', *Parliamentary Affairs*, Special Hansard Society Fiftieth Anniversary Issue (1994).

Parry, G. and G. Moyser, 'A Map of Political Participation in Britain', *Government and Opposition*, vol. 25, no. 2 (1990).

Parry G. and G. Moyser, 'Political Participation in Britain', *Politics Review*, vol. 3, no. 2 (1993).

Parry, G., G. Moyser and N. Day, *Political Participation and Democracy in Britain* (Cambridge: Cambridge University Press, 1992).

Pattie, C., R. Johnston and A. Russell, 'The Stalled Greening of British Politics', *Politics Review*, vol. 4, no. 3 (1995).

Peele, G., 'The Constitution' in P. Dunleavy, A. Gamble, I. Holliday and G. Peele (eds), *New Developments in British Politics 4* (London, Macmillan, 1993).

Pierson, C., *Socialism after Communism* (Oxford: Polity, 1995).

Pimlott, B., 'The Myth of Consensus', reprinted in B. Pimlott, *Frustrate Their Knavish Tricks* (London: HarperCollins, 1995).

Plant, R., 'The Resurgence of Ideology' in H. Drucker, P. Dunleavy, A. Gamble and G. Peele (eds), *Developments in British Politics* (London: Macmillan, 1983).

Pliatzky, L., *Getting and Spending* (Oxford: Blackwell, 1982).

Pliatzky, L., *Paying and Choosing* (Oxford: Blackwell, 1985).

Pollard, S., *The Development of the British Economy 1914–1980* (London: Arnold, 1983).

Porter, B., *The Lion's Share: A Short History of British Imperialism 1850–1983*, 2nd edn (London: Longman, 1984).

Pugh, M., *State and Society (British Political and Social History 1870–1992)* (London: Arnold, 1995).

Pyper, R. and L. Robins (eds) *Governing the UK in the 1990s* (London: Macmillan, 1995).

Rasmussen, J., 'They Also serve: Small Parties in the British Political System' in F. Muller-Rommel and G. Pridham (eds), *Small Parties in Western Europe* (London: Sage, 1991).

Reed, B. and G. Williams, *Denis Healey and the Policies of Power* (London: Sidgwick and Jackson, 1971).

Reynolds, D., *Britannia Overruled British Policy and World Power in the Twentieth Century* (London: Longman, 1991).

Rhodes, R. A. W. (1987)

Rhodes, R. A. W., *Beyond Westminster and Whitehall* (London: Unwin Hyman, 1988).

Richard, I. *et al.*, *Europe or the Open Sea?* (London: Charles Knight, 1971).

Riddell, P., *The Thatcher Era and its Legacy*, 2nd edn (Oxford: Blackwell, 1991).

Riddell, P., 'Major and Parliament' in A. Seldon and D. Kavanagh (eds), *The Major Effect* (London: Macmillan, 1994).

Ridley, F. F., 'There is no British Constitution: a Dangerous Case of the Emperor's Clothes', *Parliamentary Affairs*, vol. 41, no. 3 (1988).

Ridley, F. F. and M. Rush (eds), *British Government and Politics since 1945: Changes in Perspective* (Oxford: Oxford University Press, 1995).

Robins, L., *The Reluctant Party: Labour and the EEC 1961–1975* (Ormskirk: Hesketh, 1979).

Robins, L. (ed.), *Topics in British Politics* (London: Politics Association, 1982).

Robins, L. (ed.), *Politics and Policy-Making in Britain* (London: Longman, 1987).

Robins, L., H. Blackmore and R. Pyper (eds), *Britain's Changing Party System* (Leicester: Leicester University Press, 1994).

Rollings, N., 'British budgetary policy 1945–1954: a 'Keynesian Revolution'?', *Economic History Review*, 2nd series, XLI, 2 (1988).

Rollings, N., ''Poor Mr Butskell: A Short Life, Wrecked by Schizophrenia'?', *Twentieth Century British History*, vol. 5, no. 2 (1994).

Rollings, N., 'Butskellism, the Postwar Consensus and the Managed Economy' in H. Jones and M. Kandiah (eds), *The Myth of Consensus New Views on British History, 1945–1964* (London: Macmillan, 1996).

Rosamund, B., 'Whatever Happened to the "Enemy" Within Contemporary Conservatism and Trade Unionism' in S. Ludlam and M. J. Smith (eds), *Contemporary British Conservatism* (London: Macmillan, 1996).

Rose, C. R., *The Relation of Socialist Principles to British Labour Foreign Policy*, unpublished D. Phil., Nuffield College, Oxford, 1959.

Rose, R., *The Problem of Party Government* (London: Macmillan, 1974).

Rose, R., *Understanding the United Kingdom* (London: Longman, 1982).

Rose, R., *Do Parties Make a Difference?* (London: Macmillan, 1984).

Rose, R. and I. McAllister, *Voters Begin to Choose* (London: Sage, 1986).

Rose, R. and I. McAllister, *The Loyalties of Voters* (London: Sage, 1990).

Rubinstein, W. D., *Wealth and Inequality in Britain* (London: Faber and Faber, 1986).

Sampson, A., *Macmillan: A Study in Ambiguity* (London: Penguin, 1967).

Sanders, D., *Losing an Empire, Finding a Role* (London: Macmillan, 1990).

Sarlvik, B. and I. Crewe, *Decade of Dealignment: The Conservative Victory of 1979 and Electoral Trends in the 1970s* (Cambridge: Cambridge University Press, 1983).

Saville, J., *The Labour Movement in Britain* (London: Faber and Faber, 1988).

Seawright, D. and J. Curtice, 'The Decline of the Scottish Conservative and Unionist Party 1950–1950–92: Religion, Ideology or Economics?', *Contemporary Record*, vol. 9, no. 2 (1995).

Sedgemore, B., *The Secret Constitution* (London: Hodder and Stoughton, 1980).

Seldon, A., *Churchill's Indian Summer: The Conservative Government 1951–55* (London: Hodder and Stoughton, 1981).

Seldon, A., 'The Churchill Administration, 1951–55' in P. Hennessy and A. Seldon (eds), *Ruling Performance: British Governments from Attlee to Thatcher* (Oxford: Blackwell, 1987).

Seldon, A. (ed.), *UK Political Parties since 1945* (London: Philip Allan, 1990).

Seldon, A., 'The Conservative Party since 1945' in T. Gourvish and A. O'Day (eds), *Britain since 1945* (London: Macmillan, 1991).

Seldon, A., 'Conservative Century' in A. Seldon and S. Ball (eds), *Conservative Century: The Conservative Party since 1900* (Oxford: Oxford University Press, 1994).

Seldon, A and S. Ball (eds), *Conservative Century: The Conservative Party since 1900* (Oxford: Oxford University Press, 1994).

Seldon, A., 'The Conservative Party' in A. Seldon and D. Kavanagh (eds), *The Major Effect* (London: Macmillan, 1994)

Seyd, P., *The Rise and Fall of the Labour Left* (London: Macmillan, 1987).

Seyd, P. and P. Whiteley, *Labour's Grass Roots: The Politics of Party Membership* (Oxford: Clarendon Press, 1992).

Seyd, P. and P. Whiteley, 'Conservative Grassroots: An Overview' in S. Ludlam and M. J. Smith (eds), *Contemporary British Conservatism* (London: Macmillan, 1996).

Seymour-Ure, C., 'The Media in Postwar British Politics' in F. F. Ridley and M. Rush (eds) *British Government and Politics since 1945: Changes in Perspective* (Oxford: Oxford University Press, 1995).

Shanks, M., *The Stagnant Society* (Harmondsworth: Penguin, 1961).

Shanks, M., *Planning and Politics: the British Experience 1960–76* (London: PEP/Allen and Unwin, 1977).

Shaw, E., *The Labour Party since 1945* (Oxford: Blackwell, 1996).

Shell, D., 'The House of Lords: Time for a Change?', *Parliamentary Affairs*, Special Hansard Society Fiftieth Anniversary Edition, 1994.

Skidelsky, R., 'The Fall of Keynesianism' in D. Marquand and A. Seldon (eds), *The Ideas that Shaped Postwar Britain* (London: HarperCollins, 1996).

Smith, M., 'From Thatcher to Major: Continuity and Change in Conservative Party Politics', *Politics Review*, vol. 5, no. 2 (1995).

Smith, T., 'The British Constitution: Unwritten and unravelled' in J. Hayward and P. Norton (eds), *The Political Science of British Politics* (London: Wheatsheaf, 1986).

Social Trends, 23 (1993).

Solomos, J., *Race and Racism in Contemporary Britain* (London: Macmillan, 1989).

Stacey, F., *British Government 1966–1975: The Years of Reform* (Oxford: Oxford University Press, 1975).

Stevenson, J., *Third Party Politics since 1945* (Oxford: Blackwell, 1993).

Stewart, M., *The Jekyll and Hyde Years Politics and Economic Policy since 1964* (London: Dent, 1977).

Stoker, G., *The Politics of Local Government* (London: Macmillan, 1990).

Taylor, A., 'The Party and the Trade Unions' in A. Seldon and S. Ball (eds), *Conservative Century: The Conservative Party since 1900* (Oxford: Oxford University Press, 1994).

Taylor, A. J. P., *English History 1914–1945* (Oxford: Oxford University Press, 1965).

Thain, C., 'Government and the Economy' in B. Jones and L. Robins (eds), *Two decades in British politics* (Manchester: Manchester University Press, 1992).

Thane, P., 'Women since 1945' in P. Johnson (ed.), *Twentieth Century Britain* (London: Longman, 1994).

Thomas, G., *Government and the Economy Today* (Manchester: Manchester University Press, 1992).

Thomas, H. (ed.), *The Establishment* (London: Anthony Blond, 1959).

Thornhill, W. (ed.), *The Modernisation of British Government* (London: Pitman, 1975).

Tivey, L. and A. Wright (eds), *Party Ideology in Britain* (London: Routledge, 1989).

Tracy, N., *The Origins of the Social Democratic Party* (London: Croom Helm, 1983).

Urwin, D. W., *The Community of Europe* (London: LOngman, 1995).

Wallace, W., 'Survival and Revival' in V. Bogdanor (ed.), *Liberal Party Politics* (Oxford: Clarendon, 1983).

Waller, R., 'Conservative Electoral Support and Social Class' in A. Seldon and S. Ball (eds), *Conservative Century: The Conservative Party since 1900* (Oxford: Oxford University Press, 1994).

Walters, A., *Britain's Economic Renaissance: Margaret Thatcher's Reforms 1979–1984* (Oxford: Oxford University Press, 1986).

Webb, K., *The Growth of Nationalism in Scotland* (Harmondsworth: Penguin, 1978).

Webster, C., *The Health Services since the War*, vol. 1 (London: HMSO, 1988).

Webster, C., 'Conflict and consensus: explaining the British Health Service', *Twentieth Century British History*, vol. 1, no. 2 (1990).

Weiner, M. J., *English Culture and the Decline of the Industrial Spirit, 1850–1980* (Cambridge: Cambridge University Press, 1981).

Whiteley, P., P. Seyd and J. Richardson, *True Blues: The Politics of Conservative Party Membership* (Oxford: Clarendon Press, 1994).

Whitfield, D., *The Welfare State; privatisation, deregulation, commercialisation of public services* (London: Pluto Press, 1992).

Willetts, D., *Modern Conservatism* (Harmondsworth: Penguin, 1992).

Williams, G., *When was Wales? A History of the Welsh* (Harmondsworth: Penguin, 1985).

Wilson, H., *The Labour Government 1964–1970* (London: Weidenfeld and Nicolson and Michael Joseph, 1971).

Windrich, E., *British Labour's Foreign Policy* (Stanford CA: Stanford University Press, 1952).

Wood, A. H. and R. Wood (eds), *The Times Guide to the House of Commons 1992* (London: Times Books, 1992).

Wright, A., 'The Constitution' in L. Tivey and A. Wright (eds), *Party Ideology in Britain* (London: Routledge, 1989).

Index